1

THE FIRST FRONTIER

THE
FIRST
FRONTIER

BY

R. V. COLEMAN

ILLUSTRATED

CASTLE BOOKS

This edition published in 2005 by
Castle Books ®
a division of Book Sales, Inc.
114 Northfield Avenue
Edison, NJ 08837

Copyright © 1948 by Charles Scribner's Sons

This edition published by arrangement with and permission of
Charles Scribner's Sons
An imprint of Simon & Schuster, Inc.
1230 Avenue of the Americas
New York, New York 10020

ISBN 13: 978-07858-2081-9
ISBN 10: 0-7858-2081-7

Printed in the United States of America

Foreword

WE HAD BEEN discussing the present condition of our town and country. The Judge—aged forty, successful lawyer, representative in the state assembly, typical up-and-coming young man—suddenly turned to the past.

"Coley," said he with the familiarity of youth (my contemporaries address me as Mr. Coleman), "you must have a book here that will give a busy fellow such as myself the inside story of how this country began."

"Didn't they tell you enough of that at Yale?" I countered.

"Not quite," he replied. "What I want to know is why the first settlers came, what sort of people they were, how they made their livings, how they behaved, what they thought about."

The answer seemed easy. The walls of my study were lined with books, the unoccupied chairs were filled with them, my desk was stacked with them—all on American history. I knew well enough what the Judge wanted. But each time I came up to saying, this is it, I knew it was not. One was too long, another too specialized; they were for the scholar, not the "busy" reader.

In search of a thought I looked out the window—across the fields and woods to Long Island Sound gleaming in the distance. Down there, behind that hill, ran the road along which Thomas Kellond and Captain Kirke, sore of behind, had urged their horses in a vain pursuit of the regicides. Out there, on the Sound, Governor Winthrop's ship, the *Blessing of the Bay,* had passed in her trading trips during the 1630's. Over there, on the Island itself, turning to a blue line in the setting sun, John Scott had schemed for a royal domain. All up and down the coast, from Florida to Maine, men and women had lived and died, worked and loitered, sacrificed and sinned, succeeded and failed, and their acts and thoughts had made America what it became.

That was the story the Judge wanted. "I'll have to write it for you," I finally said. It was an idle answer. My job was to publish books, not write them. Still, the idea took hold and grew. And so I wrote the story and here it is. I hope the Judge, and others who may have been wishing for such a book, will like it.

R. V. C.

December 5, 1947

Contents

ACKNOWLEDGMENTS

To the members of my staff at Scribner's: Joseph G. E. Hopkins for valued suggestions and criticism; Mary Wells McNeill for keeping me within the bounds of literacy and for competent reading of the six successive drafts of the manuscript; Ethel M. Watson for faithful and intelligent research at the New York Public Library.

To Atkinson Dymock for designing the book and supervising its production; to William Koch for laying out the illustrations; to James T. Hoar for a handsome job of composition.

To LeRoy H. Appleton for drawing the maps.

The mistakes, which I hope are not many, are all my own.

Illustrations and Maps

THE FIRST FRONTIER

The Kiva

IN THE LATE SUMMER of 1849, three years after the American conquest of New Mexico, a military expedition was plodding westerly from Santa Fe toward the Navaho country. Day after day the trail had led up and up. The heads of the streams that flowed eastward toward the Gulf of Mexico had become steadily smaller. Then, almost imperceptibly, the trail tipped down and a trickle of water was running west—on the long trip toward the Pacific. The men and horses and mules had crossed the Continental Divide. They were on the headwaters of the Rio Chaco, a tributary of the San Juan River, which in turn flows through deep canyon walls into the deeper-canyoned Colorado of the West.

To the weary soldiers this Chaco region of northwestern New Mexico seemed about the last place any one would have wished to live—a waste of drifting sand covered with sagebrush. Yet, off to the right of the line of march, Lieutenant Simpson of the Topographical Engineers sighted a "conspicuous ruin." With R. H. Kern, an artist accompanying the expedition, Simpson rode over to investigate. The "ruin" which he had first seen proved to be the outpost of a dozen great buildings strung along the sides of the canyon through which the river ran—uninhabited, ravaged by neglect, but revealing "a combination of science and art" beyond anything known to the Mexicans or the Indians then living in New Mexico.

Typical of the ruins was one which the Pueblo Indian guide called Chetro Ketl. It occupied a circuit of 1300 feet. The walls, both outer and inner, were of stone so skillfully laid that they had successfully defied time. Simpson thought that it had originally been four stories high. Subsequent excavation has revealed that it was at least five stories high, one story having become buried under the drifted sand. On what Simpson took to be the ground floor he counted over one hundred rooms. One room he found in a fair state of preservation. It was fourteen feet long by seven and a half feet wide and ten feet high. The ceiling was made by logs laid from wall to wall and embedded in the walls. Across the logs, at right angles to them, were laid poles, and over these, to make the floor of the room above, was spread bark covered with a layer of mud cement. There were doors from one room to another on the same story, but none for entry from outside, nor were there stairs or other provision for going from the lower floors to the upper. Simpson correctly judged that the entrance to each story of the building had been through holes in the roofs, reached by ladders raised against the outer walls; also that each story had been terraced back from the one below. In addition to the rectangular rooms he found six circular rooms about the origin and use of which we shall learn more later.

From his Indian guide Simpson inquired, "Who built these structures?" The guide's reply was, "The Montezuma," by which he meant the people whose descendants were found by Cortez in the Valley of Mexico in 1519.

Eleven days later, and a hundred miles to the west in the Canyon de Chelly, another tributary of the San Juan, Simpson saw, perched in a cave in the side of a canyon, a group of ancient stone buildings—but he had no time to examine them.[1]

*   *   *   *   *

On a snowy December day in 1888 two cowboys, Richard Wetherill and Charlie Mason, were looking for stray cattle

Above. The "conspicuous ruin," first of the Chaco Canyon pueblos sighted by Lieutenant Simpson in 1849.
From a sketch made at the time by R. H. Kern, and reproduced from *U. S. Senate Executive Document No. 64, 31st Congress, 1st Session.*

Below. Restoration of Chetro Ketl, one of the Chaco Canyon pueblos examined by Lieutenant Simpson in 1849.
By R. M. Coffin in Edgar L. Hewett, *The Chaco Canyon and Its Monuments. Courtesy,* School of American Research, Santa Fe.

3

on the Mesa Verde, a high plateau in southwestern Colorado. Through the mesa the Mancos River slashes its way
from the northeast to join the San Juan, some thirty miles
below the place where the Chaco enters that same stream
from the southeast. By following the canyons, which would
have been the natural route of prehistoric travelers, the distance between Mesa Verde and the Chaco "ruins" would
not exceed two hundred miles. Both places—the Mesa Verde
and the Chaco Canyon—were parts of the great San Juan
drainage basin. In the Mesa Verde district, however, the
main canyon was much deeper than that of the upper Chaco
and the distance between the canyon walls was much less;
also there were more and deeper side canyons.

Riding across the mesa Wetherill and Mason were stopped
by one of these side canyons, yawning two hundred feet deep
before them. But what they saw in the opposite wall banished all thoughts of the hazards involved in hunting stray
cattle. There, right in front of them, in a vast cave in the
side of the canyon stood a miniature city—square houses,
round houses, some four stories high, all built of stone, all
silent as the stones themselves.

Rounding the head of the canyon, Wetherill and Mason
were soon on the mesa directly above the cave city. There
they found the ancient trail leading down the side of the
cliff. Down they scrambled—and two American cowboys
stood among the homes of a people who had left those homes
two hundred years before Columbus sailed for America.
Wetherill and Mason at Mesa Verde in 1888 were face to
face with the same civilization that Simpson and Kern had
met in the Chaco Canyon in 1849. In the Chaco the people
had built their houses in the wide bed of the canyon. In the
Mesa Verde they had built them in the walls of the canyon.
The purpose was the same in each case: community life for
protection—in defensible walled pueblos in the Chaco—in
easily defended caves in the Mesa Verde.[2]

The inhabitants of both places were of the same racial
stock. They visited and traded with each other. They doubtless intermarried. And there were hundreds of similar related
communities: in the Mesa Verde itself; on the main San

Above. The cliff dwelling at Mesa Verde first seen by Wetherill and Mason in 1888. They called it Cliff Palace and the name has persisted. Photograph by W. H. Jackson.

Above. Stone axe from Cliff Palace.

From *Bureau of American Ethnology, Bulletin No. 51.*

Right. Typical pottery from cliff dwellings at Mesa Verde.

Courtesy, Mesa Verde National Park.

5

Juan; in the Canyon de Chelly; along the Little Colorado River; over the Continental Divide on the upper Rio Grande; southwesterly on the Gila River; southward into Mexico—and still southward.[3]

Since Simpson puzzled over the Chaco Canyon "ruins" there has been much study of these and other ancient houses of our southwest, and of their contents. From the customs and traditions of the Pueblo Indians who still live in adjoining regions comparative deductions may be safely made. All of this when put together has enabled us to reasonably reconstruct the life of the people who lived and worked, laughed and worried and died in the Chaco Canyon and at Mesa Verde seven centuries ago.

Corn was their staff of life. In the Chaco Canyon the fields were in the bed of the canyon itself and were irrigated from the river. At Mesa Verde the fields had to take the chance of sufficient rainfall since they were on the mesa above the cave—reached by paths that wound up the side of the cliff. Squashes and beans supplemented the corn; domesticated turkeys furnished meat for food and feathers for blankets.

The corn was ground on slightly hollowed-out slabs of stone. The grinder was a sort of rolling pin, also of stone. For cooking, for storing grain, and above all, for carrying water and for storing it against the dry season, pottery was made in great quantities and varieties of shapes. Since the women did the cooking and most of the carrying, the privilege of making the pottery fell to them. Evidently they took real pride in the forms and patterns of their products. Many of the designs are of great beauty.

Mosaics of turquoise, inlaid work and carved beads attest the taste and skill of the inhabitants of the pueblos. The lignite frog with turquoise eyes and collar, shown on page 7, ranks with the best art work of prehistoric people anywhere.

In the making of blankets from feathers the pueblo people were expert. Cloth woven from cotton was also common, although for much of the region the cotton had to be imported, as it did not grow locally.

Bones found many uses, particularly for the various sorts

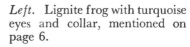

Left. Lignite frog with turquoise eyes and collar, mentioned on page 6.

Courtesy, American Museum of Natural History, New York.

Right. Garland of beads found in the remains of an older building buried beneath the foundations of Chetro Ketl.

Courtesy, School of American Research, Santa Fe.

Left. Typical masonry of the Chaco Canyon pueblos.

Courtesy, School of American Research, Santa Fe.

7

of needles. But most of the pueblo implements were of stone. Trees were felled with stone axes and with stone axes beams were shaped. Stone hammers were used to shape the stones from which the houses were built.

Nor were these great houses the out-of-hand products of any Montezuma. They were the result of thousands of years of slow advance. Each of the houses, or pueblos, had within it one or more circular rooms, entirely or partly below the ground level, or at least made to appear so. Although there might be slight variations in the method of construction, in general the structure of these rooms was always the same. They were entered from the top—by ladders. Into the room through an outside vertical shaft and a horizontal tunnel came an opening which we call a ventilator—a sort of reverse chimney which formed a draft that carried smoke out of the room through the opening at the top. Near the center of the room was a fire pit, and in the floor near it was a hole about three inches in diameter and a few inches deep. We call these rooms *kivas* and the hole in the floor is called a *sipapu*. During the period of the great houses the *kivas* were used as ceremonial rooms or as loafing places for the men. It was in them that the young men learned from the lips of the older and wiser ones the traditions and wisdom of the clan. It was in them that the ceremonial paraphernalia—feathers, beads and such—were kept. It was from these rooms that the various ceremonial dances issued. These *kivas* represented the cultural background of the community. And well they might. In shape and form and construction they were patterned after the first permanent houses built in this region—circular pits dug in the ground, covered over with poles and sod, and entered from the top by ladders. Even back of this goes the meaning of the *sipapu*. That hole in the floor was the symbol of the exit of the first people from the earth, and it served to keep the pueblo dwellers in contact with the spirits of their ancestors.*

From such beginnings—covered holes in the ground—these people had slowly advanced to a point where they learned to build their houses above ground and of stone. Then having started on the road of progress, they suddenly, like other

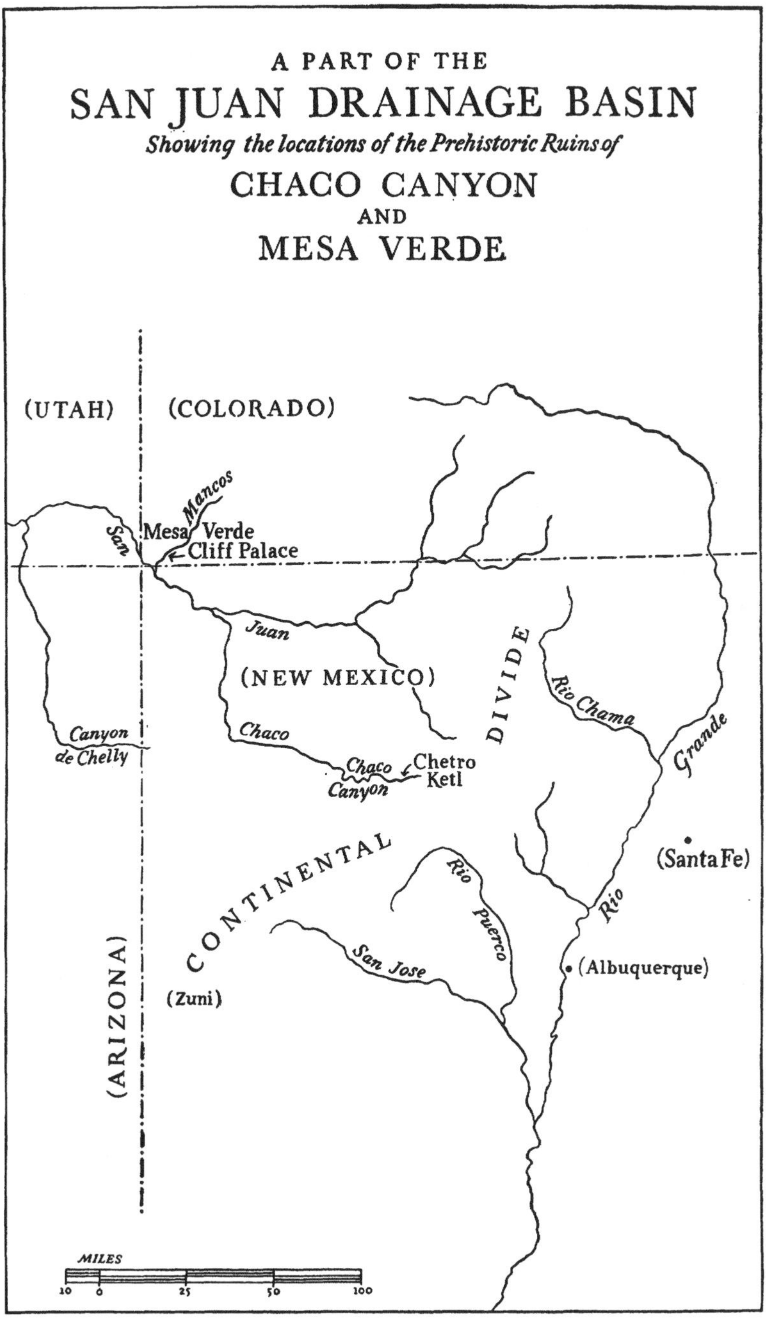

A PART OF THE
SAN JUAN DRAINAGE BASIN
Showing the locations of the Prehistoric Ruins of
CHACO CANYON
AND
MESA VERDE

(UTAH) | (COLORADO)

Mancos

San

Mesa Verde
Cliff Palace

Juan

(NEW MEXICO)

Chaco

Canyon
de Chelly

Chaco
Chaco
Canyon

Chetro
Ketl

DIVIDE

Rio Chama

Grande

(Santa Fe)

CONTINENTAL

Rio
Puerco

Rio

(ARIZONA)

(Zuni)

San Jose

• (Albuquerque)

MILES

10   0   25   50   100

people before and since, developed an obsession for progress. Bigger and better grew the community houses. More and more rooms were added. Higher and higher went the terraces. More and bigger *kivas* were incorporated in the bigger and better houses. Prodigious effort went into the construction of their houses, much more than utility demanded. And then the people vanished, and only their houses and pottery and axes and a few mummified bodies remained.[5]

Why did they leave? We do not know. There is nothing to indicate that war, either foreign or domestic, was the cause. It may be that a change of climate was the reason—insufficient rain, failure of crops. It may be that they simply progressed too fast, wore themselves out and vanished.

In 1200 A.D. they were at their zenith. A century later they were gone. Their houses were left as though the inhabitants had locked the door and gone away expecting to return. But they never came back.

Of Europe they knew nothing, nor Europe of them. In 1200 A.D. there was no Spain. The forefathers of Ferdinand and Isabella were still at grips with the Saracen. France was a collection of small independent dukedoms. England was suffering with King John, who was soon to be forced to accept the Magna Charta. Almost three centuries went by; the marriage between Ferdinand of Aragon and Isabella of Castile created a Spain; the last stronghold of the Saracen fell; new conquests for Spain and Holy Church beckoned. At that moment Christopher Columbus was present with the proposal to find a new world which knew not the Church—and which might be rich in things that Europe wanted.

The Cross

I N AUGUST, 1492, Columbus sailed west from Palos, Spain. He bore a commission from Ferdinand and Isabella as high-admiral and as viceroy in lands which he might discover. His fleet consisted of three tiny ships carrying less than a hundred men. On October 11 he sighted land. The place was an island in what we now call the Bahamas. Within a quarter of a century Hispaniola (Haiti), Cuba and other islands of the Caribbean had been conquered, and approaches were being made toward the mainland. Destiny rode with Hernando Cortez when in 1519 he began his march to the Aztec capital at Mexico City. There the Spanish met and destroyed the most advanced and most formidable civilization in sixteenth-century North America.

The vast treasure of gold that fell into the hands of the conquerors at Mexico City created an appetite for gold and ever more gold. North, south, east and west the conquest was extended, always with the hope that other rich hordes of gold would be found. Where gold was not to be had Indian slaves had a commercial value. Up the west coast of Mexico, with fire and sword for the natives who resisted, and with chains for those they could catch, the conquerors were pushing their way northward when a curious event occurred. Into the camp of the slave hunters came, from the north, three Spaniards and a negro.

These four men were the survivors of an expedition which eight years before had landed with all the pride of power on the peninsula of Florida sixteen hundred miles to the eastward. On April 14, 1528, Panfilo de Narvaez came ashore near the present city of Tampa with three hundred men and forty-two horses. The ships which brought the expedition were ordered to find a harbor farther up the coast and to be available when needed.

Trouble began immediately. The exploring party had expected to live off of the country, but little was found on which to live. Moreover, the Indians proved hostile, which was not remarkable in view of their previous experience with Spanish slave hunters and their immediate treatment by Narvaez, who chained and marched along as slaves or guides such of the natives as he needed and who appropriated all the corn on which he could lay his hands.

Constantly the Spaniards inquired for gold. To the northwest at a place called Apalache the captured Indians told Narvaez he would find it. The march was therefore directed toward Apalache—through a country described by a member of the expedition as "difficult to travel and wonderful to look upon." But when the hungry Spaniards arrived at Apalache (near present-day Tallahassee) they found only a squalid Indian town. Corn, however, they did find, and the Spaniards moved in and stayed nearly a month, which sojourn the dispossessed natives did their best to make unpleasant.

Then something had to be done. Food was giving out. Many of the men were sick. The ships could not be found. It developed later that they had gone back to Tampa Bay. However, the explorers found the coast—at St. Marks Bay. There, without knowing how to build boats, they built five. The horses were killed for food; from their tails and manes the Spaniards made ropes. From their own shirts they made sails. From the skins of the horses they made bottles to hold water.

Some fifty of the men were already dead either from disease or from the arrows of the natives, when on September 22, 1528, the two hundred and forty-three survivors embarked in the five boats. The plan was to follow the shore of the Gulf of Mexico westward to a Spanish settlement near Tampico, Mexico. For six weeks they struggled along, paddling, sailing, fighting with the Indians for food. They passed the mouth of the Mississippi and bailed up fresh water—a hundred and fifty-four years before La Salle "discovered" it. And then came the inevitable storm. Three of the boats were lost, including the one with Narvaez. Two other boats with eighty survivors, among whom was Cabeza de Vaca, were driven ashore somewhere along the coast of Texas. Cabeza de Vaca and his companions had stripped preparatory to relaunching their boat, in which they had put their clothing and weapons and food. It was November; there was a cold north wind blowing; their hands became numb; the boat got away from them. And there they were, these men who, when equipped with guns and coats of mail, with horses and lances and swords, had been accustomed to lording it over and enslaving the naked Indians—there they were on a savage shore, themselves utterly and completely naked, hungry and cold. During the winter most of them died, the living devouring the bodies of their dead companions—to the scandal of the heathen Indians. By spring only fifteen were left. These the Indians divided among themselves. They did not put them in chains, as the Spaniards would have done had the conditions been reversed, but the need to eat served quite as effectively as chains.

Thus for six years the diminishing number of Christians lived as slaves of the Indians—carrying wood for fires, digging roots and shellfish for food, naked in the blazing sun of summer and the bitter cold of winter, beaten by the savage natives, some killed, some dying of cold and hunger. Yet there were occasional flush times, as, for example, when Cabeza de Vaca was put to work scraping deerskins. He scraped and scraped and had a regular feast from the bits of meat that he scraped off the skins.

Finally Cabeza de Vaca and two other Spaniards made their escape. With them went Estevan, a negro slave belonging to one of them. Their plan was to work westward until they reached a Spanish settlement in Mexico.

They had already tried their hands at healing, or "medicine." Now that mystery became the key to their welcome as they passed from tribe to tribe, their prestige growing until they acquired the stature of messiahs whose very touch healed. Nor did they lack for guides. As they left one village, every one turned out and escorted them to the next, from which, as they approached, the inhabitants came to meet them, laying at their feet all the movable property they owned. For themselves the Spaniards took nothing, but turned the offerings over to the Indians who had escorted them from the preceding town. This procedure worked satisfactorily so long as each tribe collected from the next enough to make up for what they had given the tribe that brought the Spaniards to them. However, as other more civilized people have frequently discovered, there is a flaw in such schemes; the last one out loses, and so it was in this case.

On westward went the three Spaniards and the negro—across western Texas, across northern Chihuahua, over the Sierra Madres. Finally they began to hear of other Christians and soon were led into their camp—the frontier slave-hunting post mentioned on page 11. The Spanish slave hunters, who for weeks had been unable to find an Indian, suddenly found in their camp hundreds of Indians trustfully delivering to them three Spaniards and a negro, and expecting a reward for doing it. The reward that most of them received, despite all that Cabeza de Vaca could say or do, was to be rounded up and marched off in chains. Down the road toward Mexico City, joyfully rescued from the wilds, went three Spaniards and a negro; clanking along with them were five hundred Indians destined to a life of slavery.[1]

On their arrival at Mexico City the three Spaniards made an official report of their experiences, after which Cabeza de Vaca sailed for Spain. The report told only of savage Indians and the lowest order of living, certainly nothing to encourage further exploration. But Cabeza de Vaca and his companions when they wrote that report were still insulated from the impact of a phenomenon which in 1536 put golden spectacles on the Spanish world. While Cabeza de Vaca had been carrying wood in Texas for his savage masters, Francisco Pizarro had forced his way through an Indian frontier to the south and had found gold in unbelievable quantities. If beyond one Indian frontier there was an Inca empire, why not a similar empire and horde of gold behind another Indian frontier?

Cabeza de Vaca, himself, after he reached Spain, seems to have revised his estimate of the region he had formerly accounted of so little value. At any rate he asked for the governorship of "Florida," meaning all of the southeastern part of the later United States. But this prize fell to Hernando DeSoto, who had been with Pizarro in Peru and who had done well. Nor was the area lying west of "Florida" to be ignored. The Viceroy of New Spain (Mexico), whose domain it adjoined on the north, moved to find out what was there.

Within four years two great exploring expeditions, directly influenced by stories credited to Cabeza de Vaca or members of his party, were pushing into the lands which that party had traversed.

DeSoto, organizing his expedition in Spain, was the first to get under way. On May 30, 1539, with nine ships, some five hundred men, two hundred and thirteen horses, a pack of bloodhounds, and a drove of hogs, he landed on the west coast of Florida not far from where Narvaez had landed eleven years before. And the same scenes were repeated: Indians were captured for guides; Indians were capriciously killed; the food and homes of the Indians were coolly appropriated. From an account written by a member of the expedition, we see it all too clearly. ". . . some of the youngest [of the captured Indians] the Governor gave to those who had good chains and were vigilant; all the rest were ordered executed." And again, "Two captains having been sent in opposite directions, in quest of Indians, a hundred men and women were taken, one or two of whom were chosen out for the Governor, as was always customary for officers to do after successful inroads, dividing the others among themselves and companions. They were led off in chains, with collars about the neck, to carry luggage and grind corn, doing the labor proper to servants."

Following much the same route as Narvaez and lured by
the same stories of gold ahead, DeSoto moved northward.
The need for food led him, as it had led Narvaez, to the
Indian town of Apalache—near which place his men saw
where Narvaez had built his boats to escape from Florida.
But DeSoto was of sterner stuff. Gathering up all the grain
he could load onto the horses (most of the Indian slaves
having died of hard work and exposure), he turned inland,
north and east through present-day Georgia.

Again food proved scarce. The captured natives disclaimed
knowledge of where corn could be found. However, after one
of them had been burned, the others directed the Spaniards
to a town named Cofitachequi—on the Savannah River about
eighty miles from where it enters the ocean. The chief of
Cofitachequi turned out to be a woman. She came out of
the town, says the chronicler, "seated in a chair, which some
principal men having borne to the bank, she entered a canoe.
Over the stern was spread an awning, and in the bottom lay
extended a mat where were two cushions, one above the
other, upon which she sate; and she was accompanied by her
chief men, in other canoes. . . ." Still other canoes brought
shawls and skins which the chieftainess presented to DeSoto,
while from her own neck she took a string of pearls and threw
them around his neck. These pearls interested the Spaniards,
and from the burial places in some nearby deserted towns
they unearthed three hundred and fifty pounds of them.

"The country was delightful and fertile," the chronicler
tells us. The natives were "brown of skin, well formed and
proportioned." They wore clothing from the bark of trees
and from feathers, and shoes and leggings made from deer
skins. All in all they were the most civilized people the Spaniards had met thus far.

But good soil and pearls did not satisfy DeSoto. He wanted
gold. The people of Cofitachequi told him of another large
town to the northwest, so on he went. With him, as a reward
for her hospitality, he dragged along on foot and under guard
the chieftainess of Cofitachequi. She carried with her a box
of very special pearls which DeSoto had in mind acquiring
in return for her release. His hopes proved vain; the sly

hussy, on the excuse of stepping aside into the woods, gave him the slip together with the pearls.

On northwesterly went the Spaniards, climbing over the Blue Ridge and arriving on the Tennessee River a little below present-day Knoxville. The natives, probably Cherokee, proved friendly until DeSoto made his usual demand for women to carry the baggage and provisions. At that the uncivilized savages rebelled, but were soon rounded up and forced to comply.

Finding no satisfactory evidences of the hoped-for gold, DeSoto now turned southward. Along the Coosa and Alabama Rivers trudged the long line: mounted Spanish dons sweating in coats of mail; foot soldiers with lances and guns; servants leading horses or driving hogs; captive Indian women chained together and loaded with heavy burdens, none destined to return to her people "save some whose fortune it was to escape."

Thus on October 18, 1540, almost five months after they had landed in Florida, the Spaniards came to Mabila, a palisaded native town some fifty miles north of the present city of Mobile. They had passed through a thickly populated district. The natives were restive. The Spaniards were holding as a hostage a very important native chief. Things looked bad. "Luis de Moscoso said that, since the Indians were so evil disposed it would be better to stop in the woods, to which the Governor [DeSoto] answered that he was impatient of sleeping out, and that he would lodge in the town."

Into the town went the Governor, taking with him the captive chief, who promptly appealed to his fellow Indians for release. "Baltasar de Gallegos, who was near, seized [one of them] by the cloak of martin-skins that he had on, drew it off over his head, and left it in his hands; where upon the Indians all beginning to rise he gave him a stroke with a cutlass, that laid open his back, when they, with loud yells, came out of the houses, discharging their bows." DeSoto ran for it and was knocked down several times before he got away. As the chronicler put it, ". . . discovering that the Christians were retiring, and some, if not the great number, at more than a walk, the Indians followed with great promptness."

Reaching his men, DeSoto ordered an assault. The Indians fought bravely, but guns and lances prevailed. The village, built of poles and brush, was set on fire. According to the Spanish account some two thousand five hundred people perished in the affair. Nor were they all Indians. Eighteen Spaniards were killed and one hundred and fifty were severely injured. Twelve irreplaceable horses were killed and all the loot which the Spaniards had so far collected, including the pearls acquired at Cofitachequi, was lost.

The loss of the pearls condemned the expedition to further wanderings. While at Mabila, DeSoto learned that his ships were waiting for him on the coast only a few days' travel distant (probably at Pensacola Bay), but rather than return empty-handed, he plunged back into his domain of "Florida."

The new line of march brought the expedition into the country of the Chickasaw, a tribe never noted for timidity. At a place called Chicaca the Christians got a taste of what they had given the Indians at Mabila. Attacking in the dead of night the natives set fire to the village in which the Spaniards were sleeping and stampeded the horses. When the morning dawned, a cold one in March, 1541, eleven more Spaniards were dead and the rest had only the clothing in which they had fled their beds. There were fifty fewer horses. Most of the saddles had been burned. Among the ashes were many blackened swords from which the temper had gone.

Repairing their losses as best they could, the Spaniards tramped on, this time almost due west—seizing the grain of the Indians and in turn assailed by the Indians, many of whom appeared painted in red, white, black, yellow and vermilion stripes. Some had feathers and horns on their heads and their faces blackened, with circles of vermilion around their eyes.

Thus welcomed, the Spaniards in the spring of 1541 arrived at the Mississippi River, about thirty-five miles in a straight line south of the present-day city of Memphis. The chief of the Indians living on the westerly side of the river paid a call "with two hundred canoes filled with men, having weapons. They were painted with ochre, wearing great bunches of white and other plumes of many colors, having feathered shields in their hands, with which they sheltered the oarsmen on either side, the warriors standing erect from bow to stern, holding bows and arrows. They were fine looking men, very large and well formed; and what with the awnings, the plumes and the shields, the pennons and the number of people in the fleet, it appeared like a famous armada of galleys." Whatever the intentions of the Indians, a few shots by the Spaniards ended friendly relations.

The river was over a mile wide. It was "swift and very deep; the water, always flowing turbidly, brought along from above many trees and much timber." This did not deter the Spaniards. They set to work and within thirty days had built four boats. And then early one morning within a space of five hours they were across, horses and all.

For a year the expedition wandered aimlessly about in the marshy lands of eastern Arkansas and northeastern Louisiana, devouring the food of the Indians and killing those who resisted. Then on May 21, 1542, DeSoto died. His body was weighted and sunk in the broad Mississippi. The Indians were told that he had ascended into the skies for a short visit.

Before he died DeSoto had appointed Luis de Moscoso as his successor in command. Moscoso called the leaders together and asked for advice. The decision was to get out and to do it as fast as they could. The best way seemed to be by marching west and south in the hope of reaching a Spanish settlement in Mexico.

Off they went across Arkansas, northern Louisiana and into Texas. Here they heard vague rumors of other Christians to the west and even found an Indian woman who said she had been in their hands. However, all these reports appeared doubtful and the country ahead was reported to be a desert. So the Spaniards turned back to the Mississippi where they hewed out planks, forged spikes, manufactured rope and built a number of boats.

On the second day of July, 1543, the expedition embarked upon the Father of Waters, which they called simply the Rio Grande, meaning big river. Of the five hundred who had entered Florida four years earlier there were left but three hundred and twenty-two. On the way down the river their number was still further reduced. The Indians attacked unmercifully and for once had somewhat the advantage of the Spaniards, the latter being unable to use their horses, while the Indians operated from canoes in the use of which they were expert.

But despite everything the little flotilla sailed out of one of the mouths of the Mississippi and headed west. Hugging the coast, battling storms, suffering from mosquitoes, they crept along, supplicating God "that He would take them to a land in which they might better do Him service." Their prayers were evidently heard, as, after fifty-two days of sailing and paddling, they arrived on September 10, 1543, at the Spanish settlement of Panuco near present-day Tampico, Mexico.[2]

Had DeSoto in the spring of 1541, after he crossed the Mississippi, kept straight on, he might well have met Coronado's party, which at that very time was not more than four hundred miles to the west. Farther south the routes of the two expeditions came even nearer together. The Indian woman who told Moscoso that she had been in the hands of the Christians may very well have been telling the truth. Moscoso was on the middle stretch of the Brazos River in Texas; Coronado had been on the upper course of the same river only a year before.

The Coronado expedition, like that of DeSoto, was inspired by stories afloat as to what Cabeza de Vaca and his companions had learned on their long trip from Florida to the west coast of Mexico. Unlike the DeSoto expedition, which originated in Spain, that of Coronado was authorized and organized in New Spain. Antonio de Mendoza, the Viceroy, was fully informed of DeSoto's proposed explorations and suspected that, if the game was worth it, DeSoto would not hesitate to exceed his instructions by pushing on westward beyond "Florida." Mendoza had bought the negro, Estevan, who had made the trip with the Cabeza de Vaca party. Also Mendoza had in his possession several of the Indians who had been captured when they delivered Cabeza

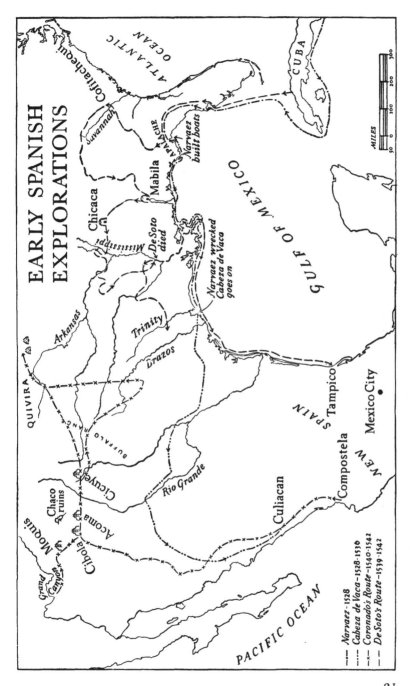

EARLY SPANISH
EXPLORATIONS

ATLANTIC OCEAN

CUBA

Culiacacui

Savannah

APACHE

Mabila

Chicaca

De Soto
died

Narvaez
built boats

Mississippi

Narvaez wrecked
Cabeza de Vaca
goes on

GULF OF MEXICO

Arkansas

Trinity

Brazos

QUIVIRA

BUFFALO PLAINS

Cicuye

Rio Grande

Chaco
ruins

Acoma

Cibola

Moquis

Grand
Canyon

Tampico

NEW SPAIN

Mexico City

Compostela

Culiacan

PACIFIC OCEAN

MILES
0   100   200   300

--- Narvaez-1528
·-·-· Cabeza de Vaca-1528-1536
-x-x- Coronado's Route-1540-1542
— — De Soto's Route-1519-1542

de Vaca to his fellow Christians. What Estevan and the Indians told Mendoza can only be surmised, but whatever it was it seemed worth investigating further. Mendoza had no intention of being outdone by the ruthless DeSoto, he who in Peru had participated in finding and looting a rich civilization where the chances seemed no more promising than in the country just north of Mendoza's own viceroyalty.

So, early in the year of 1539, while DeSoto and his men were in Cuba preparing for their descent on the coast of Florida, Mendoza directed Friar Marcos de Niza, in whom he had full confidence, to go north into the Indian country, see what was there and report. With Friar Marcos went Estevan and some of the captured Indians as guides and interpreters. They started from Culican, where the Cabeza de Vaca party had arrived three years earlier. Just what route they followed is uncertain, but with Estevan and the Indian guides ahead spying out the route, they seem to have advanced very directly toward the Seven Cities of Cibola, the name applied to what we now call the Zuni pueblos in western New Mexico. Thus we may assume that the fame of Cibola as picked up by the Cabeza de Vaca party was the basis for the rumors of a rich people to the north. Well may Mendoza have had misgivings as to DeSoto's real objective.

And now Estevan, who had seen Cabeza de Vaca treated as a messiah by the Indians some years earlier, was himself approaching the wonder cities of the north. Evidently he attempted a little messiah business himself but failed to impress the Cibolans. A terrified Indian fled back to Friar Marcos with the news that Estevan and several of the Indians accompanying him had been killed. The Zuni tradition is that they "gave him a powerful kick, which sped him through the air back to the south, whence he came." Whatever the means, this appears to have been the end of Estevan.

Friar Marcos prudently decided to omit an immediate visit to the Seven Cities, but he did get close enough to view one of them from a distance—and what he saw lost nothing in the telling, either by the good Father or by those who told it second or third or fourth hand. The country, says a contemporary writer, "was so stirred up by the news which the friar had brought back from the Seven Cities that nothing else was thought about."

Mendoza promptly organized an expedition for the conquest of the Seven Cities. One hundred and fifty or so young fellows recently arrived from Spain in quest of loot and glory constituted the spearhead of the little army. Reckless, well mounted and well equipped with arms and coats of mail, they were a formidable force as against almost any number of natives. With them went some two hundred foot soldiers armed with guns and crossbows, and several hundred friendly Indians. Francisco Vasquez de Coronado, also a relatively new arrival in the New World, was appointed to the command.

On February 23, 1540, while DeSoto was still wintering at Apalache in far-away Florida, Coronado started his army northward up the west coast of Mexico, following the route marked out by Friar Marcos. Progress was slow; the long train of pack horses required grain and grain was scarce; so, leaving the army to follow, Coronado took Friar Marcos as guide and with fifty horsemen and a few foot soldiers pushed on ahead. Through the valleys of the Sierra Madre of northern Mexico they went; into the present southeastern Arizona; across the Gila River; through the mountains along the Arizona-New Mexico boundary; and finally they stood before the first of the Seven Cities. When they saw it "such were the curses that some hurled at Friar Marcos, that I pray God may protect him from them," wrote a member of the expedition, adding, "It is a little, unattractive village, looking as if it had been all crumpled up together."

What in fact they saw was a sprawling community house designed somewhat after the manner of the great stone houses in the Chaco Canyon, which houses even then stood silent and empty scarcely one hundred miles to the northeast. But the people of the Chaco would have looked upon the houses of Cibola with quite as much contempt as did the men from Spain. Each succeeding story was terraced back like the houses of the Chaco; each terrace was entered by ladders as had been the custom at Chaco; but the houses were poorly constructed of adobe rather than from stone, and in every way lacked the finish and style of the Chaco houses. Whether they represented a primitive approach to the Chaco standards or a stage of degeneration from that standard we cannot say.

But whether primitive or degenerate, the Cibolans were ready to defend their homes against what must have appeared a pretty amazing enemy. Never before had they seen a horse. To go up against men encased in shining armor and those men mounted on great strange beasts, also somewhat sheathed in armor, took courage. Nonetheless the Indians stood to it. Coronado himself was knocked off his horse by a stone and for a while the battle was lively. However, the "fury of the Spaniards could not be resisted and in less than an hour they entered the village and captured it," says Castaneda, who later wrote an account of the expedition.

The Indians had had enough fighting and left the Spaniards in possession of the pueblo. Meantime the rest of the army, which Coronado had left to follow, came up. Exploring parties were sent out. One visited the Moqui villages to the west, and, still farther west, peered down into the Grand Canyon of the Colorado. Another party went eastward, passing by the great rock of Acoma, on the top of which was perched a pueblo accessible only by a stairway up the sheer side of the rock. One hundred and twenty-five miles east of the Seven Cities the Spaniards reached the Rio Grande in the vicinity of present-day Albuquerque, New Mexico. Here they found numerous large pueblos and plentiful supplies of food. Still farther east, on the Pecos River, they visited Cicuye (Pecos), the largest pueblo in the region. And from there they went out to see the "cows," by which they meant the vast buffalo herds which ranged down into eastern New Mexico. But the guide to the buffalo range told stories which were much more interesting to the Spaniards than a sight of the humpbacked cows of the plains.

This guide, the "Turk" they called him because he looked like one, discoursed freely about gold, silver and other riches which abounded in Quivira, his home country—location somewhat indefinite. Here was the sort of news they had been looking for, and the Spaniards, taking the Turk with

Above. Zuni, one of the Seven Cities of Cibola visited by Coronado in 1540.

From the Bureau of American Ethnology, *Fourteenth Annual Report.*

Right. The Grand Canyon of the Colorado—over a mile deep—down which a party from Coronado's expedition peered in 1540.

From Joseph C. Ives, *Report upon the Colorado River of the West.*

them, hastened back to the Rio Grande to report to Coronado.

And the report that Coronado got was surely enough to have inspired any prospective conqueror. "In his country," said the Turk, "there was a river in the level country which was two leagues wide in which there were fishes as big as horses and large numbers of very big canoes, with more than twenty rowers on a side, and that they carried shields, and that their lords sat on the poop under awnings, and on the prow they had a great golden eagle." He added that "everyone had their ordinary dishes made of wrought plate, and the jugs and bowls were of gold."

In part the story was true enough. DeSoto's men had seen large canoes with rowers and awnings such as the Turk described. And at times the Mississippi was even more than two leagues (roughly five miles) wide. For the rest, stranger stories had proved true in Mexico and Peru. Why doubt the Turk? When a native chief ventured to contradict some of the Turk's statements, all he got for it was to be chained up and led off to the Spaniards' camp.

But however much Quivira beckoned, winter was at hand and no extended expedition could be made. So the Spaniards went into camp on the Rio Grande. By what sort of arrangements they got food for themselves and their horses is not clear, but it is sure that the Indians supplied it either willingly or unwillingly. How the Spaniards got winter clothing is recorded in some detail. Soldiers were sent to the various pueblos along the river to collect blankets and cloaks—and what they saw they took, even if it was off the back of the leading man of the village. This did not make for good feeling. Other incidents added to the unhappiness of the natives. A Spaniard saw a pretty woman on the terrace of one of the pueblos. He had her husband come down and hold his horse while he climbed the ladder to the terrace.

Well-justified complaints failing of redress by Coronado, the Indians undertook their own. Apparently reasoning that the horses gave the Spaniards their superiority, the first attack was made on these unoffending beasts. In turn the Spaniards besieged the pueblos. In the end the natives had

Above. Herd of buffalo.

From Henry R. Schoolcraft, *Information Respecting the History, Condition and Prospects of the Indian Tribes of the United States.*

Below. Grass houses such as Coronado found at Quivira in 1541.

From *United States Senate Executive Document No. 54, 32nd Congress, 2nd Session.*

to give up and many were killed, or burned at the stake after having been promised mercy. Finally the long bloodstained winter came to an end. The ice in the Rio Grande broke up. About the 1st of May, 1541, the little army of Spaniards started for Quivira—with the Turk leading the way. Circling north and east around the Staked Plains, they were soon in the buffalo range, where they saw "such great numbers of cows [buffalo] that it already seemed something incredible," wrote Castaneda. Here, too, they found Indians who lived by following the buffalo herds—whose only food was the flesh of the buffalo, whose clothing and shelter were from the hide of the buffalo.

Some of these Indians told the Spaniards that Quivira was to the north rather than to the east, as the Turk was leading them. This confirmed statements made by Ysopete, an Indian who accompanied the expedition and who all along had insisted that the Turk was a liar. Failing provisions added to the growing uncertainty. In a council of the leaders it was decided that Coronado with thirty horsemen and a half dozen foot soldiers should push on to Quivira while the rest of the army returned to the Rio Grande.

With Ysopete as the guide and the Turk along in chains, Coronado's men rode due north. At the end of forty-two days they arrived at Quivira—and found a tribe of Indians living in circular grass-made lodges. Of gold or other wealth they found none. The Spaniards took it out on the poor Turk. "They garroted him, which pleased Ysopete very much," says the chronicler.

The exact location of Quivira is uncertain, but most authorities place it along the northern bank of the Arkansas River between Great Bend and Wichita, Kansas. Wherever it was, it held no attractions for Coronado. He made a bee-line back to the Rio Grande and his disappointed fellow conquerors. Nor did they delay long there. The following spring, that of 1542, saw the expedition trudging back along the route over which they had gaily traveled north two years before—leaving only a few priests whom the Indians promptly knocked in the head. Peace again reigned in the pueblo country.[3]

The Heretic

CORONADO'S MEN ON THE Rio Grande and DeSoto's on the Mississippi were not the only Europeans who shivered out the winter of 1541–42 in North America. Far to the north, huddled in a rude fort on the St. Lawrence River, were Jacques Cartier and a company of Frenchmen—there under the authority of the King of France. Twice before Cartier had explored the bay and entrance to the river, first in 1534 and more extensively in 1535. No permanent settlements were made. Nevertheless his explorations served to establish a French claim on the Atlantic shores of North America.[1]

But Spain recognized no French claims in America. She, Spain, had discovered America. Pope Alexander VI in 1493 had confirmed the title, except for the eastern hump of South America which went to Portugal. When Francis I of France authorized the explorations of Cartier, Spain protested. Unfortunately for the solidarity of Christian princes France questioned the Pope's certificate of title and "much desired to see Adam's will to learn how he partitioned the world."[2]

Spain did not push her protest; the St. Lawrence region was of little real interest to her; but the principle of the thing remained. Farther south, particularly along the eastern coast of Florida, a settlement by a possible enemy would be fatal

—for through the straits of Florida went the Spanish plate ships bearing to Spain the loot of Mexico and Peru. This was the only route by which the sailing ships of the day could get out of the Caribbean. The westerly blowing trade winds that so providentially wafted Spanish ships through the eastern portals of that sea made a return by that same route impossible. On the other hand, the Gulf Stream, flowing out of the Caribbean between Cuba and the tip of Florida, provided a natural seaway for Europe-bound ships. And except for Havana, on the northern coast of Cuba, Spain had no base in this area to protect her valuable and tempting cargoes.[3]

Nor was Spain oblivious to the need for such bases. As early as 1526 Vasquez de Ayllon had been encouraged to found a colony on the eastern shores of Florida—Florida being an elastic term at that time. With over five hundred men, women and children; with priests; with domestic animals; in fact, with all that went to make a permanent settlement Ayllon landed somewhere between the Savannah River and Chesapeake Bay. The exact site is uncertain, but in 1540, while at Cofitachequi, DeSoto's men saw in the hands of Indians articles of European manufacture which had evidently been secured from the Ayllon colony. The colony itself had long before disappeared—due to hardship and dissension.[4]

Again in 1561 a search was made along the east coast for a suitable location for a settlement. On the shores of present-day South Carolina the explorers found a pleasant harbor which they called Santa Elena. It may have been the site of Ayllon's colony. But after careful examination the expedition sailed back to San Domingo with an unfavorable report.[5]

Hardly were the Spaniards off the coast before two little ships came poking along. They looked in at the mouth of the St. Johns River in northern present-day Florida and worked on northward. But in those ships there were no Spaniards. They were Frenchmen. Worse yet they were French Huguenots—Lutherans or heretics, the Spaniards would have called them.

And had the Most Catholic King of Spain known what

these French Huguenots had in mind or what their backers had told the King of France they had in mind, he would have had something more serious than trespass to worry about. They were, so they said, hunting for a place in which to found a Huguenot refuge from the persecutions to which their nonconformity subjected them in Europe—the fountainhead of which persecution was the Most Catholic King of Spain in whose American domain they intended to find a haven. Perhaps their only thought was that of founding a Huguenot colony, but they were locating in a place that could very easily be used as a base for raiding the Spanish treasure fleets on their way home. In command was Jean Ribault of Dieppe, a French port from which had sailed, with the blessing of its Huguenot officials, many of the freebooting expeditions which for the past twenty years had roamed the Caribbean, capturing Spanish ships and sacking Spanish towns.

On May 27, 1562, Ribault's ships passed between the headlands now called Hilton's Head and St. Helena—and into the calm water within. They called it Port Royal, and it is still called Port Royal. It was the same harbor that the Spanish expedition had recently examined under the name of Santa Elena and reported unsuitable for a settlement.

Whatever Ribault thought of Port Royal as a permanent site for his proposed colony, it was here that he started a rude fort, named Charlesfort in honor of the King of France. And here he left thirty men as the nucleus of the future settlement. Then he sailed back to France to make his report and to bring colonists and supplies.

Except for some few survivors of wrecked ships in the hands of the Indians along the Florida coast, these thirty Frenchmen were the sole European inhabitants of the future United States during the autumn and winter of 1562 and 1563. Having completed the fort and eaten up their food, they became both bored and hungry. The Indian villages were nearby; the inhabitants were hospitable—as Indians ever have been where food is concerned. The Frenchmen had a way of getting on with them—as Frenchmen ever have had with Indians.

King Audusta, an Indian chief, invited them to a religious festival of his tribe. Doubtless it was the prospect of food rather than an opportunity for anthropological research that prompted an acceptance. However, their report of what they saw gives us a vivid picture of Indian customs prior to the coming of the white man.[6]

The day before the feast the Indian women swept and cleaned the place where the festival was to be held—". . . a great circuit of ground with open prospect and round in figure. On the morrow therefore, early in the morning, all they which were chosen to celebrate the feast, being painted and trimmed with rich feathers of divers colours, put themselves on the way to go from the kings house toward the place of Toya; whereunto when they were come they set themselves in order and followed three Indians, which in painting and in gesture were differing from the rest; each of them bare a Tablet in their hand, dancing and singing in a lamentable tune when they began to enter into the middest of the round circuit, being followed of others which answered them again. After that they had sung, danced and turned 3 times, they fel on running like unbridled horses, through the middest of the thickest woods. And then the Indian women continued all the rest of the day in teares as sad and woful as was possible and in such rage they cut the armes of the yong girles, which they lanced so cruelly with sharpe shels of muskles that the blood followed which they flang into the aire, crying out three times, He Toya. . . . Those that ran so through the woodes returned two days after: after their returne they began to dance with cherefull courage in the middest of the faire place. . . . When all these dances were ended they fell on eating with such greedinesse that they seemed rather to devoure their meate then to eate it, for they had neither eaten nor drunke the day of the feast, nor the two dayes following."

At this point the chronicler adds, "Our men were not forgotten at this good cheere."[7]

But there came a day when these jovial Frenchmen had worn out their welcome. Their food was gone. They were homesick. They could not stand each other. They killed their commanding officer, and from materials which they could get together they made a boat and embarked for France. Starvation overtook them. Lots were cast. The loser was slain and eaten. But finally they reached European waters. In November, 1563, an English ship picked them up and carried them into England, where their story was listened to with interest.[8]

And what of Jean Ribault, who had left these Frenchmen to rot at Port Royal or to make the best of their way home as they had done? He, too, was in England—a refugee. On his way back from Port Royal in 1562 he had sailed into Dieppe only to find France engaged in a civil war over religion—Catholic against Huguenot, Huguenot against Catholic. For the moment Dieppe was in Huguenot hands, but within three months it fell to the Catholic forces and Ribault fled to England where he published an account of Florida and flirted with the idea of an Anglo-French Protestant settlement there. However, the religious wars in France quieted down, and in the spring of 1564 Rene de Laudonniere sailed from France to re-establish the colony while Ribault returned to Dieppe and arranged to follow Laudonniere with supplies and reinforcements.[9]

In June Laudonniere was off the coast of Florida. A site just within the mouth of the St. Johns River, which Ribault had entered two years before and named the River of May, was selected for the new settlement. Men and tools were landed and a fort called Caroline was constructed. Among the colonists was an artist named Jacques le Moyne, from whose pencil we have what may be accepted as an authentic, if somewhat glorified, representation of this fort.

As soon as possible Laudonniere got to the main business of the settlement, which apparently put little emphasis on tilling the soil. Like DeSoto, a quarter of a century earlier, Laudonniere asked the Indians about gold, and like DeSoto he heard of gold—always just beyond. Soon he was embroiled in the intertribal wars of the natives. Worse yet, some of his men became mutinous; they knew a better way to find gold, and taking one of the ships went on a freebooting expedition against the Spanish, the news of which did not contribute to the popularity of the colony among its Spanish neighbors.

Months had passed since the colonists had landed. Again food was running low. The Indians were hostile and refused to supply corn. The French tried taking it by force and got more wounds than corn. Ribault and the long-expected supply ships had failed to arrive.[10]

Had the colony been forgotten? Far from it. The westerly-blowing trade winds of 1565 were bringing across the Atlantic three separate expeditions from three different countries, each of which expeditions had very much in mind this forlorn little fort back of a sand bar on the coast of Florida.

In October, 1564, four ships had sailed out of Plymouth, England. Towering over her three sister ships was the *Jesus of Lubeck,* loaned by Queen Elizabeth's navy in expectation of profits to be made. The venture was financed by a group of traders who had sold shares to a considerable number of people including some highly placed in Her Majesty's councils. In command of the ships was John Hawkins, who two years before had invaded the Caribbean contrary to all Spanish regulations and disposed of a cargo of negro slaves contrary to a contract between Spain and those to whom Spain had granted a monopoly of the slave trade.

Before leaving England in 1564, Hawkins took on board a French pilot who had been with Ribault on the Florida coast in 1562. Then dropping down the west coast of Africa, Hawkins collected some four hundred negroes. Late in January, 1565, he headed west into the trade winds, and two months later was on the Spanish Main (the northern coast of South America). Here he asked permission to trade his negroes for the gold, silver, pearls and hides which were the medium of exchange on the Main. Naturally the local Spanish officials had to refuse the request. However, ways were found, for the Spanish planters wanted the negroes. One of the ways was for Hawkins to land an armed party and "force" the Spanish to trade. After which he would "force" the official to give him a certificate of good conduct. Having finished his business, Hawkins headed for the Florida straits.[11]

At about the same time Ribault, with supplies and men for Fort Caroline, sailed westward from Dieppe, France.

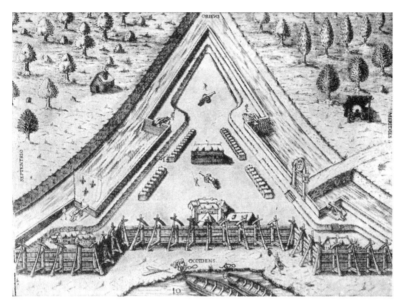

Above. Fort Caroline.

Below. A fortified village of the Florida Indians.

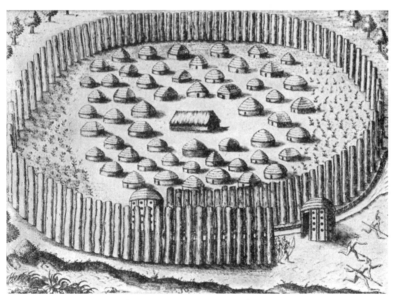

Both of the pictures shown *above* were made by Jacques Le Moyne, and are reproduced from Theodore De Bry's *Grands Voyages.*

And close behind Ribault, out of the harbor of Cadiz, came an armada of the King of Spain, commanded by Pedro Menendez. He, too, was headed for the coast of Florida.

On August 3 the starving and seemingly forgotten garrison of Fort Caroline saw a great ship standing in toward the mouth of the river. It turned out to be the *Jesus of Lubeck* and was accompanied by three smaller vessels. John Hawkins, the English slave trader, was making a call. Courteously he inquired as to their needs and offered to take them back to France. Laudonniere asked for supplies and a ship, all of which Hawkins provided, taking in payment some cannons and a note that was probably never redeemed. Then the Englishman sailed on northward. He had done a good deed and he had an interesting report for his fellow traders in England, who were beginning to eye the possibilities in the western waters.[12]

Twenty-five days later another fleet was off the mouth of the river. It was Jean Ribault with seven ships, three hundred men and ample supplies. The colony was saved—so thought the French at Fort Caroline.[13]

Another week went by and on the dark night of September 4 the watchmen on Ribault's ships lying at the mouth of the river were startled by strange craft, bristling with guns, bearing in upon them. Pedro Menendez was there. Locking prows with the French ships, he inquired who they were. Subjects of the King of France, they told him.

"Catholics or Lutherans?" asked Menendez.

"Lutherans," they replied.

Then Menendez stated his business. "I come to hang and behead all the Lutherans I may find on this sea and in this land."

The French, who were unprepared for a fight and not inclined to be hanged or beheaded, slipped their cables and stood out to sea. Menendez could not catch them nor on his part did he have strength enough to risk attacking the heavily garrisoned fort up the river. So he retired down the coast some thirty miles and began disembarking at a place which he named St. Augustine.

Meanwhile the French ships had come back to their sta-

SIR JOHN HAWKINS.
From *Herologia Anglica.*

tions off Fort Caroline. Ribault recognized that in Menendez he had an antagonist who would "hang and behead" the French unless they "hanged and beheaded" him first. Action was the only solution. Loading onto his ships practically all the able-bodied men from the fort, Ribault started for St. Augustine. The following morning the Spanish saw the French armada approaching—and prayed to the Virgin for deliverance. Instantly a howling wind came out of the north. The overloaded French boats were driven past the inlet to St. Augustine and, out of hand, went hurtling southward along the treacherous sands of the Florida coast. That they would not be back soon was a certainty in the mind of Menendez, who moved promptly to profit by their misadventure.

Into the teeth of the blinding storm, overland through swamps and tangled forests the grim old Spaniard led his men to a surprise attack on the now defenseless Fort Caroline. To oppose him there were left at the fort only the aged, the disabled, the women and the children. Sheer butchery took the place of hanging and beheading. Some few got away. Le Moyne, the artist, tumbled out of bed, dashed past his assailants, jumped the ditch surrounding the fort and made for the woods. With Laudonniere and a few others who had similarly escaped, he was picked up by one of the ships that had been tied near the fort—and they sailed hastily for France.

Leaving most of his men at the captured fort, Menendez hurried back to St. Augustine. The five or six hundred men who had been swept southward in the storm were still to be accounted for. Within a couple of days some Indians arrived at St. Augustine with news. A few miles to the south they said were many Christians afoot and stopped on their northward march by an arm of the sea. With only forty men, all that were at his disposal, Menendez went to meet them. And there they were, two hundred survivors of Ribault's armada bottled up at the end of a sand reef. Their ships had been wrecked and they were trying to get back to Fort Caroline. Menendez sent a boat which brought some of the leaders across to him. He informed them that their fort had already

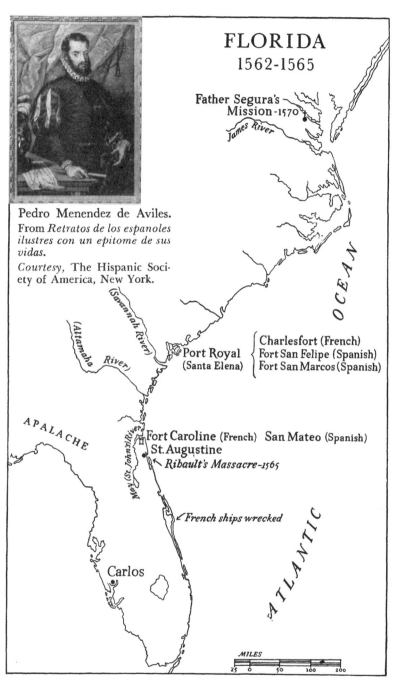

FLORIDA
1562-1565

Father Segura's
Mission -1570

James River

OCEAN

(Savannah River)

(Altamaha River)

Port Royal
(Santa Elena)

⎰ Charlesfort (French)
⎱ Fort San Felipe (Spanish)
⎱ Fort San Marcos (Spanish)

APALACHE

May (St. John's River)

Fort Caroline (French) San Mateo (Spanish)
St. Augustine
↖ *Ribault's Massacre-1565*

↙ *French ships wrecked*

ATLANTIC

Carlos

MILES
25 0   50   100   200

Pedro Menendez de Aviles.
From *Retratos de los espanoles
ilustres con un epitome de sus
vidas.*
Courtesy, The Hispanic Society of America, New York.

Based on Plate 8, *Atlas of American History.*

been captured and that since they were Lutherans he must regard them as enemies. If on these terms they wished to surrender, they might do so. The alternative was starvation, and the French surrendered. Menendez had them brought over in a boat ten at a time. As each boatload landed, he marched them behind the sand dunes and had their hands tied behind their backs. Finally they were all across, two hundred and eight of them. Then Menendez asked if there were any Catholics among them. Eight professed themselves to be true sons of the Church. The rest were marched into an open place among the dunes and "put to the knife."

Two days later the Indians reported an even larger body of Christians at the same place where the first group had been discovered. Again Menendez went down to meet them. Again the French leaders, this time including Ribault himself, parleyed with Menendez. There were about three hundred and fifty Frenchmen there. Half of them, with Ribault at their head, surrendered and were brought across the inlet ten at a time, tied up and marched back of the dunes. And they, too, were "put to the knife, understanding this to be expedient for the service of God Our Lord and Your Majesty," as Menendez reported the affair to his master, King Philip II of Spain; and Philip replied, ". . . you have done this with entire justification and prudence, and hold Ourselves greatly served thereby." There remained now only the one hundred and seventy-five who had refused to surrender. Soon the Indians brought word of them—farther down the coast near Cape Canaveral. After them went Menendez with three hundred men, some in boats and some along the shore. He found the French trying to rebuild one of the wrecked ships. At the sight of the Spaniards they fled, but on the promise of their lives most of them surrendered—and suffered no worse treatment than to have to pull an oar in a Spanish galley. Twenty fled to the woods, announcing that they "would rather be eaten by the Indians than surrender to the Spaniards."

With the French threat thus eliminated, Menendez, who among other titles held that of Governor of Florida, turned to the survey and administration of his colony. Many Spanish ships had been driven by storms onto the coast of Florida in years past. It was hoped that some survivors might be found among the Indians. To rescue these was one of the first concerns of the Governor; he, himself, had lost a son in one of the wrecked ships. Sailing up the west coast of Florida, he heard of several Christians, both men and women, in the hands of a local chief known as Carlos. By various wiles the chief was lured aboard a boat, whereupon Menendez told him to produce the captives or be killed. Carlos produced them; also a sizable amount of gold and silver which had been salvaged from wrecked ships. In fact, Carlos took quite a fancy to Menendez, so much so that he insisted upon giving him his sister, mature and plain, for a wife. Menendez demurred. "Christian men," he explained, "could not sleep with women who were not Christians." Further he "told them who God was, and His wisdom, power and goodness, and that all creatures who are born on earth must worship Him alone." Carlos readily agreed and assured the Governor that he and his sister were already Christians because he, Carlos, had taken the Governor as his elder brother, and besides there were four thousand Indians present who would be scandalized, even troublesome, if Menendez jilted the girl. There seemed no way out, so, as a member of the expedition tells the story, ". . . the Christian women [that is, those who had been held by the Indians] bathed and clothed her, and she appeared much better than before, when she was naked. . . . The supper, the music and the merriment took place on land, in some tents the Governor had set up, near his ships, and lasted until two o'clock in the morning. The Governor had her seated next to him, and said many things to her through the interpreter which pleased her. . . . Her Indian women and the Christian women danced with the soldiers, and when that was ended, they conducted her to rest on a bed which the Governor ordered to be made, and he followed her; and in the morning she arose very joyful and the Christian women who spoke to her said she was very much pleased."

Shipping his new wife to Havana, Menendez sailed back to the east coast of Florida; reinforced St. Augustine; repaired and garrisoned the former French fort, which he gave the name of San Mateo; and, going on up the coast, built a new fort named San Felipe at Port Royal near the ruins of the French Charlesfort.[14]

To further his plans for the subjugation and christianization of the Indians Menendez called in the Jesuits to establish missions at strategic points—from the tip of Florida to Chesapeake Bay. The latter mission, presided over by Father Segura, was not far from the present capital of the United States. The harvest of souls, however, was disappointing, and the fate of Father Segura, martyrized at his very altar, was all too typical of this effort to save the savages from eternal damnation.[15]

Except for the Spanish outpost at St. Augustine and a fleeting garrison or mission here and there Florida slipped back to its former more or less tranquil existence as the abode of the naked Indian and the ungainly alligator.

Above, from the pencil of Jacques le Moyne, is a view of tranquil existence in Florida in the sixteenth century. The Indians accosted the alligator by poking a sharp pole down its throat. Then turning the alligator over on its back, they beat it on the belly with sticks until it was dead. The alligator, shiftless descendant of the dinosaurs who for a hundred and forty million years lorded it over the earth, was on his part not beyond slapping a careless Indian into the water and chewing off a leg or arm while the rest of the organism protested.

The English

FLORIDA HAD YIELDED neither gold nor souls in sufficient quantity to justify the effort which Spain had expended in holding it. But in another way the effort justified itself. It gave pause to the growing inroads of Spain's most dangerous and most persistent competitor in the New World. For a quarter of a century Frenchmen, with or without the blessing of their rulers, had been persistently pounding at Spain's Caribbean lifeline.

The pitiless finality with which Menendez disposed of Ribault's colony was stark warning that Spain would and could defend her title. True, three years later a privately organized French expedition descended upon San Mateo, the former Fort Caroline, and massacred the Spanish garrison, reserving a few to be hanged under the inscription, "Not as to Spaniards, but as to Traitors, Robbers and Murderers." This, however, was sheer bravado and the avengers wasted no time in getting away.

Other factors than fear of Spain contributed to the lessening of French assaults upon the western world during the next thirty years. The Huguenots, from whose restless ranks the marauders mostly came, were very busy at home. It was a question whether Protestantism would survive at all in France. Admiral Coligny, the head of the Protestant faction

43

and Ribault's backer in the Florida adventure, was one of the many prominent victims of Catholic fury on St. Bartholomew's Day, 1572.

But as Protestantism bowed before the hosts of the Church in France, a new champion, and a new antagonist of Spain, arose across the Channel. England, which had been only mildly anti-Catholic when earlier in the century Henry VIII broke with Rome, was now becoming aggressively and even fanatically anti-Catholic. And Spain was the target. To break the power of Spain was to break the power of Rome. English freebooters took up where the French had left off. Their activity partook of the nature of a crusade. The lust for loot entered in, but it was secondary to the enthusiasm for doing harm to Spain.

Outstanding but on the whole typical of the leaders of this crusade was Francis Drake, a young cousin of John Hawkins, the slave trader who had called at Fort Caroline in 1565. Two years later Hawkins went on another slaving expedition. With him in command of one of the ships went Drake. Again the Queen's tall warship, the *Jesus of Lubeck*, led the way. Again negroes were picked up on the African coast. Again in the face of well-known Spanish regulations to the contrary and only through an even more drastic show of force than in 1565 the negroes were traded along the Spanish Main for gold, silver, pearls and hides.

As the fleet was returning homeward, a storm forced it deep into the Gulf of Mexico, and with the *Jesus of Lubeck* in distress Hawkins reluctantly put into San Juan de Ulua, the harbor of Vera Cruz, to make his repairs. Of all the places in Spanish America this was the one in which he was least welcome. At that very moment silver in great quantities was being accumulated at Vera Cruz for shipment to Spain in the annual plate fleet, which fleet arrived at the mouth of the harbor the day after the Englishmen sailed in. Hawkins refused to let the Spanish fleet into its own harbor until the commanding officer agreed to be peaceable. The Spaniard agreed, and the six ships of the English "pirate" and thirteen ships of King Philip of Spain tied up in a line along the rocky island inside the harbor. The following morning the Spaniards made a surprise attack. Drake got his ship out and did not wait to see how his fellows fared. Hawkins, while the fight raged, transferred what he could to his one seaworthy ship and got out with it. The *Jesus of Lubeck,* property of the Queen of England, along with three other ships, an uncertain amount of booty and a considerable number of prisoners, fell into the hands of the Spaniards.

By the grace of God and great fortitude Hawkins and Drake made Plymouth—but they were in no good humor. They were certain that they had been wronged by the Spaniards. Whatever they had saved from the affair at San Juan de Ulua it was less than they had expected to make out of the voyage. Besides they had been humiliated. Unquestionably they had a claim against Spain. Drake followed a procedure common at the time. He asked for and received from the Queen "letters of reprisal" which authorized him to recompense himself from any unwary Spanish ship or town that might fall within his power. Under this thin veneer of legality he proceeded to collect, with interest, on the Spanish Main. His methods differed little from those of the former French pirates.[1]

Then in December, 1577, Drake sailed out of Plymouth, England, with five ships on a voyage the purpose and destination of which was somewhat indefinite, though it was said to be a trading venture. The Queen had a share in the enterprise as did other highly placed persons and a number of merchants. In March, 1578, Drake was off the coast of Brazil, down which he slowly felt his way. On September 6 he emerged from the western end of the Straits of Magellan and was in the broad Pacific. Of his fleet only the *Pelican* remained, which he now rechristened the *Golden Hind.* The other ships had either turned back or been lost in the stormy passage of the Straits. Drake turned northward. Before him lay the coasts of Chile and Peru from whose mines came the gold and silver that supported Spain's vast empire in Europe. The Spaniards had not an inkling of his presence until he struck. He raided the coastal towns; captured and plundered a rich silver ship; loaded onto the *Golden Hind* all the gold, silver and jewels that it could carry—and sailed on northward.

In June, 1579, he was off the coast of present-day Washington or Oregon, possibly looking for a sea passage from the Pacific to the Atlantic, which was then thought to exist in that latitude. Naturally he did not find it, and sailing southerly down the coast to a point not far above San Francisco Bay, he found and put into "a convenient and fit harbor." There he built a sort of fortification, set up tents, lightened his ship and spent a month cleaning and repairing it.

His presence soon attracted the neighboring Indians. They were a friendly, naked lot dressed mostly with feathers in their hair. Their houses were described by Drake's men as being circular pits dug in the earth and roofed over with poles on which sod was laid. The opening at the top where the poles came together in a sort of peak served both for door and chimney. In other words their houses were very similar to the pit houses in which had lived the ancestors of the pueblo dwellers of Chaco Canyon and Mesa Verde and which pit houses had furnished the design for the *kivas* of the more advanced pueblo people. Chetro Ketl and Cliff Palace had flourished and died some hundreds of years before Drake was born. Not for other hundreds of years before that had the inhabitants lived in pit houses, and yet here in northern California, in 1579, the natives were living in just such houses.[2]

By the latter part of July the *Golden Hind* was in shape for further adventures. But before leaving New Albion, as he called the region, Drake took formal possession in the name of the Queen. According to his story, he nailed to a post a duly inscribed brass plate. Three hundred and fifty-seven years later there was found on the western shore of San Francisco Bay a battered brass plate bearing the following inscription, "BEE IT KNOWNE UNTO ALL MEN BY THESE PRESENTS JUNE 17 1579 BY THE GRACE OF GOD AND IN THE NAME OF HERR MAJESTY QUEEN ELIZABETH OF ENGLAND AND HERR SUCCESSORS FOREVER I TAKE POSSESSION OF THIS KINGDOME WHOSE KING AND PEOPLE FREELY RESIGNE THEIR RIGHT AND TITLE IN THE WHOLE LAND UNTO HERR MAJESTIES KEEPEING NOW NAMED BY ME AN TO BEE KNOWNE UNTO

Sir Francis Drake.
From *Herologia Anglica*.

The brass plate supposedly left in California by Francis Drake.
Courtesy, California Historical Society.

ALL MEN AS NOVA ALBION. FRANCIS DRAKE." Eminent scholars believe that it is the identical plate.[3]

Sailing westward across the Pacific, Drake visited the East
India Islands and rounding the Cape of Good Hope reached
England in September, 1580. He was the first Englishman
to have circumnavigated the globe in his own ship. This
ship, weighed down with gold, silver, jewels and perhaps
a few boxes of spice, was tied up in the Thames River at
London. It had been a very successful trading voyage. The
Queen accepted her share and knighted Drake.

While Drake and his fellow captains were assailing Spain's
empire by sea, thousands of other young Englishmen such
as Humphrey Gilbert and his half brother, Walter Raleigh,
crossed over to the continent to aid the Protestant cause in
the Lowlands or in France. They came back with not only
an increased hatred of Spain but with a conviction that it
was the wealth of America that supported Spain's armies.
The best way to beat Spain was to take away from her the
source of her power. More English eyes turned westward.

Gilbert became the spokesman for a group who held that
by sailing northwest around North America a passage
would be found to the Indies and unlimited wealth. It was
the same passage that Drake was looking for when he was
off the west coast of North America. In 1576 Martin Frobisher, acting for private backers interested in finding this
northwest passage, made the first attempt to get through,
but was turned back by ice near Baffin's Bay. The following
year he tried again—this time with the active and open aid
of the Queen, though the objective was gold rather than the
Indies. None the less Frobisher went through the formality
of taking possession of the northern shores of eastern North
America in the name of the Queen of England. The establishment of a colony does not seem to have been thought of.[4]

In 1583 Gilbert himself was at St. Johns, in Newfoundland, reading to the doubtless slightly puzzled fishermen
from the Grand Banks a patent issued to him by the Queen
of England, directing him to discover new lands and take
possession in her name. The fishermen had been drying fish
at St. Johns for perhaps a hundred years, but Gilbert pro-

ceeded to make his discovery and to take possession through the ancient ceremony of being handed a piece of Newfoundland turf. His patent further authorized him to make grants of land, to bring settlers from England and to create and administer a local government, subject however to the laws of England. One of the laws which he made on the spot probably indicates the manner in which his pronouncement of title was received by the fishermen, many of whom were doubtless French. This law stated that "if any person should utter words sounding to the dishonour of Her Majestie, he should loose his ears, and have his ship and goods confiscate."

Thus on the shores of Newfoundland, among the boisterous fishermen of the Grand Banks, England made her first approach toward the establishment of permanent colonies in the New World. So far as immediate settlement in Newfoundland was concerned nothing came of Gilbert's enterprise. He was lost at sea on the way home and his patent lapsed. However, the ideas expressed in this patent recurred again and again and were the frame within which England colonized America.

Edward Hayes, captain and owner of one of the ships in Gilbert's fleet and historian of the expedition, clinched England's title to North America thus: ". . . the English nation onely hath right unto these countreys of America from the cape of Florida Northward by the privilege of first discovery, unto which Cabot was authorized by regall authority; and set forth by the expense of our late king Henry the seventh." In this statement Captain Hayes was repeating a formula which became common in his day, and which has persisted.[5]

The story briefly is as follows: In 1496 John Cabot or Caboto, a Venetian residing in Bristol, England, was granted a patent to discover unknown lands. In 1497 he sailed, discovered land and took possession for the King of England. The following year he started again to visit the lands he had discovered—and sailed into oblivion for a matter of eighty years. Then as English adventurers turned their eyes to the northwest and a possible open-water passage to the Indies, they felt the need for a title that would give them rights in this area similar to the rights which Spain enjoyed in the

Caribbean due to the discovery of Columbus. Cabot's discoveries, now definitely located in the area which England wished to control, served to give respectability to England's claim.[6]

The Queen's ministers, however, sensing possible future embarrassment in accepting simple discovery as a basis of permanent title, put forth a more practical formula. If Spain or any other civilized nation had actual possession of a place with evidence thereof in the nature of power to prove their possession, well and good; otherwise remote and barbarous lands were open to those who could take and hold them. This formula was clearly set forth, time after time, by Sir William Cecil, the Queen's first Minister. England recognized no Spanish monopoly in the Americas "either because of donations from the Pope or from their having touched here and there upon those coasts, built cottages, and given names to a few places." This, by the law of nations, as interpreted in England, "could not hinder other princes from freely navigating those seas and transporting colonies to those parts where the Spanish did not actually inhabit." In other words, "prescription without possession availed nothing."[7]

This interpretation of the "law of nations" appeared in Gilbert's patent and reappeared in a new patent issued on March 25, 1584, to Walter Raleigh authorizing him ". . . to discover, search for, finde out, and view such remote heathen and barbarous lands, countries, and territories not actually possessed by any Christian princes, nor inhabited by Christian people, as to him shall seem good. . . ." Promptly Raleigh dispatched two ships to find a suitable place for a colony—as near Florida as possible without violating the clause in his charter forbidding him to injure any nation at peace with England. His ships struck the American coast somewhat above Cape Fear and worked northward looking for a harbor. The first inlet they found was through the line of reefs inclosing Pamlico Sound. Landing cn one of the sandy islands, they took possession "according to the ceremonies used in such enterprises." Then they proceeded to explore the other islands and get acquainted with the Indians, who were not only friendly but gave them a good deal of information about the adjoining mainland. The natives on an island called Roanoke were particularly hospitable. By the middle of September Raleigh's scouts were back in England with two of the natives as exhibits and a report which on the whole was favorable.[8]

Apparently Raleigh was satisfied with the place selected. Queen Elizabeth thought so well of it that she named the region Virginia in commemoration of her virgin estate. By spring all the arrangements were complete for sending out the first group of settlers, and on April 9, 1585, they sailed from Plymouth for "Virginia." Seven ships carried the one hundred and seven colonists—all men—together with food, clothing, saws, axes and other things necessary to build and sustain a permanent settlement. With the colonists went the two natives who had been carried to England the previous autumn. Sir Richard Grenville, Raleigh's cousin, was in command of the fleet and of the expedition until the colonists were landed, which occurred late in June, whereupon Ralph Lane, acting under Raleigh's directions, took over with the title of Governor, and Grenville shortly returned to England to bring more colonists and more supplies.

Building rough houses and a temporary fort, the colonists were soon established on the northern end of Roanoke Island. Then they began an intensive exploration of the mainland opposite. Their objectives were the discovery of gold or a waterway to the South Sea, as they called the Pacific Ocean. ". . . for that the discovery of a good Mine, by the goodness of God, or a passage to the South-sea, or some way to it, and nothing els can bring this Countrey in request to be inhabited by our nation," said Lane, the Governor. Neither Lane nor those who sent him on this quest had any conception of the distance or of the great mountain ranges between the sandy shores of Roanoke Island and the sea to the west.

Their explorations yielded neither a mine nor a water route, but from the Indians they heard of a better place for a colony—on Chesapeake Bay, where there were also pearls.

As the winter and another spring wore along, food commenced to run low. Grenville, who had been expected back with supplies, failed to show up. Lane had shown little sense in dealing with the Indians, and no help was forthcoming

Above. A well-appointed native dinner-table on Roanoke Island.
Below. When the natives needed a new canoe, they felled a suitable tree by burning it at the base. Then they applied rosin and burned the log to the shape desired.

The pictures are from De Bry's *Grands Voyages* and were engraved from water-color paintings made at Roanoke Island by John White in 1586. The following year White returned to Roanoke as Governor of the colony.

from them. The crisis came on the 1st of June, 1586, when rowing across to the Indian town of Dasamonquepeuc with twenty-five of his men, Lane asked the natives to meet him, and when they did so, his men shot them down in retaliation for an attack which Lane suspected they were hatching up against him.

Eight days later, with starvation staring them in the face and the Indians watching their backs for a good place to land an arrow, the colonists sighted "a great fleet of three and twentie sailes" coming up the coast. It could hardly be Grenville, in that strength. It might be Spanish. The following day their fears were relieved. The ships were English under the command of Sir Francis Drake.[9]

Drake was in fact on the way home after another raiding expedition against the Spanish settlements in the Caribbean. Coming up the Florida coast, he decided to look in at St. Augustine, the Spanish post founded by Menendez in 1565. A watchtower on the shore betrayed the location of a fort protecting the little settlement. Drake took a couple of shots at it by way of introduction and during the night sent a reconnaissance party ashore, whereupon the Spaniards abandoned their fort. It was found to be a rough, stockade affair, still unfinished. The garrison, amounting to not more than one hundred and fifty men, had retired to the town, into which the English pursued them. The only known casualty was Anthony Powell, Drake's sergeant-major, who "leapt upon one of the horses they [the Spaniards] had left behind and pursued them; having advanced rashly beyond his company, over rough ground covered by long grass, a Spaniard, lying in wait for him, shot him through the head."

The town had a prosperous appearance, with a council house, a church and other public buildings, all of which Drake burned in retaliation for the killing of Powell. The inhabitants and the soldiers had fled to San Mateo, the former Fort Caroline of the French, which Drake could not get at because of the sand bars at the mouth of the river. The only real plunder that he got at St. Augustine was a chest containing money intended for the payment of the soldiers.[10]

Sailing on up the coast, Drake began watching for signs of Raleigh's colony at Roanoke—and there he was, like Hawkins at Fort Caroline twenty-one years earlier, offering assistance if they wished to stay or transportation if they wished to go home. Lane in his report to Raleigh told a not very convincing story of having first asked for supplies and then on account of a storm having reluctantly accepted the offer to be taken home. Another account gives what is perhaps a more accurate version: ". . . a great storme arose, and drove the most of their fleet from their ankers to Sea, in which ships at that instant were the chiefest of the English Colony: the rest on land perceiving this, hasted to those three sailes which were appointed to be left there; and for feare they should be left behinde they left all things confusedly, as if they had bene chased from thence by a mighty army: and no doubt so they were; for the hand of God came upon them for the cruelty and outrages committed by some of them against the native inhabitants of the countrey." [11]

Hardly was Drake's fleet, with the Roanoke colonists aboard, well headed for England before a lone ship anchored off the inlet to Roanoke Island. It had been sent by Raleigh with supplies for the colony. Finding no colony, it turned back to England. A few days later still another relief expedition was at Roanoke. This was the long overdue Richard Grenville. He found the abandoned huts of the colonists but nothing to tell him what had become of them. With a view to retaining possession of the region, he left fifteen men on Roanoke Island with supplies sufficient to maintain them for two years. Then he too sailed back to England.[12]

It might seem that Raleigh would have lost a little of his enthusiasm for Virginia and especially for Roanoke Island. Evidently such was the case, since in the year following the return of the Lane colonists he did not personally equip another expedition. Instead, in 1587, he let out the colonizing project to a company made up of merchants willing to risk their capital and of individuals willing to risk their persons by going overseas and serving the colony.

As a matter of fact practically all of the early English explorations, voyages or colonies were financed by companies of one sort or another. Those who wanted a share in the venture contributed money or goods or services against the cost of the venture. Cabot did not sail "by the expense" of Henry VII, as Captain Hayes said. All the King did was to authorize Cabot to go and Cabot was probably financed by a group of Bristol merchants who, if there had been any profits, would have divided them among themselves according as each contributed—a ship or victuals or money to pay the sailors or insurance or whatever it was. The King or Queen, unless they were shareholders by having put in something, stood to receive only the usual royal fifth of the commodities or precious metals that might be found and brought out.

Hawkins' slaving voyages were financed by a group of merchants and other speculative-minded persons each of whom put up a proportion of the expenses, and probably subdivided their respective shares among their friends or where they would do good in high places. The Queen, or rather her navy, ventured a ship or ships. Drake's voyage around the world was financed by many shareholders with many different interests in the venture. Some of these venturers even had their representatives aboard Drake's ships, and their evident apprehension when they discovered the real destination and purpose of the voyage caused no end of trouble. Frobisher's voyages in search of a northwest passage were likewise financed by various backers, including the Queen, whose contribution may have been only prestige but would have been taken in profits had there been any. Gilbert sold shares in his Newfoundland venture. Raleigh, himself, had contributed both his time and his money in that failure.

Thus in 1587 we find a newly formed company preparing to establish a new colony in Virginia under a lease of rights from the proprietor, namely, Raleigh. Funds for the purchase of supplies and equipment, for the payment of employees, for the rental of ships and for all the other things that went into equipping the colony came from a central treasury into which the shareholders had each paid their separate assessments—in cash or in goods or in the use of ships or in contracts for personal services. Profits, if any, also went into this central treasury, and dividends, if any, would be paid out of this central treasury to each shareholder in proportion to his contribution. Only the shareholders could make a profit out of the venture. Colonists who were not shareholders were simply hired help, and whatever they produced went into the company treasury.

There were thirty-two members of this new company known as The City of Raleigh in Virginia. Nineteen of the members were London merchants; they footed the costs. Thirteen members had contracted to go to Virginia and direct the operations of the colony; they ventured their time, ability and lives. John White, one of the thirteen, was chosen Governor of the colony, which is to say that in the management of the settlement to be established in Virginia he was to be Governor, though as to the management of the affairs of the company as a whole he might have very little to say. He had been a member of Lane's colony, had taken part in the explorations of 1585–86, and had made numerous water-color views of the Indians, their houses and their customs, two of which views are reproduced on page 52.

The colony sailed from England on April 26, 1587, in three ships, the largest being of one hundred and twenty tons. There were about one hundred and twenty-five colonists in all—ninety-some men, seventeen women, nine children and two natives who had piled into the boats with the Lane party the year before and had been carried to England. The colonists, from the Governor to the youngest child, were merely passengers until they were landed in America. In command of the ships and of the crews and perhaps of the route was one Simon Ferdinando, a name which sounded odd among all those Englishmen. He may have been hired for the job because he knew the way. Anyhow he dropped south and followed the usual Spanish path into the Leeward Islands; coasted along San Domingo; and then turned northward for Virginia. In view of the tension between England and Spain at the time, Ferdinando either took a very great chance or was exceedingly able in avoiding the eyes of the Spanish.

On July 16 the coast of Virginia was sighted and six days

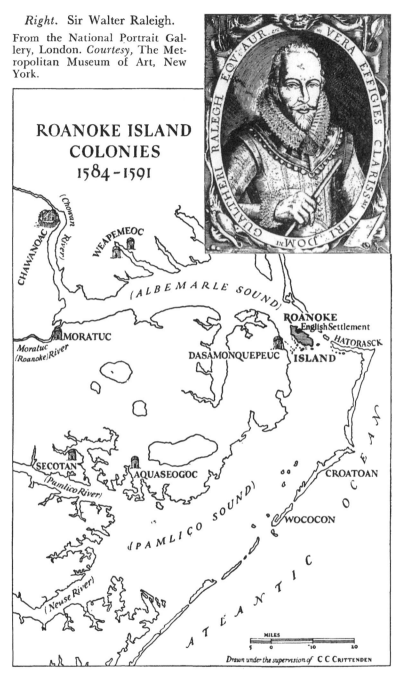

ROANOKE ISLAND COLONIES 1584-1591

(*Chowan River*)

CHAWANOAC

WEAPEMEOC

(ALBEMARLE SOUND)

ROANOKE
English Settlement

HATORASCK

MORATUC

Moratuc
(Roanoke) River

DASAMONQUEPEUC

ISLAND

SECOTAN

AQUASEOGOC

(*Pamlico River*)

CROATOAN

WOCOCON

(PAMLICO SOUND)

(*Neuse River*)

ATLANTIC

OCEAN

MILES

5   0   10   20

Drawn under the supervision of C C CRITTENDEN

From the *Atlas of American History.*

57

later they were off Roanoke Island. In an account of the voyage White says that "according to the charge given us among other directions in writing, under the hand of Sir Walter Ralegh," the ships were to stop at Roanoke only long enough to pick up the fifteen men left there the year before by Grenville and then were to go on to Chesapeake Bay, where the new colony was to be established. However, Ferdinando dumped the colonists ashore at Roanoke, and White seemingly lacked the gumption to insist that Raleigh's directions be carried out.

Instead of being greeted at Roanoke by the fifteen men left there by Grenville the new colonists found the bones of one and from the Indians of Croatoan, an island a few miles south of Roanoke, they got the rest of the story. It appeared that the Indians from the mainland had come across to Roanoke in their canoes, caught the Englishmen off guard and killed two of them. The rest had fled in a small boat to an adjoining island and had later disappeared no one knew where. The houses that Lane's men had built the year before were still standing. White set his people to work repairing them. In the midst of this activity a blessed event took place —the date August 18. It was a girl and, to quote White, "because this child was the first Christian borne in Virginia, shee was named Virginia." The proud parents were Ananias and Eleanor Dare. We can understand White's pleasure in telling us about the little girl. She was his granddaughter, Eleanor Dare being his daughter.

But White had little time in which to beam upon the little Virginia. Simon Ferdinando was going back to England with the ships. Some member of the company had to go along to arrange for supplies. The Governor agreed to go. And so on August 27, 1587, John White, Governor of The City of Raleigh in Virginia, stood on the deck of a dingy little sailing vessel and watched the low sandy island, whereon were his colony and his daughter and his granddaughter, slowly merge with the sky and disappear.[13]

Even before the White colony had left England a vast war fleet was being fitted out in the ports of Spain for the conquest of England. What with her Drakes, and Raleighs and other unpleasant people and habits King Philip of Spain had had all he could stand from his heretic half-sister-in-law of England. The Spanish preparations had become so evident that in the very month in which the White expedition sailed for Virginia Sir Francis Drake was "singeing the King of Spain's beard" by destroying naval supplies and ships in Cadiz harbor. However, the persistent Philip repaired his losses, and in July, 1588, the great Armada bore down on England—and disaster.

It was into the midst of feverish preparations to meet this impending Spanish onslaught that White got back to England in November, 1587. Through Raleigh's influence he was able to get two ships, load them with supplies and start for Virginia in April, 1588. The hovering screen of the Armada lashed him back under the guns of the English forts. Thereafter until the Armada was disposed of there was no possible chance of getting either men or ships to carry anything anywhere away from England. England needed every ship and every man.

Nor could White get a ship in 1589. The following year he practically hitchhiked a ride with three privateers which were going on a voyage into the West Indies and which agreed to circle up to Roanoke and see how things stood there.

With what must have been to White tantalizing slowness the expedition dropped down the coast of Africa, turned westerly into the trade winds, slipped in among the Leeward Islands, lay in wait for Spanish prizes, chased some and caught some. On the 15th of August they dropped anchor at Hatorasck (see map on page 57). The larger ships were unable to get over the bar at the inlet and had to stand outside. There was a high wind from the northeast. The sea was heavy. Only after great difficulties and the loss of seven men by drowning did the small boats get White ashore at Roanoke.

As he stepped up the bank, he was confronted by a tree on which "were curiously carved these faire Romane letters C R O." Going on to where the settlement had stood, he found that the houses had been taken down and "the place very strongly enclosed with a high palisado of great trees, with curtains and flankers very Fortlike, and one of the chiefe trees or postes at the right side of the entrance had the barke taken off, and 5 foote from the ground in fayre Capitall letters was graven CROATOAN." He found where the colonists had buried some chests, later dug up and rifled by the Indians; but of the boats, ordnance and other equipment of the colony he found no trace.

Before sailing for England in 1587 White had arranged with the colonists that should they leave the settlement they would indicate their destination by signs just such as he had found on the tree and post. Therefore to him it was evident that they had moved over to Croatoan, the natives of which island had always been friendly.

But the following morning, just as White and his party were leaving the ships to go to Croatoan, a storm came up. They were driven out to sea, they were short of water and of food, and, seemingly, of much persistence—and they sailed for England.

Three years later, in giving a written account of the expedition to Richard Hakluyt, the collector of English voyages, White ended with these words, "Thus committing the reliefe of my discomfortable company the planters in Virginia, to the merciful help of the Almighty, whom I most humbly beseech to helpe and comfort them, according to his most holy will and their good desire, I take my leave." [14]

History, however, has refused thus meekly to take leave of the Lost Colony and of little Virginia Dare. Their fate has been a recurring subject of speculation and theory. One widely accepted rumor was that the colonists did betake themselves to the Chesapeake Bay region and were there massacred by Powhatan only a short time before the arrival of the English at Jamestown in 1607.

But that story lacked documentation, which defect was handsomely compensated for in a discovery that startled the academic world in 1937—the year following the discovery of the Drake plate in California. A tourist walking along the east bank of the Chowan River (note the location in the upper left of the map on page 57) stumbled upon a stone slab on one side of which was inscribed, "Ananias & Virginia Dare went hence unto Heaven 1591. . . . Anye Englishman shew John White Govr Via." On the reverse side was a message seemingly from Eleanor White Dare reciting the miseries of the colonists and telling where most of them were buried. Here at last was a partial solution of the three-hundred-and-fifty-year-old mystery. Perhaps the burial place would yield further records, and sure enough it did.

So impressive were the discoveries that distinguished scholars gathered to examine the evidence and to seek for more stones—which also were found. Across the Carolinas and into Georgia went the trail of engraved stones, each with its message from the dwindling survivors of the Lost Colony. How many stones might have been found, and with what additions to our knowledge, is a matter only for speculation. When nearly fifty had come to light, enthusiasm for further discovery waned. The weight of evidence was becoming top-heavy—over a ton of it, in fact. And the stones were left to rest, unregarded, in the basement of a southern college, an unique monument to the enduring interest in little Virginia Dare, still known to history for but nine days.[15]

The King Is Dead

DRAKE'S ASSAULT UPON St. Augustine in 1586 had a more far-reaching effect than that hard-hitting sea captain could have foreseen. It brought about a prompt contraction of the formerly undefined "Florida" to approximately its later geographical dimensions. Even by Spain the name ceased being applied to all southeastern North America. Actually Florida no longer extended to Port Royal; that outpost was abandoned. The region known as Guale in southern Georgia became the northern limit of Spanish influence, an influence kept up largely through the missionary activities of a group of Franciscan monks who had replaced the unsuccessful Jesuits.

But, even in this limited sphere, the Cross could not maintain Spanish dominance without some aid from the sword. In 1597 Juanillo, a conservative if enterprising young native of Guale, took issue with Father Corpa on the subject of polygamy. The good father was firm. So was Juanillo, who settled the controversy by a crude imitation of the way by which his white Christian brothers of the time often settled their differences. Hiding in the mission chapel with several of his friends, Juanillo brained the father with a club just as he finished his devotions. Then, having initiated his private counter-reformation, Juanillo headed a general uprising against all the missionaries in Guale. Five Franciscans were killed and one was captured. Flushed with this easy success, the insurgents attacked the large mission of San Pedro on Cumberland Island (off the coast of Georgia). There, however, they were ignominiously defeated.

Naturally the Spanish authorities at St. Augustine were disturbed over all this uproar. A company of soldiers marched northward to restore order. The Indians took to the woods and only a few, mostly boys, were captured. With the exception of one who admitted his guilt the prisoners were pardoned with an injunction to behave better in the future. Spanish nature seems to have changed since the days when Narvaez and DeSoto dealt with the Indians of Florida. And again the patient Franciscans went to work, striving by gentle measures to bring their charges to an understanding of the less brutal side of the white man's civilization. However, their spiritual conquest was extended westward across the peninsula rather than northward toward Virginia.[1]

But as Spain drew back in Florida she was expanding from Mexico. Up through the sand dunes of Chihuahua, that spring of 1598, creaked a long line of wagons headed for *el paso* (the pass) where the Rio Grande breaks out of the mountains and turns eastward toward the sea. Leading the caravan was Juan de Onate, newly appointed Governor of "New" Mexico. With him were several hundred colonists —men, women, children and a few Franciscan missionaries.

On April 30, 1598, on the banks of the Rio Grande, Onate took formal possession "of all the kingdoms and provinces of New Mexico, on the Rio del Norte [Rio Grande] in the name of our Lord King Philip. There was a sermon and secular celebration, a great salute and much rejoicing. In the afternoon a comedy was presented and the royal standard blessed." Thus was born New Mexico—a province comprising not only the present State of New Mexico but also Arizona, Nevada, Utah and parts of Wyoming, Colorado, Kansas, Oklahoma and Texas.

Following the river northward from *el paso*, Onate and his colonists traveled nearly two hundred miles before they found any permanent settlements. Then, a little below a place which they called Socorro, and which is still called by that name, they began to see pueblos, at first small and scattered, but farther on increasing in number and in size, many being four and five stories high. The pueblos were similar in construction to those which Coronado had seen fifty-eight years before and, except for the material of which they were built and the workmanship, were much like the houses which for three hundred years had been standing vacant in the Chaco Canyon. And each of these houses along the Rio Grande had its *kiva* just as at Chaco Canyon or Mesa Verde or the Seven Cities of Cibola.

The people, of whom there were many thousands at each of the larger groups of pueblos, wore clothing made from cotton and shoes made from deerskins. The women were not indifferent about their appearance—their skirts were embroidered with colored thread; the maidens wore their hair arranged in large coils on either side of the head as shown in the picture on page 67. The men were armed with bows and flint-pointed arrows—quite as effective as the guns which the Spaniards carried. In their gardens corn, beans, and squashes were growing. Domesticated turkeys were everywhere. All in all, life in the pueblo country seemed prosperous, comfortable and satisfactory.

Continuing on up the river through villages which lined its banks and extended east and west for a considerable distance, Onate established his headquarters not far from where Santa Fe was founded eleven years later. His colonists began building a church; the missionaries were assigned to their charges among the various pueblos; and the government of the Province of New Mexico was put into operation.

On September 8 these Spanish colonists celebrated the completion of their church—which must have been a very temporary affair at best. Five days later, in the Escorial, that vast convent-palace-mausoleum raised by his direction high on the mountains of New Castile, Philip II, who for forty-two years had been King of Spain, died. Whether in his last moments he thought of his colonists in far-away New Mexico no man knows—but it was Philip's nature to think of everything concerning the welfare of his kingdom, and perhaps he did. With him, unknown to Spain, passed the greatness of Spain.

Oblivious of what had occurred or its meaning, and with his own affairs in order, Onate proceeded to explore New Mexico. One party was sent eastward to the buffalo range where Coronado's men had first seen the *vacas de Cibola,* meaning cows of Cibola, which name was later contracted to simply cibola—from a corruption of which our name of buffalo is derived. Now, in 1598, as in the time of Coronado, the Spanish party found immense herds, accompanied by nomadic Indians who moved along with the buffalo and lived on them. The visitors were particularly entertained by the use which these roving Indians made of dogs as carriers. What they saw in fact was the Indian travois—poles fastened on either side of the animal with the ends dragging behind and the load strapped across the poles. "It is a sight worth seeing, and very laughable," said the chronicler, "to see them travelling, the ends of the poles dragging on the ground, nearly all of them snarling in their encounters, travelling one after another on their journey." Also the Spaniards learned something about buffalo. They attempted to drive some of them into a corral, but the buffalo, after starting off nicely, "turned back in a stampede upon the men, and, rushing through them in a mass, it was impossible to stop them, because they are cattle terribly obstinate."

Meanwhile Onate himself visited the Zuni pueblos, which were the ones that, under the name of the Seven Cities of Cibola, had lured Coronado northward in 1540. There he found a son of one of the Indians who probably had guided Cabeza de Vaca to the Spanish slave-catching camp, been captured by the Spaniards, and later used as a guide to bring the Coronado party to Cibola. From Zuni Onate went on westward to the Moqui villages which Coronado's men had also visited. There the inhabitants received him "scattering fine flour upon us and upon our horses as a token of peace and friendship." But the real objective of this western trip was a silver mine believed to be somewhere beyond the Moqui towns. Nine men were sent out to find it and, plunging southwestward through present-day Arizona, they discovered, some fifty miles west of present-day Prescott, a very rich silver outcrop. Here was what the colonists came to New Mexico to find. The produce of farms would not repay the cost of the long haul to markets; gold and silver would. But even so an outlet to the sea would help.

On this trip to the silver mine Onate's men began to hear stories of the South Sea (Pacific Ocean)—not far distant— and of pearls to be had along its shores. That report interested Onate. But other ventures claimed his attention. Quivira, which the Turk had extolled and Coronado scorned, must be explored. So in the spring of 1601, from his base at San Gabriel on the western side of the Rio Grande about opposite the present town of Santa Fe, Onate himself led a party eastward into the buffalo country. Following the Canadian River into the Texas Panhandle, he turned northward and struck the Arkansas River in southern Kansas. Somewhat west of the present city of Wichita he entered the region known as Quivira at "a settlement containing more than twelve hundred houses . . . all round, built of forked poles and bound with rods, and on the outside covered to the ground with dry grass. Within, on the sides, they had frameworks or platforms which served them as beds on which they slept. Most of them were large enough to hold eight or ten persons"—just such houses as are shown in the picture on page 27.

The inhabitants had fled eastward where, as he moved forward, Onate found the river lined with quickly deserted villages and was told that ahead the population was even greater. It was evident that the Indians did not care for the callers and that it was no place for a mere seventy Spaniards, even though they had four pieces of artillery mounted on carts. In fact, the Indians started the row, and apparently Onate retreated rather fast. By the end of November he was back at San Gabriel. But he recognized that the land which he had seen would "enrich thousands of men with suet, tallow and hides," and was suitable for "founding many important settlements."

In October, 1604, with thirty well-armed and mounted men Onate started on his long-deferred journey to the west-

Left. Pueblo Indian maiden.

Courtesy, Bureau of American Ethnology.

Dog travois in tumult. Except for the horses the scene might be identical with that observed by Onate's men in 1598.

From George Catlin, *Manners, Customs, and Condition of the North American Indians.*

Right. Indians of lower Colorado River region.

From *Senate Executive Document No. 78, 33rd Congress, 2nd Session.*

67

ern ocean. He followed the old route through Zuni and Moqui to the silver mine. Then, keeping on down the Bill Williams' Fork, he came to the Colorado of the West and followed its western bank through a procession of Indian villages, to ". . . a wonderful port . . . so large that more than a thousand vessels can anchor in it." In short they were at the mouth of the Colorado where it empties into the Gulf of California. On January 25, 1605, Onate "took possession of this port in the name of his Majesty."

Onate did not *discover* the lower course of the Colorado River. That had been done, and done much more extensively, by Hernando de Alarcon and Melchior Diaz, in connection with the Coronado expedition of 1540. What Onate did was to determine the relationship between the Rio Grande and the Colorado, which latter river, where it is joined by the Gila, subsequently became a jumping-off place for the overland journey to California. At the time Onate was there the officials of Mexico were intensely interested in the coast of California. Three years before, ships had been sent up the west coast to search for ports and had discovered not only San Diego but the very much better harbor of Monterey Bay. Onate might himself have won through to San Diego by a hard march of three weeks, but he neither knew the way nor could he get guides. He may even have thought, as many did later, that California was an island. Probably he had no authority to go on. Anyway, after a superficial examination of the river and the usual inquiries of the Indians about gold, he started back for the Rio Grande.[2]

Nearly a century was to elapse before it was proved that California could be reached by a land passage from Mexico —and that important piece of information was then provided not by captains of armed forces or by captains of ships but by a man in a black robe, urged on and protected only by his zeal and his faith.[3]

"The Means, Under God"

A S ONATE and his men were urging their horses back over the mountains of Arizona in the spring of 1605, a ship named the *Archangel* was fighting its way westward across the Atlantic. It had left England on the 5th of March, dropped southward to the Azores, and evidently intended holding a course toward the southerly coast of North America. That course, however, for a sailing vessel of the time, was contrary to the habits of the Atlantic Ocean, and, as the historian of the voyage put it, ". . . when our Captaine by long beating saw it was but in vaine to strive with the windes, not knowing Gods purpose heerin to our further blessing . . . he thought but to stand as nigh as he could by the winde to recover what land we might first discover."

The captain was George Waymouth. Aboard were twenty-nine men in all. The principal backer of the voyage was Thomas Arundell, a prominent English Catholic who presumably was trying to find a haven in the New World for his fellow Catholics, then under a particularly severe persecution in England.

Captain Waymouth's first landfall, made on May 13, was at Nantucket Island, whose shoals proved so disconcerting that he pulled off and again let the wind be his guide. Five

NEWFOUNDLAND

A M E R I C A

GRAND
BANKS

St. Lawrence

Gulf of
St. Lawrence

Kennebec

St.Croix

ACADIA

Bay of Fundy

Monhegan Is.

Cape
Cod

Nantucket Is.

N O R T H

N O R T H

Chesapeake Bay

Roanoke Is.

Stream

BERMUDA

St.
Augustine

Gulf

Gulf of
Mexico

CUBA

HISPANIOLA

LEEWARD IS.

Westerly
Trade

C A R I B B E A N   S E A

SPANISH MAIN

SOUTH

AMERICA

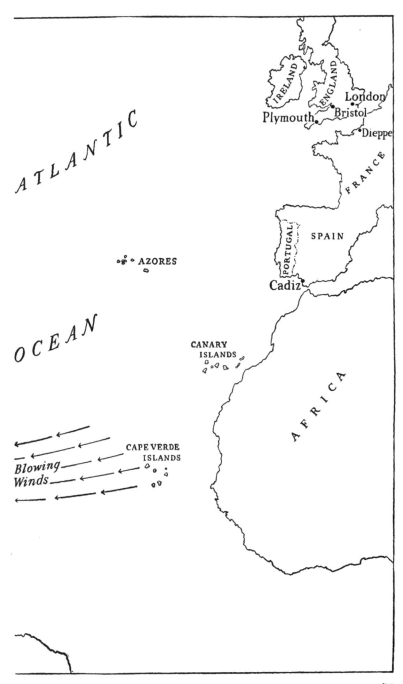

ATLANTIC

OCEAN

AZORES

IRELAND

ENGLAND

London
Plymouth Bristol
Dieppe

FRANCE

PORTUGAL SPAIN

Cadiz

CANARY
ISLANDS

AFRICA

CAPE VERDE
ISLANDS

Blowing
Winds

days later he anchored at Monhegan Island within sight of the coast of Maine. The following day he moved in closer to the shore among the cluster of islands and jagged headlands east of the Kennebec River.

Waymouth had brought along in his ship, stowed away in sections, a smaller boat suitable for use in shallow water. This he now had put together and with half his men started out to explore the adjoining mainland. Meanwhile Indians began to appear and to take an interest in the ship anchored off shore. First they looked it over from a distance, and then approached in their canoes "made without any iron, of the bark of a birch tree, strengthened within with ribs and hoops of wood, in so good a fashion, with such excellent ingenious art, as they are able to bear seven or eight persons. . . ."

The Indians themselves were well set-up men. Their faces were painted in red, black, and blue—doubtless in honor of the occasion. They were clothed in beaver and deer skins "cast over them like a mantle, and hanging down to their knees, made fast together upon the shoulder with leather." When it is considered that this was in the month of May, it is evident that they were far from being naked savages. Soon friendly relations were established between Indians and Englishmen. The natives brought beaver, otter, sable, and other skins which they traded for knives, combs, mirrors, and candy. They liked the Englishmen's rum, but there is no evidence that it was used as an article of trade.

However, immediate trade was not the prime purpose of this voyage. Waymouth and those with him had been sent to find a suitable place for a colony and to bring back a full report. The likelihood of a profitable trade in furs of course was of interest, as were also the natural resources of the region such as fish and lumber, samples of all of which they were preparing to take back with them. And among these exhibits they wanted some Indians.

Three friendly and trustful natives were lured on board the ship and held there. Two others, whom the captain wanted, became suspicious, so the crew "suddenly laid hands upon them. And it was as much as five or six of us could do to get them into the light horseman [small boat]. For they were strong and so naked as our best hold was by their long haire on their heads."

With the five captive Indians "stowed below," Waymouth sailed for England on June 16.[1]

Two days later, on June 18, 1605, another exploring party, in a boat not much larger than Waymouth's light horseman, started on a trip along the coast of Maine from an island at the mouth of a river some one hundred and fifty miles to the northeast. At the helm was Samuel de Champlain, and with him was the Sieur de Monts, Lieutenant-General, by grace of the King of France, of Acadie, a vast piece of northeastern North America—almost as elastic in area as had been "Florida" in the southeast. De Monts was authorized to bring in colonists and found settlements, but the backbone of his authority was a monopoly of the fur trade—if he could enforce it.

Since the day in 1583 when Humphrey Gilbert read his patent to the unimpressed fishermen at Newfoundland, the French shipmasters—and every spring they came in flocks —had discovered that furs made quite as good a cargo as fish. From an occasional trade with a stray Indian at a drying stage the traffic had developed into a regular business with attempts at permanent trading posts up the St. Lawrence River—where Cartier had explored for the King of France sixty years before.

So profitable was this trade that those with favor at court asked, and often received, the exclusive right to exploit it. De Monts was but one such favorite in a procession that had preceded him. With two ships and a miscellaneous collection of colonists he sailed from France in the spring of 1604. With him came Champlain, already a veteran of one trip to the St. Lawrence. De Monts himself was no stranger in the region and did not relish the prospect of spending a winter on that icebound river. Accordingly he sent one of his ships, in charge of a subordinate, to pick up any available furs along the St. Lawrence while he directed his own course along the southern shore of Nova Scotia and into the Bay of Fundy, where he thought it would be warmer. On an island at the mouth of a river flowing in from the west he

established his colony—the capital of Acadie, with pretensions extending as far south as the future city of New York.
He named the place St. Croix.

One winter at St. Croix was enough, and the expedition
southward along the coast in the spring of 1605 was presumably for the purpose of finding a better location. It is
just possible that De Monts and his party were looking for
Waymouth and any furs that he might have collected contrary to their monopoly. Anyway, on down the shore they
came—past the place from which Waymouth had just departed, into Massachusetts Bay, past the harbor where the
Pilgrims settled fifteen years later, on around the tip of Cape
Cod and part way down the ocean side of the Cape. Then
they turned back to St. Croix and simply moved across the
Bay of Fundy to a place which they called Port Royal.[2]

The die was cast—that summer of 1605. The French advance into America was to be from the north, through the
Gulf of St. Lawrence. Mostly it was to be a quest for the
skins of animals rather than for the produce of the soil, which
fact was to have its consequences too.

Waymouth, with his five Indians, was back in England
by the middle of July. The England to which he returned
was a different England from that to which John Hawkins
and Francis Drake returned from their voyages. Now John
Hawkins was but a fading memory. Nine years had passed
since Francis Drake, to the accompaniment of roaring cannon, muffled drums, and flaming ships, had gone to his last
rest off Puerto Bello. William Cecil, Elizabeth's great minister, he who had made good the dictum that "prescription
without possession availed nothing," was dead. Elizabeth
herself ruled over only a little space in Westminster Abbey.
On the throne of England sat James of Scotland, "the wisest
fool in Christendom." Walter Raleigh, Elizabeth's erstwhile
favorite, stripped of his wealth and privileges, was in the
Tower of London under a delayed sentence of death.

It was a less heroic England but withal a stronger England. From being a pirates' nest on half an island off the
coast of Europe it had won recognition as a participant in
the untold wealth of an unexploited world. It was not a rich

England, but from the markets which it had already won it was accumulating a reservoir of capital which was available for further ventures. England was on the way up. On the other hand Spain, with whom England had contested the monopoly of the wealth of the world, was on the way down. When, in 1604, Philip III, indolent son of a great father, agreed to a treaty of peace with England in which the question of English settlements in North America was intentionally avoided, the significance of that fact was not lost on the English.[3]

Waymouth's Indians were not the first natives of America to visit England. Manteo of Croatoan Island had commuted back and forth with the Raleigh colonists in the 1580's. But these Indians who arrived in the summer of 1605 were the first to attract widespread attention—and they are credited with having so extolled their homeland that the ever-grasping white man took it for his own.

Waymouth docked near the port of Plymouth of which Sir Ferdinando Gorges was military governor. Apparently the group that backed the voyage was disorganized and failed to make the most of the reports or of the exhibits which were brought back. In any case three of the Indians were, to use his own words, "seized upon" by Gorges while the other two came into the custody of Sir John Popham, Chief Justice of the King's Bench in London.

Worse yet for the Catholic group, Gorges and Popham seized upon their idea of a colony on the coast of Maine. Gorges spent a fortune and most of the remaining years of his life on projects having to do with settlements in what came to be called New England. And in his old age he stated that the accident of his getting hold of those Indians "must be acknowledged the means, under God, of putting on foot and giving life to all our plantations"—by which he meant the English colonies in America.[4]

Jamestown and Sagadahoc

I
T IS PROBABLY true that the tales which Gorges and Popham heard or thought they heard from the captive Indians had some part in bringing about the first permanent English settlements in America. "The longer I conversed with them," said Gorges, "the better hope they gave me of those parts where they did inhabit, as proper for our uses."[1]

The Spanish ambassador in England, who kept himself exceedingly well informed of all that went on, reported to his government that Gorges and Popham were "teaching and training [the Indians] to say how good that country is for people to go there and inhabit it."[2]

Doubtless what really stirred Gorges and Popham to action was recognition of the fact that if they did not move and move fast the group that had backed Waymouth's voyage would be ahead of them in asking for a grant on the coveted coast of Maine. And back of that lay the recognition by the statesmen of England that if *they* did not move and move fast, France might well pre-empt the whole northern coast of North America.

Thus apparently men of greater vision and influence used the enthusiasm of Gorges and Popham to enlist the financial support of the merchants, and then rushed through a patent which created much more than the anticipated trading company.

By this patent, which was issued on April 10, 1606, England staked out for herself practically all of the habitable eastern coast of North America that could be claimed without actually colliding with Spain in the south or with France in the north. The limits set forth in the patent stretched from the 34th to the 45th degrees of latitude, which is to say from about Wilmington, N. C., to the Bay of Fundy, with the extent inland left conveniently vague—all of which was called Virginia. Within this thousand-mile stretch of territory two plantations, each one hundred miles square, were authorized, one to be operated by the merchants and venturers of London and the other by a group from Plymouth, Bristol, and other West of England ports.[3]

Of the eight men, four for each colony, whose names appear as patentees none was outstanding in the sense that Gilbert or Raleigh had been. None of them on his own account could have aspired to particular favor from the King. They must be looked upon as agents for greater men who were back of the enterprise. The fact of their being named as patentees neither gave them the authority to govern the people living in their respective colonies nor did it give them title to the lands within the colonies.

The "superior management and direction" of the two colonies, or any others that might be established within the limits of the patent, was placed in the hands of a Council appointed by the King and residing in England. This Council in turn appointed, for each of the colonies, sub-councils the members of which were expected to reside in the colonies and govern, or manage, them. Title to the land was vested in the King, who, however, stood ready to make grants upon the recommendations of the councils for the respective colonies. Thus, although the merchants and other adventurers put up the money which made the colonies possible, the King kept under his control both the management and the allotment of the land.

Actually, all that the patent granted to the investors was the privilege of exploiting the territories assigned to them. It seems evident that the colonies were not thought of as places where people might, through their own efforts, create a self-sustaining society, but rather as plantations which, while supported by the companies, would work for the investors.

Among those who signed up to go in person to the new colonies some doubtless had an interest in the enterprise, but the greater part were simply hired men sent by investors who were willing to pay wages against the possible income from a share in the companies. However, all who went were guaranteed by the King that they and their children should "have and enjoy all liberties, franchises, and immunities, within any of our other dominions, to all intents and purposes, as if they had been abiding and born, within this our realm of England. . . ." In short, the colonists might live or be born thirty-five hundred miles across the ocean, but they would be just as truly Englishmen as though they lived or had been born in London.⁴

Royal guarantees of "liberties, franchises and immunities" were fair enough. Queen Elizabeth had inserted similar clauses in the patents to Gilbert and Raleigh. But royal supervision of commercial enterprises was a novelty to seventeenth-century English merchants and some of them lost their enthusiasm about providing the supplies and shipping which were needed to launch the expeditions. Evidently with a view to allaying this dissatisfaction, the King, late in the autumn of 1606, directed that for a period of five years all the trade of each of the colonies should be conducted in joint stocks, which is to say that all the supplies—food, clothing, tools, arms, the rental of ships and the payment of crews—were to be handled by central purchasing agencies and paid for out of central treasuries controlled by the trading companies. In the same way all the produce of the companies was to go into central pools and be sold for the benefit of the companies. At the end of five years the joint stocks, whatever they were, would be distributed to the stockholders in money, land or other assets. This was a system of trading well understood by the merchants and investors of the time. It was the system that had been followed in most of the previous trading ventures, and it had worked.⁵

It may be assumed that even before the patent was drafted

each of the groups had decided where it wished to establish its plantation. The London Company had turned its eyes toward the Chesapeake Bay region—where Raleigh had advised moving his plantation after Roanoke Island had proved unsatisfactory. The Plymouth Company, as the West Country group came to be called, had set its heart on the coast of Maine. In fact Gorges and Popham had each sent out a ship to check up on the reports of Waymouth and the captive Indians. One of these ships, with one of the Indians aboard, had taken the southern route and been captured by the Spanish. The other, under the command of Captain Martin Pring, with another of the Indians aboard, had followed the northern course and arrived safely. Pring explored the mouth of the Kennebec River with some care and left the Indian with his fellow tribesmen of that vicinity—to welcome the colony which now seemed assured.[6]

What the Indian told his friends in Maine about England and Englishmen unfortunately remains unknown, but his return must have cleared up one misunderstanding. The Indians had told Champlain, when he passed along the coast in the summer of 1605, that the English had treacherously killed five of their people. Here was one of the five returned to life and able to give some account of the other four, though he did not know that one of them was at that moment in the hands of the Spanish far to the south.[7]

By early December the London Company was ready to try its fortune in the New World. ". . . the good ship called the *Sarah Constant* and the ship called the *Goodspeed,* with a pinnace called the *Discovery* are now ready victualed, riged and furnished for the said voyage."[8]

On December 20, 1606, the little fleet sailed. Christopher Newport, famed as a privateer, was in command of the voyage by appointment from the superior Council. With him he carried a sealed box containing the names of those whom that Council had appointed to be members of the sub-council in Virginia and who were to govern the colony after its landing. Perhaps in the same box was a very detailed set of orders prepared by the Council in England for the guidance of Captain Newport and the sub-council. In any case they had the orders, and from them it is evident that the main objective in 1606 was the same as it had been twenty years earlier, namely, the finding of gold mines or a passage to the East Indies. The possibility of an agricultural plantation was not so much as thought of. The colonists were warned to plant themselves well up a river and not to get caught as the French had at Fort Caroline in 1565. Nor were they to set themselves down in an unhealthy place. "You shall judge of the good air by the people, for some parts of that coast where the lands are low have their people blear eyed, and with swollen bellies and legs," the Council gravely cautioned them.²

Despite the danger of being intercepted by Spanish warships, Newport followed the old familiar southern route. Entering the Caribbean through the Leeward Islands, he passed between Puerto Rico and San Domingo and then turned northward toward the mainland of North America. With all the information which the Spanish ambassador in London had about the plans of the venturers he apparently missed the date of this sailing; otherwise the results might have been different.

The voyage took more than four months. Not until April 26, 1607, did the colonists see the two capes which guard the mouth of the Chesapeake. That night they opened the sealed box and read the names of the seven men, of whom Newport was one, commissioned to govern or manage the other hundred or so members of the colony. But the government could not yet be organized because they did not know with any certainty where they would establish their colony.

The following day they built or put together a small boat and started exploring inside the capes. Finding a point of land which, due to the depth of the water near it, "put us in good comfort," they named it Cape Comfort and moved the ships up to its southern shore. Thus they came to the mouth of the James River, which in the next few days they examined as far as the entrance of the Appomattox—without serious resistance from the Indians who thronged the banks.

Of all the places they saw along the river one on the

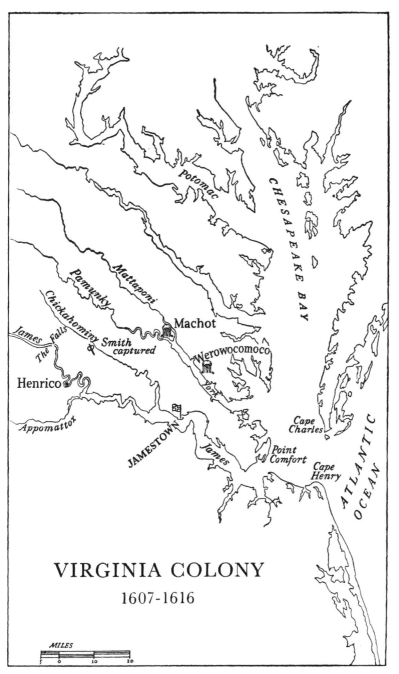

VIRGINIA COLONY
1607-1616

MILES

northerly side, some thirty miles above Point Comfort, seemed best suited to their requirements—partly because the channel ran close beside it with sufficient water to float the ships. At this spot, on May 13, they began unloading their supplies and clearing away the trees to make space for the tents in which they had to live until more permanent quarters could be built. They called the place James Fort, and it soon came to be known as Jamestown.

Here the local council—with the exception of Captain John Smith, with whom the others were at odds—was sworn in and the government of the colony put into operation. Some went to work building a fort. Others began cutting clapboards (barrel staves) to be carried back to England for sale. And, at the same time, a party of twenty men went to explore the upper courses of the river—looking for a connection with a westward-flowing river that would lead to the Pacific Ocean and the Indies. For six days they pushed up the winding stream and then came to a falls which put an end to further navigation. There, where the city of Richmond now stands, was an Indian town called Powhatan, "consisting of some 12 houses pleasantly seated on a hill." [10]

Being unable to go on, the explorers returned to Jamestown, where they found that during their absence the Indians had made a surprise attack, injuring several men and killing one boy. For the moment there was to be no more exploring; all hands were needed to build a palisade around the fort and to clear the adjoining land for planting corn; also to load the ship with something to justify the voyage, which something was mostly clapboard.

By June 15 the fort was finished. It was built "triangle wise, having three Bulwarkes, at every corner, like a halfe Moone, and foure or five pieces of Artillerie mounted in them. We had made our selves sufficiently strong for these Savages," reported George Percy, one of the adventurers." [11]

A week later Captain Newport sailed for England to report the progress of the plantation and to bring back more supplies. He left one hundred and five men and boys huddled behind the palisades of the fort on the steaming banks of the James River. Six of them were members of the council. They were the government, or rather the managers or overseers—and they were already quarreling among themselves. Only with the prospect of Newport's leaving had they admitted Captain John Smith to a place among them, though his name had been included in the list brought over in the sealed box. Twenty-nine were classified as "gentlemen." There were one preacher, one doctor, and four carpenters. There were a blacksmith, a barber, two bricklayers, a mason, and a tailor. The rest were either laborers or just colonists.

In the newly cleared fields around the fort they had some corn growing, but otherwise their food supply was low. The long outward voyage had made deep inroads in what seemed ample when they left England. They were surrounded by hostile natives and their nearest Christian neighbors were the Spanish at St. Augustine, who so far as they knew already had orders to wipe them out. What would happen before Newport got back, if he ever got back, was the question which must have been in the minds of most of the colonists as they watched the ships disappear down the river.

Five weeks later, on July 29, 1607, Newport dropped his anchor in Plymouth Harbor, England. That same day he wrote a letter to the Earl of Salisbury reporting that he had successfully planted the colony in Virginia and that he had "discovered into the country near two hundred miles, and a River navigable for greate shippes one hundred and fifty miles. The contrie is excellent and very rich in gold and Copper, of the gould we have brought a say [assay] and hope to be with your Lordship shortlie to show it to his Majesty and the rest of the Lords." [12]

Making due allowance for Newport's optimistic report, it is worthy of note that the Earl of Salisbury, to whom Newport wrote his letter, was at the time not only Secretary of State for England but also Lord Treasurer. That fact gives us a glimpse of the influence behind those one hundred and five men sweating on the banks of the James River thirty-five hundred miles away.

By Newport's ships the Council in England received a letter from the local council in Virginia apologetically calling attention to the cargo of clapboards sent back, and pleading for supplies "least that all devouring Spaniard lay his ravenous hands upon these gold showing mountains"—which last was at least a careful statement.[13]

As the promoters of the London Company were reading the reports brought by Newport, the Plymouth Company's colony was already well on its way to the coast of Maine, which was still referred to by Englishmen as Northern Virginia. In two ships the expedition had left England the latter part of May, 1607. In command of the *Gift of God* was Captain George Popham, a nephew of the Chief Justice, while the *Mary and John* was commanded by Captain Raleigh Gilbert, son of Sir Humphrey Gilbert and nephew of Sir Walter Raleigh. With Captain Gilbert went Skidwarres, one of the five Indians who had been brought to England by Waymouth.

The captains followed the northern route and on August 7 met near the mouth of the Kennebec River, which they called the Sagadahoc. Here Captain Gilbert, with Skidwarres and a number of his men, went ashore in search of information. Skidwarres led them to a village the chief of which turned out to be the Indian that Captain Pring had brought back the year before. Through the good offices of these two widely traveled natives amicable relations were easily established.

After a few days spent in exploration along the coast and up the river, the colonists chose for their plantation a place "at the very mouth or entry of the Ryver of Sagadehocke." On August 19 they all went ashore and listened to a sermon after which the patent and the instructions from the superior Council for Virginia were read to them. Apparently their local government was organized before the expedition left England, with Popham designated as president, or chairman, of the council.

At Sagadahoc, as at Jamestown a few months earlier, some of the men went to work constructing a fort while others explored the river. Up the Sagadahoc, as up the James River, they found a falls barring further navigation, near which place stood a large Indian village. Today the city of Augusta, Me., occupies the approximate spot. And at the

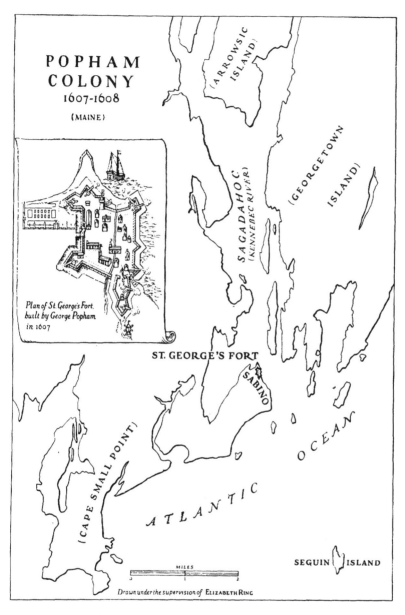

POPHAM
COLONY
1607-1608
(MAINE)

Plan of St. George's Fort,
built by George Popham
in 1607

(ARROWSIC ISLAND)

SAGADAHOC
(KENNEBEC RIVER)

(GEORGETOWN ISLAND)

ST. GEORGE'S FORT

(SABINO)

(CAPE SMALL POINT)

OCEAN

ATLANTIC

MILES

SEGUIN ISLAND

Drawn under the supervision of ELIZABETH RING

From the *Atlas of American History.*

falls on the Sagadahoc, as at the falls on the James, immediate attempts to reach the Pacific Ocean by a short portage came to an end. The road to the Indies was longer than the great men in England had realized.

Meanwhile the fort, named St. George's, at the mouth of the river was nearing completion and into it from the ships were carried the food and clothing, the Indian trading goods and the arms that had been brought over for the colony. Among the latter were twelve cannons to be mounted on the walls of the fort—for the benefit not only of unfriendly Indians but also of any unfriendly Frenchmen who might come down in ships from their settlement a couple of hundred miles up the coast. With the same idea in mind the *Gift of God* was kept at Sagadahoc much longer than had been intended.[14]

On October 6, 1607, the *Mary and John* sailed for England. With her went reports about the settlement and samples of the various products of the country—among them some pods "in which they supposed the cotton wooll to grow." Thus did the milkweed of America aspire to a place in the world's commerce. And while the *Gift of God* lingered on the coast, George Popham learned an important fact from the Indians. ". . . they positively assure me," he reported in a letter addressed to the King, "that there is a certain Sea in the opposite or western part of this Province, distant not more than seven day's journey . . . a sea large, wide and deep of the boundaries of which they are wholly ignorant; which cannot be any other than the Southern Ocean, reaching to the regions of China, which unquestionably cannot be far from these parts." It was probably Lake Ontario that he was hearing about.[15]

Late on the night of December 1, Sir Ferdinando Gorges, Governor of the Port of Plymouth and a member of the superior Council for Virginia, was writing a hurried letter to the Earl of Salisbury, Secretary of State and Lord Treasurer of England. The *Mary and John* had just arrived in Plymouth Harbor. Along with more formal reports Gorges had collected a good deal of gossip about what was going on at Sagadahoc.

It appeared that George Popham, president of the local council, was old and fat and too easy-going; that Gilbert was going around among the men saying that the colony really belonged to himself because Queen Elizabeth had granted that part of the world to his father. In addition Gorges' informant charged Gilbert with having little zeal for religion, of living a loose life and of being "prompte to sensuality." That word sensuality raises a somewhat shocking thought. Is it possible that the son of Sir Humphrey Gilbert could have fallen a victim to the wiles of the Indian maidens —out there on the coast of Maine, so far from home? All in all, the Plymouth Company's colony at Sagadahoc was not doing so well.[16]

Six hundred miles down the coast from Sagadahoc the London Company's colonists at Jamestown were in an even worse state. They were short of food when Newport left for England late in June. What with improvidence and bad management the situation soon became desperate. A pint of wheat and barley, well mixed with weevils, was their daily ration. Their cabins and bedding were damp. The location was unhealthful. Their only drinking water was from the river, then at flood tide. Cramped in the fort as they were through fear of Indian attack sanitary conditions must have become increasingly bad.

Naturally sickness developed—malaria, dysentery and other diseases. By August men were dying at an alarming rate. "If there were any conscience in men," wrote one of them, "it would make their harts to bleed to heare the pitifull murmurings and out-cries of our sick men withoute reliefe, every night and day, for the space of sixe weekes, some departing out of the World, many times three or foure in a night; in the morning, their bodies trailed out of their Cabines like Dogges to be buried."

Dissension was rife. Even among the members of the council there was constant bickering. The president, or chairman, of this the governing body of the colony was accused of withholding for his own use the common supply of oatmeal, beef, eggs, and, worst of all, brandy. He was voted out of office by the other councilors. Another member was accused of heading a conspiracy to seize the pinnace and sail for England. He was tried, condemned and shot.[17]

Other troubles hung over the colony, of which those squabbling men at Jamestown knew nothing. Pedro de Zuniga, the Spanish Ambassador at London, had reported Newport's arrival from Virginia and the preparations being made for his return. Zuniga had advised his master, Philip III, "not to be too slow; because they will soon be found there with large numbers of people, whereupon it will be much more difficult to drive them out than now." On September 27, while Gilbert was exploring up the Sagadahoc and men were dying of the dysentery at Jamestown, Zuniga had an audience with King James of England. In behalf of his master Zuniga protested against the English settlements in America, which land, he said, belonged to the King of Spain. James professed to know little of what was going on, but held to his right to authorize the founding of colonies there. A few days later Zuniga suggested to Philip that, "It will be serving God and Your Majesty to drive these villains out from there, hanging them in time which is short enough." Philip's father probably would have acted on this advice, but Philip III was not Philip II, nor had he a Pedro Menendez to do the business for him.[18]

The Indians could have finished off the colony very easily that autumn of 1607. More than half of the men had died. The rest were too sick and too beaten out to have put up much resistance. But at just that point the savages, deficient in the niceties of civilized warfare, took pity on the sickly settlement and brought enough corn to ward off starvation. Moreover, cooler weather was at hand. Those that had not died were immune to almost anything except hunger, and with reviving strength they began to think of ways to meet that situation.

Newport had left the pinnace with the colonists. Captain John Smith with a few men took this small boat and dropped down the river to the Indian village at Point Comfort. There he traded for a cargo of corn. Having made this promising start, Smith began trading up the river, and along the Chickahominy, which flows into the James only a few miles above Jamestown.

Captain John Smith.

From his map of
New England, 1614.

Below we see Captain John Smith
being saved by Pocahontas—as
the story is told by Smith in his
Generall History of Virginia, etc.,
published in 1624.

On one of these trips up the Chickahominy Smith explored a little too far and was captured by the Indians. By a roundabout route they conducted him to the Indian town of Werowocomoco, on the north bank of the York River only twelve miles distant from Jamestown. There they delivered him to Powhatan, head chief of all that region. As Smith was led into Powhatan's presence he saw him "proudly lying uppon a Bedstead a foote high, upon tenne or twelve Mattes, richly hung with manie Chaynes of great Pearles about his necke, and covered with a great Covering of [raccoon skins]. At [his] heade sat a woman, at his feete another; on each side, sitting uppon a Matte uppon the ground, were raunged his cheife men on each side the fire, tenne in a ranke, and behinde them as many yong women, each [with] a great Chaine of white Beades over their shoulders, their heads painted in redde; and with such a grave and Majesticall countenance, as drave me into admiration to see such state in a naked Salvage. Hee kindly welcomed me with good wordes, and great Platters of sundrie Victuals, assuring mee his friendship, and my libertie within foure days." [19]

Thus Smith told the story in 1608. Eight years later, when Pocahontas had become a celebrity in England, Smith told a somewhat different story, in which the daughter of Powhatan played a prominent part. "At the minute of my execution," Smith related, "she hazarded the beating out of her owne braines to save mine; and not onely that, but so prevailed with her father, that I was safely conducted to James towne." [20]

This later version has greatly enriched American history, and we can agree with Smith that if it did not happen, it could or should have happened, and let it go at that. In any case, guided by four of Powhatan's Indians, and loaded down with food and other evidences of good will, Smith got safely back to Jamestown early in January, 1608.

That same day a ship came feeling its way up the James River and tied up to the trees lining the bank at Jamestown. Captain Newport was back from England with supplies and recruits for the settlement. Of the one hundred and five colonists that he had left there in June he found only thirty-eight still alive. The supply ship had arrived none too soon.

Hardly had they got the food, clothing, tools and other supplies out of the ship and within the palisaded walls of the town before a fire broke out. Much of the newly landed food was destroyed; many of the colonists lost their clothing and bedding. One young fellow who had just come over in the ship wrote home asking for any old hand-me-downs that might be available whether they fit him or not. The preacher lost his library. The loss of housing during a bitterly cold winter was accountable for many deaths in the next few weeks.[21]

Smith's new-found friend, Powhatan, interested Newport, and Newport interested Powhatan. Each wanted something that he figured the other could supply—and both were good traders. Newport wanted the good will of an outstanding native chief who could perhaps point the way to gold mines and the South Sea. Powhatan wanted some of the white man's guns, swords and tools. Smith, who arranged the meeting at Powhatan's town of Werowocomoco, felt that Newport spoiled the market by being too liberal. But Newport was playing for higher stakes than the few bushels of corn which the practical Smith wanted in order to bolster up those all too scant supplies across the peninsula at Jamestown.

Nor was Smith happier about another enterprise which to Captain Newport and to his fellow members of the council seemed much more important than the prosaic business of swapping for corn or cutting barrel staves. They had found gold. ". . . There was no talke, no hope, nor worke, but dig gold, wash gold, refine gold, loade gold." Smith referred to this gold as "gilded durt"; perhaps it came from those "gold showing mountains" that the council had written home about. Anyway they loaded the ship with it and on April 10 Newport sailed for England.

Ten days later another ship, the *Phoenix,* was tying up alongside the fort at Jamestown. It had left England with Newport, but had become separated in a storm and was supposed to have been lost. Now four months later it came safely in with additional supplies and colonists. Between Newport's ship and the *Phoenix* over a hundred people had been added to the thirty-eight survivors, though deaths had already reduced the number.

Of the original seven members of the council which directed and governed the colonists, one had died; one had been shot; one had returned with Newport, who was himself one of the members; and another was returning on the *Phoenix*. As an offset to these losses Matthew Scrivener had come over with Newport bearing a commission from the Council in England to act as a member of the local council. Smith, who had few good words for the other leaders, referred to Scrivener as "a very wise understanding man," and it is evident that the two got along together. They saw to it that the *Phoenix* took back a cargo of lumber rather than more of the "gilded durt."

Still, whether his gold was real or not, Newport was on the right track in putting his main effort on a search for some such cargo. Lumber would not justify the colony. It took up too much cargo space as against the sale price. The adventurers had to find something that had a high value in a small space; precious minerals would do that. Or, as a transshipping point for the silks and spices of the East, cargo space could be made to pay; a short route to the South Sea (Pacific) would do that. Otherwise, the investment of the adventurers was lost and additional investments would not be forthcoming. Thus reasoned the merchants who had put up the money for the colony, and they were right.

During the summer of 1608 Smith, doubtless on orders from London, spent much of his time exploring Chesapeake Bay to see what it offered in the way of a connection with the "South Sea." In an open boat, with a dozen men, he examined the eastern shore, looked in at the Potomac, and pushed on up toward the head of the Bay. There in the hands of the Indians he saw knives and hatchets of European manufacture, which he was told had come from the French in Canada. The account was doubtless true. Champlain was at just that time laying the foundations of the city of Quebec on the St. Lawrence River—less than two hundred and fifty miles northwest of the English colony at Sagadahoc, and right on the road to that "sea large, wide and deep" of which Captain George Popham had written King James.[22]

But George Popham was no more. The winter of 1607–1608, which had been cold enough on the James River, had been vastly colder up there on the coast of Maine, and old George Popham and a few others had succumbed. Otherwise the colony had fared well enough. They had finished their fort. They had "framed a pretty Pynnace of about some thirty tonne" which they named the *Virginia*. They had got a good store of furs through trade with the Indians. There seemed to be no reason why the colony should not take root.

Yet, even as John Smith was looking at the French hatchets in Chesapeake Bay, fateful news was on the way to Sagadahoc. Chief Justice Popham, uncle of the dead leader and one of the principal backers of the colony, was dead in England. Dead, too, was Raleigh Gilbert's elder brother, leaving an estate that called for the immediate presence in England of the younger brother. There was no one else who could hold the men together and keep the colony going. So some of them piled into the supply ship and others into the "pretty pynnace" and back they all went to England, "by which means," said Sir Ferdinando Gorges, "all our former hopes were frozen to death." [23]

The leaders of the London Company were a more persistent lot. As the Plymouth Company colonists were on their way home, Captain Newport was, for the third time, heading westward for the James River. His cargo of gold had turned out to be only "gilded durt," but the company was ready to try again. With Newport were seventy new settlers including Mistress Forest, gentlewoman, and Anne Burrows, her maid. There were a number of Dutch and Poles experienced in making pitch, tar, glass and other products. There was a boat, in sections that could presumably be carried over the falls and put together for a voyage to the South Sea. And there was a crown for Powhatan.

Early in October, 1608, Newport arrived at Jamestown. His first job was to win Powhatan as an ally. That was where the crown came in. Powhatan was to be recognized as the "emperor" of all the Indians; then the emperor was to aid Newport in the conquest of the territory above the falls, from which the voyage to China was to start—in the boat that the men would carry up in sections.

So Smith was sent to Werowocomoco to invite Powhatan to his coronation. The emperor-elect was not home, but his people, not to be outdone by the Europeans in the matter of pageantry, put on a show for Smith and his friends. "Thirty young women came naked out of the woods (only covered behind and before with a few greene leaves) their bodies al painted, some white, some red, some black, some partie color; but every one different. Their leader had a faire paire of stagges horns on her head, and an otter skinne at her girdle, another at her arme, a quiver of arrowes at her backe, and bow and arrowes in her hand. The next, in her hand a sword; another, a club; another, a pot-stick; all horned alike. The rest, every one with their severall devises.

"These fiendes, with most hellish cries and shouts, rushing from amongst the trees, cast themselves in a ring about the fire, singing and dauncing with excellent ill varietie, oft falling into their infernall passions, and then solemnely againe to sing and daunce. Having spent neere an houre, in this maskarado; as they entered, they in like manner departed.

"Having reaccomodated themselves, they solemnely invited Smith to their lodging: but no sooner was hee within the house, but all these Nymphes the more tormented him than ever, with crowding, and pressing, and hanging upon him, most tediously crying, *love you not me.*"

The next day Powhatan arrived and coolly informed Smith that if the Englishmen wanted a coronation they would have to come to him, not he to them. Accordingly, Newport loaded up the crown and other paraphernalia and went to Werowocomoco, where the coronation duly took place. Powhatan accepted a scarlet cloak willingly enough, but when they tried to get him to kneel for the putting on of the crown he balked. However, by leaning hard on his shoulder they got him to stoop a little and the crown was clapped on his head. At that moment the soldiers fired a royal salute which so scared the new emperor that the ceremonies almost ended there and then. And they might as well have ended. Powhatan flatly refused to join in an attack on the Indians above the falls. Still he was not wholly un-appreciative of the honors showered upon him or the pres-ents given to him. In return he gave Newport his old shoes.

Nor did Newport have better luck with his sectional boat. Even in five pieces it was more than the men could carry, so the discovery of the route to China had to be deferred. Meanwhile the patient Dutchmen and Poles had turned out a little pitch, tar and glass which, together with the usual clapboards, provided a cargo—and Newport sailed for Eng-land.[24]

The cargo was disappointing enough to the merchants who had ventured their money on the voyage, but the re-ports which Newport brought of lack of harmony among the members of the local council were even more disturbing. What the colony needed was one competent boss instead of three or four bosses each pulling a different way. As the merchants had feared, royal control of the government and management of the plantation was making a mess of what might otherwise still be a good investment.

Accordingly the Company asked for, and received on May 23, 1609, a new patent which placed the Superior Council in England under the control of the stockholders and di-rected that the colony should be governed by a single gov-ernor with dictatorial power instead of by a council in which none of the members had real responsibility. At the same time the territorial limits of the colony were extended to reach two hundred miles north and the same distance south from Point Comfort, and "up into the land, through-out from sea to sea, west and northwest." This "west and northwest" extension of the boundary followed the current notion that the shortest route to the Pacific was in that direction; it later gave Virginia title to a vast area of land lying back of the northern colonies. In addition to extending the boundaries the new patent definitely granted the land to the Company, but with an injunction that it be distributed by the Company to the individual adventurers and planters.[25]

So reorganized, the Company, now commonly called the Virginia Company, offered shares of stock in denominations of £12 10s. Subscriptions poured in—from the great lords, from bishops, from the gentry, from the merchants, from ironmongers, from grocers, from widows, from ministers, and from the City Companies of Brewers, Carpenters, Musicians and many others. As in 1606, so again in 1609 it was agreed that for a period of years, seven being the number decided upon, the operation of the colony should be carried on jointly —the Company retaining title to all the land, paying all the costs and receiving all the profits.

Along with its drive for adventurers who would subscribe money, the Company made attractive offers to prospective planters who would venture their service in the colony. They were assured of "meate, drinke and clothing, with an howse, orchard and garden, for the meanest family, and a possession of lands to them and their posterity, one hundred acres for every man's person that hath a trade, or a body able to endure day labour, as much for his wief, as much for his child, that are of yeres to do service to the Colony, with further particular reward according to theire particular meritts and industry"—all this in return for seven years' service to the Company.[26]

Thus, for a period of seven years, the Company, sitting in London and presided over by Sir Thomas Smith, was to be the sole owner of the lands in the colony of Virginia. It was to be the sole owner of the produce of the lands. It was to be the sole owner of the houses, livestock, tools and shipping in the colony. It was to be the sole owner of the food and clothing sent to the colony, and it was to all intents and purposes to be the sole owner of the people who lived in the colony. Through a Governor living in the colony but appointed by the Company in London, the people in the colony were to do what the Company told them to do.

As Governor of the colony under this new patent the Company designated Sir Thomas West, Lord Delaware. Whether he was expected to go personally, or whether the intent was merely to use his name and send a deputy, may be questioned. In any case he did not go at once. In his stead Sir Thomas Gates received authority to act as Governor, and a great expedition prepared to sail for Virginia.[27]

Meantime, without any idea of what was going on in England, the colonists at Jamestown went about the business of cutting clapboards and of making pitch, tar and glass with which to load the next ship that might come from England. In the midst of all this Mistress Forest lost her maid. John Laydon, a laborer who had come with the first settlers, who had resisted malaria and dysentery, who had survived on short rations and avoided Indian arrows, fell a victim to the charms of Anne Burrows. Virginia had its first Church of England wedding.

Tragedy visited the colonists, too. Matthew Scrivener and ten other men were caught in a violent squall while in a small boat, and all were lost. This left Captain John Smith the only member of the council still in Virginia. He had a difficult situation to meet, that spring of 1609, and he met it with vigor—more perhaps than was necessary. Corn was scarce. Not even the Indians had any to spare. With starvation facing the colony Smith took by force from the Indians what corn he could find and he compelled the colonists to eat food that they did not relish. "This Savage trash you so scornfully repine at, being put in your mouthes, your stomacks can digest it," he told them, and added that those who would not work would be put out of the fort, "and live there or starve." [28]

On July 13 a strange ship appeared in the James River. It brought neither supplies nor colonists and had made the voyage from England in sixty-nine days, which was a record. In command was Captain Samuel Argall, who had been sent by the officers of the Virginia Company to find a more direct route than the well-known one through the West Indies. He had demonstrated that by keeping just south of the easterly flowing Gulf Stream a much quicker crossing could be made. [29]

From Argall the colonists learned of the reorganization of the Company and the impending change in the government of the colony. From him they learned that Sir Thomas Gates, with a commission as governor of the colony, was probably already on his way with a number of ships and several hundred new colonists. John Smith, who had enough enemies among the colonists, must have had some misgivings when he learned that three of his former fellow councilors, with whom he had quarreled, were accompanying Gates.

On August 11 four badly battered ships limped into the James River. They were a part of the Gates fleet. Their captains reported that they, with five other ships, had left Falmouth harbor on the 8th of June; that they had followed a course similar to that taken by Argall; that on July 23, when only a few days from the Virginia coast, they had run into a hurricane; and that the ships had become separated. These four had met later and made the best of their way to Virginia. They did not know what had happened to the other ships, on one of which, the *Sea Venture,* was Sir Thomas Gates, the Governor.

Within a week or ten days two more of the ships arrived. This accounted for six of the nine vessels that had left England with Gates. But still no word of the *Sea Venture.* Here was a pretty situation. Among the three hundred or so people who had arrived on the six ships there were a number who expected to hold preferred positions under the new governor. There were three members of the old local council who had looked forward with pleasure to Captain John Smith's deposition and who were ready to present all sorts of charges against him. And here they were without the Governor or anything to prove that any one had the authority or the wish to depose Smith. With legality all on his side Smith refused to relinquish his power. However, he was now but one among several councilors and the others were making it very unpleasant for him. Doubtless he, even more than some of the others, would have welcomed the arrival of the new Governor. But where was the *Sea Venture?* A month had gone by and no one knew more of its fate than the first arrivals had been able to tell.[30]

Neither did the survivors of the storm know, nor would they have been greatly concerned if they had known, that on the very days during which they were wallowing through the blinding hurricane on the Atlantic, another pioneer of another nation, in a very different sort of boat, was making a voyage fully as fateful as theirs. Crouched in a birch-bark canoe, with Indians wielding the paddles, Samuel de Champlain was gliding southward along the western shore of the lake which now bears his name. We last met him on the coast of Maine in the summer of 1605. Now, with a trading post established at Quebec, he was spearheading a westward push for France which would ultimately collide with a westward push by the Colony of Virginia.

There were twenty-four canoes in Champlain's flotilla. They were manned by sixty Algonquin Indians from the St. Lawrence country, and there were two other Frenchmen along. For Champlain the expedition afforded an opportunity to explore the country. For the Algonquins it offered a hope of revenge upon their deadly enemies the Iroquois, whose confederation stretched across upper central New York. By themselves the Algonquins were no match for the Iroquois, but with the help of those terrifying guns of the Frenchmen they might win a victory.

Somewhere near the spot where Fort Ticonderoga later came into being the Iroquois challenged a further advance of the Algonquin fleet—and the following day (July 30, 1609) the battle was on. The Iroquois advanced confidently, but when the Algonquin ranks opened and Champlain appeared, in armor and with his strange-looking gun, they stared in amazement. A shot or two and the whole thing was over. The Iroquois fled in panic leaving several dead and ten or a dozen prisoners in the hands of the invaders.

And then Champlain was introduced to the niceties of Indian warfare. One of the prisoners was selected for the ceremony. A fire was kindled "and when it was well burning, they each took a brand, and burned this poor creature gradually, so as to make him suffer greater torment. Sometimes they stopped, and threw water on his back. Then they tore out his nails, and applied fire to the extremities of his fingers and private member. Afterwards they flayed the top of his head [scalped him], and had a kind of gum poured all hot upon it . . ." and so on for quite a long time, when Champlain, to the disgust of his Algonquin friends, shot the poor devil in mercy. The rest of the prisoners they took home for their wives and children to play with, being kind husbands

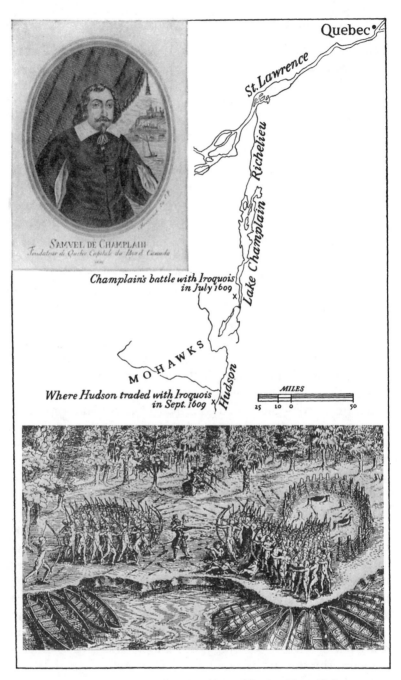

SAMVEL DE CHAMPLAIN
Fondateur de Québec Capitale du Nouvel Canada

Quebec

St. Lawrence

Richelieu

Lake Champlain

Champlain's battle with Iroquois in July 1609 ×

M O H A W K S

Where Hudson traded with Iroquois in Sept. 1609 ×

Hudson

MILES
25   10   0   50

Above. Defeat of the Iroquois at Lake Champlain.

and indulgent fathers according to their understanding.[31]

Champlain had made himself and his fellow Frenchmen solid with the Algonquins, but he had made an enemy which was to cost France dearly in the years to come. And hardly had the Iroquois finished licking their wounds before there came sailing up one of their rivers an expedition which was to be the means by which they would get the guns to meet the Frenchman with his own kind of warfare and worse.

Henry Hudson, an Englishman, had in some way come into possession of maps of the American coast made by Captain John Smith during his exploration of the Chesapeake Bay during the summer of 1608. Early in 1609 Hudson entered into a contract with the Dutch East India Company to search for a northeast passage around Europe to the East Indies. In April he sailed from Amsterdam in a little ship of some sixty tons named the *Half Moon,* manned by a mixed crew of Dutch and English sailors.

Ice blocked his further progress somewhere north of Norway and, apparently on his own responsibility and perhaps with Smith's maps in mind, Hudson turned west to the coast of North America where he hoped to find a passage to the Indies. From Newfoundland to the entrance to the Chesapeake, which he did not enter, he cruised the coast. Then turning back toward the north he entered Delaware Bay. It offered no route to the East Indies, so he backed out and tried a little farther north.

On September 12, 1609, while John Smith was still clinging to a semblance of control of the disorganized colony in Virginia, Hudson entered the river which today bears his name. For eight days he sailed up the river—past the Palisades, through the Highlands and on to a point near present-day Albany. There he found the Indians friendly and traded beads, knives and hatchets for beaver and otter skins. These Indians were the same Iroquois some of whose braves, less than two months before, had fled from the mysterious thunder-stick of Champlain along the shores of a lake less than a hundred miles to the north.

Doubtless Hudson fired his guns, too, but for the entertainment rather than the destruction of the Iroquois. Better yet, he invited the head chiefs aboard the *Half Moon* and gave them all the brandy and wine they could drink. They liked that and would have been happy to have had the ship stay longer. But Hudson's voyage up the river was at an end; shoals stopped further navigation; and he turned back down stream. He had not found the hoped-for passage to the East Indies but he had found a place where within a few years the Dutch began planting a colony. On October 4, 1609, Hudson passed out through the Narrows and sailed for Europe.[32]

On that same day, two hundred and fifty miles to the south, another ship poked its prow out of Chesapeake Bay and sailed eastward. It was one of the survivors of the Gates fleet which had reached Jamestown the previous August and was now on its way back to England. Aboard was Captain John Smith. His enemies had been too much for him and he was on his way home "to answere some misdeamenors." He never came back to Virginia, but he had ample revenge on his enemies and gave ample credit to himself in the pages of his *Generall Historie of Virginia, New-England, and the Summer Isles,* published in London in 1624 and long accepted by scholars as an authentic source for information regarding the early years of the colony.[33]

And, as Smith sailed out of Chesapeake Bay, the sturdy little pinnace *Virginia,* built at Sagadahoc two years before, sailed in. She had started from England as a part of the Gates fleet and had been given up for lost. Here she was, however, with a second trip across the Atlantic to her credit —the first ocean-going vessel ever built by English people in America. Her arrival accounted for seven of the ships in the Gates fleet. But still there was no word of the *Sea Venture.*[34]

The arrival of these seven ships had dumped upon the colony, already short of provisions, some three hundred additional people who had to be fed. In all, in the autumn of 1609, there were nearly five hundred colonists scattered along the James River, most of them at Jamestown. They had five or six hundred hogs; about the same number of chickens; and a few sheep and goats. They were short of corn or other cereal, and all too many of the supplies which had been sent from England were aboard the missing *Sea Venture.*

More serious than the immediate lack of food was the lack of an able leader. The three members of the old council, who had come back with the fleet, joined with some who had expected to serve under Governor Gates, and this group attempted to manage things, with most unfortunate results. One of them tried to establish a settlement near the present-day city of Norfolk, and lost several men through an attack by the Indians. Another, in trying to build a fort at the Falls (where Richmond now stands), lost even more men in a brush with the irritated natives. Still another of these leaders took one of the pinnaces, with thirty or forty men, and went around to Powhatan's town of Werowocomoco on the York River to trade for corn; the Indians wiped them out almost to a man. Captain Francis West, a younger brother of Lord Delaware, took another of the pinnaces on the excuse of looking for corn and, having no luck, sailed for England. However, he lived to become Governor of Virginia seventeen years later.[35]

Captain West arrived home to find his brother preparing to go in person to Virginia. The directors of the Company had evidently come to the conclusion that the *Sea Venture* was lost, and with it Governor Gates. This mishap, together with reports of the disorganized condition of the colony, had dampened the enthusiasm of the subscribers to the Company's stock. Many had failed to pay their installments. Something had to be done and the best solution seemed to be a show of confidence from high places. If Lord Delaware, "a Baron and Peere of this Kingdome, whose Honour nor Fortune needs not any desperate medicine," was willing to risk his life and comfort for Virginia, the Company figured that the subscribers ought to be willing to risk their money. Accordingly Delaware received a commission as Governor for life, with almost dictatorial powers, and three ships were shortly being put in order to carry him and many new colonists to Virginia.[36]

Meanwhile, as the winter and spring of 1610 wore along, the situation in Virginia became truly desperate. At James-

town the starving people had devoured every living animal
of every description within their reach—hogs, chickens, sheep,
goats, horses and even snakes. One man had killed his wife,
salted her down and was eating her as his appetite directed.
The hostility of the Indians kept the colonists close to the
fort; if they tried to forage in the woods, they were more apt
to be knocked in the head than to find food. At Point Comfort, the only other outpost, a few men fared somewhat
better. But of the almost five hundred men, women and children in the colony in the autumn of 1609 only about sixty
woebegone creatures were still alive on May 23, 1610.[37]

On that day the men at the little fort at Point Comfort
saw two pinnaces approaching from the east. They were
crowded with people, and as they came closer it was seen
that there were women and children among the passengers.
As the leading boat eased in beside the fort, there was no
need for a query as to who they were. Towering over the
gunwale was the figure of Sir Thomas Gates, Governor of
the Colony of Virginia.

And there they were—the one hundred and forty colonists
who had sailed on the *Sea Venture* and who had long been
given up for lost. The story was soon told. The *Sea Venture*
had been driven northward by the storm and wrecked on
one of the islands of the Bermudas. The passengers had got
safely ashore where they had not only managed to live com-
fortably but, from the timbers of their wrecked ship and
from the forests of the island, had built the two pinnaces
in which they arrived at Virginia.

The next day the new arrivals sailed on up to Jamestown,
the goal of their long trip, the haven where, after all their
troubles, they had expected to find succor. And what they
found were some fifty half-dead creatures so weak from
hunger they could hardly stand. The town itself was falling
to pieces. The palisade had been torn down for fuel. Houses
stood empty without doors. The church was a ruin. Of food
there was none. Only by sharing the small supply that the
two pinnaces had brought from Bermuda was immediate
starvation averted.[38]

Something had to be done and done fast. Gates made the

Sir Thomas Gates.

From a portrait by C. Janssen. *Courtesy,* The Right Honorable
Lord Brassey, Apethorpe Hall, Peterborough.

decision. Besides the two pinnaces in which he had come from Bermuda there were available at Jamestown the *Virginia* and one other pinnace. Into these four small boats he would load the two hundred people and sail for Newfoundland where he hoped to find relief among the fishing fleets. From there he hoped to get the colonists back to England. Virginia was to be abandoned. Gates may have thought of the smug smile on the face of the Spanish ambassador in London when he heard the news. He doubtless thought of the sour looks on the faces of the investors in the Virginia Company when they heard the news. But everywhere before his eyes were the drawn faces and wasted figures of men and women whose very lives hung on his decision.

The *Virginia* was sent ahead to pick up the men at Point Comfort, and on the morning of June 7 those at Jamestown were put aboard the other three boats. Some wanted to burn the town but this Gates would not permit. A dreary farewell salute was fired, and the tiny fleet started dropping down the James River. The next morning, while still some distance above Point Comfort, they saw a strange longboat coming up the river. She carried a message for Sir Thomas Gates. He was no longer Governor of Virginia. Lord Delaware, with his ships and ample supplies, was off Point Comfort.

Gates swung his boats sharp about; a fair breeze came out of the east; and by nightfall the colonists were back within the dilapidated town which they had left the day before. Two days later Delaware and his new colonists were also at Jamestown. They all listened to a sermon by the preacher; Delaware formally took over the government from Gates; and then the new Governor "delivered some few wordes unto the Company, laying some blames on them for many vanities and their idlenes, earnestly wishing that I might no more find it so, leaste I should be compeld to drawe the sworde of Justice, to cut off such delinquents. . . ."[39]

In these stern words Delaware was speaking for the Company, which had learned by sad experience how much "it hurteth to suffer Parents to disburden themselves of Lascivious sonnes, masters of bad servants and wives of ill husbands, and so to clogge the businesse with such an idle crue, as did thrust themselves in the last voiage, that will rather starve for hunger, than lay their hands to labor." [40]

The Company did not altogether live up to its ideals about "lascivious sonnes" and "ill husbands," but it did during the ensuing critical years have governors who, though sometimes harsh, saw to it that the colonists took care of themselves. Never again was there a possibility that Virginia would be abandoned. England had achieved a permanent settlement in America.

Virginia and New England

ALTHOUGH THE ENGLISH COLONY on the James River was firmly established, it was still far from prosperous. The question naturally arises as to why the adventurers kept on pouring good money after bad.

Spain had her own ideas on the subject. She had been convinced from the first that the real and only purpose of the settlement was to provide a pirates' nest from which to raid Spanish shipping. As word of the disaster of 1609 leaked into London, the Spanish ambassador suggested to Philip III that he send "a few ships to finish what might be left in that place, which is so important for pirates." [1]

Nor can it be said that Spain lacked grounds for her conviction. Many of those now active in the Virginia Company had, within the not too distant past, backed or even taken part in raids upon Spanish shipping in the New World. King James himself recognized these habits of his subjects by inserting in the Virginia patent a clause withholding his protection from the colonists if they robbed or spoiled the subjects of any other Christian prince, by which he meant Spain.

The route which the earlier expeditions took in going to Virginia lent color to the Spanish suspicion. Newport had consistently dropped south into the trade winds and passed through the West Indies on his way to the Chesapeake Bay. There is no record of his having engaged in piratical activities during these voyages, but had an opportunity presented itself, he might have been tempted. It was in part with a view to removing both the suspicion and the temptation that Argall was directed to find a more direct route in 1609.[2]

It is true that England did look upon the Virginia settlement as a "bit in the mouth of Spain" in case war should break out between the two countries. But, aside from that, Spain's suspicions as to the intent of the adventurers in establishing the colony appear to have been unfounded.

Then why, after the hope of finding gold or a passage to the Indies had waned, did the Virginia Company stick to it? In part it was national pride. England was in an expansive mood. She had just pushed into the East India trade, which, incidentally, was paying very large profits. The investors were willing to risk in the West some of the profits they made in the East—and perhaps Virginia would ultimately pay out. Anyway, if Spain and France were going to have colonies in America, so was England.

Another reason for the persistence of the Company was that it had become fashionable to support such ventures. Outstanding among the backers of the Virginia Company was the Earl of Southampton. He had been Shakespeare's patron and the money he spent on that popular dramatist had brought dividends in vanity. Colonization now provided a new and worthy "cause." Into it Southampton threw his influence and his purse. Others followed suit.

Still another reason, and one that always influenced responsible public officials, was the belief that the colony served a useful purpose "by transplanting the rancknesse and multitude of increase in our people; of which there is left no vent, but age; and evident danger that the number and infinitenesse of them will out-grow the matter, whereon to worke for their life and sustenation, and shall one infest and become a burthen to another."[3]

But the "real and substantial food" which nourished Virginia during this period came from lotteries authorized in a new charter which was issued to the Company in 1612.

Held in various parts of England, these lotteries were publicized in pamphlets, poems, and sermons; all sorts and conditions of people and corporations bought tickets; and lucky ticket holders sometimes received as much as four thousand crowns. The losers were consoled with the assurance that they had helped a worthy cause. And the Company made its profit out of the difference between the total take and the prizes.[4]

So much for the promoters of the colony. But why did colonists continue to come to Virginia in the face of what must have been common knowledge of the fate of so many of their predecessors? Some came in the hope of bettering their economic condition. Men like John Rolfe stuck it out and ended up with good estates. But the great majority of the colonists were of a different sort. They were gathered up from "riotous, lasie and infected places," said Governor Dale, who added that they were of "sutch diseased and crased bodies as the Sea hither and this Clime here but a little searching them, render them so unhable, fainte, and desperate of recoverie as of 300 not three score may be called forth or imploied upon any labour or service." In short they were mostly a worthless lot who came because they were assured of food, clothing, and shelter—none of which they were sure of in England. And they stayed in the colony because they were not permitted to go home. During their term of service they did what they were told to do and as little of that as they could.[5]

Most of them lived at Jamestown, where there were "two rowes of houses of framed timber, and some of them two stories and a garret higher," which together with the storehouses and the fort were enclosed by a palisade of logs planted upright in the ground. Within the houses women cooked and washed, while children played on the floors or in the street outside. The men worked in the corn fields or felled and split trees for clapboards, or gathered sassafras which had a high value on account of its supposed medicinal properties. Life was strict. Twice daily upon the tolling of the bell every one was required to go to church and hear divine service. Swearing was frowned upon; whoso offended a second time might have a bodkin (large needle) stuck through his tongue, and if he kept it up, the penalty was death. Nor was slovenliness tolerated. No one was permitted to "throw out the water or suds of fowle cloathes, in the open streete, within the Pallizadoes, or within forty foote of the same, nor rench, and make cleane, any kettle, pot, or pan, or such like vessell within twenty foote of the olde well, or new Pumpe; nor shall anyone aforesaid, within lesse than a quarter of one mile from the Pallizadoes, dare to doe the necessities of nature," upon pain of whipping.⁶

Despite the improved sanitation at Jamestown a very large proportion of the colonists died within a few months of their arrival. Not even Lord Delaware was exempt from the fevers which were prevalent. To effect a cure he went on an ocean voyage which ended in England. But the plantation went on. Ships came into the James River from England with new colonists and cattle and horses and supplies. They sailed back loaded mostly with lumber and sassafras. Delaware's departure was more than made good by the arrival in May, 1611, of Sir Thomas Dale, who took over the management of the colony with both sense and energy. He put the colonists to planting corn; he repaired the houses at Jamestown; and up the river toward the falls he laid out a new plantation known as Henrico, with "three streets of well framed houses, a handsome Church . . . besides Store-houses."⁷

In the midst of all this activity the colony had visitors. Up what we today call Hampton Roads came a lone Spanish ship. Just off the fortification at Point Comfort it dropped a small boat which pulled in toward the shore, and landed three men—who were promptly captured and disarmed by the Englishmen at the fort. The captives admitted being Spanish and their leader, Don Diego de Molina, explained that they were looking for a missing ship. The story seemed a little too good, and the captain at the fort sent John Clark, his pilot, to the Spanish ship to bring it up to the fort. Clark was in turn made a captive aboard the ship, and with him it sailed out of the Bay. Spain had accomplished her purpose. She had planted three spies in the English colony and had in her possession an Englishman who knew the approaches to the colony and might talk. However, nothing came of it. Molina was held at Jamestown for several years, and Clark was released by the Spanish in time to help pilot the *Mayflower* across the Atlantic in 1620. Nonetheless the incident gave Dale something to worry about in 1611.[8]

It will be recalled that, under the arrangement entered into between the Company and the planters in 1609, there was to be no private ownership of land or of its produce until 1616. For a period of seven years all the planters, by which name the colonists were now generally called, were to work for the Company, and during that period the Company was to support the planters. The program naturally did not encourage individual effort, so Dale tried an experiment. To a number of industrious men he allotted three-acre plots of good cleared land. The result is told in the words of Ralph Hamor, one of the planters: "When our people were fed out of the common store, and laboured jointly together, glad was he could slip from his labour, or slumber over his taske he cared not how, nay, the most honest among them would hardly take so much true paines in a weeke, as now for themselves they will doe in a day: neither cared they for the increase, presuming that howsoever the harvest prospered, the generall store must maintaine them, so that wee reaped not so much Corne from the labours of thirtie, as now three or foure do provide for themselves."[9]

Whether from one of these three-acre plots or simply because of the improved spirit in the colony there was begun at this time the cultivation of a plant destined to solve all of Virginia's economic problems and to bring greater riches than could have been derived from many gold mines. John Rolfe, who had left England aboard the *Sea Venture* in 1609 and arrived in Virginia on one of the pinnaces built in Bermuda, was so improving the native tobacco that it had become almost as good as the tobacco which England was buying from Spain at very fancy prices.[10]

But at the moment the colonists wanted corn rather than tobacco. The Indians, and particularly Powhatan's people, were still unfriendly, and refused to supply the needs of the settlement. To meet this situation Captain Argall, who had come to Virginia with a ship strong enough to take care of any visiting Spaniards, was sent up the Potomac River in the spring of 1613 to trade for such corn as might be available in that region. While there he discovered that Pocahontas, Powhatan's daughter, was in one of the villages. By treachery he got her aboard his ship and sailed for Jamestown, sending word to Powhatan that his daughter would be released upon the return of some English captives whom the Indians were holding. Powhatan somewhat grudgingly complied. The English then made further demands and emphasized them by burning Werowocomoco. And they still held Pocahontas, or possibly she did not want to go home.[11]

Anyway Pocahontas stayed on at Jamestown. From all accounts she was an attractive girl, and unattached women were scarce in the English community. John Rolfe, the tobacco farmer, had recently lost his wife. He felt moved to save Pocahontas' soul by instructing her in the catechism. Soon one of the great romances of history was under way. From a letter in which Rolfe asked Sir Thomas Dale's blessing we may sense the passion of the ardent suitor. He was courting the daughter of Powhatan, said Rolfe, not because of "unbridled desire of carnall affection, but for the good of this plantation, for the honour of our countrie, for the glory of God, for my owne salvation, and for the converting to the true knowledge of God and Jesus Christ, an unbeleeving creature, namely Pokahuntas." He realized that she was "one whose education hath bin rude, her manners barbarous, her generation accursed," but, "What should I doe? Shall I be of so untoward a disposition as to refuse to leade the blind into the right way?"[12]

It would have taken a harder-hearted man than Dale to refuse such an appeal, so as the blossoms opened along the James River that spring of 1614, John Rolfe and Pocahontas were joined in marriage. The ceremony was held in the church at Jamestown. The Reverend Buck officiated. Powhatan sent some of his people to see that everything went off all right. And from that day onward, so long as Powhatan lived, there was peace between the Indians and the English.[13]

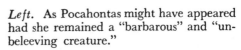

Left. As Pocahontas might have appeared had she remained a "barbarous" and "unbeleeving creature."

From a painting by John White. *Courtesy,* The William L. Clements Library, Ann Arbor.

Right. Pocahontas, from a portrait painted in England in 1616 by Simon de Passe.

114

Peace with the Indians fitted in with Dale's plans for expansion of the colony. The success of the Rolfe-Pocahontas alliance evidently gave him an idea. If one marriage between the English and the Indians could help so much, two might help more. Accordingly he sent Ralph Hamor with a message for Powhatan. Hamor found the savage chieftain at Machot, between the forks of the Pamunkey and Mattaponi rivers, where he had been living since the English burned Werowocomoco. Powhatan received him courteously, asked about Pocahontas, and demanded the purpose of the visit. Hamor requested a private audience. Instantly Powhatan dismissed the two hundred bowmen who surrounded him. Then Hamor disclosed his mission. Governor Dale wished to marry the younger sister of Pocahontas, aged about twelve years. To show that his intentions were honorable the Governor offered in return for the girl's hand two pieces of copper, five strings of white and blue beads, five wooden combs, ten fishhooks, a couple of knives, and a grindstone. Powhatan had long wanted a grindstone. Nonetheless he declined. One white son-in-law was enough. Probably it was better so. Two years later, when Dale returned to England he was accompanied by John Rolfe and Pocahontas and their baby son. Had he had along, as his own wife, the sister of Pocahontas, it might well have proved embarrassing when he introduced the party to his English wife and children who had remained in England.[14]

As it was, when the Dale party arrived, all proper and in order, Lady Delaware took Pocahontas in hand and saw that she met the right people, including the King and Queen. But the poor girl did not flourish in England, nor did she last long. Within the year John Rolfe was again a widower.

In the spring of 1613, while Pocahontas was still being held captive at Jamestown, along with Molina and his fellow Spaniards, fifteen more prisoners were added to the colorful group. These new arrivals were Frenchmen and among them were two black-robed Jesuit priests. They were brought in by Captain Argall who, shortly after his capture of Pocahontas, had sailed northward on what was said to be a fishing trip. Off the coast of Maine, not far from where the

English in 1607 had built their fort at Sagadahoc, he learned from the Indians that there was a French settlement to the eastward—on the island which we now call Mount Desert. The Indians, being friendly with the French and supposing Argall to be of the same nation, readily guided him to the place.

The French, wholly unprepared for an attack, saw Argall's ship "coming from afar off with full sails." On it came, reported Father Biard, who was on the receiving end, "swifter than an arrow, being favored by the wind, with the Flag of England displayed, all dressed in red and three trumpets and two drums making a great noise." To the Frenchmen's questioning hail the English replied with a blast of artillery and muskets, followed by more until all possible resistance was silenced. Then Argall investigated.

The settlement turned out to be the pioneer effort of the Jesuits north of "Florida." Argall charged them with being trespassers on the domain of King James of England. They were there under a commission from the King of France, but as Argall had all their papers in his possession, together with much other loot, they were in no position to argue. Their ships were part of the loot, but Argall allowed them one small boat into which were crowded as many as possible, and turned loose to make their way northward to the fishing fleet or perish. The rest, including two priests, he took aboard his ships and carried back to Jamestown.

Jesuits were not popular among Englishmen at that time, and Dale's first idea was to hang them. However, they suffered no worse fate than that of having to spend a few weeks among the unsympathetic planters at the tiny settlement on the banks of the James River, after which they were again marched aboard the ships of Captain Argall. He had been ordered back to the Maine coast to finish the job of cleaning out all French settlements in that area. There is reason to think that the priests were taken along as guides. In any case, Argall not only put the final touches on what was left at Mount Desert but destroyed Port Royal to his own profit.[15]

The following summer our old acquaintance, Captain John Smith, late of Virginia, was on the coast of New England. In fact it was he who gave it the name of New England. Prior to 1614 the region had been called Northern Virginia by Englishmen and Canada by the French. Smith thought that it was directly opposite the place on the Pacific which Francis Drake had visited in 1579 and which he had named Nova Albion. Therefore Smith decided that the proper name for the Atlantic shore between 41° and 45° would be New England. To clinch the name he made a map of the area and labeled it New England. To the various physical features on this map Prince Charles, the future King Charles I, gave suitable English names. Some of these names stuck, as for example Plymouth, Charles River and Cape Anne. Others, such as Boston, were placed quite a distance from the localities where cities bearing the names later came into being.[16]

It was a fishing and fur-trading voyage that brought Smith to New England. His part of the job was to trade with the Indians for furs, of which he obtained eleven thousand beaver and a couple of hundred marten and otter hides at a trifling cost in trade goods. Above the Penobscot he found the trade unprofitable, due to French competition.[17]

Smith was impressed with the wealth to be had from fishing, but thousands of fishermen from France and Spain and the west of England had been aware of that for perhaps two hundred years. Since the failure of the Sagadahoc colony Sir Ferdinando Gorges and other members of the Plymouth Company had used their patent rights in the northern country to send out from year to year expeditions similar to that in which Smith was engaged in 1614. Often the fishermen would establish temporary quarters ashore while drying their catch. However, life around the fishing stages lacked the refinements of organized society. ". . . in their manners and behaviour they are worse than the very savages," said Gorges, "impudently and openly lying with their women, teaching their men to drink drunk, to swear and blaspheme the name of God, and in their drunken humor to fall together by the ears, thereby giving them occasion for revenge."[18]

Smith himself just missed being a party to one piece of skulduggery that the Indians did not soon forget. There were

Above. Fishing boats on the Grand Banks.

Below. Fishing stage.

Both pictures are from Duhamel du Monceau, *Traité général des pesches*.

two ships in the venture with which he came to the New England coast in 1614. At the end of the season Smith sailed for England in one of the ships, laden with furs, oil and salted fish. The other ship, under the command of Captain Thomas Hunt, stayed on to dry its fish for sale in the Spanish market. Naturally the Indians gathered around the drying stages—which were erected along the shore of Cape Cod Bay. As he was stowing the last of the fish in his hold Captain Hunt lured twenty-four of these friendly natives below deck, clapped down the hatches and took them along to Spain. There he sold some of them as slaves; others were taken in charge by the kindly friars and released. One of them, named Squanto, finally got to England, was put aboard an out-bound fishing ship and dropped off in New England, where he proved more kindly to the white men than they had been to him. However, the incident did not make for either confidence or good feeling among the natives generally.[19]

To the north of Nova Scotia, then called Acadia, the French ruled the fur trade and most of the fishing. Quebec was now solidly established as a French trading post and Samuel de Champlain was again pushing his explorations westward. But despite his victory over the Iroquois in 1609 he knew better than to again venture southward along the lake that bore his name. The Indians that he had met there were the Mohawks, an eastern branch of the Iroquois confederacy. West of them, strung along the southern shore of Lake Ontario, were the other Iroquois nations—the Oneidas, Cayugas, Onondagas and Senecas. Together they constituted the most formidable and most advanced native confederation in North America. North of Lake Ontario were the Hurons, with whom Champlain established friendly relations.

Now, in the autumn of 1615, as in 1609, Champlain's new friends asked him, with a handful of other Frenchmen, to aid them in a foray against one of the hated Iroquois nations, probably the Oneidas. Skirting the eastern end of Lake Ontario in canoes the raiding party landed somewhere near present-day Oswego, N. Y., and marched inland to attack a village located south of Oneida Lake. They found their enemy well fortified within a palisaded enclosure. Nor did the Frenchmen's guns cause a panic this time. The Iroquois fought well and skillfully. In the end the attackers gave it up and retreated, Champlain himself so badly wounded that he had to be carried in a basket on the back of one of the Indians. It was evident to his Indian allies that the Frenchman was not invincible, and to the Frenchman that, if he wanted to push west, he would have to by-pass the hardfighting Iroquois. To make the situation worse, Champlain learned from his Huron friends that the Iroquois were getting help from the Dutch, who had established a trading post up the river that Hudson had discovered six years before.[20]

The Dutch, or more properly the United Netherlands, were at this time in an even more expansive frame of mind than the English. On the seas they had worsted Spain, their former master, and, even as Hudson was skirting the coast of America in 1609, they were wringing from Spain a truce that was equivalent to freedom. Their trade with the East Indies was bringing them great wealth, some of which the Virginia Company had tried to lure into its empty treasury by offering the Dutch an interest in their Colony. This invitation was declined, but at the same time the States General, *i.e.,* the government of the United Netherlands, encouraged its own sea captains to explore the region about the mouth of the Hudson River.

As a result, in 1614, Adriaen Block ranged eastward from Manhattan Island, through Long Island Sound, while Cornelis May explored southward to the bay that was later named for Lord Delaware. Still another Dutch captain was examining the Cape Cod region. What they saw convinced their backers in Holland that a profitable trade in furs could be carried on. A company was formed with the blessing of the States General; ships and men were sent out; and the lands "situate in America, between New France and Virginia" became officially known, in Holland, as New Netherland.

The United New Netherland Company, as the Dutch traders called themselves, had a post on the lower end of Manhattan Island, but their best source for furs was at the head of navigation on the Hudson River. There, in the midst of the Mohawk Indians, near where the city of Albany now stands, they had a stockaded fort though the traders lived on terms of complete friendship with the fierce Iroquois hunters and warriors. These were the Dutchmen that Champlain, spending a miserable winter in a smoke-filled wigwam north of Lake Ontario, heard about in 1616.[21]

With the Dutch clapping the name of New Netherland on everything between New France and Virginia it behooved Gorges and the other members of the now almost forgotten Plymouth Company to do something to prove that they had some rights to the land as well as to the fish in that area. Since the cold winter of 1607–08, when Popham's men had almost frozen to death at Sagadahoc, no Englishman had wintered in New England. They fished or they traded for furs, but when the leaves turned red they headed for England. Now, in 1616, Gorges decided to prove that New England winters were not as bad as they had been painted. He hired Richard Vines and a group of traders to spend the winter on the coast of Maine, which they did. Their favorable report infused new life into what remained of the Plymouth Company. The day of permanent settlements in New England was approaching.[22]

Meanwhile in Virginia the year was at hand when the planters expected to receive their individual allotments of land. The seven years during which they had worked and the adventurers waited had run their course. At this time, namely 1616, Governor Dale sailed for England and Captain Samuel Argall was sent over to take his place. It was a sorry exchange so far as the planters and investors were concerned. Not only did Argall refrain from making the general allotments of land but, under the system of martial law then existing in the colony, he forced even those who already had individual allotments to work on the Company lands. Nor did this profit the Company. All that the plantation produced or accumulated went to the private enrichment of Argall, who probably divided with his patron and backer, Sir Robert Rich.[23]

This man Rich, soon to succeed to the title of Earl of

Warwick, was a dominant figure in England's overseas expansion during those early years of the seventeenth century. One of the richest men in England, he had semi-piratical ships operating from the Indian Ocean to the Caribbean. He was a member of the Virginia Company and had a hand in most of the other colonizing ventures of the day. Typical of his enterprises was the voyage in 1618 and 1619 of the *Treasurer.* It arrived in the James River under the command of one of Rich's captains and with a commission from the Duke of Savoy who was then at war with Spain. It was the same ship that Argall had commanded when he made his raid on the French at Mount Desert, and now, as Governor of Virginia, and under the pretense of sending it on a peaceful trading voyage, he filled out its crew with Virginia planters—and off it went to the West Indies to prey on Spanish shipping.

The marauding activities of previous expeditions backed by Rich had already brought him into collision with Sir Thomas Smith, the responsible head of the Virginia Company in London. Factions had developed among the stockholders and early in 1619 Smith was forced out of office. The outcome, however, was not altogether to Rich's advantage, as the new head of the Company, Sir Edwin Sandys, promptly ordered Argall's arrest for his mismanagement in Virginia; also that his property be attached in behalf of the Company.

But Rich was not a man who failed his henchmen in time of trouble, particularly where it affected his own pocketbook. Before the Company could get a ship under way, Rich sent a pinnace scudding across the Atlantic; and when in April, 1619, Sir George Yeardley, the new Governor, arrived at Jamestown, Argall was gone.[24]

With Yeardley's arrival a new day dawned for Virginia. From the Company in London he brought instructions, orders and even a frame of government which changed Virginia from a plantation worked by overseers to a colony of free men governed, in part at least, by themselves. The impending changes were foreshadowed in a proclamation issued by the new Governor shortly after his arrival, in which he is said to have stated that "all those which were resident here before the departure of Sir Thomas Dale [in 1616] should be freed and acquitted from such publique services and labours which formerly they suffered, and that those cruell lawes by which we had soe longe been governed were now abrogated, and we were now to be governed by those free lawes which his Ma^{tys} subjects live under in Englande. And farther that free libertie was given to all men to make choice of their dividents of lande and, as their abilities and meanes w^d permitt, to possesse and plant uppon them. And that they might have a hande in the governinge of themselves, it was granted that a general assemblie should be helde yearly once, wherat were to be present the Govr and Counsell with two Burgesses from each plantation freely to be elected by the inhabitants thereof; this assembly to have power to make and ordaine whatsoever lawes and orders should by them be thought good and proffittable for our subsistance." [25]

In accordance with his instructions the Governor began making allotments of land to those who had earned them, with the result that now "knowing their owne land, they strive who should exceed in building and planting." [26]

Promptly too the Governor called for the election of two burgesses from each of the eleven separate plantations strung up and down the James River. How they were elected or who was allowed to vote is, unfortunately, unknown. On July 30, 1619, in the church at Jamestown, the duly elected burgesses met with the Governor and his Council in the first General Assembly of the representatives of the people ever to be held in America. Mr. John Pory, formerly a member of the English Parliament, was elected Speaker, and the Assembly went to work. It considered and improved a body of laws sent over by the Company in London; it added some laws of its own (subject to approval by the Company in London); and it gave thought to the state of the colony. The session lasted only six days but it established a most persistent precedent. It may be called the mother of representative government in America. [27]

Hardly had the newly made freemen finished discussing

the newly made laws of the new General Assembly when up the James River came the *Treasurer,* back from a successful voyage in Spanish waters. The captain had expected to be welcomed by Governor Argall, and when he learned of the change of administration he wasted no time in getting out. He may have been accompanied by a Dutch man-of-war as he came up the river. John Rolfe, again in Virginia, reported that there "came in a dutch man of warre that sold us twenty Negars," which may have been a tactful account of a transaction that would have brought the wrath of King James upon the Virginia Company had it been admitted that the negroes, doubtless picked up at the point of a gun in the Spanish waters, were acquired from the *Treasurer.* Be the facts as they may, this episode marks the beginning of negro slavery in Virginia.[28]

Along with recognition of the fact that white bond servants working for a master would never make a colony the directors of the Company in London began to realize that a few hundred shiftless inhabitants would never make a colony. In line with the more liberal and statesmanlike point of view in London it now became the policy of the Company to get the colony filled with people, and with people of a better kind. In 1619 eleven ships sailed from England to Virginia with some twelve hundred new colonists.[29]

Among these newcomers were sixty "young and uncorrupt" maidens who it was hoped would be the "meanes to make the men there more setled." If these young ladies married men who were employed on the Company's lands, they were to be transported at the expense of the Company; if, however, they married independent planters, then the husbands were called upon to pay the transportation. Also, many boys and girls of twelve years of age and over were brought in and placed as apprentices until they should reach the age of twenty-one, after which they were to be employed as tenants on the Company's lands unless, in the case of the girls, they married first.[30]

With all this activity the finances of the Company were still in a bad way. Seventy-five thousand pounds had been spent on the colony with no dividends paid and very little in the way of assets to show for it. The merchants who had supplied food and clothing for the colonists had doubtless made a profit. The owners of the ships that went back and forth had doubtless made their profit. But the adventurers who had subscribed for shares had seen no returns or were they likely to.

To shift some of the burden from their shoulders and at the same time to continue the policy of peopling the colony as rapidly as possible the Company had begun the practice of making sub-grants of land to smaller companies that would agree to send over settlers at their own expense. Thus, an "association" or "society" of public-spirited or speculatively minded persons in England would subscribe enough money to hire servants, transport them, feed and clothe them, and to buy the necessary tools and stock for a plantation. Then they would secure a grant of land from the Virginia Company and proceed to operate their plantation as a small private domain. Sometimes they got the patent first, and with it as an asset tried to get the funds and people to start a plantation.[31]

On May 26, 1619, the Virginia Company held one of its regular meetings in London. Present were Sir Edwin Sandys, the Treasurer, and twenty other stockholders of the Company. Before them, at that meeting, appeared one John Wyncop "comended to the Company by the Earle of Lincolne intending to goe in person to Virginia, and there plant himselfe and his Associats. . . ." He asked for a patent for a private plantation of the sort that the Company was then granting. Two weeks later, during another meeting of the Company, "By reason it grewe late, and the Court ready to breake up," it was agreed that this patent should be passed without taking the trouble to have it read, and if it was not all right, they could cancel it later.[32]

In this offhand manner, late of an afternoon, came into being the patent which, while never used, started on their way to America the company of people known to American history as the Pilgrims.

The Pilgrims

"SO THEY LEFTE that goodly and pleasante citie, which had been ther resting place near 12 years; but they knew they were pilgrimes and looked not much on those things, but lift up their eyes to the heavens, their dearest cuntrie, and quieted their spirits." Thus, said William Bradford, who was one of them, did the Pilgrims depart from Leyden in the summer of 1620.[1]

Their spiritual pilgrimages had begun many years earlier. For them, as for thousands of other people throughout England, the Genevan Bible, published in 1560, had opened wide vistas for spiritual perambulations. With God's Word available to all who could read or were willing to listen the possibilities of interpretation became almost limitless. No longer did salvation depend upon the "popish trash" and other mummeries of the Church of England. In fact, it appeared to these people, many of whom were ministers holding their parishes under the Church establishment, that, by conforming to the ritual and discipline of the Church, they were endangering their own salvation and, in the case of the ministers, that of their parishioners.[2]

But there was more involved in this controversy than a matter of conscience. King James saw clearly enough that from dispensing with the Bishops of the Church of England it was but a step to dispensing with the temporal rulers of England. At a famous conference between the Bishops and the Non-conforming ministers at which the King presided he turned to the Bishops and said, ". . . if once you were out and they in, I know what would become of my supremecy, for *No Bishop, No King.*" And then to both the Bishops and the ministers he summed up his decision: "I will make them conform themselves, or else I will harry them out of the land, or else do worse." [3]

In the face of this royal pronouncement the great majority of the Non-conformists clung to the Church and strove to reform it from within. Some gave lip service to the Book of Common Prayer and read their Bibles in their own way. Others openly separated from the Church and took the consequences—sometimes rotting in filthy prisons. A few, of which Bradford was one, separated from the Church and were "harried out of the land." They fled to Holland where some of them disagreed with and separated from each other. In short, they were Separatists and by that name known.

In Holland the particular congregation of which Bradford was a member finally settled down in the city of Leyden —held together by a beloved pastor. Most of them were desperately poor, but by taking such jobs as they could get, they managed to live and to have the comfort of worshiping according to their convictions. Still they were an island of piety surrounded by worldly interests. Their children were being lured from the ways of salvation. The fathers longed for a place where all could live without danger of contamination. And as they searched their Bibles they found that those who "confessed that they were strangers and pilgremes on the earth" might desire a better country, "that is an heavenlie: wherefore God is not ashamed of them to be called their God: for he hathe prepared for them a citie." [4]

The advantages of a heavenly city on this earth became an obsession with them. But where could such a city be reared? Naturally their thoughts turned toward the New World. They considered Guiana but decided upon Virginia. The patent for a private plantation taken out by John Wyncop in June, 1619, was a preliminary to their intended settlement along the James River. Doubtless this patent was applied for and secured in all good faith, but when it became known that a compact body of honest, hard-working people was available for a plantation, salesmen rushed in with competitive bids.

The Dutch offered them a home in the Hudson River region where New Netherland was not making much progress. Over from London hustled one Thomas Weston, who had in his pocket another patent from the Virginia Company. If they would use his patent, his associates would back them financially. It was an attractive offer, for the prospective colonists needed financial assistance. Weston was representing a group of merchants or speculators who had money to invest in any promising venture.[5]

At the same time word got around that members of the old Plymouth Company, they who had backed the short-lived settlement at Sagadahoc in 1607, had applied for a new and enlarged patent and that settlers would be welcome in New England. The fact was that Sir Ferdinando Gorges had reached the conclusion that New England was habitable and that the time had come to settle the coast and control the valuable fishing and fur-trading resources. Associating with himself a number of men influential at court, he petitioned the King for a patent in March, 1620. Just when the Leyden people first got word of this is uncertain, but certain it is that as early as June, 1620, their leaders had made up their minds that New England was their destination—this despite the fact that two patents for plantations in Virginia had been made out in the expectation that they would settle there.[6]

The actual decision to go to New England instead of Virginia was probably made by the London merchants rather than by the Leyden people. In fact, in accepting the financial support of Weston and his associates, the Leyden group became only a part of a larger project. With them to America were to go a number of other people not Separatists at all but gathered up in England by Weston primarily as man power for a plantation. The Leyden leaders were keenly interested in the character of these prospective fellow colonists but do not appear to have been greatly disturbed about them.

In any case the Pilgrims went ahead with their preparations. Those who had property turned it into money. Two of their number, John Carver and Robert Cushman, were sent over to England to buy supplies and work out financial arrangements with the merchants. It was proposed that the business affairs of the venture be handled through a joint stock partnership along somewhat the same lines as that followed by the Virginia Company. Each share was to have a par value of £10. Each person over sixteen years of age who emigrated to the new colony was to be rated as holding one share in consideration of his or her prospective service to the company. If, from available funds, an emigrant also paid into the treasury £10 in money, he was to be rated as holding two shares and so on. The merchants and other investors, who had no thought of emigrating, were to put in money only—£10 or £100 or whatever they wanted to risk, and were to be credited with shares accordingly.[7]

All of the money was to go into a central treasury from which the expenses of the venture would be met, including the fee for a patent, the purchase or rental of ships, the wages of the crews, and food and clothing for the colonists. The colonists on their part, in consideration of their shares in the enterprise and their support, were to work exclusively for the company. All the profits from their work—fishing, fur trading, or anything else—were to go into the central treasury. At the end of seven years the assets of the company —money, fish, furs, ships, whatever there might be—were to be divided according to the shares that each investor, merchant or colonist, had in the venture.

And here came a hitch. The Leyden people objected to having houses which they might build for themselves included in the common stock to be divided seven years hence. Also they wanted two days a week to work for themselves. The merchants stood pat on their terms. If the colonists built houses on company time, the houses should be company property. Without settling this controversy, the Pilgrims went ahead with their plans to emigrate. They bought, in Holland, a small ship called the *Speedwell,* which was designed not only to help transport them to New England but to be kept there for use in fishing and fur trading.

At the same time another ship, the *Mayflower,* was being fitted out at London under the joint direction of the agents of the emigrants and of the merchants, the latter of course being the heavy investors of actual money. On this ship were being collected the other people signed up by Weston in England and destined to be fellow planters with the Pilgrims.[8]

Late in July, 1620, such of the Leyden people as were still willing to make the venture—and only a part of them were willing—sailed from Holland aboard the *Speedwell* to meet the *Mayflower* and its passengers at Southampton, England. While they were making this short voyage, the King's Council handed to the Solicitor General of England a warrant for a new patent for New England.[9]

The Pilgrims, on arriving at Southampton in the *Speedwell,* found the *Mayflower* and the other emigrants waiting for them. There too, at Southampton, was Weston, who had come down from London to get the Leyden people to sign the proposed agreement between themselves and the merchants. The Pilgrims raised their former objections. Weston bluntly informed them that the terms were the best that the merchants could offer. The Pilgrims just as bluntly refused to sign. Weston then told them that they would have to "stand on their owne leggs" so far as any more help from the merchants was concerned. The meaning of this became immediately evident. The Pilgrims needed £100 in ready money to clear their commitments before they sailed. They did not have the money and to get it they had to sell thirty or forty tubs of butter which they were carrying with them.

So off they went—the *Speedwell* and the *Mayflower*—with a release from the port authorities because they had a patent for settlement in Virginia and were presumably going to Virginia. They had not gone far before the *Speedwell* started leaking. They put in at Dartmouth and had the leak fixed. Again they went out to sea and again the *Speedwell* developed a leak. They turned back to Plymouth and there they were informed that the *Speedwell* was not up to making

Above. Departure of the *Speedwell* from Delftshaven.
From a painting attributed to Albert Cuyp.

Below. Model of the *Mayflower.*
Courtesy, The New York Historical Society.

the voyage. There was nothing for it but to leave her; also some of the Pilgrims, including Cushman, had to give up the voyage, probably without too great regret. The rest were packed aboard the *Mayflower,* and on September 6, 1620, they "put to sea againe with a prosperus winde." [10]

Aboard as passengers were one hundred and one emigrants: men, women, and children; masters and servants; shareholders and hired men; Separatists and non-Separatists. In command of the ship was Captain Christopher Jones. One of the mates was John Clark, the James River pilot who had been captured by the Spanish off Point Comfort in 1611. In addition there were some forty other members of the crew. The ship was of one hundred and eighty tons, broad of beam, double-decked, and with three masts. Below and on deck she was crammed with food, furniture, baggage and all sorts of supplies and equipment. But the *Mayflower* was a sturdy little tub and with no worse mishaps than were usual to such a voyage she went pounding across the Atlantic. [11]

So far as the Pilgrims were concerned they were being carried toward a strange new world in a ship which they did not control; they had little money or credit at home; they had no agreement as to how they would be supported in the New World; they had no patent authorizing them to settle where they were going; many of them did not know where they were going; and winter was approaching.

Meanwhile, in London, on November 3, when the *Mayflower* was still eight days off the coast of America, the Great Seal of England was attached to a patent creating a "Councill established at Plymouth, in the County of Devon, for the planting, ruling, ordering, and governing of New-England, in America." To this Council, which soon came to be known as the Council for New England, the King granted all of North America between 40° and 48° (from Philadelphia to Newfoundland) and from the Atlantic to the Pacific. In making the grant the King specifically directed that the region should be called "by the Name of New-England." Thus did Captain John Smith's designation receive royal confirmation. The patent gave Gorges and the old Plymouth

Company all that they had asked for, including a monopoly of the fishing, which latter stirred up a hornet's nest. The Virginia Company had long been in the habit of sending its fishing vessels into the waters off the New England coast and it did not intend to be pushed out of the sea, it "beinge to all as ffree and common as the Ayre." The day following the issuance of the patent there was a meeting of the directors of the Virginia Company. Gorges came in for a sound rating and it was decided to petition the King for redress.[12]

Ignorant of what was happening in London, the people aboard the *Mayflower* sailed on westward. On November 9 they sighted Cape Cod and two days later were at anchor in Provincetown Bay. They all knew where they were then, and the fact of their being in New England instead of in Virginia was evidently somewhat of a shock to some of them, particularly the non-Separatists. A few of them took the attitude that since they were not in Virginia, where they had signed up to go, they could do as they pleased. To meet this situation the more responsible men drew up a compact pledging the signers to combine together in one body and to submit to such laws as would be "for the generall good of the Colonie." Forty-one of the men, being a heavy majority of both Separatists and non-Separatists, signed this Compact before any one went ashore. At the same time John Carver, a leader of the Leyden group, and "a man godly and well approved amongst them," was chosen Governor.[13]

For ten weeks—from Plymouth, England, to Cape Cod— these people had been cramped up aboard the ship. Even now, at anchor back of the Cape, they had to wade three-quarters of a mile to reach land. And what then? As Bradford says, "they had now no freinds to wellcome them, nor inns to entertaine or refresh their weatherbeaten bodys, no houses nor much less townes to repaire too, to seek for succoure." Their nearest white neighbors were possibly some few late-lingering Dutchmen at the mouth of the Hudson River. The Virginia settlements were more than four hundred miles down the coast. To the northward the fishermen and fur traders had all turned homeward. At Quebec and possibly two or three other points in the St. Lawrence region there were some Frenchmen. Otherwise it was "but a hidious and desolate wildernes, full of wild beasts and willd men."[14]

But somewhere in this "hidious and desolate wildernes" they had to find a place to live. Obviously the bay in which they were anchored was not suitable. So while the women waded ashore to do a much-needed wash and the carpenter started putting the shallop (small boat) into condition, some of the men went exploring.

For a solid month, with the weather growing steadily worse, these exploring parties crept around the inside of the hook that is Cape Cod. They dug up hidden hoards of corn belonging to the "willd men"—"goodly ears, some yellow, and some red, and others mixed with blue, which was a very goodly sight." So they took as much as they could carry, assuring themselves that "it was God's good providence" that they had found it, and that they would square it with the Indians later. They found Indian houses—made by sticking both ends of long thin saplings into the ground and covering the dome-shaped frame with grass mats. Inside the houses they found wooden bowls, pots, baskets, and other household stuff. "Some of the best things we took away with us," one of them reported. During all this time they saw very few Indians and had only one slight brush with them.[15]

In the end they decided to make their settlement at a place which on John Smith's map, a copy of which they had along, Prince Charles had given the name of Plymouth. It was a pleasant if shallow harbor on the mainland almost directly across the Bay from where their ship was anchored. On December 16 the *Mayflower* was brought across. Building lots were laid out and assigned to each family and there was shortly under way the construction of a community house in which they could store their supplies and in which some of the men could live until the separate houses were finished. On Monday, December 25, 1620, they "went on shore, some to fell timber, some to saw, some to rive, and some to carry; so no man rested all that day." At night all but a guard of twenty men went back to the ship—anchored a mile and a half out in the shallow harbor. The fact that it was Christmas meant nothing to the Leyden people, who looked upon any special recognition of that day as a sin. But Captain Jones of the *Mayflower* felt differently about it and opened a barrel of beer which the tired Pilgrims gladly joined their non-Separatists friends in drinking—all except those twenty poor fellows left to guard the new building on shore.[16]

Besides the common house, which was twenty feet square and pretty well finished by the first week in January, each family built its own house, the unmarried men being assigned to some particular family. The houses were in two rows along a single street. The construction was partly of hewn frame and partly of woven brush filled with mud. The roofs were of thatch. Naturally there were some accidental fires, but none of them serious.[17]

So far the planters had seen Indians only at a distance. Then on a warm day in March, 1621, there strode into the little town a tall savage clad only in a belt with a narrow —very narrow the Pilgrims felt—fringe. He bade the new-comers "Welcome," in passable English; told them that his name was Samoset; and asked for beer. He explained that he too was a stranger in those parts, being from farther up the coast where he had picked up his English words from the fishermen. A few days later he brought in another Indian named Squanto, who was a native, in fact the last surviving native of the place where the town of Plymouth was being built. All the rest had died of a plague some four years earlier. Doubtless he too would have died had he been there. But it so happened that he had been living in London at the time. In short he was one of the twenty-four Indians that Captain Hunt had kidnapped in 1614 and carried to Spain for sale as slaves. Squanto had fallen into the hands of the priests, had been returned to England, and only a few months before the arrival of the *Mayflower* had been dropped off at Cape Cod by one of Gorges' trading ships. Through the good offices of Samoset and Squanto the Plym-outh people got acquainted with the neighboring Indians and discovered that they were neither strong enough nor aggressive enough to be greatly feared.[18]

Far more dangerous than the Indians was an epidemic

of influenza that swept through the colony that winter. Poor diet on the ship had weakened them. Wading through the cold water back and forth to the ship had done its part. Inadequate shelter and exposure to inclement weather had brought on colds and related ills. Between the beginning of the settlement at Plymouth and the end of March half of the colonists had died. Nor was the crew of the ship exempt. The deaths among them had been almost as serious. On April 5, 1621, Governor Carver, who had been working in one of the fields, came in complaining of pains in his head. Within a few days he was dead.[19]

On the day that the Governor was taken sick the *Mayflower* sailed for England. It had not been the intention of the London adventurers that she should stay longer than was necessary to unload the colony and take on a return cargo of something that would defray the costs of the voyage. But between the Leyden people and the other colonists there were enough shares of stock at Plymouth to persuade Captain Jones to stay until the emigrants were reasonably settled and housed. And by that time so many of the crew were down with the sickness that he could not have sailed if he had wanted to. Nor were the planters in condition to get together a cargo of even the usual clapboards. So except for perhaps a few beaver skins the *Mayflower* started home under ballast. In May she was back in England.

As may be imagined the London merchants were far from happy about the lack of cargo. Weston probably expressed their sentiments when he wrote to the colonists: "That you sent no lading in the ship is wonderfull [*i.e.*, amazing], and worthily distasted. I know your weaknes was the cause of it, and I beleeve more weaknes of judgemente, then weaknes of hands. A quarter of the time you spente in discoursing, arguing, and consulting, would have done much more." Weston apparently knew the habits of the Pilgrims.[20]

However, as soon as he was assured that the colonists were settled in New England Weston acquired a patent for them from the newly created Council for New England, and stirred up his associates to equip and send off another ship with more planters, though with few supplies. Probably he was moved to this action because he wanted the signatures of the Leyden people on the articles of agreement. He had not dared to admit to his fellow backers of the colony that he had failed to close this contract before the *Mayflower* sailed.[21]

The patent which Weston procured from the Council for New England, dated June 1, 1621, legalized the settlement already made at Plymouth. It granted one hundred acres of land for each settler transported to New England and allowed an extra fifteen hundred acres for the support of a church, schools, hospitals, and other public works. It did not specify where the land should be located or give any definite boundaries. However, it stipulated that at any time within seven years the patentees might, by surrendering the existing patent and providing a survey of their land, receive a duly bounded deed to it, subject only to the payment of a nominal quitrent or annual tax to the Council for New England. The patent gave the colonists the privilege of trading with the natives and of fishing, which enterprises were looked upon by the Council as being the main source of support for any colony in their territory; and as a matter of fact the fur trade turned out to be the main support of Plymouth Colony.[22]

At practically the same time that the Council for New England was granting its patent to the Plymouth people the High and Mighty Lords, the States General of the United Netherlands, were granting a charter to the Dutch West India Company which gave to that company the exclusive right, so far as Dutch citizens were concerned, to trade in America. This charter did not claim or give title to any area of land nor did it promise such title. None the less it did direct the company to "advance the peopling of those fruitful and unsettled parts" and authorized it to erect "fortresses, fortifications and settlements." Thenceforth New Netherland —the straggling Dutch trading posts along the Hudson River and Delaware Bay—was to be in experienced and capable hands.[23]

Meanwhile, with the *Mayflower* gone, the English colonists at Plymouth, or New Plymouth as they called it, were at last wholly on their "owne leggs." The epidemic had about run its course, but there were scarcely fifty people still alive when corn planting time came around. Many of these were women and children. In the place of the late Governor Carver they chose thirty-one-year-old William Bradford, already a leader among the Leyden group. The fifty-four-year-old William Brewster, former elder of the Leyden church, had also weathered the sickness; in the absence of a minister he was looked upon as the leader of the Separatist congregation at New Plymouth. Edward Winslow, the best-educated of the Leyden people and the owner of nine shares of stock in the company, was still alive. Very much alive too was Isaac Allerton, former London tailor and a long-time member of the Leyden church. But both Winslow and Allerton had lost their wives during the epidemic.

Outstanding among the non-Separatists who had survived was Steven Hopkins, a man of substance and highly regarded by his fellow colonists. In addition to his wife and family he had brought along two servants. Captain Miles Standish, hired in London to be the "army" of the colony, and later dubbed "Capt. Shrimp" on account of his diminutive size, had proved too tough for any epidemic, though his wife had succumbed. Young John Alden, who also had been hired in England—to look after the casks of beer in the hold of the *Mayflower*—was now staying on at Plymouth, held there by the charms of Priscilla Mullens, only survivor of her family. The Billingtons, who had joined up at London, and were known as the "profanest" family in the colony, were the only ones who entirely escaped the sickness, although old John was destined to be hanged nine years later, "a mater of great sadnes unto them," recorded Governor Bradford.[24]

And there they were, in the spring of 1621, these fifty people, living in their flimsy, thatched, oil-paper-windowed houses on either side of The Street which ran up from the harbor toward the hill. On the Sabbath they gathered in the twenty-by-twenty common house and listened while Elder Brewster "taught," or they joined in singing praises to Jehovah—

"Confess to him, bless ye his name.
Because Jehovah he good is:
his mercy ever is the same:
and his faith, unto all ages." [25]

Around the 1st of May they began to think about planting their corn—the corn that they had lifted from the Indians the previous autumn. Corn was new to them. They neither knew how to plant it nor tend it. In this emergency the ever-helpful Squanto came to the rescue. He showed them how it was done and added a trick worked out by his people through years of experience. With each hill of corn Squanto had them plant two or three dead fish. Fish were plentiful; other forms of manure were not. [26]

Since among his Sabbath-day teachings Elder Brewster probably did not stress the "providence" involved in the following coincidences, it may be of interest to note that had the colonists not stolen the seed corn from the Indians there would have been no corn to plant; had Captain Hunt not stolen Squanto, it is probable that he would have died with his fellow Indians and there would have been no Squanto to show the Pilgrims how to plant the corn; and had there been no corn crop in the autumn of 1621, there would have been no Plymouth Colony. The lesson is *not* from Exodus 20:15.

The corn crop turned out all right. Also the colonists learned something about the fur trade. A party of ten men was sent up to the Massachusetts Bay region to get acquainted with the natives and to do a little trading if they could. The trade had not been too good, but as they were starting to leave a number of squaws arrayed in and only in some very nice beaver skirts followed them to their boat. The Englishmen coveted the beaver. The squaws coveted some shiny gewgaws which the English had brought along. A brisk trade quickly developed. The Pilgrim Fathers got the furs and to supply their lack the squaws "tied boughs about them, but with great shamefacedness," reported Winslow, who apparently was not looking the other way. [27]

Almost a year had passed since the colonists arrived in

Cape Cod. Seven months had passed since the *Mayflower* sailed away, and no supplies had come for them. It began to appear that the London merchants meant to leave them on their "owne leggs" permanently. Pulling in their belts they prepared to face the winter. Then on November 9 an Indian brought word of a ship approaching. She turned out to be the *Fortune,* sent from England by Weston. Aboard were Robert Cushman and thirty-five people for their plantation, but little in the way of food or other supplies.[28]

It soon developed that Cushman had come over only to persuade the Pilgrims to sign the agreement with the merchants—the one that they had refused to sign at Southampton. Also he had brought along a letter from Weston telling them that he had secured a patent for them and that if they would sign up and produce a cargo for the *Fortune,* he would see that they got supplies. They signed up. In fact, they almost had to, for the merchants by having the patent in their possession held the only legal title to the plantation. Nor is it likely that the Pilgrims could have secured a patent on their own account. Their questionable religious beliefs were against them. In any case to get a patent some one had to apply for it and they had no one to act for them; nor probably did they have the ready money which was required in the way of a fee to the Council for New England.

In addition to signing the agreement the Pilgrims helped load the ship with clapboard "as full as she could stow." On board too went the beaver skirts they had acquired from the "shamefaced" squaws of Massachusetts—in all a fairly valuable cargo. And off went the *Fortune* for England. Cushman and the signed agreement went with her.[29]

With thirty-five extra mouths to feed, but assured that relief would come in the spring, the colonists starved through the winter. The last snowdrift melted, the robins came back, and the maple leaves opened but still there was no supply ship. Then one day toward the end of May, 1622, a shallop pulled up at the Plymouth landing. In command was Master Mate Gibbs of the ship *Sparrow,* lying one hundred and fifty miles up the coast at Damariscove. The ship belonged to Weston and another of the London merchants who had un-

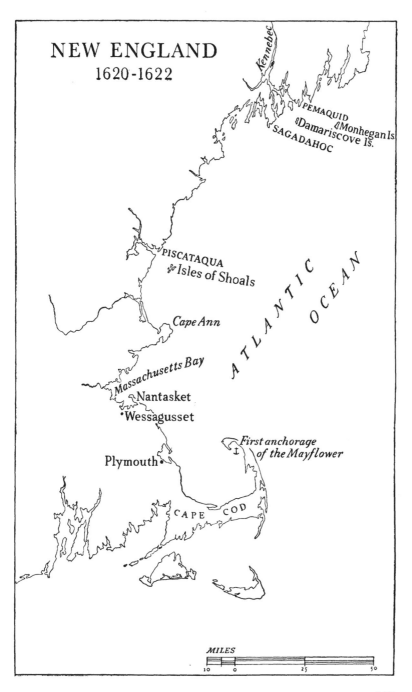

NEW ENGLAND
1620-1622

Kennebec

PEMAQUID
◊Damariscove Is. ◊Monhegan Is.
SAGADAHOC

PISCATAQUA
✲ Isles of Shoals

ATLANTIC   OCEAN

Cape Ann

Massachusetts Bay

⌇Nantasket
•Wessagusset

*First anchorage
of the Mayflower*

Plymouth•

CAPE   COD

MILES

10   0   25   50

141

dertaken to finance and feed the colonists. But the shallop brought "no vitails, nor hope of any." Instead it brought seven men to make salt—the vanguard of a larger number of men whom Weston was sending to establish a separate plantation of his own near Plymouth. So far as supplies for Plymouth were concerned a letter from Weston summed up the situation thus: the merchants would "doe great maters, when they hear good news; Nothing before," which, observed Governor Bradford, was "cold comfort to fill their hungrie bellies." [30]

But by God's providence the arrival of this shallop did help fill their "hungrie bellies." In addition to the letter from Weston the shallop brought a letter from John Hudlston, Captain of the *Bona Nova,* who the previous spring had been licensed by the Virginia Company to carry passengers to the James River and then go fishing. He had delivered his passengers and was now up Monhegan way getting his cargo of fish. He had no personal acquaintance with any of the Plymouth people but he had a piece of information which he thought they ought to know. His letter told of an Indian uprising in Virginia and warned Plymouth to be on its guard against similar attack. [31]

The facts of the massacre in Virginia were even worse than Captain Hudlston had related. Since 1619 the colony had grown rapidly. More than thirty-five hundred new colonists had come in. Captain Hudlston's ship was but one of many which had been licensed to bring planters, artisans, and servants to Virginia. Many new plantations had been established up and down the James River. The government of the colony had been liberalized. The Company had confirmed the right of the General Assembly to meet at least once every year and had vested it with administrative powers equal to those of the Company itself. [32]

The Indians had long been peaceful and were allowed to mix freely with the settlers. But now Powhatan was no more and his brother, Opechancanough, had no love for the crowding white people. He figured that it would be best to get rid of them before they got too thick. With great secrecy the Indians laid their plans and on March 22, 1622, struck all the plantations at practically the same time. Between three and four hundred people, among whom was John Rolfe, fell before the savage fury. Jamestown was saved through the warning of a friendly Indian, but in the outlying plantations the destruction was often complete. It was a heavy blow for the colony, setting back its growth just at the time when its prospects seemed brightest.[33]

Indian Massacre of Virginia Colonists.
From an engraving by Theodore De Bry.

The news of this was all very disturbing to the people at Plymouth, but at the moment their empty bellies were their chief worry. From Gibbs they learned that food was available up there at Monhegan, where the *Bona Nova,* the *Sparrow,* and many other ships were filling their holds with fish. Winslow and one or two others volunteered to go and find out what could be had, but neither he nor any one else at Plymouth knew the way. So apparently Master Mate Gibbs took them up in the *Sparrow's* shallop and brought them back again.

Winslow found at least thirty ships on the fishing grounds around about Damariscove and Monhegan. Some of them probably were there under license from the Council for New England, but we may be reasonably certain that such was not the case with the *Bona Nova;* she had a license from the Virginia Company—and the Council for New England might collect if it could. Captain Hudlston received Winslow hospitably and "not only spared what he could, but writ to others to doe the like"—and the openhearted fishermen loaded down the shallop. It did not amount to much among the many hungry mouths at Plymouth, but it meant the difference between living and starving.[34]

Meanwhile Bradford acted upon Captain Hudlston's warning about the Indians. On the hill above the town the men at Plymouth built a strong fort on the roof of which they mounted several heavy guns. The lower part of the building became their church in place of the common house. The building of this fort meant a lot of work for hungry people, and the contributions from the fishermen helped.[35]

In the midst of all this there came into Plymouth Harbor another of Weston's ships, the *Charity,* loaded with passengers and accompanied by a pinnace. A letter from Weston informed Bradford that the *Fortune,* with all those furs on board, had been captured and looted by a French pirate. This letter also informed them that Weston had sold his shares in their company; in other words he, their main reliance, was "quit" of them. But here, aboard the *Charity,* were the men for his new plantation—sixty of them—big, husky fellows. Would the Plymouth people kindly take care of them while the *Charity* went on down to Virginia with some passengers she had for that colony?

So the long-suffering Pilgrims moved over and provided beds and houses for these sixty "rude fellows" in addition to the seven that had arrived before. The *Charity* went on its way to Virginia, and some of Weston's men in the pinnace went searching up the coast for a good place to establish his new colony. In the end they decided upon Wessagusset, on the south shore of Massachusetts Bay, where the Pilgrims had got some of their best furs and had looked forward to

Peregrine White, born on the
Mayflower, was rocked in the
cradle shown *above*. His father
died in the epidemic of 1621,
and his mother shortly after
married Edward Winslow.

Elder Brewster's chair.

Both pictures are by the *courtesy* of Pilgrim Hall, Plymouth.

getting more. However, Plymouth was relieved of its un-
welcome guests.[36]

Harvest time was now at hand, when for once "all had
their hungrie bellies filled." But as Governor Bradford
thought of the long months before the next harvest, he knew
that starvation still faced the colony.

At this very time God vouchsafed another "providence"
to the colonists. Into Plymouth Harbor sailed Captain
Thomas Jones in his ship, the *Discovery*. He, like Captain
Hudlston, had been licensed by the Virginia Company to
carry passengers to Virginia and then go fishing, which latter
generally included a little fur trading on the side. He apparently had been delayed in Virginia and only now, late in
August, was reaching the fishing banks—too late for much
fishing or trading. Thus he had some food and quite a lot
of Indian trade goods—knives, hoes, mirrors, beads, and such
—to spare. He drove a hard bargain but the Plymouth people
got from him the things that they had been unable to get
through their own financial backers in London, and they got
them by giving in exchange beaver skins which they had
somehow acquired by their own efforts. The trading goods
enabled them to lure some corn from the Indians along with
enough beaver skins to more than replace those they had
parted with.[37]

Aboard the *Discovery,* as a passenger on his way to England, was Mr. John Pory, whom we last met in the Speaker's
chair during the session of Virginia's first General Assembly
in 1619. His brief visit at Plymouth was evidently a great
treat to Elder Brewster and Governor Bradford since it provided some one with whom they could discuss recent theo-
logical publications. And they loaded him up with Separatist literature to read on the voyage home.[38]

As the autumn air sharpened and the forest turned to
gold, Weston's ship, the *Charity,* came back from Virginia,
left some supplies at Wessagusset but none for Plymouth,
and sailed for home. Home to the firesides of old England.
To pigeon pies and plum puddings. To snug taverns and
jolly good fellows and buxom barmaids. To spired churches
and stately services. To a big spree and all the rum yer

skin can 'old. Give her the sail. Home, boys, home! So doubt-less felt the captain and the mate, the passengers and the crew of the eastward-bound ship as the savage coast of America faded from their view.[39]

But to the people of Plymouth the vanishing sails of the *Charity* brought no homesickness. Plymouth was their home. In the thatched houses along The Street kettles simmered over wood fires; women sang hymns and mended clothing; children prattled and played—except on the Sabbath. In the cemetery by the harbor lay their husbands and wives and children and friends. Many families had been broken by deaths, but marriage had joined some of the breaks. Edward Winslow had taken the Widow White to wife. Johnny Alden had won the orphaned Mullens girl. In their store-house was possibly enough corn to see them through; if not, they would manage. Of adversity they had tasted until it had no bitterness. If the merchants, yea if the whole world, should forsake them, there was One who would never for-sake them, "For the Lord thy God is a merciful God: he will not forsake thee."[40]

Fish and Furs

THE COUNCIL FOR NEW ENGLAND, sole proprietor of America from present-day Philadelphia to the southern tip of Newfoundland and westward to the Pacific, had made a good start by having one colony, that on the *Mayflower,* well on its way to New England before the Council itself was legally in existence. Nor had the planting of this colony cost the Council a penny; on the contrary its financial backers had very promptly paid to the Council a fee for the privilege of letting the *Mayflower* people settle in its domain.

And this payment for the privilege of planting a colony was in accord with the policy of the Council. Unlike the Virginia Company the Council for New England had no intention of entering directly into the business of establishing colonies. It was not a mercantile company made up of any one who could lay down £12 10s. It did not admit to its membership any Tom, Dick, or Harry who was willing to risk his hide in New England. Membership in the Council was restricted to "persons of Honour or Gentlemen of blood." True, the members were called upon to pay £110 into the treasury, but "honour and blood" came first. To its individual members or to others of proper standing the Council would grant parcels of land; and those grantees, personally or through sub-grantees, were expected to carry on the practical business of getting colonists; of making contracts with them; of buying shoes and shirts; of shipping and selling the fish or furs that their colonists produced. The Council would make its profits from fees for rights to establish plantations, from licenses for the privilege of fishing, and from quitrents on all the land granted.[1]

The directing head of the Council for New England was Sir Ferdinando Gorges. The young Earl of Warwick was a member and occasionally attended the meetings. The Duke of Lennox and other great lords lent their names. The King improved the opportunity to do a good turn for his loyal servant, Sir William Alexander, Scottish poet and former tutor in the royal household. Alexander yearned to found a "New Scotland" in America. Accordingly when the grant of land was made to the Council, the northern boundary of New England was pushed northward to include the region which the French called Acadie. Then the King sent a "gracious message" to Gorges suggesting that this northern area be transferred to Alexander. Naturally the message was heeded, and Alexander (later to become the Earl of Stirling) undertook the colonization of his Nova Scotia as a separate province. New England returned to the limits assigned to it by John Smith in 1614.[2]

Through Alexander's interest in Nova Scotia, Gorges became acquainted with Captain John Mason, who, after six years as Governor of Newfoundland, was back in England ready for a new adventure in the New World. He joined energetically with Gorges in plans for the development of New England. He asked for and received, on March 9, 1622, a patent for the land between the Naumkeag River (Salem, Mass.) and the Merrimac River. Five months later Mason and Gorges jointly took out a patent for the land between the Merrimac and the Kennebec rivers. Thus these two men made themselves responsible for planting settlements along a stretch of coast more than a hundred and twenty-five miles in length.[3]

The first and in fact the only immediate result of the Mason and Gorges patents was the establishment, in the

spring of 1623, of a small colony at the mouth of the Piscataqua River, near where the city of Portsmouth, N. H.,
stands today. At the time the region was indifferently known
as Piscataqua, Pascataqua or Pascataquack. There, in the
spring of 1623, David Thomson, a Scotchman, brought his
wife and a number of settlers together with the necessary
equipment for a plantation.[4]

Another plantation had its beginnings in 1623 through
the direct action of the Council. Its rule as to "honour and
blood" had not brought in the subscriptions needed to meet
its expenses and the members decided to admit a few merchants—along with their fees of £110 each. One of these
merchants, Abraham Jennings of Plymouth (England), took
in return for his fee a patent to the island of Monhegan, the
well-known and advantageously situated fishing base off the
coast of Maine.[5]

With Plymouth and Wessagusset colonies actually in existence; with all these other colonies in prospect; and with
many fishing ships to be examined for licenses the Council
came to the conclusion late in 1622 that New England needed
a resident Governor. Robert Gorges, son of Sir Ferdinando,
received the appointment. To support his dignity he was
given a patent to the land lying just south of Mason's province and extending to the northern shore of Massachusetts
Bay. Within this area he was expected to establish a colony
of his own.[6]

The hope of profits from fishing laid the foundation for
still another plantation. On February 18, 1623, "Mr. William Darby of the Towne of Dorchester, Agent for Richard
Bashrode [Bushrode] of the same, Merchant, and his Associates, propounded unto the Councell that the said Mr. Bashrode desired that either himselfe or some one of his Associates
might bee admitted a pattentee, and for that they propose
to Settle a plantation in New England, they now prayed to
have a Lycence granted unto them to send forth a Shippe
for Discovery and other Imployments in New England for
this yeare, which the Councell ordered accordingly." For
their license the Bushrode Associates paid the Council £13
6s. 8d., with the understanding that if they found a place

at which they wished to plant a colony and the location did not conflict with any existing settlement, then they would be entitled to a patent, with bounds duly set forth, upon submission of a survey and the payment of an additional fee that would bring the total up to £110, the amount required for such a patent.[7]

On the authority of this license the Bushrode Associates sent out a fishing ship that summer and established a base on Cape Ann. This was within the grant made by the Council the previous year to Captain John Mason. Thus it would appear that the Bushrode Associates were not so much thinking about planting a permanent colony as they were about fishing. However, when the ship returned in the autumn fourteen men were left at Cape Ann to look after the fishing stages and to get together provisions for the ship when it came back the following spring. Thus, perhaps unintentionally, was begun a settlement destined to have far-reaching consequences.[8]

Other prospective fishermen were not so respectful of the Council's monopoly of the sea off New England. The Virginia Company, having received no satisfaction as a result of its petition to the King, appealed to Parliament. Through adroit action, a bill for free fishing was introduced in the House of Commons. The Council's patent was ordered to be brought in to the Committee of Grievances, and Gorges was called to defend its privileges. The upshot was that Parliament voided the clause in the patent which permitted the Council to confiscate any ship caught fishing in New England waters without a license from the Council. This action by Parliament was a severe blow to the Council. It cut off anticipated income and it discouraged prospective applicants for membership.[9]

And at the very time that Gorges, in England, was defending his colonization program, one of the existing colonies in New England was going to pieces. Weston's men at Wessagusset had put up substantial living quarters and storehouses; they had received sufficient supplies from the *Charity;* they had traded with the Indians for some corn. But they apparently did not know how to manage what they had;

Governor Bradford of nearby Plymouth heard that their overseer wasted the supplies "keeping Indean women," how truly he knew not. Anyhow along in February, 1623, they were out of food. Plymouth could not help them, so the overseer took one of their boats and, like Winslow the year before, went to Monhegan to see what he could get. While he was gone some of the men ran away to live with the Indians and one, Phinehas Pratt, ran away to Plymouth, where he told a wild story of an impending massacre by the Indians.[10]

To Bradford, Winslow, and others at Plymouth, this was the last straw in a long line of grievances against Wessagusset. From its beginning that settlement had been a sore spot with them. Weston, they felt, should have been spending his money on supplies for Plymouth instead of starting a new colony next door. Nor did the make-up of his colony approve itself to them. The men at Wessagusset were "rude fellows," not at all interested in their own salvation and inclined to laugh at the brand of salvation practiced at Plymouth. Also, the plantation at Wessagusset was monopolizing the fur trade from the Massachusetts Bay region. Now, to top it all, there was this threat of an Indian attack, which might extend to Plymouth—and all because of the shiftlessness of the Wessagusset people. It was time for Plymouth to act.

Promptly Captain Miles Standish with a number of men started for Wessagusset. There they found Weston's colonists associating with the Indians on friendly terms and unaware that any danger existed. However, the Plymouth captain had been sent to do a job and he did it. Luring four of the naked Indian leaders into a room and locking the door, Standish and his men, who were doubtless encased in armor, hacked three of them to pieces. The other, a boy of eighteen, they hanged. This beginning was followed up by killing a few more of the Indians after which the rest ran away, giving evidence of unfriendliness, which of course proved that they had intended to massacre the whites. With the Indians hostile the only immediate source of food for Weston's men was cut off. Standish offered them the choice of going to Plymouth or elsewhere. The majority elected to embark on

Edward Winslow.

Courtesy of Pilgrim Hall, Plymouth.

GOOD
NEVVES

FROM NewEngland

OR

A true Relation of things very remarkable at the Plantation of *Plimoth*
in New-England.

Shewing the wondrous providence and good-
nes of God, in their prefervation and continuance,
*being delivered from many apparant
deaths and dangers.*

Together with a Relation of fuch religious and
civill Lawes and Cuftomes, as are in practife amongft
the *Indians*, adjoyning to them at this day. As alfo
*what Commodities are there to be rayfed for the
maintenance of that and other Plantations in the faid Country.*

Written by *E. W.* who hath borne a part in the
fore-named troubles, and there lived fince
their firft Arrivall.

LONDON
Printed by *I. D.* for *William Bladen* and *John Bellamie*, and
are to be fold at their Shops, at the *Bible* in *Pauls* Church-
yard, and at the three Golden Lyons in Corn-hill
neere the *Royall Exchange.* 1 6 2 4.

their boat for Monhegan. The buildings were left standing. What happened to their equipment and store of furs is not clear. It was clear, however, that Weston's colony was at an end.

Standish, after seeing the departing colonists well out of Massachusetts Bay, "took leave and returned to Plymouth; whither he came in safety, blessed be God! and brought the head of Wituwamat with him." Wituwamat was one of the Indians that Standish's men had butchered. The head was taken "to the fort, and there set up"—for reasons that seemed obvious to Winslow as he told the story in a little book entitled *Good Newes from New England*. The more reticent Bradford did not mention this particular incident in his *History of Plymouth Plantation*.[11]

A short time later Weston himself arrived at the fishing grounds to the eastward. Here he heard of the disaster to his colony, and in a small boat started down the coast to investigate. His boat was wrecked and he was stripped to his shirt by the Indians. Nothing daunted he made his way to Piscataqua, where David Thomson and his colonists had just arrived. Thomson loaned him a boat and fitted him out with clothing suitable for a call at Plymouth.

Governor Bradford's account of what transpired between Weston and the Plymouth leaders is far from convincing, but he admits that they gave him a hundred beaver skins. He said they did it out of the goodness of their hearts. If so, it was more than a generous action; it was a case of giving away what did not belong to those who gave it, for the partnership between the planters of Plymouth and the merchants of London was still in force and those skins, if acquired by the labor or trade of the colonists, were the property of the company treasury. The thought must arise that their transfer to Weston represented some claim that he had on account of the part played by Plymouth in the affair at Wessagusset.[12]

If the Governor in parting with company furs did violate the terms of the contract with the merchants, it was not the only independent action he took that spring of 1623. Like Governor Dale in Virginia nine years earlier, Bradford came to the conclusion that people would not work as hard for the community welfare as they would for their own. Accordingly he allotted individual corn fields to each family with the promise that what they raised would be their own. "This had very good success," he said, "for it made all hands very industrious, so as much more corne was planted than other waise would have bene . . . and gave farr better contente." Then the Governor, who felt that he knew whereof he spoke, ventured a generalization: Their experience at Plymouth, he said, evinced "the vanitie of that conceite of Platos and other ancients, applauded by some of later times;—that the taking away of propertie, and bringing in communitie into a comone wealth, would make them happy and florishing; as if they were wiser than God." [13]

When the corn was knee-high at Plymouth and the best fishing was about over at Monhegan, the vanguard of the Council's new government arrived. Captain Francis West, he who had so unceremoniously ducked out of Virginia during the hungry winter of 1609–10, now came to New England with the title of Admiral—to see that no ship fished there without license from the Council. But, as Governor Bradford summed up the Admiral's ill-success: "He could doe no good of them, for they were too stronge for him, and he found the fisher men to be stuberne fellows." [14]

It was now getting on toward three years since the Plymouth colonists had left England. A year and eight months had passed since the Pilgrims had signed the contract brought over by Cushman. And still no supplies had come for them from their London backers and partners. True, all that the colonists had produced for the merchants had been lost to the French pirate, but the fact remained that their clothing was in tatters and they had neither the equipment nor the supplies with which to do more than eke out a bare existence. However, the merchants had not wholly forsaken them. As Weston, their original backer, passed out of the company, others took hold; and while Bradford worried about the 1623 corn crop, supplies and reinforcements were already on the way from the London merchants. Late in July the lookout at the fort on the hill saw a ship and a pinnace approaching Plymouth. The ship proved to be the *Anne* with new colonists and supplies. The pinnace had been sent for use by the Plymouth people in fishing and fur-trading ventures.

Sixty of the newcomers had been sent over at the general expense of the company—to work for the company and share in its profits, if any. Among these were the wives of some men who had come on the *Mayflower*. Then, too, there were Fear and Patience Brewster, daughters of Elder Brewster. Fear was soon married to the widowed Isaac Allerton. Another passenger on the *Anne* was Alice Southworth, widow of a former member of the Leyden congregation. Within three weeks she was the wife of Governor Bradford. Thus the *Anne* brought consolation as well as strength and equipment to the struggling colony.

Also aboard the *Anne* were a number of men who came at their own expense, to live at Plymouth but not to be under the contract between the colonists and their London backers. They were spoken of as being on their "perticular," which may be translated as meaning that they were on their own. Among these were John Oldham and probably Roger Conant, both of whom left their impress on the history of New England, although to Governor Bradford of Plymouth they brought no comfort.

On September 10 the *Anne* was on her way back to England—loaded with clapboard and carrying what beaver had been collected. With her went Edward Winslow to arrange with the merchants for more supplies. Things were looking up for Plymouth Colony.[15]

At about the time Winslow sailed for England, Robert Gorges, the new Governor-general, and his colony arrived in New England. They came as passengers on a ship that was going on to Virginia and which could not be held indefinitely while they searched out a place to establish themselves. The north shore of Massachusetts Bay, where the Governor's province lay, was still an unexplored country. On the south shore, however, the buildings vacated by Weston's men only six months earlier were still standing. So Gorges' people moved in, and here was another colony, slightly out of place, but of great promise. In addition to several anonymous families of working people there were the Reverend William Blackstone, M.A., Cambridge University; Samuel Maverick, gent.; and Thomas Walford, blacksmith, each destined in his own way to play a colorful part in the early life of the Massachusetts Bay region.[16]

The commission of the Governor-general provided for a local council to be composed of himself; of the Governor of Plymouth Colony; of Captain Francis West, the Admiral; and of Christopher Levett, who the previous spring had been granted six thousand acres of land for a plantation. West had already departed for Virginia. Levett had not yet arrived. So Gorges, while his colony was getting settled at Wessagusset, made a call at Plymouth.[17]

And at that very time Thomas Weston again arrived at Plymouth—this time in his small ship that had been wrecked up the coast, but was now salvaged and in condition. Governor Gorges promptly lodged a series of complaints against him. For one thing he had mismanaged the Wessagusset plantation; this Weston readily admitted; worse yet he had sold some ordnance that did not belong to him. One gets the impression that Gorges pressed the charges when he needed Weston's ship for his own use and forgave him when he was through with it.[18]

Anyway it was in Weston's ship that Gorges sailed eastward in the late autumn to call on David Thomson at Piscataqua. There Levett, who had just arrived on the coast to look for a suitable place to locate his colony, found them. And there, at Piscataqua, during the early winter of 1623 those three, Robert Gorges, the son of Sir Ferdinando; David Thomson, a former employee of the Council for New England; and Christopher Levett, a patentee of the Council, doubtless made great plans for the future settlement of the country—with the kind of people and under a form of government that would have been unsympathetic to Governor Bradford's colony at Plymouth.[19]

Success seemed within their grasp. Where a year before there had been but two colonies in all New England there now were five. It would be but a matter of a few more years before the whole coast would be filled with plantations which, through a series of feudal overlords, would pay homage and quitrents to the Council for New England. At the mouth of the Sagadahoc, where Popham and Gilbert had failed in 1607–08, would be a "State County" forty miles square within which would be the capital city of New England—and all the building lots would be owned by the members of the Council.[20]

However, God willed that Bradford's humble colony at Plymouth should endure while all the great plans of the Gorges family should come to naught. The hard winter of 1623–24 had cooled whatever enthusiasm the Governor-general ever had for New England. His father too was discouraged by the action of Parliament in voiding the Council's fishing monopoly. Early in the new year Robert Gorges sailed for England. Some of his colonists returned with him; others went to Virginia; some stayed on at Wessagusset. The Reverend Blackstone shortly established himself with his books in a solitary home on the peninsula where a few years later the city of Boston was founded. Maverick and Walford and probably some others moved across the Bay and settled within the lands granted by the Council to Robert Gorges for his colony.[21]

Meanwhile Levett, with seven or eight men, was exploring the coast northeastward from Piscataqua in a couple of small boats. In Casco Bay, near the site of the present-day city of Portland, Me., he found a place that suited him: good land, good fishing, and Indians with furs to trade. So here, on an island, he built a fortified house and tried to take possession under his patent.

But others had found Casco Bay before Levett arrived there. In fact, although it was the dead of winter, there were several fishing and fur-trading ships in the vicinity, and they had no intention of being done out of any furs by a mere patentee of the Council for New England. The captain of one of the ships informed Levett that "he cared not for any authoritie in that place and though he was forbid to trucke [*i.e.,* trade] yet would he have all he could get: in despite of who should say to the contrary," and he backed up his remarks with seventeen pieces of ordnance and a crew

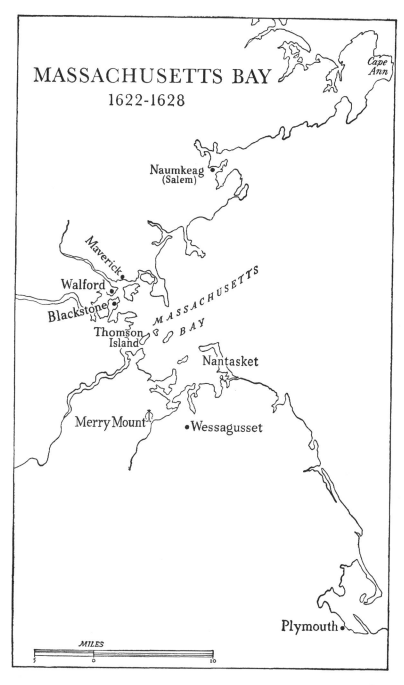

MASSACHUSETTS BAY
1622-1628

Cape
Ann

Naumkeag
(Salem)

Maverick

Walford

Blackstone

Thomson
Island

MASSACHUSETTS
BAY

Nantasket

Merry Mount

•Wessagusset

Plymouth•

MILES

5   0   10

of fifty men. Levett did not argue the point.

And indeed, the captain's practice, says Levett, "was according to his words, for every Sunday or once in the weeke, he went himselfe or sent a boat up the river and got all the trucke before they could come downe to the Harbour. And so many savages as he could get to his stage, hee would enforce them to leave their goods behind them." One day two Indians started to carry their furs to Captain Levett. The captain of the ship ordered them to do their trading with himself. "Levett," he told them, "was no captaine, but a *Jacknape,* a poore fellow, &c." The Indians told the captain "that he was a *Roague,* with some other speeches, whereupon he and his company fell upon them & beate them both. . . ." Such was the fur-trading business along the coast of New England in 1623 and 1624.[22]

However Levett appears to have been able to take care of himself, and the prospects for a successful plantation in Casco Bay seemed good. Leaving ten men to hold the fortified house and to carry on the fur trade, Levett returned to England in quest of capital for the expansion of his colony. But he found no enthusiasm for New England among English investors. This was due partly to the action of Parliament in censuring the Council's monopoly of fishing and partly to the uncertainty of the times.

Nor could Levett get any support from Sir Ferdinando Gorges or Captain Mason. England was drifting into war with Spain and later with France. Both of these men held important military positions which required all their time and energy. The affairs of New England became incidental and for five years the Council was inactive.[23]

As the Council for New England sank into inactivity, the Dutch West India Company burst into life. Although its charter had laid no claim to any territory in America, none the less the Dutch company in establishing trading posts up the Hudson River was trespassing on land granted by King James of England to the Council for New England. Another Dutch trading post, Fort Nassau, established on the Delaware River in 1623, lay in the no-man's land between the grants made to the Virginia Company and the Council for New

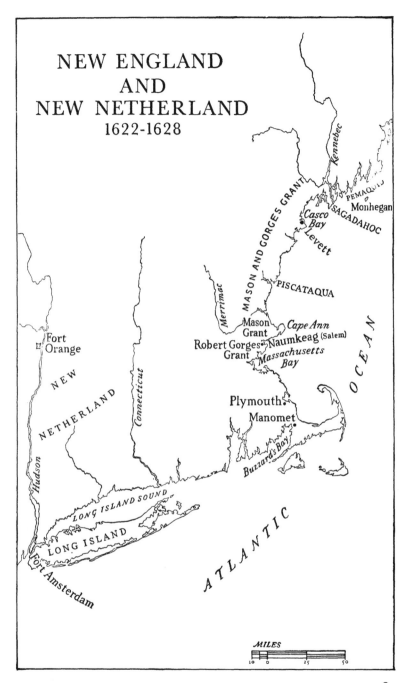

NEW ENGLAND
AND
NEW NETHERLAND
1622-1628

Kennebec

PEMAQUID

SAGADAHOC

Monhegan

*Casco
Bay*

Levett

MASON AND GORGES GRANT

Merrimac

PISCATAQUA

Mason
Grant *Cape Ann*

Robert Gorges· Naumkeag (Salem)
Grant *Massachusetts
Bay*

Fort
Orange

N E W

N E T H E R L A N D

Connecticut

Plymouth

Manomet

Hudson

Buzzard's Bay

O C E A N

LONG ISLAND SOUND

LONG ISLAND

Fort Amsterdam

A T L A N T I C

MILES

10   0   25   50

161

England but none the less in territory claimed by England under the Charter of 1606. The English government had complained to the High and Mighty Lords of the United Netherlands but without result.

Now, in the spring of 1624, the Dutch company added colonization to trading. Thirty families were brought over, most of whom were settled up the Hudson River where today the City of Albany, N. Y., stands. There they built a pretentious trading post to which was given the name of Fort Orange. A few families remained on Governor's Island at the mouth of the river. The following year as other emigrants arrived, they moved over to the tip of Manhattan Island and built Fort Amsterdam. Thus began the city later called New York. To manage the affairs of this growing colony a governor or director was sent over. Houses grew up around the forts; more settlers arrived; horses, cattle, sheep and hogs were shipped in. Increasingly, Dutch ships, loaded with supplies and trade goods, arrived at Fort Amsterdam, went on up to Fort Orange, and sailed back to Holland laden with cargoes of furs. New Netherland was beginning to justify its name.[24]

Also, in that spring of 1624, fishing and fur-trading ships came to the coast of New England as usual. The fourteen men who had stayed the winter on Cape Ann had a longer wait for their returning ship than they expected. The fact was that the venture of 1623 had turned out badly for the Bushrode Associates. However, their fellow townsmen of Dorchester were willing to back another attempt. A meeting of the merchants was held; more than £3000 was subscribed; a second ship was bought; and late in the spring the Dorchester outfit was on its way to Cape Ann.[25]

At Wessagusset the remnant of the Robert Gorges colony was still holding on, and in the spring of 1624 they had neighbors. Into the mouth of a small river three miles to the west of them, where the city of Quincy now stands, came the not-too-good, in fact quite leaky, ship *Unity,* out of London: Captain Wollaston, master, and Humphrey Rastel, merchant in charge of the venture. Among the passengers was Thomas Morton, a London lawyer who had recently been engaged in a very lively family row and probably cared little where he was, provided it was away from England.[26]

Another passenger aboard the *Unity* was Captain John Martin, proprietor of Martin's Hundred, Virginia Colony. He had come to Virginia with the first planters in 1607. He had been a member of the first local council in that colony, had quarreled with Captain John Smith, and had gone back to England. Later he had returned to Virginia with the Gates fleet. In recognition of his services to the colony his good friends in the Company had not only granted him a large piece of land along the James River but had also granted him privileges which practically exempted his holdings from control by the governor or the laws of the colony. From the time of the arrival of Governor Yeardley in 1619 there had been a steady stream of complaints against Martin's Hundred with its ". . . divers exorbatant pryveledges and transcendent liberties . . . repugnant to justice and good Government of the generall Plantation. . . ." The Company in London began putting pressure on him to surrender his patent and take one more in line with those which had been given other landholders of Virginia. For some time Martin had been in England arguing his case but in the end had been forced to yield and take a new patent. He was now, in 1624, on his way back to Virginia. Mr. Rastel of the *Unity* had agreed to carry him and several of his servants to the James River. Instead on one excuse or another the ship had headed for New England.[27]

And there they were—on the south shore of Massachusetts Bay. And there they stayed for nine weeks while Captain Martin fumed and raged. In the end Martin and his men and supplies were transferred to Weston's little ship and off they went to Virginia. Morton and a bunch of wild fellows who had come over in the ship, and some of whom were indentured servants intended for Virginia, turned their camp into a trading post which, appropriately, they named Merry Mount.[28]

Martin arrived in Virginia too late to get in a crop of tobacco and too late to contribute his bit of damning testimony to a royal commission then in the colony investigating the operations of the Company. However, the recommendation of the commission was all that Martin could have wished. The Company's charter was revoked and the King instead of the Company ruled in Virginia.

This result was probably inevitable. At the time the charter of 1606 was granted, the King had intended that the colony should be under his direct control. Only at the insistence of the merchants had he assented to the corporate charter of 1609. Now the corporation was bankrupt. Abuses unquestionably did exist. Nor did the King have any goodwill for those in control of the Company. So when he sent over his commissioners in the spring of 1624 it was a more or less foregone conclusion that they would find ample reasons for stripping the Company of its powers. On May 24 the King's Bench in London annulled the charter so far as the Virginia Company was concerned and from that time forth the King rather than a commercial corporation appointed the Governor and the Council of Virginia Colony. After eighteen years of existence; after having financed and founded the Colony; after having nursed it to success, the Virginia Company was dead.[29]

Plymouth Colony was having its difficulties too but they were of a different sort. It will be recalled that Winslow went to England in the fall of 1623 to present the needs of the colonists to their London backers. Now in the spring of 1624 he returned to Plymouth on the good ship *Charity,* bringing supplies of various sorts including three heifers and a bull; also he brought a preacher. These heifers and this bull were the first cattle the Plymouth people had received and they were most welcome. The Reverend John Lyford was the first preacher they had received but he was looked upon with grave suspicion by Governor Bradford and his Separatist brethren. They had hoped that their own preacher from Leyden might be sent to them, but the London partners would not listen to that suggestion. If they, the merchants, put up the supplies, the colonists would have to take the preacher that they, the merchants, sent them—and they would stand for no Separatist. Winslow yielded.

Trouble soon started. The Reverend Lyford was a Church

of England preacher. The majority of the colonists and especially the "perticulars" were Church of England people. On the other hand the control and the management of the colony were firmly in the hands of the Separatists. The Reverend Lyford lent a sympathetic ear to the complaints of those who were dissatisfied with the Separatist regime. Twenty-four-year-old John Oldham made himself the leader of the opposition. He and the Reverend Lyford wrote long letters of complaint to the London partners and gave their letters to the captain of the *Charity* for delivery. When the ship sailed, Governor Bradford accompanied it a short distance, opened and copied the letters, and returned to Plymouth in a shallop which he had taken along.

With the copies of these letters in his pocket the Governor shortly called a general meeting of the colonists. There he charged Lyford and Oldham with seditious behavior—and read their letters to prove it. Evidently the majority sided with him and against the malcontents. Oldham was sentenced to immediate expulsion. Lyford on account of his family was permitted to stay six months and then he too must depart.[30]

Bradford by his prompt and forceful, if somewhat unethical, action had saved New England for Separatism. The entering wedge of Episcopacy had been cast forth. Had only a few men backed Lyford and Oldham in that general meeting at Plymouth in the summer of 1624, the course of New England history might have been very different.

When Oldham departed from Plymouth he did not go alone. A number of others, including Roger Conant, went along, disgusted with the government of Bradford. At Nantasket, on the southern shore of Massachusetts Bay, a little to the northeast of Wessagusset, they established a temporary settlement which drew still others from Plymouth, among them the Reverend Lyford when his period of grace expired.[31]

It would have been better for Lyford's reputation had he gone to Nantasket at once. The Pilgrim Fathers disliked and feared him. They knew that there would be repercussions when the story of their action reached London. So they went to work to blacken whatever good name the poor preacher had. From his wife they extracted a story to the effect that before she married him he had brought a bastard into the world. Further she set forth, so they said, that "she could keep no maids but he would be medling with them, and some time she hath taken him in the maner, as they lay at their beds feete, with shuch other circumstances as I [*i.e.,* Governor Bradford] am ashamed to relate." Nor was this all. The Governor dug up a story of how before the Reverend Lyford came to America he had been requested by a young parishioner to act as his solicitor for the favor of a fair damsel. The preacher, so the story went, had carried out his mission all too well. In fact he had "overcome her, and defiled her body before marriage." The Governor forbare the details "for they would offend chast ears to hear them related, for though he satisfied his lust on her, yet he indeavoured to hinder conception."[32]

The Governor may have believed all this, but the merchants in London did not. In fact, there was an explosion when the news of Lyford's treatment reached London. Most of the partners washed their hands of the colony instantly and permanently. The company as a common-stock partnership ceased to exist. When the next supplies came over they were consigned not to the colony but to Winslow and Allerton personally. Whoso wanted to buy a cow or a pair of shoes or some cloth might buy them, but he bought them for cash (or beaver skins) and at a 40 per cent advance on account of the cost of sending them over, plus a 30 per cent discount on the skins for the risk of bringing them back, or a total of 70 per cent above the purchase price of the articles. The deficit on past transactions remained as a debt, and the outstanding shares of the company as a liability.[33]

Trouble with their London backers was not the only mishap that the Lyford incident brought to the Plymouth people. They had secured a somewhat doubtful patent to the Cape Ann region and had erected some fishing stages there or thought they had a right to the fishing stages which were already there. But the Dorchester people looked upon Cape Ann as their own. They had left a number of men there in the winter of 1623–24, and when their fishing ships sailed for home in the fall of 1624, some thirty men stayed on to take care of the stages and plant corn and raise provisions against the return of the ships. Also, in the spring of 1625 they invited Conant and the other settlers at Nantasket to join them, which they did, Conant being put in charge of all their operations on Cape Ann. At just this moment along came the Plymouth fishermen and demanded the stages. The Dorchester men told them to take them if they could. Captain Standish raged—"a little chimney is soon fired" as one chronicler put it—but he had to back down, and Conant held control at Cape Ann for the Dorchester company.[34]

However, this rebuff turned out to be a "providence" for Plymouth. If they could not fish at Cape Ann, they would try something else somewhere else. So after their corn was harvested and they found that there was some to spare, they loaded it into a shallop and went trading up the Kennebec River far to the north. They came back with over seven hundred pounds of beaver plus the knowledge that corn was good trading stock with the Indians in the Kennebec region.[35]

Nor did the Dorchester company profit by holding Cape Ann. The fishing was good that summer of 1625 but the price was very bad. Catholic Spain had always been the best market for fish, but now England was at war with Spain. The price of fish fell to a level that made even the best haul a loss. Thus for the third straight year the Dorchester venturers spent more than they made. The £3000 trading stock was gone and the company was broke.[36]

There were at this time perhaps fifty people living the year around at Cape Ann. They had substantial houses and barns. They had a few cattle and possibly other livestock. They had cleared enough land to raise the grain they needed. When the Dorchester company dissolved, some of the people were taken back to England and some went to Virginia, but Conant with a few others stayed on—encouraged by the Reverend John White, Rector of Holy Trinity parish, Dorchester, England.

White had been interested in the plantation from its beginning, and now came to the conclusion that, even though fishing did not pay, a colony in the New World might be profitable in spiritual values. In short he was thinking along much the same lines as had the Pilgrims six years earlier, though he would have resented being compared with them; to him the Separatists were objectionable fanatics. What White envisioned was a refuge for moderate people who could not conform to the practices of the Church of England and who might as a colony, far removed from England, create a purified church.

So the Reverend White wrote to Conant asking him to hold on while he and his friends in England tried to get a patent and financial backing for such a colony as he had in mind. In the meantime White arranged to have more cattle and more supplies sent over, and Conant moved his little settlement from the barren shores of Cape Ann to the more fertile land at Naumkeag, later rechristened Salem. This move placed the settlement within the land granted to Robert Gorges rather than within that granted to Captain Mason.[37]

The Dorchester company was not the only fishing venture that went out of business in 1626. Abraham Jennings, who it will be recalled had a plantation on Monhegan Island, was also feeling the fall in the price of fish—and he now sold out. Abraham Shurt, just then starting a trading post at Pemaquid, eastward of the Kennebec, proved the high bidder for most of the stock and equipment. But Shurt did not have it all his own way; Bradford and Winslow were also there, as was David Thomson from Piscataqua. And despite all competition Bradford and Winslow came away with over £500 worth of goods, including goats and French blankets, the latter having fallen into the hands of the Monhegan people, so Bradford said, through a French ship having been wrecked at Sagadahoc.[38]

And well might the Plymouth leaders bid at an auction. Their traders were doing an extremely good business on the Kennebec—swapping surplus corn for beaver. The goods that Bradford and Winslow got at Monhegan enabled their traders to acquire still more skins. Business was booming and the Plymouth colonists were at last in a position to bargain with the merchants of London. Allerton was sent to England to

THE TOWN
OF PLYMOUTH

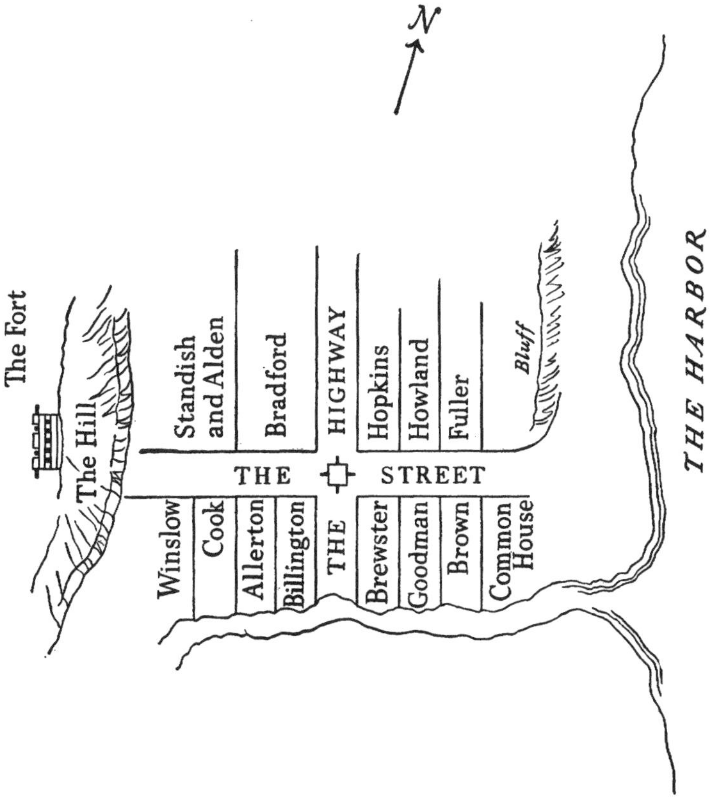

N

The Fort

The Hill

Standish
and Alden

Bradford

THE HIGHWAY

Hopkins

Howland

Fuller

Bluff

THE STREET

Winslow

Cook

Allerton

Billington

THE

Brewster

Goodman

Brown

Common
House

THE HARBOR

pay old accounts and buy out the London shareholders—which he did for £1800, payable £200 a year, with a few of the Plymouth leaders made personally responsible for the installments. Thus after seven years of struggle Plymouth Colony belonged to the Plymouth colonists.[39]

To meet these installments and at the same time to pay cash for the shoes, shirts, guns, cows and other supplies which they needed the Plymouth people had to find a new source of income. This they did by establishing a base at Manomet on Buzzard's Bay (see map on page 161) from whence their trading boats began tapping the fur-rich Narragansett region. There they came into contact with the Dutch traders working out from Fort Amsterdam. To the Pilgrims the Dutch speech brought memories of the sympathetic treatment they had received while exiles in Holland. A profitable trade soon developed between Plymouth and Fort Amsterdam.

In the fall of 1627 Isaack de Rasieres, Secretary of the colony of New Netherland, made a call at Plymouth. Going by boat through Long Island Sound and along the shores of present-day Rhode Island, he landed at Manomet and walked across the narrow neck of land to Cape Cod Bay. There a boat from Plymouth met him and escorted him and a few of his men to the town. "The houses," he wrote to a friend in Amsterdam, "are constructed of hewn planks, with gardens also enclosed behind and at the sides with hewn planks, so that their houses and court-yards are arranged in very good order, with a stockade against a sudden attack; and at the ends of the streets there are three wooden gates. In the center, on the cross street, stands the governor's house, before which is a square stockade upon which four patereros are mounted, so as to enfilade the streets. Upon the hill they have a large square house, with a flat roof, made of thick sawn plank, stayed with oak beams, upon the top of which they have six cannon, which shoot iron balls of four and five pounds, and command the surrounding country. The lower part they use for their church, where they preach on Sundays and the usual holidays. They assemble by beat of drum, each with his musket or firelock, in front of the captain's

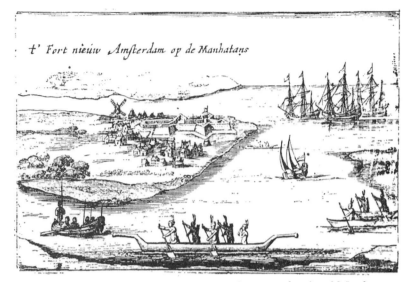

Above. New Amsterdam or Fort Amsterdam—on the tip of Manhattan Island.

From Joost Hartgers, *Beschryvingbe van Virginia, Nieuw Nederlandt.*

Below. Wampum, the Indian money.

Courtesy, Museum of the American Indian, Heye Foundation, New York.

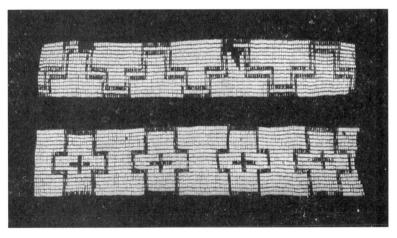

door; they have their cloaks on, and place themselves in order, three abreast, and are led by a sergeant without beat of drum. Behind comes the governor, in a long robe; beside him, on the right hand, comes the preacher with his cloak on, and on the left hand the captain with his side-arms, and cloak on, and with a small cane in his hand; and so they march in good order, and each sets his arms down near him. Thus they are constantly on their guard night and day." [40]

From these Dutch traders the Plymouth men learned that beads made from shells and known as wampum were in great demand among the Iroquois Indians and passed as money. The Plymouth traders secured a supply of this wampum and tried it out along the Kennebec River, where it soon proved so popular that it would extract beaver from the savages after corn had ceased to appeal. In fact, the Kennebec trade became so important to the welfare of the Plymouth colonists that in 1628 they applied for and received a grant of land some thirty miles up that river. The grant was made by the dormant Council for New England, but it had sufficient authority to warn off competition. That summer Plymouth established a permanent trading house at an Indian town near the falls of the Kennebec, where twenty-one years earlier Gilbert had ended his search for a portage to the Pacific Ocean and where the city of Augusta, Me., stands today. [41]

It was high time that the Plymouth people were getting some sort of title to their trading grounds on the Kennebec. Their neighbor, Thomas Morton of Merry Mount, was also trading there—and Morton had a way of getting on with the Indians. This might have had something to do with an attack which Plymouth launched against him at this time. "The first precept in their Politique," observed Morton, "is to defame the man at whom they aim." Be that as it may, the governor of Plymouth not only defamed Morton but he put an end to him as a competitor for the fur trade either on the Kennebec or along the shores of Massachusetts Bay. [42]

Even without the element of competition Governor Bradford would have viewed Merry Mount with disfavor. Morton was a well-educated man of the world who treated the Separatists with amused contempt. Most of the other men at Merry Mount were indentured servants who had broken their contracts. Bradford said that, after kicking out their overseer, "they fell to great licenciousnes, and led a dissolute life, powering out them selves into all profanenes. And Morton became lord of misrule, and maintained (as it were) a schoole of Athisme. And after they had gott some good into their hands, and gott much by trading with the Indeans, they spent it as vainly, in quaffing and drinking both wine and strong waters in great exsess, and, as some reported, 10*li* worth in a morning. They allso set up a May-pole, drinking and dancing aboute it many days togeather, inviting the Indean women, for their consorts, dancing and frisking togither, (like so many fairies, or furies rather,) and worse practises. As if they had anew revived and celebrated the feasts of the Roman Goddes Flora, or the beasly practieses of the madd Bacchinalians. Morton likwise (to shew his poetrie) composed sundry rimes and verses, some tending to lasciviousnes, and others to the detraction and scandall of some persons, which he affixed to this idle or idoll Maypolle." [43]

Morton himself viewed the Maypole episode with considerable pride. The pole, he said, was "a goodly pine tree of 80 foote long . . . with a peare of buckshorns nayled one, somewhat neare unto the top of it." Morton also fancied his poem. It was loaded down with classical allusions, and those were what bothered Bradford. He did not know what they meant and suspected that they were aimed at himself and his fellow Separatists. "There was likewise," said Morton, "a merry song made, which (to make their Revels more fashionable) was sung with a Corus, every man bearing his part; which they performed in a daunce, hand in hand about the Maypole, while one of the Company sung, and filled out the good liquor like gammedes and Jupiter." [44]

All in all it was a creditable re-enactment, on the shores of Massachusetts Bay, of an "old English custome." It undoubtedly horrified the Pilgrim Fathers, but it would have evoked favorable comment from the average Englishman of the day. The Indians too liked the idea and brought their beaver to Merry Mount rather than to Plymouth.

In the eyes of the Plymouth people the Maypole, the poem, and the competition in the fur trade were ample grounds for the expulsion of Morton. However, Bradford recognized that these charges would not impress an English court. Accordingly he accused Morton of having sold guns and ammunition to the Indians. This may or may not have been true. It was, however, a charge on which the Governor could act with the full support of the other settlers in New England. "Captain Shrimp," as Morton ungraciously called Miles Standish, was sent with eight men to make the arrest; Morton was brought back to Plymouth and shipped to England for trial.[45]

Morton had accepted arrest with the understanding that his men and his trading house should not be bothered; even the Maypole was left standing. Nearby at Wessagusset there was still a small settlement, the remnant of the Robert Gorges colonists. On the north side of Massachusetts Bay, in the Robert Gorges grant, Thomas Walford, the blacksmith, and a few others were farming and trading. On the peninsula that later became Boston the Reverend William Blackstone was living with his books. David Thomson had given up at Piscataqua and had moved to an island in Boston harbor where he died about 1627. Samuel Maverick, who had come over with Robert Gorges in 1623, appears to have maintained his headquarters on the north side of the Bay while acting as agent for the Gorges grant and for Christopher Levett's plantation in Casco Bay. Shortly after Thomson's death Maverick married his widow and moved in with her on Thomson's island. John Oldham, who had stayed on at Nantasket after Conant and the others went to Cape Ann, was on his way to England with, or in charge of, Thomas Morton.[46]

At Naumkeag (Salem) Roger Conant with about thirty people—men, women and children—was holding on, hoping for the patent which the Reverend John White was trying to get for them. White had done what he could. He had retained the support of a few of the original members of the Dorchester company and had interested a number of London merchants in his idea. Through their assistance cattle and supplies were being forwarded to Conant in quantities which seemed to indicate that some were for purposes of trade.[47]

But none of these merchants associated with White was sufficiently outstanding to qualify for a patent from the Council for New England. They lacked "honour and blood." At this point Roger Conant from faraway New England may have put in the decisive word. His brother, the Reverend John Conant, held his parish through the recommendation of Sir Henry Rosewell. Sir Henry was not personally interested in colonization but was apparently willing to let his name head an application to the Council for a grant of land to the friends of the Reverend John Conant's brother. On March 19, 1628, a patent or some sort of title was passed by the Council in favor of Sir Henry and five associates, one of whom was John Endecott.[48]

It is doubtful whether the Council could legally have passed a patent at this time. Sir Ferdinando Gorges was still wholly occupied with his military duties. The old Duke of Lennox was dead. The other members were scattered. The Earl of Warwick was acting as President and had the Council's seal in his possession. He may have issued a patent on his own responsibility. But if so, what did he grant? The land occupied by Conant in 1628 had already been granted by the Council to Robert Gorges in 1622, all of which Warwick well knew. Nor as successors to the Bushrode Associates and the Dorchester company could the new patentees have established any title to a particular piece of land. Those companies were based on a license to search for a place in which to plant a colony, but they do not appear to have applied for or received a patent for any definitely located or bounded lands. There remains the possibility that, instead of granting a patent from the Council, Warwick assigned to the Rosewell associates a shadowy title that he had acquired to the Massachusetts Bay region through an unconfirmed division of the Council's lands among its members in 1623.

JOHN ENDECOTT.

". . . a fit instrument to begin this Wildernesse-
worke, of courage bold undanted, yet sociable,
and of a chearfull spirit, loving and austere,
applying himselfe to either as occasion served."

—Captain Edward Johnson, in
Wonder-Working Providence.

All in all, this so-called patent of March 19, 1628, was a very elusive document. It was never produced when called for by those with the authority to make such a demand; it was never exhibited when such exhibition would have been conclusive refutation of damaging testimony; nor apparently does it exist today.[49]

Thus came into being the New England Company, by which name this group of colonizers was known. Whatever the Company received title to, it was good enough to attract prompt subscriptions to its stock from some twenty hardheaded Dorchester and London merchants who, along with a sprinkling of gentlemen and two ministers, put up £2915 with which to finance the proposed plantation. Matthew Cradock, skinner, of London was made Governor of the Company. It is safe to assume that the beaver and otter skins of New England had something to do with his interest. The Reverend John White was of course a subscriber. The other minister was the Reverend Hugh Peter, then or shortly a refugee in Holland because of his nonconformist views. The avowed purpose of the subscriptions was "the propagation of the Gospel of Jesus Christ, and the particular good of the several Adventurers," the latter part of which statement was broad enough to cover either a financial or spiritual objective.[50]

The new Company moved swiftly. John Endecott was chosen to go as resident governor of the plantation and to make preparations for the coming of more colonists. On June 20, 1628, with some forty people, mostly workmen, he sailed from Weymouth, which was the natural port for the inland city of Dorchester. On September 6 he stepped ashore at Naumkeag (Salem). All that Roger Conant had hoped for and waited for—a patent, financial backing and reinforcements—had been achieved, but Conant was no longer governor. Henceforth the colony was to be in less kindly but more efficient hands.[51]

The Great Migration

JOHN ENDECOTT WAS GOVERNOR at Massachusetts Bay and of that fact the few inhabitants of the region were soon made aware. Calling at Merry Mount, he caused Morton's Maypole to be cut down and admonished his men "to looke ther should be better walking." Nor was he much less blunt with Conant and the other Old Planters at Naumkeag. Their houses and livestock and growing corn and almost themselves were taken over as the property of the new company—all subject to the orders of Governor Endecott. This was reasonable enough in the case of men sent over as servants by the Company, but to take such an attitude with Conant and others who had joined the settlement on their own account was manifestly unfair and caused much hard feeling.[1]

But Endecott went vigorously ahead. Men were set to work building new houses at Naumkeag. Exploring parties were sent out to seek sites suitable for other towns when more colonists should arrive the following spring. Along the north shore of the Bay some of these scouts found Thomas Walford, the blacksmith of Robert Gorges' colony, living in a palisaded house. The location was reported favorably to Endecott.[2]

Then winter closed in and the sickness usual among new arrivals in America began taking its toll. There was no doctor at Naumkeag, and Endecott appealed to Plymouth, forty miles down the coast, for help. There was no doctor there either, but Samuel Fuller had acted in that capacity during the almost eight years since the *Mayflower* had returned to England—and apparently with considerable success. So off he went to Naumkeag. Morton, doubtless prejudiced, tells us that Fuller was a butcher by profession and that on this visit to Naumkeag he cured Endecott of a disease known as a wife. Whatever his skill as a doctor of medicine, Fuller proved an able advocate for the Separatist church organization as it existed at Plymouth. On May 11, 1629, the Governor at Naumkeag wrote to the Governor at Plymouth, thanking him for sending Fuller, and added: ". . . I am by him satisfied touching your judgments of the outward forme of Gods worship. It is, as farr as I can yet gather, no other then is warrented by the evidence of truth, and the same which I have proffessed and maintained ever since the Lord in mercie revealed him selfe unto me; being farr from the commone reporte that hath been spread of you touching that perticuler."[3]

This outstretched hand of fellowship from the new colony must have been a great satisfaction to Bradford, but, as so often happens, it was offset by a blow from another direction. Isaac Allerton had been in England attending to the affairs of Plymouth Colony. Now, in the spring of 1629, he returned —and with him came Thomas Morton. None of the charges made by Bradford against the "Host of Merry Mount" had been of the slightest interest to the authorities in England, so here he was back in New England. Worse yet, Allerton, the son-in-law of Elder Brewster, was entertaining him at his house in Plymouth. This was going altogether too far and Bradford ordered Allerton to "pack him away."[4]

Meantime in England the New England Company had "with great cost, favour of personages of note, & much labour" transformed its questionable title from the Council for New England into a patent from the King himself and attested by the Great Seal of England. In short, the enterprise that five years earlier had started as a fishing venture under a license from the Council for New England now, under the name of the Governor and Company of Massachusetts Bay, occupied exactly the same legal position as the Council for New England—and it had back of it influence and wealth and ability such as the Council never had known.[5]

While the Council for New England had found it necessary to beg great men to support its projects, the Massachusetts Bay Company, as the new company came to be known, was being eagerly watched over and guided by many "personages of note." While the Council was ever under the necessity of urging its members to pay their subscriptions, the Massachusetts Bay Company had money poured into its treasury. While the Council had depended for advice and counsel on a little clique of men of "honour and blood," the Bay Company had at its call many of the ablest minds in England.

This widespread and generous support of a colonial venture which gave no particular promise of financial success was largely due to the working of a ferment which King James had defined in the terse phrase, "No Bishop, No King." Growing resistance to the authority of the Church had crystallized into opposition to the King and his government. Puritanism was taking on a political tinge. Nor was the movement confined to a few poor tenants and nonconforming ministers; it extended into every level of society; and where religion was concerned the bond transcended social lines.

Thus when the Reverend John White and his associates proposed a Puritan refuge in the New World, they found no difficulty in interesting the great interlocking fellowship of Puritanism—noblemen and gentry, ministers and merchants, tenants and servants. The influence back of the seemingly not very important John Humphry was typical. He was a friend of the Reverend John White; he had been a member of the old Dorchester company; he was named as a patentee in the New England Company. Then came the move to get the royal patent. Suddenly we discover that Humphry's wife was a sister of the Earl of Lincoln, he in whose name John Wyncop had secured the first patent from the Virginia Company for the Pilgrims in 1619. The Earl was a Puritan. So was his father-in-law, Viscount Saye and Sele, who was in turn closely related to other great families with Puritan leanings. If John White wanted a patent for a colony, they would see that he got it. But this was not all. The interest of the Earl of Lincoln brought into the new company as a patentee and heavy subscriber the husband of another of his sisters, Mr. Isaac Johnson. Naturally, too, Thomas Dudley, business manager of the Earl's estates, became a subscriber and active member of the company. Truly the "favour of personages of note"·had its advantages.[6]

Almost as important as the family networks were the professional relationships centering at the Inns of Court in London. There every practicing lawyer of England had a legal residence. There the Puritan guardians of the legal interests of the Puritan landowners and merchants met and talked. There such men as John Winthrop of Suffolk, a neighbor of the Earl of Lincoln, came into contact with such men as Roger Ludlow of Wiltshire, a neighbor of the Reverend John White of Dorchester. There they discussed what they considered the corrupt condition of the Church and State of England. There they read and added their "Reasons" or "Objections" or "Answers" to the hand-written tracts that passed from hand to hand concerning White's proposed Puritan colony in America. These shrewd men of the law, many of them, each contributing his bit, saw to it that the new patent for the Massachusetts Bay Company was worded as they wished it to be worded, and that it moved through the legal mill without mishap.[7]

This royal patent, or charter, passed the last legal hurdle on March 4, 1629, and was shortly delivered to the patentees in an original and a duplicate copy. It recounted the creation of the Council for New England in 1620 and stated that on March 19, 1628, the Council had granted to Sir Henry Rosewell and five associates (*i.e.,* the New England Company) all the land lying between a point three miles south of the Charles River and a point three miles north of the Merrimac River, extending from coast to coast. It will be recalled that within these bounds lay the two grants of land made by the Council to Captain Mason and to Robert

Gorges in 1622; also that considerable doubt exists as to whether the grant to the Rosewell group was actually in the nature of a patent from the Council or whether it was merely an assignment of a title held by the Earl of Warwick. None the less the present patent from the King confirmed to the Massachusetts Bay Company, as successor to the Rosewell associates, all the title claimed in the possibly non-existent and certainly irregular patent of 1628.

In form the patent was similar to those usually granted to trading companies, with the one important exception that it did not specify where the Company was to have its official residence. It provided for a Governor, Deputy-governor, and eighteen Assistants all to be elected from the freemen (stockholders) of the Company. It provided for the holding of general courts (meetings of the stockholders) and for the admission of new freemen. In short, it organized a governing body for a company which would presumably hold its meetings and transact its business in England for the operation of a colony in America.[8]

On March 5, the day after the patent was issued, the officers of the new Company held a meeting. Matthew Cradock presided as President under the charter. First in the order of business was the consideration of "A newe proposition . . . in behalfe of Mr. Oldum." This was our old acquaintance John Oldham, who had been chucked out of Plymouth in 1624. We last met him on the way to England with Thomas Morton in 1628. While on this visit, or perhaps earlier, Oldham had acquired title to a part of the Robert Gorges grant which lay squarely within the lands now granted to the Massachusetts Bay Company. Although the Company was convinced that this title was "voyde in lawe," it gave them many an unhappy hour and delayed for two months the sailing of a fleet being prepared in the spring of 1629 to carry additional supplies and colonists to Massachusetts Bay.[9]

It is likely that troubles other than the Oldham claim contributed to the delay in getting off the ships in the spring of 1629. There were many details to be worked out—the buying of shoes and shovels, of swords and millstones, of

Courtesy, State House, Boston, Mass.

First parchment, or sheet, of the patent issued over the Great Seal of England on March 4, 1629, to the Massachusetts Bay Company.

horses and cows. There was the problem of selecting and making contracts with ministers. And there was the business of hiring carpenters to build houses and of finding farmers to plow the land and tend the livestock. The ships had to be heavily armed and manned since England was still at war with Spain and France.[10]

Five ships in all were to go. About the middle of April the *George* was hustled off. Aboard was Samuel Sharpe with the duplicate copy of the patent and a long letter of instructions from the officers of the Company, both of which were to be put into the hands of Governor Endecott at Naumkeag with the utmost despatch. Among these instructions was a long one regarding John Oldham, "not that we would wrong him . . . but if necessity require a more severe course . . . send forty or fifty persons to Mattachusetts Bay to inhabite there . . . the better to strengthen our possession there against all or any that shall intrude upon us, which we would not have you by any meanes to give way unto." It is evident that Oldham's claim under the Robert Gorges title had the Company worried.[11]

Trailing along behind the *George* came the other four ships. Among them was the *Mayflower,* which, in addition to passengers and supplies for Naumkeag, helped to carry thirty-five members of the Leyden congregation on a long-delayed migration to Plymouth Colony. On the *Talbot* came the Reverend Francis Higginson, one of three preachers hired to serve the spiritual needs of the colony at Naumkeag. He was a cousin of one of the patentees; he had been silenced by the Church for his nonconformist views; he had a wife and eight children and gladly accepted the Company's offer of £30 per year together with a house, food, and firewood.[12]

As the *Talbot* cleared the coast of England, Higginson is said to have assembled the passengers and expressed himself thus: "We will not say, as the Separatists were wont to say at their leaving of England, Farewell, Babylon! Farewell, Rome! But we will say, Farewell, dear England! Farewell, the Church of God in England, and all the Christian friends there! We do not go to New-England as Separatists from the Church of England; though we cannot but separate from the corruptions in it."[13]

The *George,* speeding on ahead, arrived at Naumkeag on June 23. Sharpe delivered into Governor Endecott's hands the duplicate of the royal patent and the instructions from the Company. Evidently the fact of having in his possession a title under the Great Seal of England impressed Endecott. From the pen of the sardonic Thomas Morton we get a fleeting glimpse of the reverence with which this document was looked upon by the Governor. Said Morton, "There was a great swelling fellow, of Littleworth, crept over to Salem . . . and to ad a Majesty (as hee thought) to his new assumed dignity, hee caused the Patent of Massachusetts (new brought into the Land) to be carried where hee went in his progresse to and froe, as an embleme of his authority: which the vulgar people not acquainted with, thought it to be some instrument of Musick locked up in that covered case, and thought (for so some said) this man of littleworth had bin a fiddler. . . ." Governor Bradford of Plymouth later branded Morton's literary effort "an infamouse and scurillous booke." [14]

One by one the other ships came in, adding approximately two hundred people to the hundred or so already living at Salem, no longer called by the Indian name of Naumkeag. There were only ten or eleven houses in the town so one of the first jobs for the newcomers was that of building homes for themselves. There was an unlimited supply of lumber at hand waiting for the axe and saw; nails had been brought over in great quantities; a brick kiln was set up; and the work went merrily on. [15]

In the pastures adjoining the town were forty cows and forty goats, all of which gave milk—the price a penny a quart. Higginson was impressed with the "fatness" of the land and with the amount of corn it produced. "Little children here, by setting corn," said the minister, "may earn much more than their own maintainence." [16]

Partly perhaps to crowd Oldham out of the Bay and partly because the location was good, a new town was begun at Charlestown, where Walford lived, and a hundred or so people moved there. Most of the settlers at both Salem and Charlestown were servants who had been sent over by shareholders in the Company to take charge of and improve the land which each shareholder was to have in proportion to his investment in the stock of the Company. There were, however, two outstanding exceptions among the arrivals of 1629. They were John and Samuel Browne, brothers. Their names appeared among the patentees of the Company. They were heavy investors in the colony. They, together with two other men and the three ministers, were designated by the Company to act as Councilors to Governor Endecott. But they were misfits on this Puritan frontier.[17]

By the middle of July the bustle and confusion of disembarkation was over. The ships had sailed northward to pick up what fish they could for a return cargo to England. Salem was ready to settle into a proper course of life. For the spiritual consolation and guidance of the inhabitants a pastor was desired. Under the government of the Church of England the prospective members of the church should have petitioned their Bishop to provide a pastor, and the Bishop in his discretion would have supplied one according to his judgment. Governor Endecott proceeded differently. He set apart the 20th of July "for a solemne day of humiliation for the choyce of a pastor and teacher." Three ministers had just arrived. Two of them, Higginson and Skelton, were questioned regarding their beliefs. Their answers were satisfactory. Accordingly "Mr. Higgison, with 3. or 4. of the gravest members of the church, laid their hands on Mr. Skelton, using prayer therwith. This being done, ther was imposission of hands on Mr. Higgison also"—and by this strange, unepiscopal ceremony they were installed, Mr. Higginson as teacher of the church and Mr. Skelton as pastor. The former Reverend Higginson, now simply Mr. Higginson, may not have departed from "dear England" as a Separatist, but in what manner his new church differed from that of the Separatist church at Plymouth the Archbishop of Canterbury in "dear England" would have been puzzled to understand.[18]

However, the majority of the people in Salem and Charlestown probably agreed with Mr. Higginson that their church followed the "true Religion and holy Ordinances of Almightie God," and that it had been formed in accordance with the practice of the primitive Christian churches before such corruptions as episcopal authority intervened. Nor was the preaching of Mr. Skelton without fruitful results. Edward Gibbons, one of Morton's wild crew at Merry Mount, was so affected that he confessed the error of his ways and was soon admitted to church membership.[19]

But there were those who viewed the whole procedure with cold disapproval, and among these were the highly respectable Browne brothers. They saw in it nothing but Separatism and openly said so. Not only that, they organized a small group which so far as possible without a minister followed the Church of England service. That was too much for Endecott. Patentees of the Company the Brownes might be, members of the Governor's Council they might be, but "New England was no place for such as they"—and he shipped them back to England.[20]

Had the Reverend John White, while on a visit to Cambridge University in England that summer of 1629, known what was happening at Salem, he might have spoken with less confidence about the advantages of a Puritan refuge in America. As it was, his arguments were perhaps the deciding factor in bringing into the Massachusetts Bay Company a man who was largely responsible for making it everything that White hoped for—except in the crucial matter of moderation in religion.[21]

John Winthrop, lord of the manor of Groton in Suffolk, was, as we have noted, trained to the law. He had held lucrative offices in London, but the spring of 1629 found him in debt and despondent about the future of England. "I am veryly persuaded," he wrote his wife, "God will bringe some heavye Affliction upon this lande, & that speedylye." The possibility of migration to one of the colonies was not a new thought to him. One of his sons was already attempting a plantation in Barbados.[22]

As the summer wore along, Winthrop joined with others at the home of the Earl of Lincoln, where the Massachusetts project was being discussed. As a result of these discussions Winthrop, Isaac Johnson, John Humphry, Sir Richard Saltonstall, Thomas Dudley, and seven other men, all of means

JOHN WINTHROP.
Governor of the Massachusetts Bay Company.

From the frontispiece of R. C. Winthrop, *Life and Letters of John Winthrop.*

and position, met at nearby Cambridge on August 26, 1629. There these twelve men "Upon due consideration of the state of the Plantation now in hand for New England . . . and having weighed the greatness of the work in regard of the consequence, God's glory and the Church's good," agreed to "be ready in our persons, and with such of our several families as are to go with us, and such provision as we are able conveniently to furnish ourselves withal, to embark for the said Plantation by the first of March next . . . Provided always, that before the last of September next, the whole Government, together with the patent for the said Plantation, be first, by an order of Court, legally transferred and established to remain with us and others which shall inhabit upon the said Plantation."[23]

Two days later at a General Court, or meeting, of the stockholders of the Massachusetts Bay Company, held in London, committees were appointed to consider the proposition laid before them by the signers of this agreement made at Cambridge. The following day the matter was argued in an open meeting and the question put:

"As many of you as desire to have the pattent and the government of the plantation to bee transferred to New England, soe as it may bee done legally, hold up your hands:

"Soe many as will not, hold upp your hands.

"Where, by erection of hands, it appeared by the general consent of the Company, that the government & pattent should be setled in New England."[24]

So passed the fateful vote that was to make Massachusetts not a colony of servants ruled over by a company in England but a commonwealth in which the shareholders were citizens and the officers were magistrates. On October 20 John Winthrop was elected Governor of the Massachusetts Bay Company. John Humphry was elected Deputy-governor. The leading men among the signers of the Cambridge Agreement were elected Assistants, which is to say that they became the Council for the Governor. Thus these men assumed the management of the Company in England, while Endecott carried on as Governor at Massachusetts Bay. Arrangements were made for financing and equipping the ships needed to transport the Company to America; contracts were made with servants and workmen; livestock, tools, and food were assembled; and those who planned to join in the migration began putting their affairs into order against the 1st of March, 1630.[25]

Seemingly neither Sir Ferdinando Gorges nor Captain John Mason, their time wholly taken up by the war with France and Spain, understood exactly what the creation of the Massachusetts Bay Company meant to their personal interests or to the overall authority of the Council for New England. Gorges knew that a colony was being planned and apparently looked with favor on the project as coming under the general control of the Council. He evidently was not aware that the Bay Company had secured a royal patent or that the patent extended over an area within which lay a grant made by the Council to his son Robert, a grant made by the Council to Captain Mason, and a three-mile-wide slice of a grant made to himself and Mason jointly.[26]

But now the war with France was over. Gorges and Mason had a little leisure in which to think about New England. Also there had come to light a possibility that interested them. It all went back to a privateering expedition which England had authorized as part of the war. The Kirke family, waylaying French fur-trading ships in the St. Lawrence River and co-operating with Sir William Alexander in the development of his colony of Nova Scotia, had captured Quebec. There Samuel de Champlain had fallen into their hands and been carried back to England. From him Gorges had learned that there was a rich fur trade along the "Lake of the Iroquois," lying west of the coast of Maine. This lake —probably Lake Champlain—appeared to be within the bounds of the Council for New England though to the west of any explorations so far made by Englishmen.[27]

And so for a moment the Council for New England came to life. Whether or not Mason knew that his grant of 1622 had been swallowed up by the Massachusetts Bay Company, he now asked Gorges for a division of the land which they held jointly from the Merrimac River to the Kennebec River. Gorges kept the northern part and Mason took a patent from the Council to the part from the Piscataqua to the Merrimac, apparently oblivious of the fact that the Massachusetts Bay patent extended to a point three miles north of the Merrimac. To this tract of land Mason gave the name of New Hampshire.[28]

Gorges and Mason's provinces of Maine and New Hampshire extended inland only sixty miles, but on November 17, 1629, the Council granted to them jointly an ill-defined area lying to the westward and called Laconia. Within this region was supposed to be the Lake of the Iroquois from which the partners expected to reap a fortune in furs. But they were doomed to disappointment, as were also the Kirkes and Sir William Alexander. King Charles of England, in his final peace with France, agreed to the restoration of Canada, including Nova Scotia. David Kirke was recompensed by being knighted and appointed Governor of Newfoundland, a cold and unprofitable business as Sir George Calvert, Lord Baltimore, had already discovered.[29]

Calvert had long been interested in colonial schemes. He had been a member of the Virginia Company and of the Council for New England. Since 1622 he had held an extensive grant in Newfoundland. He had spent a great deal of money and time on the venture, but it did not pay. In the summer of 1629, while on a visit to Newfoundland, he wrote to King Charles that he would like "to shift to some other warmer climate of this new world, where the wynters be shorter and lesse rigorous." And he continued, ". . . I am determined to committ this place to fishermen that are able to encounter storms and hard weather, and to remove myself with some 40 persons to your Majesty's dominion of Virginia, where if your Majesty will please to grant me a precinct of land with such privileges as the King your father my gracious master was pleased to grant me here, I shall endevor to the utmost of my power to deserve it."[30]

Without waiting for an answer Calvert sailed for Virginia, arriving there late in the fall of 1629. But he was not a welcome visitor. In part the people of Virginia suspected his design, as well they might. In part he was a Catholic where Catholics were not popular. This latter might explain why Thomas Tindall got into trouble "for giving my Lord Baltemore the lye & threatening to knock him down." The colonial authorities proceeded more diplomatically; they tendered him the oath of supremacy, in other words the declaration that the King rather than the Pope was supreme in spiritual matters. As a Catholic Calvert could not take such an oath; hence he departed. None the less he had seen the place he wanted for his colony.[31]

While Calvert was looking over the possibilities in Virginia, Winthrop and the other leaders of the Massachusetts Bay Company were preparing for their departure from England. Some few had fallen by the wayside, but others had taken their places. Roger Ludlow, member of a land-holding family of Wiltshire and, as we have seen, a lawyer by profession, was elected an Assistant of the Company on February 10, 1630. Under his leadership one hundred and forty people from Dorchester and the west of England joined in the migration. This group gathered at Plymouth (England) during the month of March. There they "kept a solemn day of fasting;" the Reverend John White of Dorchester came down and preached a farewell sermon; and they chose their ministers—without so much as a thought of the wishes of any bishop. On March 20, 1630, aboard the *Mary & John,* they sailed for Massachusetts Bay. Another ship with other colonists sailed from Bristol at about the same time.[32]

The Winthrop fleet, eleven vessels strong, was preparing at Yarmouth and Southampton. On April 8 the *Arbella,* the *Talbot,* the *Ambrose,* and the *Jewel* sailed. Aboard the *Arbella,* flagship for the voyage and named for Lady Arbella, wife of Isaac Johnson and sister of the Earl of Lincoln, was Governor Winthrop with the original of the royal patent. Three or four weeks later the *Whale,* the *Hopewell,* the *William & Francis,* the *Trial,* the *Charles,* the *Success,* and the *Mayflower,* with the last of the passengers and supplies, unfurled their sails and followed the leaders out to sea.[33]

And there they were—strung out for hundreds of leagues over the face of the uncertain ocean—the *Mary & John* leading the van and the old *Mayflower* wallowing along in the rear. From the vanishing hills of Land's End to the ice-bound headlands of Cape Sable the great Puritan migration was on. A piece of old England was crossing the Western Sea to found a New England. As the reef points slat-slatted against the taut sails on the *Mary & John,* a cow bawled in the hold of the *Hopewell;* as the timbers of the *Talbot* groaned under the strain of her masts, a mother crooned to her restless babe; as servant girls flirted with the carefree sailors, Ludlow on the *Mary & John* and Winthrop on the *Arbella* thought and thought, and wondered how it would all turn out.

Behind them as the fleet sailed, Winthrop and other leaders of the Company left a *Humble Request* "To the rest of their Brethren, in and of the Church of England." They asked to be remembered "as those who esteem it our honor to call the Church of England, from whence we rise, our dear mother . . . ever acknowledging that such hope and part as we have obtained in the common salvation, we have received in her bosom and sucked it from her breasts." They further asked their brethren in the Church of England to include them in their prayers, which, if they were "frequent and fervent, will be a most prosperous gale in our sails." We may be sure that over the fleet as it sailed westward hovered the prayers of all Puritan England.[34]

On May 30 the *Mary & John* sailed past Salem and dropped anchor off Nantasket, where Oldham and Conant had spent the winter of 1624–25. Two weeks later the *Arbella* arrived at Salem, and the other ships came trailing along. With the arrival of Governor Winthrop, Endecott ceased to be Governor of Massachusetts. He became Captain Endecott and one of the Assistants of the Company.[35]

Within a few weeks some fifteen hundred new inhabitants had been added to the three hundred people already living at Salem and Charlestown. Obviously those two places could not accommodate all of these newcomers. The leaders of the various groups searched the shores of Massachusetts Bay and up the Charles River for suitable places to establish new towns. The Ludlow group settled on the south side of the

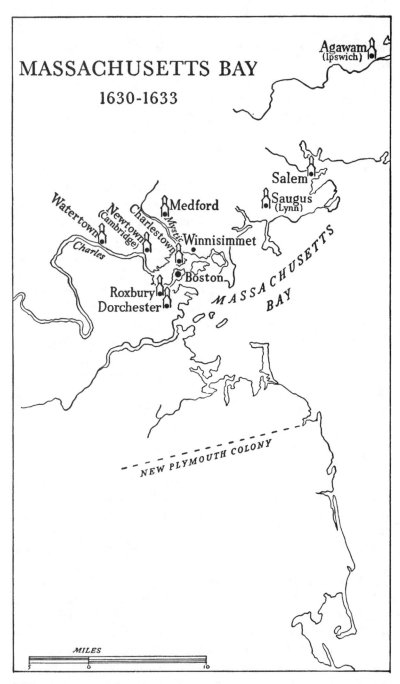

MASSACHUSETTS BAY

1630-1633

Agawam
(Ipswich)

Salem

Saugus
(Lynn)

Medford

Watertown

Charles

Newtown
(Cambridge)

Charlestown

Mystic

Winnisimmet

Boston

Roxbury

Dorchester

MASSACHUSETTS BAY

NEW PLYMOUTH COLONY

MILES

Bay and named their town Dorchester in honor of the English city from which many of their members had sprung. William Pynchon and his people settled a little to the west of Dorchester and named their town Roxbury. Sir Richard Saltonstall founded a town on the north side of the Charles River, which he named Watertown. Others settled temporarily at Charlestown, where the Governor and some of his official family made their home in the "great house" built there in 1629. Some few established themselves on the peninsula called Shawmut (Boston), where the Reverend William Blackstone had his home. Tents, wigwams made of brush and mud, and other hastily thrown together shelters protected the people and their furniture and their food until more permanent houses could be built.[36]

In 1629, while the Company was still in England, it had been decided that each shareholder who had subscribed £50 to the common stock should be entitled to two hundred acres of land and proportionately more or less for greater or lesser subscriptions. To those who went to Massachusetts Bay at their own expense, and were also shareholders, fifty additional acres were to be allowed for each member of the family; to those who went over at their own expense, but were not shareholders, fifty acres were to be allotted to the head of the family only. The allotments were to be made or confirmed by Governor Endecott at Salem. Now, in 1630, with several additional towns in existence somewhat the same procedure was followed, though the allotments to individuals were made by the towns rather than by the Company. It soon followed that the basis of these land "dividends" came to be not so much a question of shareholding in the Company as a question of social standing, size of the family, need of the recipient, or ability to make use of the land. And when a man received his "dividend" of land from the town there were no strings attached to his title. The land was his in fee simple. The Company did not require the payment of annual quitrents (acknowledgments of feudal tenure) which was the accepted custom in England and which custom was as a matter of course continued in Virginia and in the parts of New England controlled by Gorges and Mason, or granted by the Council for New England.[37]

With the people gathered into towns and settled communities through the ownership of land and houses, the organization of churches could no longer be delayed. In fact, the first matter considered at the first Court or meeting of the Company in New England, held at Charlestown on Aug. 23, 1630, was "howe the ministers should be mayntayned," and "It was ordered that houses should be built for them with convenient speede, att the publique charge."[38]

Four days later Governor Winthrop, then residing at Charlestown, recorded, "We, of the congregation, kept a fast, and chose Mr. Wilson our teacher [a position hardly distinguishable from that of pastor]. . . . We used imposition of hands, but with this protestation by all, that it was only as a sign of election and confirmation, and not of any intent that Mr. Wilson should renounce his ministry he received in England." Accepting their protestation as having been made in all good faith, the fact remains that in using the "imposition of hands" they were following separatist practices, and in choosing rather than receiving a spiritual leader, call him what they might, they were going directly contrary to the government of the Church of England, that "dear mother" from whose breasts they had sucked such hope of salvation as was theirs when they left England the preceding April.[39]

Here, at Charlestown in 1630, was an almost exact repetition of what had happened at Salem in 1629. The question must be faced. Was Higginson sincere when, upon his departure from England, he vowed loyalty to the Church? Was Winthrop sincere when he signed the *Humble Request?* And if so, why did they become separatists when they organized their churches in New England a few weeks later?

The answer seems to be that while Higginson and Winthrop and the majority of the colonists frankly left England because they wished to escape from the discipline and government of the Church of England—from its corruptions, as they put it—few of them anticipated separating from it entirely. But when they reached Massachusetts Bay and were faced with the problem of organizing their own churches they discovered that there was no way to do it except by a form that partook of the separatist pattern. If they were not to ask a bishop to act for them, they had to act themselves —and that was separatism. In part, too, they were undoubtedly influenced by the already existing church at Plymouth. And so, somewhat to their own evident astonishment, they went farther than they intended. But they did not admit that they had separated from the Church nor did they call themselves Separatists. They spoke of their churches as congregations, with the result that they came to be known as Congregationalists.[40]

The fact remains, however, that in the organization of their churches as in the distribution of their land, the first colony that stood squarely on its own responsibility in the New World broke with the long-established institutions of England. No feudal lord stood between the landowner and his title; no ecclesiastical lord stood between the church member and his salvation.

Under whatever form it functioned it was well that spiritual help was at hand. It would have been well if a few physicians also had been at hand, for the sickness which always descended upon new arrivals in America was upon them. About the 1st of September the Lady Arbella, Isaac Johnson's wife, died. Johnson himself died a month later. Hardly a family escaped. Officers of the Company, ministers, and servants were afflicted alike. Thomas Dudley, who was there and may be looked upon as knowing something about it, attributed this sickness to "the want of warm lodging and good diet, to which Englishmen are habituated at home, and in the sudden increase of heat which they endure that are landed here in summer, the salt meats at sea having prepared their bodies thereto."[41]

There was no "starving time" at Massachusetts Bay as there had been at Virginia and Plymouth. However, during the first confused and unhealthy winter, food was scarce and bread was almost nonexistent. Roger Clap of Dorchester tells us that "many a time if I could have filled my belly, though with mean victuals, it would have been sweet unto me." But fish, clams, mussels, and nuts with an occasional bag of corn from the Indians kept the people going until better came.[42]

Governor Winthrop, foreseeing the shortage, had sent a ship under rush orders to Ireland, and just when things seemed worst it came back well loaded with supplies. Also a ship came in from Virginia with a cargo of corn. The price was high but the corn was welcome. The lack of fresh fruit had aggravated a tendency towards scurvy, but this too was met by a shipment of lemons. Massachusetts Bay took care of itself. It was not dependent upon any group of merchants nor the whim of a distant company. The Bay leaders *were* the company and they owned and controlled their own ships; also they had ample means to pay for what was needed.[43]

More serious than the shortage of food that first winter of 1630–31 was a succession of fires resulting from the flimsy character of the hastily built houses. Many families lost not only their homes but their clothing, their furniture, and their food supplies. So obvious was the reason for the disasters that the installation of wooden chimneys and thatched roofs was forbidden in the new town which the Company was planning to establish the following year.[44]

This "new town," already laid out between Charlestown and Watertown on the north side of the Charles River, was intended to be the capital city of the colony. The Governor and most of the Assistants had agreed to build their homes there, and it was to be called Boston. However, the name of Boston was in a short time officially bestowed upon the peninsula where the Reverend Blackstone lived and which was becoming increasingly attractive to the newcomers. Even Governor Winthrop picked up the frame of the house he was building at Newtown and transferred it to Boston. However, many stayed on at Newtown, including Dudley, the Deputy-governor; and the location later came to be known as Cambridge. At Boston the Reverend Blackstone stood his Puritan neighbors as long as he could and then moved out, explaining, "I came from England because I did not like the lord-bishops; but I can't join with you, because I would not be under the lord-brethren."[45]

Since the landing of the Company, Courts of Assistants had been held from time to time as occasions for action had

Above. Restoration of English wigwams as constructed at Massachusetts Bay in 1630.

Below. English wigwams when completed.

Both pictures by the *courtesy* of the Society for the Preservation of New England Antiquities, Boston.

arisen. Justices of the peace had been appointed; wages, particularly of carpenters and masons, had been limited; inquests had been held. Thomas Morton, of Merry Mount, had been condemned to be set in the bilboes (see page 354), his goods confiscated, his house burned, and himself sent to England—all of which was carried out.[46]

But Morton was not the only misfit in the colony. Sir Christopher Gardiner had arrived with a comely young woman who was affirmed by one of his wives in England "to be a known harlot"—at least such was the account of her which Isaac Allerton, agent for the Plymouth plantation, picked up in England and promptly passed along to the authorities of the Bay. The real trouble was that Winthrop suspected Gardiner of being a spy for Sir Ferdinando Gorges and greatly feared the report he might make. Without being specific as to the charge, a Court of Assistants ordered him deported but hesitated to execute the sentence. And while Gardiner lingered on at the Bay, one Thomas Purchase came down from his lonely home on the Androscoggin River, near Sagadahoc, and either claimed or wooed and won the comely young lady, taking her back with him as his lawfully wedded wife. Gardiner went along and consoled himself through the cold winter with a borrowed warming pan. The following spring he returned to England, taking the warming pan with him. The young lady remained with her husband as a respected matron of the Androscoggin, ultimately to win a place in our literature as "the little lady with golden hair" of Longfellow's poem. Nine years after Gardiner's departure, the owner of the warming pan sued Purchase for its value—twelve shillings, six pence—and the jury decided that he must pay.[47]

Although the Court of Assistants could chuck out Morton and order out Gardiner, it was not the final authority in the Bay. The patent directed that four General Courts should be held each year, in which the freemen (stockholders) had equal power with the Governor and Assistants both in admitting other freemen and in making "lawes and ordinances for the good and welfare of the saide Company, and for the government and ordering of the saide landes and plantation

Above, from the Household Edition (1886) of *Longfellow's Poetical Works,* is A. B. Frost's conception of

> ". . . the little lady with golden hair
> Who was gathering in the bright sunshine
> The sweet alyssum and columbine."

Below. Warming Pan.

Courtesy, The Metropolitan Museum of Art, New York.

and the people inhabiting and to inhabit the same." In accepting these provisions of the patent the King's officials had assumed that they would apply to a trading company sitting in England and making rules for a plantation across the ocean. But here was the company sitting in its own plantation with the inhabitants of the plantation as its prospective freemen. At the first General Court, held at Boston on October 19, 1630, one hundred and eight men applied for admission as freemen. That is, on the basis of their contributions to the colony, these inhabitants applied for the right to vote in the courts of the Company. Since the Company was the government of the colony, this meant that they were applying for the right to vote in the affairs of the colony. Among them were Samuel Maverick, Roger Conant, the Reverend William Blackstone, Edward Gibbons, and a number of others who had from long residence in the region acquired titles in the land which the Company dared not ignore.[48]

Most of these applicants, together with a few others, among whom was John Oldham, were duly admitted at the meeting of the next General Court on May 18, 1631. Not all of them, however, were in full sympathy with the form of church organization existing in the Bay. This the Company realized, and at this Court it was voted that in the future "noe man shalbe admitted to the freedome of this body polliticke, but such as are members of some of the churches within the lymitts of the same." Since there were no churches except of the Congregational variety, this meant that only those of the Congregational persuasion would be allowed to vote.[49]

Thus we see a trading company being transformed into a commonwealth. The patent of the Company became a constitution; the freemen became citizens; the Assistants became a judiciary and, between the meetings of the General Court, a legislature; the Governor, from being chairman of a board of directors, became the chief executive of a body politic. It was but a step to the assumption of power to levy taxes—from the towns, not from the individuals—for the support of the central government. And with the franchise limited to members of the only type of church allowed to exist, it was but natural that a Congregational government should be perpetuated. Known as the "New England Way" this combination of church and state soon attracted the favorable attention of a body of reformers in Old England who offered it as a model which should be adopted there.

Evidently Oldham had made his peace with the Company, but some of the Old Planters did not care to bow their necks to the new government. Among these was Thomas Walford, the blacksmith, who had been living at Charlestown before Winthrop had probably so much as heard of Massachusetts Bay. Early in 1631 he and his wife were ordered by a Court of Assistants "to departe out of the lymits of this pattent before the 20th day of October nexte . . . for his contempt of authority." [50]

Nor were all the newcomers as respectful as the Court desired. Philip Ratcliffe, who had been sent over by Matthew Cradock, the first Governor of the Company, to work on his farms, was sentenced on June 14, 1631, to be "whipped, have his eares cutt of, fyned 40^t, & banished out of the lymitts of this jurisdiction, for uttering mallitious & scandulous speeches against the government & the church of Salem." Roger Clap of Dorchester assures us that the first two items of the sentence were fully carried out; "I saw it done," he says. [51]

The stories which Morton, Gardiner, and Ratcliffe told when they got back to England substantiated other accounts that had been coming in with every returning ship. And they provided Sir Ferdinando Gorges with the testimony he needed in an attack which he was preparing against the Massachusetts Bay patent.

Peace had now been made with Spain as well as with France. Gorges and Mason were ready to again plunge actively into the business of colonization in New England. A base for their joint colony of Laconia was already established in the stone house built at Piscataqua by David Thomson in 1623 and later abandoned. Captain Walter Neale, in charge of the enterprise, had explored some distance inland but had failed to find the "Lake of the Iroquois." In 1631

Mason had caused the plantation to be moved slightly up the river to a place which they named Strawberry Bank. Additional people had been sent over; vines and livestock were being cultivated; but the settlement was not prospering. Somewhat farther up the Piscataqua was another plantation under the supervision of Captain Thomas Wiggin, and still farther up the river was the town of Dover, under the direction of Edward Hilton. (See map on page 205.) Such was New Hampshire in 1632.[52]

In Gorges' province of Maine, between the Piscataqua and the Kennebec, there was a plantation at Agamenticus (present-day York) under Colonel Walter Norton. On the south side of the Saco River (present-day Biddeford) was a plantation owned jointly by Richard Vines, who had stayed in New England during the winter of 1616–17 to prove that the region was habitable, and John Oldham, who had just been admitted a freeman at the Bay. Across the Saco River from Vines and Oldham was another plantation belonging to Thomas Lewis and Richard Bonython. Five or six miles to the north, at Black Point, Thomas Cammock, a nephew of the Earl of Warwick, had a grant of land; and across from him, at Richmond's Island, Robert Trelawny and Moses Goodyear, merchants of Plymouth, England, were starting a plantation under the management of John Winter. Christopher Levett's trading house at Casco Bay seems to have disappeared. On the Androscoggin lived Thomas Purchase, who had married Gardiner's young lady. Up the Kennebec was the Plymouth Trading Grant. And at Pemaquid, to the eastward of the Kennebec, Abraham Shurt still maintained his fur-trading station.[53]

All of these settlements along the coasts of New Hampshire and Maine were based on patents from the Council for New England, most of them passed during the year 1631 with only the Earl of Warwick and Sir Ferdinando Gorges present at the meetings. And this same year, partly because of reports of highhanded behavior and seditious speeches at Massachusetts Bay, and partly because he wished to regain control of New England, Gorges persuaded the King to permit the Council to stop all sailings for Massachusetts Bay

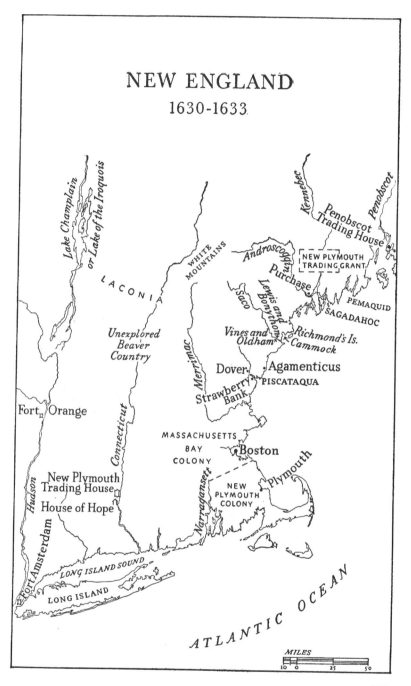

NEW ENGLAND
1630-1633

Penobscot

Kennebec

Penobscot Trading House

NEW PLYMOUTH TRADING GRANT

Lake Champlain or Lake of the Iroquois

WHITE MOUNTAINS

Androscoggin

LACONIA

Purchase

Lewis and Bonython

Saco

PEMAQUID

SAGADAHOC

Unexplored Beaver Country

Vines and Oldham

Richmond's Is. Cammock

Merrimac

Dover

Agamenticus

Strawberry Bank

PISCATAQUA

Fort Orange

Connecticut

MASSACHUSETTS BAY COLONY

Boston

Plymouth

Hudson

New Plymouth Trading House

House of Hope

Narragansett

NEW PLYMOUTH COLONY

Fort Amsterdam

LONG ISLAND SOUND

LONG ISLAND

ATLANTIC OCEAN

MILES
10 0   25   50

205

until the passengers had taken an oath to support the Church. This was an oath which the majority of the emigrating Puritans—"multitudes of discontended persons," Gorges called them—would not take.[54]

On June 26, 1632, there was a meeting of the Council at the Earl of Warwick's house in London. Present were the Earl, Sir Ferdinando Gorges, Captain John Mason, and five others. It was the best attended meeting in several years. To it came Mr. John Humphry, brother-in-law of the Earl of Lincoln, signer of the Cambridge Agreement, and patentee of the Massachusetts Bay Company. He complained to the Council "for not permitting ships and passingers to pass from hence for the Bay of Mattachusetts without Licence first had from the President & Councell or their Deputy, they being free to goe thither, and to transport passingers, not only by a patent granted unto them by the President & Councell of New England, But also by a Confirmation therof by his Majesty under His Great Seale."[55]

Through this statement by Humphry most of the members of the Council evidently learned for the first time that the Council had granted such a patent and that it had been confirmed by a royal patent. Some of them ". . . desired to see the Pattent which [the Massachusetts Bay Company] had obtained from the President & Councell, because, as they alledged, it preindicted former grants." In that word "preindicted" the whole question of the prior grants to Robert Gorges and Captain Mason was brought into the open. In short, the validity of the Massachusetts Bay Company's title was challenged.[56]

Two days later the Council again met at Warwick House —but this time the Earl of Warwick was not present. Humphry and Cradock appeared for the Massachusetts Bay Company and from them the Council demanded a map showing the limits of their patent. The following day there was another meeting of the Council at Warwick House—but again the Earl was not present. The other members "agreed that the Earl of Warwick should be entreated to direct a course for finding out what Pattents have been granted for New England." They also sent their clerk to the Earl "for the

Councell's great seale, it being in his Lordship's keeping."
The Earl sent back word that he would attend to these matters later, whereupon it was "agreed that the place of meeting for the Councell of New England shall be hereafter at
Captain Mason's house." Thus ended the Earl of Warwick's
connection with the Council for New England. It would seem
that his fellow members strongly suspected that he had acted
irregularly in granting a patent to the Bay Company in the
name of the Council, or that he knew something he did not
wish to tell. It will be recalled that this patent, which Warwick was supposed to have granted from the Council, was
the basis upon which the royal patent had been issued to
the Bay Company.[57]

Gorges and Mason wasted no time in pushing their attack.
The ill reports coming from the Bay were grist for their
mill. Morton, Gardiner, and Ratcliffe were all back in England, and together with them Gorges and Mason worked out
a damning statement of conditions at the Bay. They charged
that the colony had cast off its allegiance to England; that
it had already separated from the Church and laws of
England; that their ministers and people continually railed
against the English State, the English Church, and the English bishops. This statement, together with supporting documents, was laid before the Privy Council, which appointed
a committee to investigate and report.[58]

At that point friends of the Bay colony, including Captain
Wiggin of Piscataqua, who happened to be in England,
sprang to its defense and made so good a case for the government of the colony and so bad a case against its accusers
that the Privy Council decided in favor of the Bay. When
the news reached Massachusetts, Winthrop records that "A
day of thanksgiving was kept in all the congregations for
our delivery from the plots of our enemies."[59]

During the first years the colonists at the Bay lived to
some extent upon the capital which they had accumulated
from the sale of their property in England. Many supported
themselves in part by raising corn and garden stuff. Millstones had been an important item among the equipment
brought from England. Some of these mills were operated

by water power, and by 1632 there was at least one operated by wind power, although the wind did not always blow the right way. Corn was brought into the Bay to be ground from as far away as Piscataqua. A steady stream of new colonists with ready money in their pockets created a market for surplus corn, while their payments for transportation helped to recompense those of the Company who had underwritten the purchase or rental of ships.[60]

Fish and furs were the staple exports. They provided credits in England from which necessary imports could be purchased. Winthrop, Dudley, Cradock, and seven other members of the Company held a limited monopoly of the fur trade in consideration of their having financed the migration of 1630. Samuel Maverick, still living on an island in Boston harbor, traded up and down the coast as did also William Pynchon, John Oldham, and many others. We get some idea of the magnitude of this fur business when we learn that on one ship sailing out of the Bay in 1632 there were between five and six thousand pounds of beaver worth twenty shillings a pound in England—and this was but one of many ships going out, most of them doubtless carrying skins.[61]

As early as 1629 a bark for use in fishing and the fur trade had been built at the Bay—probably by workmen sent over by Matthew Cradock, who, although he never came to America, operated farms and engaged in ship building on the Mystic River near Medford (see page 194). Winthrop, too, had land along the Mystic, and there on July 4, 1631, he launched the *Blessing of the Bay*, a thirty-ton bark.[62]

In the autumn of 1633 the *Blessing* went around Cape Cod into Long Island Sound and called at the Dutch settlement of New Amsterdam. Peter Minuit, who had sent De Rasieres to open up trade with New Plymouth in 1627, was no longer Director-general of New Netherland. During the five years, from 1626 to 1631, that he had been in charge of the Dutch colony, its fur trade had grown from five thousand to fifteen thousand skins a year. It had bought Manhattan Island from the Indians—for a sum estimated at $24—and had firmly established itself at Fort Orange on the

Hudson River where Albany stands today. On the other hand Fort Nassau, on the Delaware River across from where Philadelphia later came into being, had been abandoned. And nowhere had the colony taken root in the soil.[63]

With a view to encouraging permanent settlements the Dutch Company in 1629 offered large grants of land to such of its members as would bring in at least fifty people and establish agricultural plantations. As a result Kiliaen van Rensselaer, a pearl merchant of Amsterdam, acquired a vast patroonage, as the holdings were called, on both sides of the Hudson River around about Fort Orange. Other patroonages were taken at various places within the area claimed by New Netherland—in present-day New Jersey, on the Connecticut River, and along the Delaware River. In the latter region the promising plantation of Zwaanendael (Valley of the Swans) was started in 1631. A palisaded building was put up, the land was cleared, crops were planted; then the Indians descended upon the place, and that was the end of Zwaanendael.[64]

Where there were no Indian troubles the patroons proved less interested in farming than in the fur trade, which latter was reserved exclusively to the Company. Naturally disagreements resulted and, caught between the quarreling stockholders, Minuit was discredited and ordered back to Holland to answer charges. On his way home his ship put in at Plymouth, England, and there Captain John Mason caused both Minuit and the ship to be arrested. The charge was that the Dutch West India Company had been trespassing within the limits of the Council for New England. Minuit appealed to the Dutch ambassador at London, who came to the defense of the Dutch colony with the same argument that England fifty years earlier had used against Spanish pretensions: Prescription without possession availed nothing. England had claimed the American coast but had failed to effectively occupy it; Henry Hudson, under a Dutch commission, had discovered the river; the Dutch Company had occupied it for many years. The argument was one that was hard to answer. And Minuit was allowed to go on his way to Holland—where the Dutch Company dismissed him as

Director-general of its trading posts in New Netherland.[65]

In Minuit's place the Company sent over, in 1633, Wouter van Twiller. At about the same time some English merchants sent out a ship with orders to trade with the Indians in the Hudson River. Hardly had van Twiller reached Fort Amsterdam when this English ship arrived. Van Twiller inquired its business and was informed that it was going up the Hudson to trade. This the new Director-general forbade. The merchant in charge of the English ship then informed the Director-general that the Hudson was within the territory of the King of England and that his was an English ship and that he was going up the river—which he did. Anchoring just below Fort Orange, the English set up a tent, spread out their trade goods, and soon were doing a brisk business with the Indians. The Dutch traders from Fort Orange came down and set up a tent beside the English with a display of their own goods. It was bargain day for the Iroquois on the Hudson. But the English were getting most of the furs. So the Dutch pulled down the Englishmen's tent, took their ship in charge, sailed it back down the river, and told them to get out—which they did. The West India Company was still boss on the Hudson.[66]

Despite this unpleasant incident van Twiller received the *Blessing of the Bay* courteously enough when it arrived at New Amsterdam in the autumn of 1633. He permitted its master to carry on a proper trade with the Company, as New Netherland had long permitted Plymouth and Virginia to do. On the way back to Massachusetts the *Blessing* looked in at the Connecticut River up which the Dutch had already established a trading post and New Plymouth was getting ready to do the same.[67]

The New Plymouth colonists were no longer squatters on Cape Cod Bay. On January 13, 1630, after sticking it out for nine years with only a license to look for a place at which to settle, they had received from the Council for New England a patent confirming their plantation and bounding their lands. Starting from a point on the coast just south of Massachusetts Bay their northern boundary ran some thirty miles inland, thence south along the Narragan-

sett River to the sea and around the hook of Cape Cod—
a very liberal grant for a colony which did not exceed three
hundred people. Nor was this all. This patent of 1630 confirmed the somewhat doubtful grant which New Plymouth
held on the Kennebec River.[68]

It would seem that New Plymouth should have been satisfied. But fur was what made the colony go, and from
Narragansett Bay to Sagadahoc the number of skins brought
in by the Indians was growing less year by year. To adorn
fair ladies and fine men at the courts of Europe the middle
coast of New England had been skinned. New sources for
beaver must be found if New Plymouth was to pay off its
debts.[69]

Eastward of the Kennebec, at Pemaquid, Abraham Shurt
had for some years been monopolizing the trade from the
region more or less deserted by the French traders during the
late war. New Plymouth now joined with some London
merchants and established a trading post at the mouth of
the Penobscot River between Shurt and the former French
hunting grounds. But the enterprise did not prosper. First
there was trouble with the traders; and then the Frenchmen,
returning to their old stations, began making up for lost time
by raiding the English trading houses. At about this time
word got around that the Dutch were doing well on the Connecticut River—taking out as many as ten thousand skins
a year. And when in the spring of 1633 the Dutch established their trading post on that river—where Hartford stands
today—New Plymouth decided it was time to compete. Bradford and Winslow went to the Bay and asked Winthrop to
join with them. The Bay people declined, but the ever-enter-
prising John Oldham made a hurried trip overland to Connecticut and came back significantly uncommunicative. Also,
as we have seen, the *Blessing of the Bay* did a little investigating on its own account.[70]

While the Bay thought about it, New Plymouth acted.
William Holmes, with a few men, loaded the frame of a
house onto a small boat, sailed down to the mouth of the
Connecticut, and started up the river. When this strange
cargo arrived opposite the House of Hope, as the Dutch had

named their post, Holmes was challenged. Where was he going and what for? Holmes replied that he was going up the river to trade. In other words, by getting above the Dutch, he was aiming to intercept for New Plymouth the rich fur trade that came down the Connecticut from the wild country above. Quite naturally the Dutch traders ordered him to turn around and go home; otherwise they would begin shooting. He told them to shoot away, and without further opposition went on up the river. There, only four or five miles above the House of Hope, he unloaded his house, built a palisade around it, and was ready for business.[71]

When news of this affair reached Director-general van Twiller at New Amsterdam, he sent a force of seventy men to remove the New Plymouth traders. But they refused to be removed, and as their house was well fortified and they evidently meant to stay, the Dutch thought better of the matter—and there the two trading houses stood only a few miles apart on the great fur-rich river.[72]

What the pronouncements of the King and the protests of the Council for New England had been unable to do William Holmes and a few unsmiling men from New Plymouth had done. They had called a halt to the expansion of the Dutch. And what with Frenchmen to the north and Spaniards to the south as well as Dutchmen in the middle it was high time for England to see to it that she *possessed* what she had *prescripted*.

Maryland

WHILE THE DUTCH and the English were arguing out their respective claims on the Connecticut River that autumn of 1633, there came up from the south a strange echo of the grim clash between Catholics and Protestants on the coast of Florida sixty-eight years earlier.

It will be recalled that when, in 1606, England set forth her territorial claims in America the limits were the thirty-fourth parallel on the south and the forty-fifth on the north, or from a little south of present-day Wilmington, N. C., to the present northeastern boundary of Maine. All of this vast area was called Virginia and within it two colonies, each a hundred miles square, were authorized. In the north the first effort, that at Sagadahoc, failed. In the south the Virginia Company's colony took root and grew. In 1609 its limits were increased from one hundred miles along the coast to four hundred miles—two hundred northward from Point Comfort and the same southward. This brought its southern boundary to just about the southern limit claimed by England.

But with all its increase in population the only real settlement made by the Virginia Company was along the James River—squarely in the middle of its territory. Nor had the

Company grown with the colony. Its patent had been annulled in 1624 and the government of Virginia taken into the hands of the King. The unsettled land was his to dispose of as seemed best. Still there was hope among the former stockholders that the colony would be returned to the Company, and, when in 1625 the old King died and his son Charles came to the throne, a determined effort was made to bring this about.[1]

What happened was a rude shock to the stockholders of the Virginia Company—and to the King of Spain. On May 13, 1625, less than two months after his succession to the throne, Charles not only expressed himself regarding Virginia but promulgated a colonial policy. "Our full resolution is," he said, "to the end that there may be one uniforme course of Government in and through Our whole Monarchie, That the Government of the Colonie of Virginia shall immediately depend upon Our Selfe, and not be committed to any Company or Corporation, to whom it may be proper to trust matters of Trade and Commerce, but cannot bee fit or safe to communicate the ordering of State-affaires, be they of never so meane consequence."[2]

How in the face of this pronouncement Charles approved the Massachusetts Bay patent of March 4, 1629, must remain one of the several mysteries connected with that document. Barring this one important exception there is no doubt that in his statement of 1625 the King was announcing a definite policy. And in pursuance of this policy he granted on October 30, 1629, to Sir Robert Heath, his Attorney-general, a province to be known as Carolina. Sir Robert, so the patent stated, was "about to lead thither a Colonye of men large & Plentifull." The size of Carolina certainly indicated the need of "men large & Plentifull." It extended nearly five hundred miles along the coast and included a large piece of what had formerly been the southern part of Virginia Colony, together with a still larger piece of what had previously been conceded to Spain. In fact, it swept southward to within seventy-five miles of the Spanish fortress of St. Augustine. By this grant England assumed a title far more extensive than she had dared to do in 1606. North and south

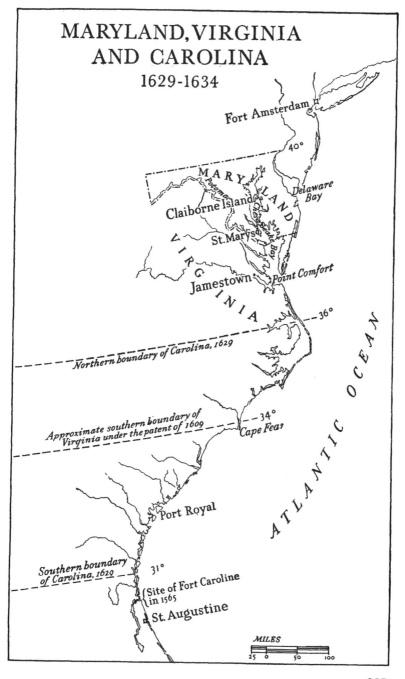

MARYLAND, VIRGINIA
AND CAROLINA
1629-1634

Fort Amsterdam

40°

M A R Y L A N D

Potomac

Claiborne Island

Delaware Bay

St.Marys

Chesapeake Bay

V I R G I N I A

Point Comfort

Jamestown

36°

Northern boundary of Carolina, 1629

A T L A N T I C   O C E A N

Approximate southern boundary of Virginia under the patent of 1609

34°

Cape Fear

Port Royal

Southern boundary of Carolina, 1629

31°

Site of Fort Caroline in 1565

St. Augustine

MILES

25   0   50   100

the Carolina of 1629 included approximately present-day
North Carolina, South Carolina, and Georgia.[3]

It soon developed that the "men large & Plentifull" who
were expected to settle in this new colony were French
Huguenots—refugees in England from the Catholic conquest
of their own country. So here, under the flag of England,
we find French Protestants seeking an asylum on the southern shores of America as in 1562–65 they had attempted to
do under Ribault. Their old Fort Caroline on the St. Johns
River did not quite fall within the new English claim, but
Port Royal, where Ribault had first thought of settling, was
well within its limits.[4]

However, the London merchants who had undertaken the
operation of the new colony defaulted and the expected
settlement did not take place. So neither the stockholders
of the Virginia Company nor the King of Spain had anything to worry about at the moment. None the less this
Carolina grant of 1629 did establish a restricted southern
boundary for Virginia Colony; it did create an English claim
extending to Florida; and it did originate the idea of a
colony to the southward of Virginia—which colony ultimately received the name of Carolina and which became
a refuge for French Huguenots.[5]

In the colonizing activities of George Calvert, Lord Baltimore, the shareholders of the defunct Virginia Company
found a more immediate menace. After his winter in Newfoundland Calvert yearned for warmth, and during his visit
to Virginia in 1629 he had found a climate that suited him.
Upon his return to England he asked the King for a grant
of the land southward from the James River to the new
province of Carolina. The King could have given the land
to Baltimore, just as he had given the southern part of Virginia to Heath, but it would have cut the settled part of the
colony in two. The protests which arose, from the colonists
as well as from the London stockholders, warned the King
to tread warily.[6]

The objections of the Virginia settlers to Baltimore's proposed colony were not wholly based upon economic or political considerations. Baltimore was a Catholic and his avowed

GEORGE CALVERT.
First Lord Baltimore.

Courtesy, Maryland Historical Society, Baltimore.

purpose in establishing the colony was to provide a refuge for his fellow Catholics from the disabilities and persecutions to which they, even more than the Puritans, were subjected in England. The Catholics, like the Puritans, refused to acknowledge the supremacy of the Church of England in matters spiritual—but for quite a different reason. To them the Pope was the supreme head of the Church. Thus they were not only in rebellion against the established Church of England but, since they gave allegiance to the same spiritual leadership as did Spain, they laid themselves open to the suspicion of possible treason to the state. Only by stealth could the average English Catholic attend the celebration of the Mass or receive the consolation of confession. Naturally great numbers yearned for a haven where they, like the Puritans, might worship as they wished. But the settlers on the James River were not prepared to offer such a haven. Most of them adhered to the Church of England; they had some sympathy for the Puritans but none for Catholics and they did not want a Catholic colony next door.

So the King's officials declined Baltimore's first request and told him to look elsewhere. To the north of the James River was plenty of unoccupied land. In fact except for a few slight settlements—by the Dutch in the north and the Virginians in the south—the whole of the great peninsula between Chesapeake Bay and Delaware Bay was unoccupied. This could be carved out of Virginia colony without too great objection, and as a buffer against the encroaching Dutch a colony located there would serve a useful purpose.[7]

Thus the grant was made. The southern tip of the peninsula was reserved to Virginia and to recompense Baltimore for this loss the boundary line was run up the southerly bank of the Potomac rather than up the Chesapeake. The northern boundary was placed at the fortieth parallel, "where," according to the patent, "New-England ends," which is to say, on a line with the present city of Philadelphia. It was a goodly province—to be known as Mary Land.

However, the patent, when it finally passed, was made out not to George Calvert, first Lord Baltimore, but to his son Cecilius Calvert, second Lord Baltimore. George Calvert was dead, at the age of fifty-two, a victim to the hardships of those cold winters in Newfoundland. But the hand of George Calvert, the experienced colonizer, had fashioned the patent for Maryland. This grant marked the first successful application in America of the King's new colonial policy as set forth in 1625. It was made not to a company of merchants or to a group of great men. It was made to one man, who was immediately dependent upon the King.

Except for his dependence upon the King, expressed by the annual delivery at Windsor Castle of two Indian arrows, Cecilius Calvert was absolute in his own province. He paid no taxes or quitrents to the King; he could make laws, appoint officials, dispose of land, collect quitrents, and assess taxes; he could establish courts, provide for churches, and appoint pastors. And to clinch his authority the patent provided "that at all times, and in all things, such Interpretation bee made thereof, and allowed in any of Our Courts whatsoever, as shall be judged most advantagious, and favorable unto the said now Lord Baltemore, his heires and assignes." Such was this remarkable document as it passed the Great Seal on June 20, 1632.[8]

There was nothing in the patent authorizing the establishment of the Catholic church in Maryland, but the powers given were ample to permit the Proprietor to do so, provided he did not persecute those who wished to follow the service of the Church of England.

Young Lord Baltimore assembled his colonists, some two hundred in number, at London. In the late summer of 1633 they were ready to sail on the good ship *Ark* and a pinnace named the *Dove*. Before clearing the Thames River they were required to take the oath of allegiance to the King, which a Catholic could conscientiously do; the anti-papal oath of supremacy apparently was not required. Some of the stricter Catholics probably joined the ships after they left London, thus avoiding even the oath of allegiance. Near Southampton three Jesuit priests were secretly taken aboard, and on November 22 "with a gentle Northerne gale" the expedition headed for the open sea.[9]

Baltimore did not personally accompany the expedition;

in fact, he never came to America. As Governor of his colony the twenty-eight-year-old Proprietor sent his twenty-seven-year-old brother, Leonard Calvert. Associated with the Governor was a still younger brother; also two gentlemen designated as Commissioners. Thirteen others were listed as "adventurers," which is to say that they were investors in the enterprise. All these leaders may be assumed to have been Catholics. The remainder of the two hundred colonists were mostly servants, many of them Church of England people.[10]

Governor Calvert and his Commissioners had been provided with a detailed letter of instructions. The first instruction was one directing them "to preserve unity and peace amongst all the passengers on Shipp-board, and that they suffer no scandall nor offense to be given to any of the Protestants, whereby any just complaint may heereafter be made, by them, in Virginea or in England, and that for that end, they cause all Acts of Romane Catholique Religion to be done as privately as may be, and that they instruct all the Romane Catholiques to be silent upon all occasions of discourse concerning matters of Religion; and that the said Governor and Commissioners treat the Protestants with as much mildness and favor as Justice will permitt. And this to be observed at Land as well as at Sea."[11]

The voyage followed the old southern route—down the coast of Africa, into the trade winds and through the West Indies, the way Captain Newport went to Virginia during the first years of that colony. It is evident that Baltimore was less fearful of the Spanish than of his fellow Englishmen of Virginia. He instructed his brother to keep away from Jamestown and not to get under the guns of the fort at Point Comfort.[12]

Despite the Proprietor's injunction the *Ark* and *Dove* anchored off Point Comfort late in February, 1634. There the colonists were courteously received by Governor Harvey of Virginia, who may have been influenced by a "Butt of sacke" which Leonard Calvert delivered to him as a present from his brother. But whatever Governor Harvey's personal feelings about Lord Baltimore's colony he had no alternative but to be helpful; Calvert had with him letters from the

LEONARD CALVERT.
First Governor of Maryland.
Courtesy, Maryland Historical Society, Baltimore. 221

King commanding the Governor of the older colony to lend all needed assistance to the newcomers.[13]

,While at Point Comfort Calvert and his Commissioners met, for the first but not the last time, Captain William Claiborne, who had a plantation up Chesapeake Bay and who was anything but happy over the prospect of being placed under the government of Lord Baltimore. Claiborne had come to Virginia in 1621 and five years later was appointed a member of the Governor's Council. He was one of those who in 1621 had hastened Lord Baltimore's departure from the colony by demanding that he take the anti-papal oath. He followed Baltimore to England in 1630, where he tried in vain to stop the issuance of the Maryland patent. On his return to Virginia in 1631 Claiborne established his trading plantation on the eastern shore of Chesapeake Bay, from which new political division a representative was promptly received by the Virginia House of Burgesses. As against the patent rights of Lord Baltimore, Claiborne was now prepared to insist upon prior occupation—and most of his fellow members of the Virginia Council were more than willing to back him. To Governor Calvert on his arrival at Point Comfort Claiborne conveyed the unpleasant news that the Indians were up in arms against the new colony—and Calvert suspected that Claiborne was back of the hostility.[14]

After this mixed reception on the threshold of his government Calvert sailed on up Chesapeake Bay and turned in at the mouth of the Potomac. There on the northerly bank of the river the colonists celebrated the Mass, erected a great cross and took possession of the province of Maryland. There Calvert made his peace with the Indians, paid them for the land needed to establish his settlement and named the place St. Mary's. There in the spring of 1634 the government of Maryland was organized; a town was built; and land was allotted to the adventurers. To those who had brought five or more servants a thousand acres or more were assigned. To those who had brought less than five servants, but who had paid for their own transportation, one hundred acres were assigned on account of each person; and for each one hundred acres allotted to them the grantees agreed to pay to the Proprietor an annual quitrent of two shillings.[15]

In Maryland, as in New Netherland and New England—and, in fact, as on every frontier of northern America—furs were an important source of revenue. It was in this field of operations that Calvert and Claiborne first clashed. Claiborne had declined an offer to operate his plantation and his trading business under a license from Lord Baltimore. The Governor was not inclined to attempt an attack on the well-fortified plantation up the Bay, but it was not long before he found an opportunity to show his authority. Several of Claiborne's men were up the Patuxent River—north of St. Mary's—trading with the Indians. Up the river after them went Calvert's men. Their boat and furs and their trade goods were confiscated, and the traders themselves were turned loose to make the best of their way home. Claiborne countered with an attack on Calvert's boats. Both sides appealed to England for support and a long-drawn-out controversy was begun.[16]

Not even Calvert's good friend Governor Harvey of Virginia was long in a position to hold Claiborne under control. In fact, Harvey was having his own troubles. The government of Virginia had been confused ever since the King had taken it in his own hands ten years earlier. First there had been a procession of more or less unofficial governors until Harvey was appointed in 1629. Throughout the period there had been a question as to the right of the Governor to call a general assembly of the House of Burgesses as had been provided by the old Company in 1619. None the less the Burgesses had continued to meet and, together with the Governor and his Council, had passed laws which were accepted within the colony but which might at any time be disavowed by the King.[17]

Governor Harvey had taken the attitude that his Council existed only for the purpose of giving him advice, which advice he might take or not as he pleased. His assistance to the Maryland colony had not increased his popularity. Quarrels with the members of the Council became more and more frequent and, when the Governor attempted to arrest some of them, he was himself placed under arrest by the Council and shipped off to England for trial.[18]

However, young Governor Calvert, in his new province across the Potomac, was amply able to maintain his rights and to take care of his colonists. From Virginia he bought hogs, poultry and cattle. From the Indians he acquired by trade more corn than his people could eat; a thousand bushels were loaded on the *Dove* and sent to Boston to be traded for salt fish. As in Virginia, tobacco soon became the staple crop. Thomas Cornwallis, one of Calvert's Commissioners, evidently tried all other ways of making a living but found them less profitable than "planting this stincking weed of America." [19]

Back in England Lord Baltimore raised funds, and sent supplies and reinforcements. The colony was soon firmly established. King Charles' new colonial policy had justified itself. A single Proprietor, immediately dependent upon the King, had proved more successful and vastly less troublesome than a company made up of merchants and adventurers.

"Against All Opposers"

LATE IN MAY, 1634, the ship *Thunder* sailed into Massachusetts Bay with a cargo of corn and goats from Virginia. From its officers and crew the people at the Bay learned the shocking facts about the new colonists at Maryland—". . . many of them Papists and did set up mass openly." When Baltimore's pinnace arrived a few weeks later to trade for fish it was received courteously enough. However, to its Church of England crew the Puritans of Massachusetts were quite as shocking as the Catholics of Maryland were to the Bay people. The sailors "did revile them, calling them holy brethren . . . and withal did curse and swear most horribly, and use threatening speeches," recorded Winthrop. Only the interference of the tactful Samuel Maverick saved the irreverent seamen from dire punishment at the hands of the outraged magistrates.[1]

Winthrop took part in this incident not as Governor but only as one of the Assistants. He had been voted out of the governorship by the very men whom he had helped to make voters. In fact, a minor revolution had taken place at the Bay. During the first four years of the colony's existence Winthrop and the half dozen Assistants—all that were in New England—had kept the government closely within their hands. They had ruled that the Governor could be elected only from among the Assistants and that laws could be made only by the Governor and Assistants.

From time to time Deputy-governor Dudley had challenged this procedure but had been overruled. Then, as the time approached for the meeting of the General Court in May, 1634, a deputation of freemen from each of the towns called upon Winthrop and demanded to see the patent. From that document they learned that four General Courts should have been held each year and that only at those courts, with themselves present, should laws have been made.

Winthrop, who had no high opinion of popular government, sensed the coming storm and tried to avert it. He called John Cotton, a much-respected minister, to the rescue with a sermon setting forth from Biblical authority that "a magistrate ought not to be turned into the condition of a private man without just cause"—but all in vain. The freemen had the power and they used it. Thomas Dudley was elected Governor and Roger Ludlow was advanced from an Assistant to the place of Deputy-governor. It was ordered that in the future Courts should be held and laws made as directed by the patent—with all the freemen present at the annual Court of Elections and with deputies from each of the towns present at the other three General Courts. Massachusetts was developing a system of popular representative government.[2]

Back in England, too, the welfare of the colonists was being thought about—but not in a way that commended itself to the leaders at the Bay. Gorges and Mason had at last forced their complaints to the attention of the King, and at just about the time that the freemen of Massachusetts were compelling their leaders to conform to the King's patent the King was appointing a Commission for Regulating Plantations. This body was headed by William Laud, Archbishop of Canterbury, and came to be known as the Laud Commission, or by the Bay people as "the archbishops." It was instructed to oversee the "rule and cure of the soules" of the colonists; to "ordain temporal judges and civill magistrates"; to "hear and determine all complaints . . . whether it be against the whole colonies themselves or any governor or officer of the same." More particularly the Commission was given authority over "letters patents and other writeings whatsoever . . . for or concerning the planting of any colonies . . . and if, upon view thereof, the same shall appear to . . . have been surreptitiously and unduly obtained, or that any privileges or liberties therein granted, be hurtful to us, our crown or prerogative royall . . . to cause the same, according to the laws and customs of our realm of England, to be revoked." All of this was aimed straight at Massachusetts Bay.[3]

Well may Thomas Morton have boasted, from London, that he had "struck the brethren into astonishment." Here appeared to be the end of the Congregational form of church organization; here appeared to be the end of any governors elected by the people of the Bay; here appeared to be the end of the Massachusetts Bay patent and of all land titles based upon it; here appeared to be a complete vindication of the overall authority of the Council for New England.[4]

First-hand news of what was going on reached the Bay in June, 1634, with the arrival of John Humphry, he who just two years before had started the trouble by telling the Council that the Massachusetts Bay Company had a patent from the Council and a confirmation from the King. He now came to the Bay bearing in one hand an urgent request from former Governor Cradock for the return of the patent and in the other hand a large consignment of ammunition.[5]

Cradock, a rich merchant of London, was in a tight place. The Laud Commission could lay its hands upon him. Without the actual patent as an exhibit to justify his actions, he stood charged with having exceeded his authority. The leaders at the Bay were in a very different position. They had the patent in their possession; their persons and their estates were beyond the immediate reach of anything the Commission could enforce; and they did not propose to surrender any of these advantages.

There is no question as to the purpose of the ammunition which Humphry brought with him. It was intended for use against the Mother Country—"dear England"—if she tried to take the patent by force. The Governor and Assistants returned a soft and evasive answer to the "archbishops" and proceeded with all haste to mount guns at strategic points in the harbor, to train the men in the use of arms, and to set up lookout stations to signal the approach of any suspicious ships.[6]

There were at this time twelve towns clustered around Massachusetts Bay. To the fifteen hundred inhabitants of 1630 each incoming ship had added. In the single month of June, 1634, fifteen "great ships" had arrived. It is estimated that by 1635 there were about eight thousand people in the Bay towns. The population had outgrown the available land; Newtown (Cambridge) was already casting about for more space in which to pasture its cattle. The crowded towns began to look longingly toward the fertile Connecticut Valley, where New Plymouth and the Dutch had their trading houses.[7]

Interest in this rich country to the westward was heightened when in the autumn of 1634 messengers from the Pequot Indians, one of the warring tribes of the region, came to Deputy-governor Ludlow and offered "all their right at Connecticut" if the Bay people would establish a plantation there. Nothing came of the proposal at the moment but it unquestionably had its influence later.[8]

And to the teeming population of the Bay an important addition was under consideration. Lord Say, father-in-law of the Earl of Lincoln, and Lord Brook, another prominent nobleman, had for some time been operating a small plantation on the Piscataqua River. Apparently the project was not very promising nor was the character of the people all that the pious proprietors might have desired. Captain Wiggin, who was in charge, complained that two of his men "had committed sodomy with each other, and that on the Lord's day, in time of public exercise."[9]

When Humphry came over in the summer of 1634, he brought "certain propositions from some persons of great quality and estate, (and of special note for piety,) whereby they discovered their intentions to join with us, if they might receive satisfaction therein." These persons were doubtless Lord Say and Lord Brook and their associates. Certainly

they did not have in mind joining their Piscataqua plantation with the Bay; it lay within Mason's province of New
Hampshire. Whether they intended settling at the Bay itself
or whether they had already hit upon a plan for settling in
the Connecticut region and joining it with the Bay is uncertain. However, within a few months they, together with
Sir Richard Saltonstall, John Humphry and several others,
turned up with a purported deed to the Connecticut country.
This deed was said to be from the Earl of Warwick and to
have been executed on March 19, 1632. The date was important since Warwick's right to dispose of the land depended upon a presumed grant to him by the Council for
New England—and subsequent to the unhappy meetings of
June, 1632 (see page 206), he had not been associated with
the Council.[10]

One difficulty at once arises. There is no record indicating
that the Council at any time granted Connecticut to the
Earl. He did, however, have the seal of the Council in his
possession on March 19, 1632, and he might have passed a
patent to himself although such an action would have been
highly irregular. He is quoted as having said that he proposed taking out some such patent. Also, it will be recalled
that, when in June, 1632, the other members of the Council
demanded from him a statement as to the patents which
had been passed, he declined an answer and withdrew from
their meetings. Be the facts what they may, no such patent
from the Council has ever come to light nor has Warwick's
so-called patent to Lords Say and Brook survived except in
a very questionable copy.[11]

The similarity between this Connecticut patent of 1632
and the Massachusetts patent of 1628 is too striking to be
overlooked. In both cases title was based upon questionable
and probably nonexisting patents to Warwick from the Council. In both cases the supposed patents from Warwick to the
grantees failed to appear when needed and failed to come
to light afterward. And in both cases nonconformist colonies
were the benefactors.

From these coincidences it may be assumed that the Earl
of Warwick was at least favorably inclined toward those

THE EARL OF WARWICK.
From a painting by Anthony van Dyck.
Courtesy, The Metropolitan Museum of Art, New York.

who for conscience sake were founding colonies in America. It was he who in 1630 had signed the long-delayed patent from the Council to the New Plymouth people, which document went out of its way to note that this pioneer nonconforming colony had prospered by "the Speciall Providence of God." Nor can it be charged that Warwick's aid to these colonies was based on mercenary ends. The ruthlessness with which he had looted Virginia fifteen years earlier nowhere appears. Simultaneously with the demand from the Laud Commission for the return of the Bay patent Winthrop records the receipt of a letter from Warwick in which he "congratulated the prosperity of our plantation, and encouraged our proceedings, and offered his help to further us in it." Such an offer from the wealthy and capable Earl was encouragement indeed. If cannon had to roar in Boston harbor, the Bay people would not be without friends in high places.[12]

And the time was at hand for a showdown between the Council for New England and her strange, lusty offspring at Massachusetts Bay. The action opened in London, where on February 3, 1635, the Council parceled out to each of its eight existing members a piece of the land covered by its patent. Captain Mason was given the area from Salem to the Piscataqua—which restored to his province of New Hampshire the slice taken off by the Massachusetts patent. Sir Ferdinando Gorges received from the Piscataqua to the Kennebec—his province of Maine. Sir William Alexander, now the Earl of Stirling, got from the Pemaquid to the St. Croix, but since the French were at this time successfully challenging all English activity east of the Pemaquid, Long Island was thrown in for good measure. The other parcels need not particularly concern us as nothing ever came of them, although it is of interest to note that Lord Gorges, a relative of Sir Ferdinando, received Massachusetts Bay and Plymouth—take them if he could.[13]

Having thus divided up the coast, the Council surrendered its patent to the King and asked that separate patents for the separate parcels be granted to the respective recipients —to be held directly from the King according to the colonial policy then being developed.

But here the scheme struck a snag. The Massachusetts Bay patent was still in the hands of the Bay people. Until that document was out of the way, the Crown could hardly put the proposed arrangement into effect. And since the Bay leaders would not return their patent for cancellation and since the King was not prepared to go and get it, the only procedure seemed to be a legal action aimed at annulling it. The records of the Council for May 5, 1635, contain the following minute: "Thomas Morton is now entertained to be Sollicitor . . . to prosecute suite at Law for the repealing of the Patent belonging to the Massachusetts Company." Shortly afterward the Attorney-general issued a writ of *quo warranto* (by what warrant are you doing what you are doing) against the patentees of the Bay Company, and the case was calendered for the King's Bench.[14]

On the day following the meeting of the Council in London, as noted above, the quarterly court of Massachusetts met at New Town (Cambridge) for the election of officers and other business. The freemen were, if anything, in a more insurgent frame of mind than the previous year when they had thrown Winthrop out of the governorship. Roger Ludlow, Deputy-governor and leading candidate for the governorship, was their target this time. He, even more than Winthrop, was unsympathetic to the growing attempts of the freemen to overrule the Governor and Assistants, and he said so with vigor. As a result he was not only defeated for the governorship but was voted out as an Assistant. "The reason was partly because the people would exercise their absolute power," commented Winthrop.[15]

The sequel came fast. Ludlow resigned all of his offices, including that of supervising the erection of fortifications in the Bay. The town of Dorchester, of which he was the leading man, asked to be allowed to remove from the Bay. And a few weeks later Ludlow, with a group of his fellow townsmen, was searching up and down the Connecticut River for a suitable place to establish a new settlement. In the end they pitched upon a spot just above the New Plymouth trading house and there, to the unconcealed dismay of the previous comers, proceeded to lay out a town which took the name of Windsor.[16]

Close on Ludlow's heels came still another group of settlers sent from England by Sir Richard Saltonstall under the
authority of the so-called patent from the Earl of Warwick
(see pages 228–229). Ludlow and his men made short work
of this competition and appear to have been none too polite
about it. Saltonstall's agent explained why his men did not
take up the desired land—they "darst not laye it out . . .
Mr. Ludloe was the cheffe man that hindered it." We get
more of the details from Saltonstall's subsequent protest
against "some abuse and injurie done me by Mr. Ludlowe
& others of Dorchester, who would not suffer Frances Styles
& his men to impall grounde where I appointed them att
Connecticut. . . ." Saltonstall goes on to say that at the time
Styles, his manager, arrived, the "Dorchester men, being then
unsettled, & seekeing up the River above the falls for a place
to plant upon, butt findeing none better to there likeing, they
speedily came backe againe & discharged my worke men,
casteing lotts upon that place, where he was purposed to
begine his worcke; notwithstanding that he often tould them
what great charge I had beene att in sending him & so many
men, to prepare a house against my coming, & enclose
grounde for my cattle, and how the damage would fall heavie
upon those that thus hindered me, whom Francis Styles conceived to have best right to make choyse of any place there.
Notwithstanding, they resisted hime, slighteing me with
many unbeseeming words. . . ."[17]

At about the same time similar groups of pioneers from
two other Bay towns were founding new settlements on the
Connecticut. Those from New Town (Cambridge) laid out
their town, soon to be known as Hartford, squarely beside
the Dutch trading house. Those from Watertown established
themselves a few miles below and shortly took the name of
Wethersfield. Such were the beginnings of the Three River
Towns from which grew the colony and state of Connecticut.[18]

New Plymouth, having no alternative, sold its Connecticut
trading house to the Windsor people and called it quits, although, as Bradford observed, "the unkindnes not so soone
forgotten." At Hartford the House of Hope was permitted

to remain in the hands of its Dutch managers, but its ultimate fate was a foregone conclusion.[19]

To the southward the Dutch were more successful in warding off the crowding English. After the expulsion of Governor Harvey from Virginia, a number of Claiborne's associates in the fur trade reached the conclusion that it would be easier to compete with the Dutch in Delaware Bay than with the fiery young brother of Lord Baltimore in the Chesapeake. Accordingly at about the same time that the men from Massachusetts were swarming into the Connecticut country an expedition sailed northward from Virginia, headed by one George Holmes, and took possession of the unoccupied Fort Nassau, situated opposite the modern city of Philadelphia. This was too much even for the easygoing Governor van Twiller. A well-armed boat was promptly dispatched from New Amsterdam; the English traders were rounded up and, after a brief captivity, were returned to Virginia with the compliments of the Dutch West India Company.[20]

And in London at just about the time that, on the Connecticut River, his men were being "resisted" and he was being "slighted with many unbeseeming words," Saltonstall and his associates were signing a commission making John Winthrop's son, also named John, "governor of the river Connecticut, with the places adjoining thereunto, for, and during the space of one whole year, after his arrival there." Some days earlier this same group had entered into an agreement with young Winthrop by which he was to repair to the Connecticut River with all convenient speed and secure men for the "making of fortifications, and building of houses at the river Connecticut, and the harbour adjoining, first for their own present accommodations, and then such houses as may receive men of quality, which latter houses we would have to be builded within the fort." The authority which lay back of all this was the questionable deed (see pages 229 and 233) from the Earl of Warwick to Say, Brook, Saltonstall, and others.[21]

Also in London during the autumn of 1635 Saltonstall's fellow patentees of the Massachusetts Bay Company—all of them that were within reach of the law—were one by one appearing before the King's Bench. There at the behest of Thomas Morton, who five years earlier had sat in the bilboes at Massachusetts Bay, they humbly made their pleas. Each and every one solemnly disclaimed any rights or responsibilities under the Bay patent. That was all they could do since they had nothing to prove their rights. The document that would have given them a defense was in the hands of the patentees at the Bay—and those patentees ignored the summons to appear in England and plead to the complaint.[22]

Early in October Winthrop, Jr., armed with his new commission, arrived at Boston and within the month dispatched men to the mouth of the Connecticut to take possession and begin the fort—which Lion Gardiner, a capable soldier and engineer, undertook to complete by the following spring. They arrived none too soon. The Dutch, too, had sent a force to take possession and build a fort at the river's mouth. However, Winthrop's men got a couple of cannon ashore, and when the Dutch boat came up, the Englishmen were firmly in possession. In honor of their two most distinguished backers, Lord Say and Lord Brook, they named the place Saybrook.[23]

Thus, in the late autumn of 1635, we find two different groups of English colonizers in the Connecticut country: forty miles up the river were the three closely associated towns of Windsor, Hartford, and Wethersfield—without a shadow of a title beyond their own good right; at the river's mouth were the Saybrook people—with a title of about the same validity as that which at that very time was being torn to shreds before the King's Bench in London.

Winter closed in early and hard that autumn of 1635. Starvation seemed inevitable for any who remained at the River Towns. Most of the pioneer settlers, leaving their cattle to the mercy of the weather and the wolves, broke a channel down the icy river and fled back to the Bay.[24]

Far to the northward on the St. Lawrence River the deadening cold also took its toll. In a dreary room of the tumbled-down fort of Quebec Samuel de Champlain, the Father of New France, breathed his last on Christmas Day, a day no different from any other to the shivering Puritans at Massachusetts Bay.

Champlain died content in the belief that a quest which he had followed for more than a quarter of a century had at last succeeded—a water route had been found through the continent. Too old himself longer to stand the hard life of the bark canoe and the Indian cabin he had trained as his successor in discovery the youthful Jean Nicolet. In a large canoe with seven Indian paddlers, Nicolet had started on his momentous trip from the Jesuit Mission on Lake Huron in the summer of 1634. He had some idea of where he was going but only the vaguest notion of the kind of people he was going to find. The eastern Indians called them "the people of the sea"; they might be Orientals; just to be prepared Nicolet took along "a grand robe of China damask, all strewn with flowers and birds of many colors."

Hugging the northern shore of Lake Huron, Nicolet passed the outlet of Lake Superior and, heading westward through the Strait of Michilimackinac, came into another great inland lake—later known as Michigan. Holding along its western shore, he entered a broad inlet which today we call Green Bay—on the eastern shore of Wisconsin. At the head of this bay Nicolet found the strange people whom he had come all this way to visit. They turned out to be only Indians, but from them he learned that by a short portage farther up the river he could transfer his canoe to another river which ran westerly to the sea. He had in fact found the Fox-Wisconsin water connection between the St. Lawrence and the Gulf of Mexico, the linking of which by missions and forts became the dream of later French explorers. Champlain, on hearing Nicolet's report, assumed that the river of the west emptied into the Pacific, and that the wealth of the Indies was within the grasp of his country.[25]

While Champlain, in Quebec, was fighting for a few more days of life, Captain John Mason, the strong man of the Council for New England, died in London. He, probably even more than Gorges, had pushed the fight against the Bay patent. In his own province of New Hampshire he had erected sawmills and was building up herds of fine cattle.

Nicolet's meeting with "the people of the sea."
From a painting by E. W. Deming at the Wisconsin State Historical
Society, Madison.

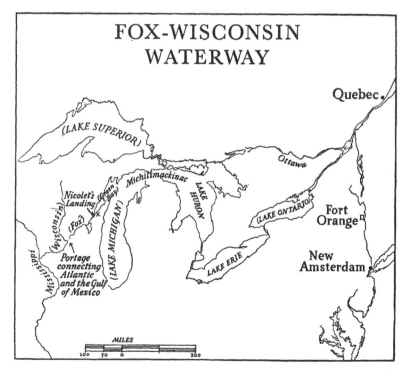

FOX-WISCONSIN
WATERWAY

Quebec.

(LAKE SUPERIOR)

Ottawa

Michilimackinac

Nicolet's
Landing
(Green Bay)

LAKE
HURON

(LAKE ONTARIO)

Fort
Orange

(Fox)

(LAKE MICHIGAN)

(Wisconsin)

New
Amsterdam

Portage
connecting
Atlantic
and the Gulf
of Mexico

LAKE ERIE

Mississippi

MILES
100 50 0   200

His death was a distinct setback to the development of the Piscataqua region—and with him died the Laconia project. However, the leaders at the Bay saw a certain providence in the matter. "He was the chief mover in all the attempts against us," wrote Winthrop, ". . . but the Lord, in mercy, taking him away, all the business fell on sleep." [26]

South of Massachusetts and in the hinterland of New Plymouth, one of the Bay's leading ministers, shivering with cold that he could feel in his bones thirty years later, was spending that terrible winter of 1635–36 in the smoke-filled wigwams of the Narragansett Indians. Roger Williams, thirty-two years old and a graduate of Cambridge University, had arrived at the Bay early in 1631—"a godly minister," Winthrop had recorded at the time. However, his pronounced separatist opinions soon made Williams unacceptable at the Bay, and he retired to New Plymouth, where he was welcomed as "teacher" in the Pilgrim church.

Two years later Williams received a call from Salem—to take the place of Francis Higginson, who had died. It will be recalled that in forming this church Higginson modeled it upon the Separatist church of New Plymouth, while the congregations subsequently organized at the Bay had followed a form less deliberately antagonistic to the Church of England. As the years went by, the difference between Salem and the other towns had widened. Nor did the teachings of Williams tend to heal the rift. Particularly his insistence that church and state should be separate and that the Indians were the real owners of the land infuriated the magistrates. After all other means of silencing him had failed, the General Court acted. On September 3, 1635, sentence was passed; "Whereas Mr. Roger Williams, one of the elders of the church of Salem, hath broached & dyvulged dyvers newe & dangerous opinions, against the aucthoritie of magistrates, as also writt letters of defamation, both of magistrates & churches here, & that before any conviction, & yet maintaineth the same without retraction, it is therefore ordered, that the said Mr. Williams shall departe out of this jurisdiction within sixe weekes. . . ."

Somewhat later the Court relented slightly and Williams

was given liberty to stay on at Salem until the spring of 1636 provided he kept quiet. But it was impossible for him to keep quiet. When he did not speak in the church, the people of Salem flocked to his house to listen to him. The magistrates decided that the only solution was to ship him off to England. But when the officers arrived, he was gone.

With one or two companions, Roger Williams was fleeing southward towards the Narragansett country. "I was sorely tossed for one fourteen weeks, in a bitter winter season, not knowing what bed or bread did mean," he recorded. But he was not wholly without friends. The Indians who had known and liked him during his stay at New Plymouth did what they could for him; other exiles from the Bay joined him; and as the winter lengthened into spring, the little group of wanderers came to rest at a point of land near the head of Narragansett Bay—only a few miles from where the Reverend Blackstone was living. In a straggling line along the shore Williams and his friends began building a town to which in recognition of God's mercy in bringing them safely through the wilderness they gave the name of Providence. Such was the beginning of Rhode Island.[27]

Around their warm firesides at the Bay that winter the leaders of the River Towns of Connecticut and the agents for the Saybrook project worked out a formula that satisfied their respective claims. The decision reached was that until Say and Brook proved their title the River Towns would proceed with their settlements. This was about the only solution possible since the River Towns were evidently going ahead anyhow; Ludlow had given Saltonstall their answer the previous summer.[28]

The fact remained however that the River Towns had no authority from any source to justify their existence or to confirm the lands which they might improve. They were clearly outside the bounds of the Bay. They made no claim of a patent from the Council for New England; nor could they hope for such a grant now that the Council had surrendered its own patent. The only legal titleholders to the Connecticut country were the individual members of the Council to whom the various parcels had been allotted when the

Council was dissolved—and they had made no move to have their allotments confirmed by the King.

To meet this situation the magistrates at the Bay, without committing themselves as to their authority, recognized that "where there are a people to sitt down & cohabite, there will followe, upon occasion, some cause of difference, as also dyvers misdeameanors, which will require a speedy redresse." On this basis of necessity the Court then commissioned Roger Ludlow and seven other men with "full power & aucthoritie to hear & determine in a judiciall way" at the River Towns. On April 26, 1636, at Hartford, five of these men met as a court, thus establishing a government which has continued for over three hundred years and whose direct descendant is the present-day General Assembly of the State of Connecticut.

Meanwhile, as the ice broke up in the Connecticut River, the pioneers of Windsor, Hartford, and Wethersfield returned to their half-finished buildings and famished cattle. They laid out their towns after the manner customary at the Bay—compact villages with houses on small home lots, the larger fields at a distance, and the pasture lands in common.[29]

In some cases the families of the settlers came overland from the Bay bringing herds of cattle and their household goods with them. Most of the traffic, however, was by boat —around Cape Cod, into Long Island Sound, and up the river. All through the spring, summer and autumn of 1636 things were humming at the River Towns, with boats coming and going, houses being built and land being brought into use.

At the river's mouth affairs were not going so well. The commission to young Winthrop had expired. No new governor had been appointed. Lion Gardiner, commander of the fort, pictured the situation in the following words, "Heare hath come many vessels with provison, to goe up to the plantations [i.e., the River Towns], but none for us. It seems that wee have neather masters nor owners, but are left like soe many servaunts whose masters are willinge to be quitt of them."[30]

One of the many boats that had been at Connecticut that

summer ran into a tragedy on its way back to the Bay. At Block Island, near the mouth of Narragansett Bay, John Oldham's trading pinnace was sighted with a number of Indians aboard but no sign of Oldham. A prompt attack scattered the savages, and in the bottom of the boat was found the hacked and mutilated body of the veteran trader. Thus passed one of the most picturesque characters of early New England—the man who had come to grips with New Plymouth in 1624, who had traded at the Bay before the Massachusetts colony had been thought of, and who was but thirty-six years of age at the time of his death.[31]

The Bay moved promptly to avenge Oldham's murder. With a hundred men in five boats, Captain Endecott descended upon Block Island. Unable to catch the Indians, he burned their wigwams and their corn and shot a few dogs. Then, since the Pequots had also committed some outrages against English traders, Endecott paid a visit to their towns —on the Connecticut shore near present-day New London— and repeated the performance.[32]

Naturally this treatment stirred the warlike Pequots to retaliation, and they took it out on the River Settlements. At Wethersfield they killed nine people and captured two girls. With the bloody clothing of their victims held aloft on poles, and with their two captives prominently displayed, they paraded in canoes past Saybrook fort, whose garrison was forced to stand and take the gibe "You are all one like women."[33]

It was life or death for the new settlements. On May 1, 1637, the General Court of the three squatter towns up the river "ordered that there shalbe an offensive warr against the Pequoitt, and that there shalbe 90 men levied out of the 3 Plantations, Harteford, Weathersfeild & Windsor. . . ." It was the act of a sovereign state; the high Parliament of England could not have done it better. Down the river went the Connecticut men. At Saybrook they were joined by a force sent from the Bay. Sailing up the Sound, they surrounded one of the Pequot forts. The rest was simply a massacre. The English were armed with guns and swords and protected by armor. The Indians were armed with bows and arrows and their only protection was a palisade around their flimsy wigwams. This structure was soon fired and "Many were burnt in the fort, both men, women, and children." Those that ran out were "entertained with the point of the sword. . . . Great and doleful was the bloody sight . . . to see so many souls lie gasping on the ground, so thick, in some places, that you could hardly pass along," recorded Captain Underhill, but he assures us that, "We had sufficient light from the word of God for our proceedings." [34]

The surviving Pequots fled westward along the coast, followed by the men from the River Towns. For seventy miles the grim chase went on, and then the wornout Indian women and children surrendered while the men stood at bay and fought it out—falling one by one in the unequal battle. It was the end of the Pequots as a tribe. There would be no more native resistance to the settlement of Connecticut.

Among the participants in this pursuit of the Indians was Roger Ludlow, forty-seven years old; an Oxford graduate; former lawyer of the Inner Temple, London; late Deputy-governor of Massachusetts and now the leading magistrate of the River Towns. To his brothers and cousins back in Wiltshire, England, the adventure would have seemed an odd one. To Ludlow the fair fields surrounding the thicket where the Pequots made their last stand proved attractive, and within two years he founded a new settlement there which took the name of Fairfield. [35]

At practically the same time that the River Towns were making their declaration of war against the Pequots the King's Bench in London was delivering its judgment in the case against the Massachusetts Bay patent. It was a complete victory for Gorges and Morton. All rights under the patent were annulled and the document itself was ordered to be delivered to the Attorney-general for cancellation. A few weeks later the King issued a manifesto taking the whole government of New England into his own hands and appointing Gorges Governor-general. [36]

So there it was—everything settled in an orderly and legal way. All Sir Ferdinando Gorges had to do was to go over to New England and take charge. But the Bay people still

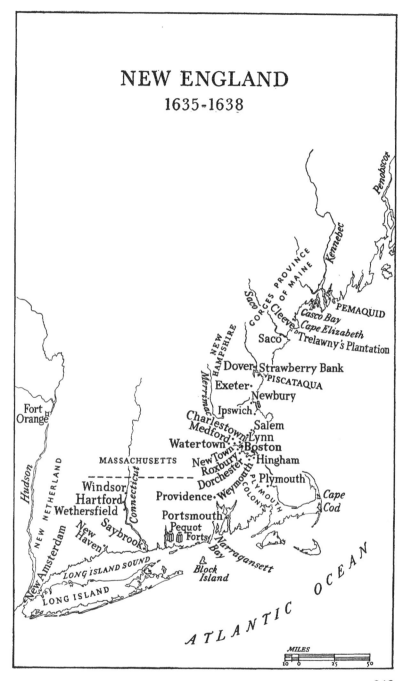

NEW ENGLAND
1635-1638

Penobscot

Kennebec

GORGES PROVINCE OF MAINE

Saco

Cleeve

PEMAQUID

Casco Bay

Cape Elizabeth

Saco

Trelawny's Plantation

NEW HAMPSHIRE

Merrimac

Dover · Strawberry Bank

Exeter ·

PISCATAQUA

Newbury

Ipswich ·

Charlestown

Medford

Salem

Watertown

Lynn

NewTown

Boston

MASSACHUSETTS

Roxbury

Hingham

Fort Orange

Dorchester

Plymouth

Hudson

NEW NETHERLAND

Windsor

Hartford

Wethersfield

Connecticut

Providence ·

Weymouth

PLYMOUTH COLONY

Cape Cod

New Haven

Saybrook

Portsmouth

Pequot Forts

New Amsterdam

LONG ISLAND SOUND

Block Island

Narragansett Bay

LONG ISLAND

ATLANTIC OCEAN

MILES
10 0   25   50

243

had the patent in their possession, and so long as they could keep it, it was valid, court decisions or no court decisions. To get the patent the prospective Governor-general would have to bring more men and more guns than were waiting at the Bay—and Gorges could not bring them. Nor could the King help him. The first faint rumblings of an approaching civil war were growing every day more distinct in England. The King having refused to summon a Parliament had received none of the customary grants of money, and his subjects were resisting what they considered illegal attempts to raise funds. In the end Gorges accepted a royal patent for his province of Maine—from the Piscataqua to the Kennebec —and left the rest of New England to get along as best it could.[37]

Among the patentees of the Bay Company still in England during the trial was Theophilus Eaton, a wealthy London merchant. He, like Cradock and the rest, had appeared before the King's Bench and there disclaimed all rights under the patent. Now in the spring of 1637 Eaton arrived at Massachusetts Bay at the head of a group reminiscent of the great migration of 1630. They came in a chartered ship; they were closely connected by ties of blood, of business and of church membership. Among them were several men of considerable means; with them were their families and household servants; prominent among them was the Reverend John Davenport, their former minister, who on account of his pronounced nonconformist views had been forced out of his church in London.

The leaders at the Bay made every effort to persuade this group to remain there; but Eaton, fresh from his experience at the King's Bench, seemingly had less confidence in the future of the Bay than was manifested by those who had faced the King's displeasure at a distance. In fact, in the summer of 1637 it was far from evident to any one that Massachusetts would get off without severe censure. The Eaton group decided to look around a bit before they settled down.

At just this time the men who had been to the west in pursuit of the Pequots were returning to their homes. They brought highly favorable reports of the land beyond Say-brook. Eaton and his associates made up an exploring party and went to see for themselves. At the mouth of a river called the Quinnipiac they found a harbor which seemed suitable for the commercial enterprises which they had in mind carrying on. And there in the spring of 1638 Eaton, Davenport and the others founded a town which soon came to be known as New Haven.

The New Haven people bought their land from the Indians—whether because of Roger Williams' doctrine or whether from their own innate goodness. They joined in a covenant of faith and organized a church—in the best Congregational manner. They agreed upon a form of government in which only the church members could vote—as was the rule at the Bay. Until they could build more permanent homes they dug caves in the ground and covered them over with earth. Michael Wigglesworth, later famous for some terrible poetry, but at the time a boy of seven, recalled that his family "dwelt in a cellar partly underground" and that "one great rain brake in upon us and drencht me so in my bed being asleep that I fell sick. . . ." [38]

Other New England frontiers were also being established during that summer of 1638. Back of it all lay the spirit of separatism that had brought the first nonconformist colony to New Plymouth eighteen years earlier. Those who for conscience sake had left their comfortable homes in England and migrated to a strange, savage land did not hesitate to extend the same privilege to those who differed with them. The Bay towns had more than the usual proportion of men and women of intellectual capacity, curiosity and certainty —which found no outlet but in the field of religion. Sermons were discussed in the utmost detail and niceties of doctrine developed beyond a point comprehensible to the twentieth-century mind.

Outstanding among the lady intellectuals was Anne Hutchinson. In the manner of later-day literary clubs she took to assembling the ladies of Boston at her house and there discussing the sermon of the previous Sabbath. Soon she began to expound her own doctrine—which turned out to be slightly unorthodox as orthodoxy had been established in Boston. Many prominent people, including some of the ministers, supported her views, but when pressure was brought to bear by the magistrates—Winthrop was again Governor—all of the ministers turned against her except her brother-in-law, the Reverend John Wheelwright. After attempts at persuasion had failed, Mrs. Hutchinson and Mr. Wheelwright were brought before the General Court and sentenced to banishment. When Mrs. Hutchinson asked the Governor on what grounds the sentence was based, he replied, "Say no more, the court knows wherefore and is satisfied." [39]

And that was that. Wheelwright, forty-five years of age and a graduate of Cambridge University, plunged northward into the winter as two years earlier Roger Williams had plunged southward under similar circumstances. A few miles beyond the Massachusetts line, in the province of New Hampshire, he bought land from the Indians; his family and a few friends joined him; and the town of Exeter came into being. [40]

Mrs. Hutchinson, being in delicate health, was given a reprieve until the following spring. However, all who had supported her religious doctrines were looked upon as potential enemies of the established government at the Bay. In fact, the controversy had created a serious rift in the colony. It probably had some influence upon the decision of Eaton and Davenport to settle their people outside the jurisdiction of the Bay. It was directly responsible for the departure of several men hitherto prominent in the affairs of the colony. William Coddington, who had been elected an Assistant in the place of Eaton just before the Winthrop fleet sailed in 1630 and who had served the colony with distinction during the seven years since his arrival at the Bay, was among those who had openly spoken in favor of Mrs. Hutchinson. In March, 1638, he, together with several others, was given an unsolicited "licence to depart" or "to answear such things as shalbee objected." They departed. [41]

Sailing around Cape Cod and up Narragansett Bay, Coddington and his friends called on Roger Williams at the new settlement of Providence. There through the good offices of

Williams they bought from the Indians the island of Aquid-
neck (Rhode Island) and on its northern end started laying
out a town to which they gave the name of Portsmouth.
At about the same time Mrs. Hutchinson and her husband
and friends arrived at Providence, having traveled overland from the Bay. They and others joined Coddington at
Portsmouth and the new town began to hum with life.

But even here Mrs. Hutchinson was not wholly forgotten
by the Bay. Strange stories began to circulate in Boston. At
his regular mid-week religious lecture John Cotton, Mrs.
Hutchinson's former minister, stated that instead of the expected child she had been delivered of a monster—which,
said the minister, "might signify her error in denying in-
herent righteousness." Stories of this sort always interested
Governor Winthrop, so he wrote to the lady's attending
physician and asked for the details. He got them in great
and nauseous quantity although not confirmatory of the al-
leged monstrous birth. "Mr. Cotton, next lecture day, acknowledged his error," the Governor informs us. Apparently
it did not occur to either Winthrop or Cotton that the treatment to which they had subjected the lady might have accounted for what happened.[12]

Nor would it have occurred to any of them, even Mrs.
Hutchinson, that a question of personal privacy was involved.
In these small communities every one knew everything about
every one else and discussed all of it with almost every one.
For example, Captain Underhill was first "privately dealt
with upon suspicion of incontinency with a neighbor's wife,
and not hearkening to it, was publicly questioned, and put
under admonition." Not even the Captain's explanation that
the young lady "was in great trouble of mind, and sore temp-
tations, and that he resorted to her to comfort her; and that
when the door was found locked upon them, they were in
private prayer together," fully satisfied the community. The
fact that Captain Underhill had joined in defense of Mrs.
Hutchinson and was soon to follow Wheelwright northward
may have had something to do with this questioning of his
behavior. The leaders at the Bay, like Bradford at Plymouth,
had a way of producing unfortunate evidence against those

who had the temerity to disagree with their decisions.[43]

As in 1635 and 1636 Massachusetts had lost able men to Connecticut for political and economic reasons, so now she lost a steady stream of people to New Hampshire and the Rhode Island region for religious reasons. Particularly did Providence and Portsmouth become refuges for those who would not accept the theocratic establishment at the Bay: government based upon the Word of God as interpreted by the ministers; and the ministers expected to interpret the Word in a way that conformed to the administrative policies of the magistrates.

Nor is it easy to see how the Bay could have compromised with these discordant elements in her population and still have preserved the purpose for which the colony had been founded. The Bay people had come to New England at great expense and great sacrifice to create a government under which *they* could live and worship as *they* wished. They had not expended their fortunes and left their homes in England to create a refuge for those who differed from themselves. Those who could not or would not conform to the "New England way" could not be tolerated at the Bay. Old Thomas Dudley, one of the founders of the colony and always a sound man among the magistrates, phrased it thus:

> "Let men of God in courts and churches watch
> O'er such as do a toleration hatch,
> Lest that ill egg bring forth a cockatrice
> To poison all with heresy and vice."

The lines may lack something in literary elegance but they tell us what the man who had put the Earl of Lincoln's affairs on a paying basis thought about tolerating tolerance.[44]

Most of those who, for religious reasons, were forced out of the Bay had for similar reasons been forced out of England. In the Rhode Island towns the clash of their strangely assorted doctrines created a clamor out of all proportion to their numbers or importance. Along with such truly liberal thinkers as Roger Williams was the man who insisted that women had no souls, and another who maintained that even the elect had the devil dwelling within them side by side with the Holy Ghost—an idea that could not be tolerated by the elect of the Bay except possibly as applying to such a case as Captain Underhill. Accounts of these strange, contending doctrines, drifting back to England, brought discredit upon all Puritan New England.[45]

In 1638 King Charles approved the preparation of a proclamation forbidding the transportation of any more people to New England except by license, on the ground that the people already there were of a "factious disposition . . . unfit and unworthie . . . of any support or Countenance from hence, in respect of the great disorders and want of Government amongst them."[46] It will be of interest to run down the New England coast and determine to what extent the King's statement was justified.

All of present-day Maine eastward of the Penobscot was dominated by the French. The English plantations began at Pemaquid. There Abraham Shurt ruled over a fur-trading post owned by English merchants. With the Council for New England dissolved and the Earl of Stirling, to whom it had been assigned, making no move to take control, the settlement came under the direct authority of the King. So far as government was concerned, Shurt bossed the post as a good and capable manager for his employers, and the inhabitants did what he told them to do.

From the Kennebec to the Piscataqua lay Sir Ferdinando Gorges' Province of Maine, or New Somerset as he was calling it at the time. Within its area were the separate plantations of Vines, Bonython and Lewis, Cammock, Trelawny, and others (see pages 204–205)—all holding their land under the Council for New England but now coming under the proprietorship of Gorges, who was taking steps to confirm his title by a patent directly from the King. In 1635 or 1636, while the trial against the Bay was in progress, Sir Ferdinando had commissioned his nephew, William Gorges, to act as Governor of Maine. Establishing his residence at Saco, where Bonython and Lewis had their plantation on one side of the river and Vines on the other, young Gorges proceeded to organize a government. For the dispensing of justice he

appointed six of the leading men from the various plantations under the title of Commissioners. Among them was
Thomas Purchase, husband of the little lady with golden
hair who probably, despite all the dirty stories circulated at
the Bay, had actually come over to marry him.[47]

On March 25, 1636, these Commissioners sat as a court.
Four men were sentenced for being drunk; "Mr. John Boni-
thon for Incontency with Ane, his fathers servant" was fined
forty shillings; George Cleeve was fined five pounds for making rash speeches. In this last item there comes to light a
controversy that in the end cost Sir Ferdinando Gorges half
his province. Cleeve had settled on the coast of Maine, near
Cape Elizabeth, as early as 1630. The following year, when
Trelawny received a patent to Richmond Island and the
adjoining mainland, John Winter, Trelawny's manager,
claimed the land on which Cleeve was planting. Cleeve
moved northward and began a new plantation on the site
of the present-day city of Portland—near the island where
in 1624 Christopher Levett had built his trading house. Soon
Winter attempted to extend the Trelawny claim to include
that area also, but this time Cleeve refused to be pushed
out. His remarks on the subject were evidently the grounds
for the fine imposed upon him by the Commissioners in
1636.[48]

In matters spiritual the people of Maine accepted the
Church of England service. For the support of their minister, the Reverend Richard Gibson, the leading men of the
province contributed from one to three pounds each in 1636.
The Reverend Gibson was, said Winter, "a very fair Condition man, & one that doth keep himselfe in very good
order, & Instructs our people well, if please God to give us
the grace to follow his instruction." Later, however, when
Gibson took to wife Mary, the daughter of Thomas Lewis,
rather than Winter's daughter Sarah, Winter lost some of
his enthusiasm for him.[49]

Thus in the province of Maine we find a certain amount
of factiousness, though it was over land titles rather than
religious doctrines. So far as government was concerned, the
Court organized in 1636 continued to function until 1639,

when Sir Ferdinando reorganized it under the royal patent which he received that year.

Between Maine and Massachusetts was Mason's province of New Hampshire. The title was based on a patent from the Council for New England. Mason was now dead. His widow had placed the management of his sawmills and stock farms in the hands of an agent and the property was slowly going to pieces. The proprietary title to the land, however, was legally vested in Mason's heirs. So far as any government was concerned, each plantation or town appears to have functioned separately. At Strawberry Bank, the oldest settlement in the province, the people had entered into what they called a "Combination" for living together in an orderly manner. This was probably a simple plantation agreement but seems to have met all their requirements for a government.

At Dover, a few miles up the river, Captain Thomas Wiggin had for some years acted as Governor—probably for the simple reason that, as agent for Lords Say and Brook, he had been instrumental in bringing in most of the settlers. In 1637 the Reverend George Burdett, a renegade minister from the Bay, got himself elected Governor in the place of Wiggin, and the following year Captain Underhill, also an exile from the Bay, defeated Burdett for the place. Then Underhill, who it will be recalled, had supported Mrs. Hutchinson's doctrines at Boston, attempted to replace Burdett by a minister of the Hutchinson-Wheelwright persuasion. The result was that the Dover church "soon after fell into factions and strange confusions, one part taking upon them to excommunicate and punish the other in the church and in the court."

At Exeter the Reverend Wheelwright and his family and friends were too busy getting settled to think about a "Combination" or to quarrel with each other. However, Dover was furnishing New Hampshire's full quota of factiousness.[50]

At the Bay the title to the land and the authority for the government stemmed from the royal patent of 1629, which patent the officers of the Company still held firmly in their hands. In accordance with the terms of that patent the freemen met at stated times either in person or through deputies and elected their officers, made laws and transacted other business of the colony. Not through any provision of the patent but as a natural and proper power derived from it the freemen levied taxes against the various towns for the support of their central government—nineteen hundred pounds being thus assessed in 1638 against the thirteen towns then within the jurisdiction of the colony. The individual property owners paid their taxes to the towns within which they lived, and from those taxes the expenses of the town governments were met and the proportional allotments made to the cost of the general government administered by the Governor and Assistants. All in all it was an efficient and orderly form of government.

The most serious defect in the government of the Bay was the lack of a code of laws. As it stood, a Mrs. Hutchinson could be convicted and sentenced for something she had no means of knowing would be looked upon as a crime; nor could the Governor justify the sentence by any better authority than the statement that "The Court knows wherefore." However, that deficiency was recognized and soon to be met.[51]

The uncertainty as to the laws probably contributed to the undeniable factiousness at the Bay, and the stern attempts to repress that factiousness doubtless accentuated it.

Southward of the Bay was New Plymouth colony. It held its lands by authority of the somewhat recently acquired patent from the Council for New England. The government of the colony was based upon the pact drawn up in the cabin of the *Mayflower* in 1620. It was a simple form of government. The men who were qualified—and the inhabitants seem to have easily agreed as to who was qualified—elected their Governor, who with a few assistants ran the affairs of the colony. With only an occasional reprieve Bradford had acted as Governor since the founding of the plantation. Once in a while there was a brawl which called for the dispensation of justice, but in general the people of New Plymouth went quietly about their business of making a living and of serving their God as they believed he wished to be served and as would assure their own salvation in the world to come.

West of New Plymouth, along Narragansett Bay, lay the two new towns of Providence and Portsmouth—without a vestige of title to their lands other than by purchase from the Indians. At Providence the government was simplicity itself. The heads of households, and somewhat later such young married men as were admitted to the settlement, met from time to time and by mutual consent settled such problems as arose. Among these problems conscience and religion were not included. It was clearly stated that the agreement entered into between them applied "only in civill things." In matters of conscience each was his or her own judge. This led, as we have seen, to much factiousness—occasionally relieved by an amusing situation, as, for example, when Joshua Verin was brought to trial for refusing to let his wife attend all of the frequent religious meetings presided over by Roger Williams. Verin was charged with interfering with his wife's exercise of conscience. He countered with the plea that it was contrary to his conscience that his wife should thus exercise her conscience. However, the husband lost. On the records of the town founded to permit freedom of conscience stands the entry: "It was agreed that Joshua Verin, upon the breach of a covenant for restraining of the libertie of conscience, shall be withheld from the libertie of voting till he shall declare the contrarie." Thus early—and fearlessly—did the exponents of liberty of conscience meet the dilemmas involved in their doctrine. Granting that the people of Providence had "factious dispositions"—one wonders how, given the conditions, King Charles would have ruled in the case of Joshua Verin *vs.* The Missus. When the story reached the Bay, John Winthrop came as near chuckling over it as his sober soul was capable.[52]

At Portsmouth the government was based upon a covenant entered into at Boston on March 7, 1638, by Coddington, Hutchinson, and seventeen others soon to be exiled from the Bay. They "solemnly, in the presence of Jehovah" incorporated themselves "into a Bodie Politick, and as he shall help, will submit our persons, lives and estates unto our Lord Jesus Christ, the King of Kings and Lord of Lords, and to all those perfect and most absolute laws of his given us in his holy word of truth, to be guided and judged thereby.—Exod. xxiv., 3, 4; 2 Chron. xi., 3; 2 Kings xi., 17." King Charles could hardly have called that a "want of Government," and strangely enough the subscribers to this covenant got along together for almost a year before the inevitable factiousness sent Coddington to the southern end of the island where he laid the foundations of a new town later known as Newport.[53]

Connecticut was New England's frontier in 1638. At the mouth of its great river Lion Gardiner and a few men still held Fort Saybrook for those who claimed title under the Warwick deed, but who apparently had lost all interest in American colonization. Neither the character of the settlement nor the number of people called for a form of government other than that of a commanding officer.

Down the coast Eaton, Davenport and their associates were just getting settled at New Haven. They had no title to their land beyond that which they had purchased from the natives. Nor had they as yet any formal government, although they were moving slowly toward the establishment of one based upon a church covenant and modeled after theories already being discarded at the Bay.

The future of Connecticut lay with the River Towns of Windsor, Hartford, and Wethersfield. They were frankly squatter settlements. In selecting the locations for the towns, their leaders had deliberately gone beyond the jurisdiction of the Bay. They had turned a deaf ear to the pretended patent of the Say and Brook group. The commission from the Bay under which they had organized their first court had long since expired, but the court continued to function.

Now, in the spring of 1638, at just about the time that King Charles in London was complaining about a "want of Government" in New England, the people of the River Towns of Connecticut met in a general assembly and considered their situation. The decision which they reached and the action which they took established something new in the constitutional evolution of America. Virginia had been handed, by its directors in London, a charter of limited representative government. The Bay had been given, by the

King's ministers in England, a patent under which its government functioned. Plantation covenants, with governmental procedure based vaguely on mutual good will or Scriptural authority, were in existence at Plymouth, Portsmouth and elsewhere. But here, on the banks of the Connecticut River, occurred America's first constitutional convention and came into being America's first written constitution.

Forasmuch as it had pleased "Allmighty God by the wise disposition of his divyne providence" to put them there, the men of Windsor, Hartford and Wethersfield worked out a detailed form of government suited to their present situation and future growth; they had it put into writing; and they voted it into being. Following a brief preamble acknowledging the supremacy of God in matters spiritual, were eleven crisp Orders creating a civil government and specifying how it should operate. The Orders provided for the calling of General Assemblies at stated intervals; for the election of deputies from the towns; for the organization of the Assemblies; and for the nomination and election of a Governor and magistrates. They placed the "supreme power of the Commonwealth" in the Assemblies, and to the end that they might exercise that power the Orders provided that, should a Governor fail to call a new Assembly as directed, the voters themselves might do so.

Such were the Fundamental Orders of Connecticut. While doubtless drafted by Ludlow, the trained lawyer, they were not the work of any one man or even of a few men. They represented the combined thought and wisdom of the freemen of the River Towns of Windsor, Hartford and Wethersfield.[54]

Reviewing the situation in New England—from Pemaquid to Connecticut—it appears that King Charles had ample justification for his belief that the people were of a "factious disposition," though a noisy few rather than the great majority were responsible for most of the disorder—even as was the case at the same time in Old England. So far as a "want of Government" was concerned, the King appears to have been in error, if we accept the needs of the people as the basis for government. With very few exceptions, and those in very small settlements, the colonists were being governed in the best interests of the majority of people in them. What the King meant was that New England lacked a uniform government patterned after the government of England—and such a government the colonists had no intention of having.

Speaking in the name of the people of Connecticut, Ludlow summed up the position of all the Puritan colonies. Their reason for coming to America, he said, "was to establish the Lord Jesus in his Kingly Throne, as much as in us lies, here in his churches, & to maynteine the common cause of his gospell with our lives & estates; and whereas wee knowe that our profession will finde fewe frends uppon the face of the earth, if occasion serve, & therefore unlikely to have any aide or succour from forraine parts, if our neede should soe require, it is our wisdom therefore to improve what wee have, to walke close with our God, & to combine & unite our selves to walke & live peaceably & lovingly togeather, that soe, if there be cause, wee may joine harts & hands to maynteine the comon cause aforesaide, & to defend our priviledges & freedomes wee nowe enjoye, against all opposers."[55]

The Dutch and Swedes

TO THE SOUTH AND WEST of New England lay the Dutch colony of New Netherland. On southward at the mouth of the Potomac was Lord Baltimore's new province of Maryland. Along the James River was Virginia. Six hundred miles on down the coast was the Spanish outpost of St. Augustine. And that was the extent of European settlement on the eastern seaboard of the future United States at the beginning of the year 1638.

Sir John Harvey, whom we last met on the way to England to answer charges placed against him by his Council, had been cleared and reinstated in the governorship of Virginia. Early in 1638 he had unexpected visitors. Standing in at the James River were two ships bearing the odd names of *Kalmar Nyckel* and *Fogel Grip*. Over them flew the flag of Sweden. In command was Peter Minuit, he who seven years earlier had been dismissed as Director-general of New Netherland. Minuit asked the privilege of taking on wood and water, which request was readily granted. When Governor Harvey asked to see his commission, however, Minuit declined.[1]

Two or three weeks later the Dutch garrison at Fort Nassau on the Delaware River, opposite the present-day city of Philadelphia, began to hear strange stories from the Indians. There were two ships a few miles down the river. Their commander had bought some land from one of the native chiefs for a "kettle and other trifles." The Dutch sent down a few men to find out what was going on. At the mouth of a creek where the city of Wilmington, Delaware, stands today they found Minuit and forty or fifty men building a fort which they had named Christina in honor of the Queen of Sweden.[2]

Queen Christina was at the time but eleven years of age. Eight years had passed since that fateful day when, commending her to the care of his people, Gustavus Adolphus, her father, had started on his meteoric career against the Imperial armies which were crushing Protestant Germany. In the midst of those campaigns the idea of a Swedish colony in America had grown in the mind of the ambitious King. Gustavus Adolphus died on the battlefield of Lutzen in 1632. But here, six years later on the banks of the Delaware, was being laid the foundation of New Sweden.

Back of the colony stood the New Sweden Company, organized in 1637. Among its Directors were several Dutchmen as well as Swedes. Minuit had been one of the active promoters of the project and was put in charge of making the settlement—partly because of his interest in the Company and partly because he knew the country and the habits of the natives. Trade for furs was a prime objective of those who put up the money that financed the colony.[3]

Fort Christina lay well within the bounds of the land granted in 1632 by the King of England to Lord Baltimore, but it was the Director-general of the Dutch colony of New Netherland who leveled the first charge of trespass against the Swedish invaders on the Delaware River. Minuit replied that his masters had as good a right there as any one else—and the Dutch were not prepared to force the issue. Though Gustavus Adolphus was dead, the flag of Sweden still inspired respect.[4]

Even had the Director-general at New Amsterdam been ordered to remove the Swedes from their fort, it is doubtful whether he could have done it at the time. Wouter van Twiller, who had taken Minuit's place at New Amsterdam

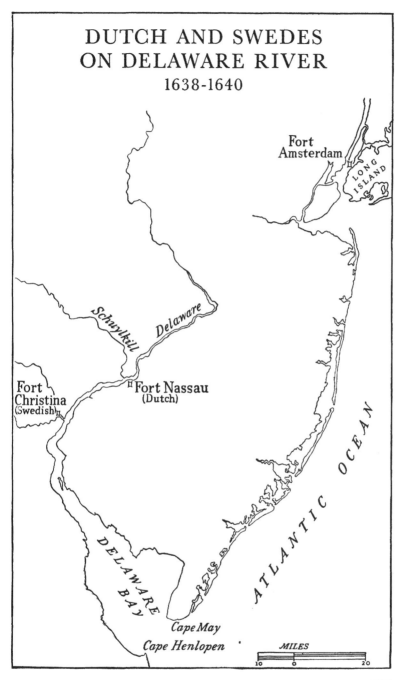

DUTCH AND SWEDES
ON DELAWARE RIVER
1638-1640

Fort
Amsterdam

LONG ISLAND

Schuylkill

Delaware

Fort
Christina
(Swedish)

Fort Nassau
(Dutch)

ATLANTIC OCEAN

DELAWARE BAY

Cape May

Cape Henlopen

MILES

10 0 20

in 1633, had proved a poor manager for the Dutch West India Company although a good one for himself. The Company buildings were in disrepair; the fort was falling to pieces; its guns were dismounted; the Company ships were unseaworthy; the Company windmills were out of order; the Company farms were not being farmed; and the Company cattle had passed into private possession.

So flagrant was the situation that a new Director-general, William Kieft, had been sent over in the spring of 1638. He arrived at New Amsterdam only a short time before the Swedes appeared on the Delaware River, and it was Kieft rather than van Twiller, who challenged Minuit's right to establish the new colony.[5]

However, Kieft had enough to do at New Amsterdam without bothering too much about losing a few furs on the Delaware. He did what he could to stop his own colonists from carrying on illicit trade in furs, this trade being claimed by the Company as a monopoly for itself. He secured tenants for the Company farms on Manhattan Island, and across the North River in present New Jersey he put the land of the defunct patroonage of Pavonia into competent hands. He bought the Indian title to a part of Long Island directly opposite Manhattan, and developed settlements there.[6]

The one part of his colony that Kieft did not have to worry about was Rensselaerswyck. Of the several patroonages granted in 1629 it alone had proved successful. Occupying both sides of the Hudson in the vicinity of present-day Albany, it was a small principality in itself. Title to the patroonage was held by Kiliaen van Rensselaer though stock in the enterprise had been sold to various associates. In part the land was leased to tenants who farmed it on shares; in part it was operated under the immediate direction of the patroon through a resident manager.

Hardly a ship arrived in the Hudson without cattle, horses or equipment for Rensselaerswyck. Gristmills turned the grain into flour; sawmills turned the forests into lumber; breweries quenched the thirst of the inhabitants. The tenants and servants lived well and the proprietors either made a fair return on their investments or had faith in the future.

More and more land was acquired until Rensselaerswyck practically surrounded Fort Orange, the Company's trading post on the upper river.⁷

Fort Orange, located as it was on the eastern edge of the great Iroquois confederacy—made up of Mohawks, Oneidas, Onondagas, Cayugas and Senecas—had been one of the Dutch Company's most profitable sources for furs. But in the early 1630's its business began to fall off. The western Indians were not bringing in their furs as they had been in the habit of doing. In December, 1634, three employees at the fort started on a visit to the Indian towns to find out what was the matter. Cutting across country to the Mohawk River, they followed its banks westward. Two days' tramp through the snow brought them to the "first castle" of the friendly Mohawk Indians. It consisted of thirty-six bark-covered houses arranged in rows. Some of the houses were as much as two hundred and fifty feet in length. In them, in addition to living quarters, were storage bins filled with corn and other provisions. The visitors were feasted on venison, pumpkins and beans, with plenty of grease.

Another short day's tramp brought the Dutchmen to the second Mohawk "castle," of sixteen long-houses. Beyond it lay the third "castle," with thirty-two of the long-houses. In every house were "four, five or six fireplaces where cooking went on." The Indians were hospitable but curious. "They pushed each other into the fire to see us, and it was more than midnight before they took their departure."

At about seventy miles from Fort Orange the three Dutchmen came to Tenotoge, the fourth and largest of the Mohawk "castles." It consisted of fifty-five long-houses, some of them more than one hundred paces in length. Here they spent Christmas while a blizzard howled through the town and medicine men howled over a sick Indian.

Tenotoge was the last of the Mohawk towns. Beyond was the "castle" of the Oneidas. The distance was not much over thirty miles, but what with the deep snowdrifts and the intense cold it took the Dutchmen three days to get there. They probably did not know that they were approaching the locality where, nineteen years earlier, Champlain and his

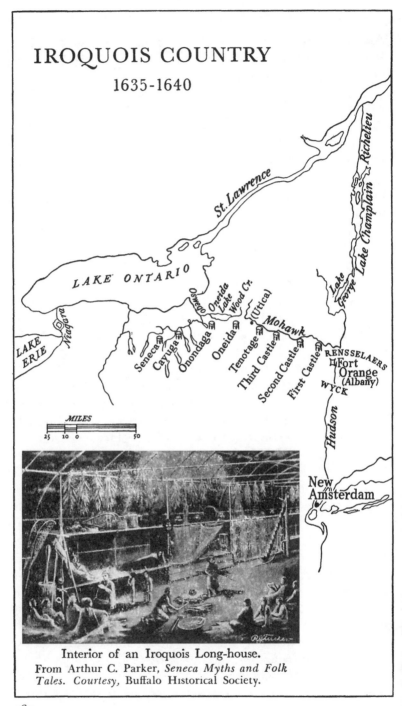

IROQUOIS COUNTRY
1635-1640

St. Lawrence

Richelieu

LAKE ONTARIO

Lake Champlain

Lake George

Niagara

LAKE ERIE

Oswego

Oneida Lake

Wood Cr.

(Utica)

Mohawk

Seneca

Cayuga

Onondaga

Oneida

Tenotage

Third Castle

Second Castle

First Castle

RENSSELAERS
Fort
Orange
(Albany)
WYCK

Hudson

New
Amsterdam

MILES
25 10 0   50

Interior of an Iroquois Long-house.
From Arthur C. Parker, *Seneca Myths and Folk
Tales. Courtesy,* Buffalo Historical Society.

Algonquin allies from across Lake Ontario had suffered defeat outside the palisades of an Iroquois town—perhaps the very one to which the Dutchmen were now going.

At the top of a high hill they saw the town. It was surrounded by a double row of palisades. The entrance was through a gate only three and a half feet wide. Above the gate were "three big wooden images, carved like men" and from them three scalps fluttered in the wind. Within the palisades were sixty-six long-houses, "better, higher and more finished" than those of the Mohawks. On the fronts of some of them were paintings of beasts of various sorts. Inside the houses the Dutchmen saw axes, razors, shirts and coats of French manufacture. Off to the northwest of the town the Indians pointed out a great river up which they said the French came in boats to trade for their furs. That "river" was Oneida Lake whose waters found their way to the sea not through the Mohawk and Hudson rivers but northerly through Lake Ontario and the St. Lawrence.

And there was the explanation of the falling off of trade at the Dutch fort. Frenchmen from Canada, working their tiny boats along the shores of Lake Ontario, up the Oswego River, and into Oneida Lake, were tapping the Iroquois trade through the back door. And they paid better prices than the Dutch offered at Fort Orange.

The three young Dutchmen returned to their fort with a message from the western Indians: If the Dutch wanted their furs they would have to come for them and they would have to pay as much for them as the French paid. This was one of the problems which Wouter van Twiller had left to be solved by the new Director-general.[8]

And while Kieft struggled to get things into some order on the Hudson, the Swedes completed their fort on the Delaware. In June, 1638, Minuit with such furs as his men had been able to collect started back to Sweden in the *Kalmar Nyckel*. He went by way of the West Indies, where he did a little trading in tobacco. At St. Kitts he called on the captain of a Dutch sloop. A storm came up. The sloop was driven out to sea, and neither it nor Minuit was ever heard of again. The *Kalmar Nyckel,* however, duly arrived in

Sweden with her cargo of furs, tobacco and other produce.

Meanwhile the men at Fort Christina were gathering up more furs from the Indians, and in April, 1639, leaving twenty-five men at the fort, the *Fogel Grip* sailed for home. The profits returned by the two ships far from met the expenses of the colony, but they were a promising start and the backers of the New Sweden Company were not discouraged. Peter Hollandaer, another Dutchman, was appointed Governor in the place of Minuit, and in September, 1639, the *Kalmar Nyckel* was again on her way to America. On April 17, 1640, she tied up at Fort Christina, where the winter's haul of furs awaited her. The usual trading goods and supplies were unloaded; the bales of furs were taken aboard; and within a month the *Kalmar Nyckel* was again on her way home with a cargo that represented a real profit. In the future the Dutch post at Fort Nassau on the Delaware would have to compete for its furs.[9]

But this competition—by the French in the north and the Swedes in the south—was probably the best thing that could have happened to the drowsy Dutch West India Company. Something drastic had to be done if New Netherland was to be more than an unprofitable fur-trading center. The upshot was that in the autumn of 1638 the trade of the colony was thrown open to all comers; immigration was encouraged; land was offered to all who would cultivate it.

Under this liberal policy the colony took on new life. Dutchmen of wealth and ability emigrated to New Netherland. New farms were established not only on Manhattan Island but north and east in present-day Westchester County. Staten Island in New York harbor was put under cultivation, and the purchase of additional titles from the Indians made possible a new expansion on the western end of Long Island.

Nor did the new settlers come exclusively from Holland. Many English servants who had served out their indentures in Virginia found greater opportunity in New Netherland than in the tobacco fields along the James River. Other Virginians came because they liked the region, among them George Holmes, who in 1635 had led the attempt to take over Fort Nassau. In 1639 he took up a farm along the East River.

From Massachusetts also came an increasing stream of Englishmen attracted as much by freedom from religious persecution as by offers of free land. Liberty of conscience had existed in New Netherland from the founding of the colony. Now, in 1638 and 1639, with the Hutchinson controversy raging at the Bay, many who could not stand conditions there but who did not care for New Hampshire or Rhode Island turned to the Dutch settlements. Captain Underhill, while still acting as Governor at Dover, asked for permission to live in New Netherland. For a time he compromised by making his home at the newly established English town of Stamford near the Dutch border, but within a few years we find him living on Long Island and giving a wavering allegiance to the Dutch.[10]

The steady encroachment of English settlements upon territory which the Dutch looked upon as their own was a matter of grave concern to Kieft and his superiors in Holland. While the Dutch West India Company had vaguely claimed the Atlantic coast from Virginia to Newfoundland, it had seriously looked upon its boundaries as including both the Delaware and the Connecticut rivers. The founding of the Plymouth trading post on the Connecticut in 1633 had been the first challenge to its limits on the east. When, two years later, the English swarmed onto that river at Windsor, Hartford, Wethersfield and Saybrook, the authority of the Dutch was reduced to one small trading house practically surrounded by the town of Hartford. In 1638 the settlement at New Haven brought the English to less than seventy-five miles from New Amsterdam. The following year Ludlow founded Fairfield—and the English were only fifty miles from New Amsterdam.

In an attempt to stave off this advance, Kieft in 1640 bought from the Indians all the land from present-day Norwalk, Conn., westward to the Hudson and southward to the land already owned by the Company around about Manhattan Island. This did not stop other Indians from selling to New Haven Colony, in the same year, a part of the same land—on which Stamford was founded, thirty miles from New Amsterdam.

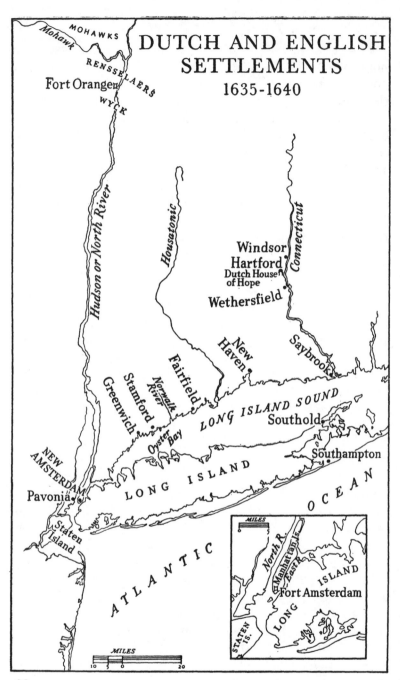

DUTCH AND ENGLISH
SETTLEMENTS
1635-1640

Mohawk

MOHAWKS

RENSSELAERS

Fort Orange

WYCK

Hudson or North River

Housatonic

Connecticut

Windsor
Hartford
Dutch House
of Hope
Wethersfield

Saybrook

New
Haven

Fairfield

Stamford

Norwalk
River

Greenwich

Oyster
Bay

LONG ISLAND SOUND

Southold

Southampton

NEW
AMSTERDAM

LONG ISLAND

Pavonia

Staten
Island

ATLANTIC

OCEAN

MILES

North R.

Manhattan Is.

East R.

Fort Amsterdam

ISLAND

STATEN
IS.

LONG

MILES

10 5 0   20

However, at Stamford the English advance along the northerly side of Long Island Sound was halted. Greenwich, only five or six miles to the west, was bought by English settlers but forced to accept the jurisdiction of the Dutch.[11]

Across the Sound on Long Island there was also a clash between English and Dutch claimants. While the latter claimed the whole island, they were not much interested in arguing the matter eastward of Oyster Bay, to which point they had purchased the Indian title. At the same time the Earl of Stirling (whom we recall as Sir William Alexander, former proprietor of Nova Scotia) claimed the entire island. It had been assigned to him by the Council for New England when, in 1635, that body divided up its land.

On the basis of this title from the Council, Stirling authorized his agent, James Forrett, to sell land on Long Island to such Englishmen as wished to buy. One of Forrett's first sales was to a group of prospective settlers from the town of Lynn in Massachusetts Colony. The site which he sold them was well to the west of the limits claimed by the Dutch through their purchase from the Indians. When the buyers started to take possession, Director-general Kieft caused them to be arrested and brought to New Amsterdam. However, on their promise not to trespass farther on Dutch territory they were released. As a recompense Forrett granted them a new site on the eastern end of the island. There, in 1640, they founded the town of Southampton, which associated itself with the River Towns of Windsor, Hartford and Wethersfield on the Connecticut mainland. At about the same time, and only a few miles distant, another group of settlers with a title acquired through Forrett established the town of Southold, which, for purposes of government, joined New Haven across the Sound. Thus the eastern part of Long Island came to be settled by English whose ties were with the Puritan colonies of Connecticut, while the western end of the island was settled largely by Dutch who gave their allegiance to the government of New Netherland.[12]

On both sides of Long Island Sound a collision between Dutch and English was bound to occur sooner or later.

The Tobacco Colonies

I N 1640, AFTER ELEVEN YEARS of arbitrary personal government, Charles I, King of England, Scotland and Ireland, called a Parliament. Scotland was in armed rebellion and the King needed aid. What he got from the Parliament was a demand for redress of past grievances. Between the stubborn King and the vindictive Parliament there was little room for compromise. Sharp words soon gave way to sharper swords. For twenty years England resounded with the clash of factions and of arms.

And as the lines of battle were drawn in the Mother Country, so also in America some of the colonies gave their loyalty to the King and some sympathized with Parliament. But beyond a slight coercion of those who backed the losers and some favors for those who stood with the winners, the colonies were for the most part permitted to remain aloof from the conflict. It was, withal, a period during which—being thrown on their own resources—they worked out their individual ways of life, and first began to think of themselves as Americans.

Up and down the coast from Maine to Virginia there were some thirty thousand English settlers. Nearly half of these were in the Massachusetts Bay Colony. Virginia stood next with eight or nine thousand inhabitants. In the Connecticut country there were about twenty-five hundred people; in

Maryland some fifteen hundred; and in New Plymouth probably less than a thousand. There may have been a thousand people in Maine; her population fluctuated—many during the fishing season and fewer in the winter. New Hampshire probably did not contain over five hundred people, and Rhode Island somewhat less.[1]

Viewed against the vast savage continent to whose eastern edge they clung, these thirty thousand pioneers hardly seemed destined to conquer and populate the future United States. And yet in Virginia the pattern which that conquest was to follow had already taken form. The possession of land had become the basis of wealth and of social standing. The hunger for land and ever more land was the urge that for more than two hundred years drove the frontier steadily onward; that turned the public domain into privately owned plantations, farms, and ranches; and that brought about the settlement of the country.

It will be recalled that all those who aided, either by money or service, in the founding of Virginia had claims to allotments of land in the colony. Most of these claimants had received their grants—in fee simple—before the dissolution of the Company in 1624. But the amount of land thus distributed—even though some of the grants were fairly large—brought into being only a thin line of plantations along the James River; uncounted acres remained in the possession of the Company. Instead of selling this surplus land to speculators the Company used it to encourage immigration into the colony, and the King continued that far-sighted policy. For each man or woman who came to Virginia fifty acres of public land was available. But the right to take title to these allotments did not necessarily, or even generally, go to the particular man or woman who arrived in the colony. Title went to the person who equipped, transported and supported the immigrant. If a man, at his own expense, brought himself and wife and two servants to Virginia, he could claim two hundred acres. The servants, being brought in at the expense of the master, had no claim to the land. Equally if a planter, already settled in the colony, brought in, at his own expense, two or three indentured servants or negro slaves, he could claim the right to take up fifty acres of land per head of people so brought in.

These "rights" to take up land soon came to be known as "head rights," and were bought and sold like any other property. Thus a planter who wanted additional land but who did not need additional servants would buy head rights from some one who had brought in people but who did not want land. For example, ship captains often transported men and women who could not pay their way but who were willing to enter into contracts to work for a specified number of years in return for having their expenses paid. On arriving in the colony the captain would sell his contracts to some planter who wanted servants. At the same time he would sell his head rights to another planter who wanted land. The procedure was simple. The captain would go before the clerk of the court in the county where the land was desired and there state under oath that he had brought in at his expense such number of people, whose names he would list. The clerk would thereupon give him a certificate for the proper number of head rights, which he would promptly assign, at a price, to the land-seeking planter. The list of names was presumably verified by the office of the Colonial Secretary, but claims were seldom denied. Meanwhile the planter would present his certificate of head rights to the county officials, point out the land he wanted, have it surveyed, and take title. There was no charge for the land, but the title was not in fee simple; it was subject to the payment —at first to the Company and later to the King—of a perpetual annual quitrent of twelve pence for each fifty acres.[2]

The value of Virginia land lay in its remarkable adaptability to the production of tobacco. Since Rolfe's experiments back in 1612, tobacco had become the staple crop. Fifty acres of tobacco land would support a family; five thousand acres would support many servants and leave a sufficient profit to enable the owner to live handsomely. There were ups and downs in prices, of course. At times the market was glutted and the amount of tobacco that could be raised was regulated by law. Occasionally there were regulations requiring the planters to destroy a part of their crop in order

to increase the price on the rest. In general, however, tobacco found ready buyers and in Virginia it passed as money.
In the London market it paid for the manufactured articles
and the luxuries required or yearned for on the plantations.[3]

The best tobacco was grown in a soil with a deep covering
of leaf mold—where trees had stood thickly. To open new
fields the trees had to be felled. The brush, and often the
timber itself, was burned on the land. The stumps were left
standing. Naturally plows could not be used in such fields.
The preparation of the soil and the cultivation of the tobacco plants were all done by hand with heavy hoes. Nor,
having cleared the land, did the planter have a permanent
return for his labor. Tobacco quickly exhausted the soil.
The old fields wore out and new fields had to be found. This
was one of the reasons for the constant demand for new
grants of land.[4]

The first expansion followed tidewater—up the rivers to
the falls line. At that point it halted, because at that point
navigation stopped; and water was the only practicable
means of transportation. By 1640 all the best land along the
James River—up to the Falls (present-day Richmond)—had
been taken. The inlets on the southern shore of Chesapeake
Bay were being settled, as was the southern tip of the peninsula opposite. The suppression of a new Indian outbreak
in 1644 was followed by the opening up to settlement of
the region between the James and the York rivers. Within
another ten years plantations dotted the banks of the Rappahannock and the southern shore of the Potomac.[5]

In the plantation system of agriculture there was no place
for towns or villages such as existed in Puritan New England.
While there were many more small plantations than large
ones, yet each was a unit in itself. From his own wharf or
plank thrust out from the river's edge, each planter delivered his tobacco to the ships that called for it, and in the
same way received direct from the ships the goods that he
had ordered from England or that were offered by wandering traders from New Amsterdam and New England.

How profitable the possession of tidewater Virginia tobacco land could be is shown by the case of George Ludlow.

At thirty-four years of age, living in England, he had been unable to support himself or his wife. In 1630 he came to Massachusetts with his brother Roger and at Roger's expense. For some years he engaged in trade but without much success. Roger Williams, from his new home in Rhode Island, complained bitterly that he could not collect for his own and his wife's "better apparell," which he had turned over to George Ludlow to sell. To avoid unfortunate experiences of this sort, Roger Ludlow, at about the time he was moving to Connecticut, had a heart-to-heart talk with brother George as to "what was the best course for the said George to betake himselfe unto, to get some livelihood, and to get something to pay his debts in England, and to relieve his Wife." The upshot was that Roger staked George to enough to get a plantation on York River in Virginia where "in Ten years by his Industrie, and Gods blessing on it, [George] procured to himselfe a large Estate both in the said Country, and a great Estate in England, paid all his Debts, and sent yearelie Considerable Mayntenaunce to his Wife, and flourished in an outward Estate, both in housing, and Household Stuffe, Plate, Servants, Corne, Cattle of all sorts and Tobacco-Plantations. . . ."[6]

George Ludlow was accounted one of the wealthy men of Virginia in the late 1640's and early 1650's. Yet his house on York River consisted only of an inner room, a small middle room, a chamber, a hall, a buttery, a kitchen, a milk house and a store—all doubtless of frame construction. Nor did Ludlow's house differ greatly in size from those of other well-to-do planters of the time. There were a few that were larger, some of twelve or thirteen rooms; but the typical houses of the period were from thirty to forty feet in length and eighteen to twenty feet in width, with only a garret in the upper story. They were generally built of wood with brick chimneys at either end. The inner walls were plastered and whitewashed. Sometimes wainscoting was used. Glass windows were not uncommon, but in the less pretentious houses shutters served for light and ventilation. In fact, a considerable number of the houses were of such temporary construction that, when the occupant wore out his land and

Above and *below*, Adam Thoroughgood house, built prior to 1640.

Courtesy, Historic American Buildings Survey, Library of Congress.

273

moved on to more fertile soil, he burned down his house to get the nails for use in building a new one. Lumber was ever at hand for the cutting; nails had to be imported from England.[7]

Brickkilns had been in operation in the colony for many years, and brick had been used for foundations and chimneys. A few houses with the outer walls entirely of brick had been erected before 1640. Adam Thoroughgood, proprietor of an estate of more than five thousand acres on the southern shore of Chesapeake Bay, built such a house, and built it so well that it has survived for more than three hundred years. Like Ludlow's home on York River it was comparatively small, only six rooms. Governor Berkeley, upon his arrival at Jamestown in 1642, encouraged the building of brick houses and set a good example by having his own house constructed of that material. Otherwise the Governor followed the custom of the country; his new home consisted of but six rooms.[8]

Usually the kitchen, the milk house and the wash house were in detached buildings, as were also the quarters for the servants. The stables, tobacco sheds and other farm buildings stood at a distance from the main house, which was surrounded by a stout fence to keep out hogs and other wandering livestock.

The furnishings of the homes depended, of course, upon the means and the tastes of the individual owners, but there was a certain uniformity. The hall, or dining room, generally had two or three or even more tables of different sizes together with a considerable number of chairs. In this room also were cupboards for dishes and silver, and chests for table linen; sometimes there was a bed. In fact, almost every room in the house, including the parlor or guest room, contained a bed or two. And in what might be called the bedrooms there would be found, in addition to beds, everything from saddles to books.[9]

Open fireplaces supplied the heat needed during the brief season of cold weather. Wood, in unlimited quantities, was the fuel. Candles, of myrtle wax or beeswax, provided light in the better homes; pine knots served where the cost of candles was prohibitive. Flints and steel served for matches.

The clothing of the colonists in Virginia was similar to that worn in England by people in similar walks of life. In fact, most of the better garments were imported ready-made, though the large number of bolts of various kinds of cloth stored in the plantation houses indicates that a considerable amount of home designing and sewing must have gone on.

The wardrobe of the average man consisted of two or three outfits—suited to the season or the occasion. The breeches—made of linen or calico for summer and of wool for winter—reached only to the knee, where they were generally fastened with tie strings. Stockings, of cotton or wool, came up to the knee and were held by garters. The shoes were of leather, ankle height, and fastened with brass or steel buckles. High boots do not seem to have been generally worn in Virginia. Ordinarily the shirt was of canvas or linen, though finer materials were used for dress occasions. Around the neck went a neckcloth, tied in a long bow in the front. The waistcoat, or vest, was of cotton or flannel and often brightly colored. The coat itself might be of cotton, wool or leather. Fastened around the neckcloth and falling over the shoulders of the coat was a wide collar of some light-colored material, called a falling band. In winter a greatcoat, or overcoat, was worn. The man of wealth wore silk stockings instead of wool or cotton; he had silver buckles on his shoes, ruffles on his cuffs, embroidery on his falling band; and the sleeves of his coat were often "slashed" to reveal a brighter fabric inserted within the slashes (see portraits on pages 221 and 339). Cloth caps, felt hats or wide-brimmed, rakish beaver hats, each according to the station in life of the wearer, topped off the fully dressed man. Underwear either was worn sparingly or seldom mentioned.

The wives and daughters of the well-to-do planters wore dresses of silk and satin, trimmed with lace—imported from England and of the latest London styles. Petticoats of serge, flannel and silk were common. Stockings were often of wool and brightly colored. Bonnets trimmed with lace were worn on dress occasions; hoods of calico or similar materials served for more ordinary wear. Aprons of various materials were

The above portrait of an English gentlewoman suggests the costume of the Virginia ladies of the period.

The subject of the portrait is Anna Wake. It was made by Anthony van Dyck. It is here reproduced by the *courtesy* of the Metropolitan Museum of Art, New York.

a part of every woman's wardrobe. Ornamental fans and bright scarves added to the feminine charm.[10]

Despite the lack of urban centers—Jamestown was but a dingy village of little more than a dozen houses—the planter and his family found ample opportunities to display their fine clothes. There was much visiting from plantation to plantation. Weddings and other special occasions brought the people together at one or another of the homes. Nor were these gatherings of a few hours' duration. The guests, traveling by boat along the rivers or by horseback through the woods, may have had to stop one or two nights at intervening plantations before they reached the home of their host. Naturally, once having arrived, they remained a day or two before they started the return journey.[11]

Naturally, too, the host dispensed the best entertainment at his command. Food was abundant and in great variety. Beef, pork and mutton were at hand from the plantation stock. Venison called only for a gun. Wild geese, ducks and turkeys crowded the swampland. The rivers were full of fish of many kinds. Sugar, spices and other delicacies came in with every ship, as did also wines, brandy and rum. Beer was brewed on almost every plantation. "Virginia wants not good victual, wants not good dispositions, and as God hath freely bestowed it, they as freely impart with it," said one who knew the colony well.[12]

What with good "victual," with enough and often more than enough to drink, with the merry tunes of a fiddle, with the youngsters tucked into the trundle beds, dancing feet flew far into the night. And when the candles were finally snuffed, all those beds—in the parlor, dining room and everywhere else—were none too many.

Attendance at church service also often called for a journey of many miles. Parishes necessarily had to include enough people to meet the cost of building and maintaining a church, as well as providing a living for the minister. In the thinly settled areas a parish might cover half a county. For the outlying planter this meant an early start on Sunday morning and a late return. For his servants it generally meant staying home—to milk the cows and to have dinner ready

St. Luke's Church, Isle of Wight County, Virginia. Restored from building erected during the first half of the seventeenth century.

Courtesy, Historic American Buildings Survey, Library of Congress.

for the family and for the guests who frequently came back with them.

Officially Virginia adhered to the Church of England, but the Church had not as yet extended its government to Virginia except in so far as the Governor could claim to represent the Bishop of London. Parishes were formed on orders from the General Assembly. The affairs of the parish were administered by a vestry selected by the parishioners. The church building was erected under the direction of the vestry. The minister was chosen by the vestry, though the Governor reserved to himself the right of induction. Not infrequently a parish would avoid formal induction and thereby leave itself free to discharge an unsatisfactory minister, which would not have been its privilege otherwise.

Whether regularly inducted by the Governor or serving at the pleasure of the vestry, a minister who proved satisfactory to his parish was assured of a reasonably permanent living and a very good one. He received a regular salary, calculated in tobacco, from a tax levied by the vestry. He received liberal fees for conducting wedding and funeral services. He was provided with a parsonage. A well-stocked farm, the property of the parish but assigned to the support of the minister, gave him food and sometimes extra income.

Through its church wardens the vestry acted as guardian over the morals and welfare of the parish. It investigated cases of drunkenness, breach of the Sabbath, sexual irregularities and similar offenses. Its findings were presented to the county court for action. One of the most serious problems with which it had to deal was that of the bastard offspring of indentured female servants. In this offense more was involved than morals. The mother naturally had no means of supporting the child and that burden might fall upon the parish. The usual punishment was both physical and economic. The woman received a goodly number of lashes on the bare back, and when her term of service expired she was required to work an additional term of years, the proceeds of which went to the parish as an offset to its expense in caring for the child. Her master might clear the fine by putting up security, in terms of tobacco of course, for the expense entailed by the parish, but he generally exacted enough additional service to repay his outlay. The father of a bastard, if a free man or the owner of property, might escape with no greater punishment than being required to build a bridge over a creek or some similar public service. The child, as soon as it could work, was bound out as a servant until it reached maturity.[13]

If servants were sometimes a moral problem, they were none the less an economic necessity. Without servants and many of them there would have been no fields of tobacco and probably no Virginia colony. The clearing of the land, the setting and cultivation of the plants, the rolling of the hogsheads to the wharves, the work about the plantation houses all called for strong arms and backs. In the early days of the colony attempts had been made to get workmen to emigrate on their own account, but without much success. Later boys and girls from the slums of English cities, or people convicted of minor crimes, had been sent over. By 1640 a system had been worked out that not only furnished a stable labor supply but helped to populate the country with what was, far and long, a sturdy English stock.

To the ill-paid English farm worker or the unemployed man or woman in the city hovels, Virginia was a land of golden opportunity. They were only too willing to go, but they lacked the means to pay their passage. To the Virginia planter their labor would be a means of raising more tobacco, and he had the money to pay their passage. Supply and demand soon got together. Through a contract, or indenture, the servant agreed to serve his master for four, five or seven years, according to his age at the time the contract was made. The master paid for his passage and agreed to feed and clothe him and to make some provision for him at the end of his service.[14]

As we have already seen, the captain of a ship would often act as a broker, making a preliminary contract with the servant and providing transportation in the certainty that when his ship reached Virginia he would be able to sell his contract, and the servant, to some planter at a profit. In such cases it was usual to allow the servant a few days after his arrival in which to pick out a master who suited him.[15]

There were all sorts of variations in the terms of the indentures, but that made in 1659 by Edward Rowzie, planter of Virginia, with Bartholomew Clarke, son of John Clarke, saddler of Canterbury, England, was probably typical. Clarke agreed to serve Rowzie faithfully for a term of four years, to keep his secrets and obey his just and lawful commands; "fornication he shall not commit, nor contract matrimony with any woman . . . at cards, dice or any unlawful games he shall not play." Rowzie agreed to teach Clarke the "mystery, art, and occupation of a planter" and to supply "competent meat, drink, apparel, washing, lodging with all other things fitting to his degree and in the end thereof, fifty acres of land to be laid out for him, and all other things which according to the custom of the country is or ought to be done." [16]

The provision of land for Clarke at the expiration of his term of service was a variation from what was customary and was therefore definitely stated. The other things "according to the custom of the country" were well understood. They consisted of two outfits of simple clothing and enough grain to support him for a year. In addition it was not unusual for a servant to build up a small estate even while in service. The average master would allow him enough land to raise some tobacco on his own account or give him a sow or a cow, the increase from which would be his own. [17]

Thus many servants, when they finished their term, were in a position to start life with more than their bare hands. Often, however, they worked as hired laborers for a year or two until they acquired enough ready capital to buy land of their own. Adam Thoroughgood, for example, who came to Virginia as a servant, bought one hundred and fifty-three acres soon after he was freed. Within three or four years he was elected a member of the House of Burgesses; and in another few years he had acquired, probably through head rights, an estate of over five thousand acres in Lower Norfolk County where he built the house described on page 274 and shown on page 273. Thoroughgood, a former indentured servant, had become one of the well-to-do men of the colony. Thousands of others did the same in a lesser degree. [18]

For seventy years a steady stream of indentured servants

flowed from England to Virginia. The number has been estimated at between fifteen hundred and two thousand a year. And these servants, together with a comparatively few negro slaves, were the man power that built the colony. African slavery had existed in Virginia since 1619, but after twenty years the total number of slaves in the colony did not amount to more than one hundred and fifty; and by 1648 the number had increased to only three hundred. Nor were these slaves held by the average planter; they were the property of a very small number of men who owned very large estates, such, for example, as Captain Samuel Mathews.[19]

Mathews had come to Virginia in 1622. By industry, courage and prudent marriage he had accumulated thousands of acres of land. In addition to tobacco he raised wheat and barley. On his home plantation he grew hemp and flax. He had his own weavers who made cloth for the clothing required by his servants. He kept eight shoemakers busy— doubtless indentured servants. He had forty negro slaves. He had large herds of cattle and a fine dairy. He kept hogs and poultry. He was a member of the Governor's Council. In short, as a contemporary expressed it, he "kept a good house" and "lived bravely."[20]

In a household such as that maintained by Captain Mathews there was generally a servant who took care of the accounts and kept records. He had been secured because of his superior education, and his spare time was often utilized in teaching the children of the family to read, write and "cypher." Children from neighboring plantations might ride over and join the class, or children of relatives might be sent for a visit of a few weeks with a view to acquiring some of the rudiments of education.[21]

For less fortunately situated youngsters there were at times, and in some places, what were known as Old Field Schools—community schoolhouses built on abandoned tobacco land with unemployed ministers acting as teachers. Sometimes the established minister himself would conduct a school in his parsonage. These were not free schools; the teacher charged a fee for each pupil.[22]

There were, however, two schools in the colony which

were endowed by individuals and served their communities without cost. Benjamin Symmes, by a will made in 1635, left the income from two hundred acres of land and the milk and increase from eight cows for the founding of such a school. Later a similar institution was endowed by Thomas Eaton. When, in 1671, Governor Berkeley thanked God that there were no free schools in Virginia, he might as well have saved his gratitude; both the Symmes and Eaton free schools were then in existence only a few miles from Jamestown, and they continued to serve their communities for nearly a century and a half.²³

Sir William Berkeley, thirty-six years of age, polished courtier, and member of an influential English family, first arrived at the dreary, tide-washed village of Jamestown in 1642. He was the new Governor of Virginia. He and the hard-bitten Captain Samuel Mathews must have looked each other over with some interest. Mathews had been the leader in packing Governor Harvey off to England seven years earlier.²⁴

As Governor of the colony Berkeley was appointed by the King and supposedly paid by the King from the duties collected on tobacco imported into England. But the King had been hard pressed for money during the past few years and the salary of the previous governors had not been sufficient to meet the demands upon their dignity—and more particularly upon their table. Governor Harvey complained that he "might as well be called the host as the Governor of Virginia." In view of this situation and because it had "an eye to the Honor" of the office, the General Assembly levied a special tax for the support of Governor Berkeley.²⁵

The General Assembly of Virginia consisted of two houses. The Governor and his Council sat as an upper house or senate; the House of Burgesses as a lower house. The members of the Council were appointed by the Governor but subject to confirmation by the King. The members of the House of Burgesses were elected by the freemen of the colony in accordance with the frame of government introduced by the Virginia Company in 1619. Following the dissolution of the Company in 1624, there had been considerable uncertainty in the minds of the colonists as to the status of their government. However, they went ahead electing houses of burgesses and conducting their affairs on the basis of acts passed by that body—always with the possibility that the King might declare the whole business illegal and void.[26]

Then, in his orders of 1639, the King directed that a house of burgesses be summoned each year "as formerly"; and in his instructions to Berkeley the order again appeared. Representative government had at last won royal recognition. It may be that gratitude for this had something to do with the generous treatment which Governor Berkeley received at the hands of the Assembly.[27]

Burgesses to the first General Assembly in 1619 had been elected from ill-defined groups of plantations. As the colony grew, there arose the need for more exact administrative divisions. In 1634 the then settled area was divided into eight counties. Subsequently, when the population increased and settlement was extended, existing counties were divided or new counties created. The county became the important local political unit of the colony. From each county one or more burgesses were elected to the General Assembly. All free males of legal age not only had the right to vote for their burgesses but were subject to a fine if they failed to do so. Indentured servants and slaves did not vote.[28]

The county also became the important unit for the administration of justice. To the county courts, sitting monthly, the parish referred its cases; to the county courts the justices of the peace presented cases beyond their jurisdiction; to these courts came servants who had grievances against their masters and masters who had grievances against their servants. The probate of wills and the care of orphans came under the county courts. Justice was dispensed in accordance with a code based partly on the laws of England and partly upon precedents established within the colony. Appeals could be carried to the General Court, consisting of the Governor and Council; and in certain cases the General Assembly acted as a court of final appeal. "More speedy Justice and with smaller charge is not in any place to be found," said a long-time resident of the colony.[29]

Thus by the 1640's Virginia had worked out an administrative system suited to its needs. The parishes were charged with supervision over purely local affairs. Above the parishes were the county officials and courts. At the top was the general government. For the support of each of these units a separate tax was levied—not against the land or the personal property of the inhabitants but rather against their persons. In other words, the levy was a head, or poll, tax. The negro slave and the indentured servant were assessed at exactly the same rate as the planter who owned thousands of acres of land. This does not mean that the negro slave or the indentured servant actually paid the tax. It was paid on their account by the planter who owned the slave or held the indenture of the servant. Thus the burden fell on the possession of manpower which was in reality the outstanding source of wealth in the colony. Land without men to work it was valueless.[30]

Usually, and as a matter of course, taxes were assessed and paid in tobacco. The levies varied from year to year but the average combined county and general tax per head would seem to have been about fifty pounds of tobacco. The average price of tobacco was two pence a pound, equivalent to four cents in United States money, and the purchasing power of money in 1640 was between four and five times greater than it was exactly three hundred years later. Occasionally other products than tobacco were specified in a tax act. The special levy in 1642 for the support of Governor Berkeley was payable in corn, wheat, beef, pork, goats, turkeys, butter and similar items—perhaps intended as a supply for the Governor's table in case he, like Harvey, should be called upon to be the "host of Virginia."[31]

With this good start, and despite his lack of previous acquaintance with frontier life, Governor Berkeley got on well in Virginia. He allied himself with the best interests of the colony, and had no difficulty in getting the leading men, such as Captain Mathews, to accept places on his Council. He gained the good will of the House of Burgesses by ready approval of its demands for broader powers.[32]

His first unpleasant experience was with a group of Puritans who had lived in the colony for many years and who took just this time to make themselves noticeable. The moment probably seemed propitious to them. Their fellow Puritans were in the ascendancy in the new English Parliament and Parliament was the boss in England. Archbishop Laud, their arch-enemy, was in prison; King Charles' chief minister had been beheaded; and the King, himself, had fled from London. It seemed unreasonable that Puritans in an English colony should longer be deprived of Puritan ministers.

So, in the autumn of 1642, these Virginia Puritans sent a letter to the elders at Massachusetts Bay "bewailing their sad condition for want of the means of salvation, and earnestly entreating a supply of faithful ministers." The church people at the Bay gladly complied, and a few weeks later three New England ministers arrived at Jamestown with a letter of commendation to the Governor of Virginia from the Governor of Massachusetts. They received anything but a friendly reception from Governor Berkeley. Neither he nor the majority of the people of Virginia sympathized with what was going on in England, and the fact that the rebellion against the King was being led by Puritans only served to prejudice the Governor and the Virginians against people of that persuasion. Within a matter of weeks the General Assembly passed a law forbidding any one to preach, either publicly or privately, who did not conform to the discipline of the Church of England. This was Berkeley's reply to Winthrop's letter. The Puritan ministers returned to Massachusetts and their prospective congregations turned their eyes to Catholic Maryland as a refuge from Church-of-England Virginia.[33]

In many ways life in Maryland paralleled life in Virginia. Tobacco was the staple crop; indentured servants, with a sprinkling of negro slaves, formed the labor supply; the plantations hugged navigable water; the same ships that brought clothing, furniture, hoes and other manufactured goods to the Virginia planters brought supplies to the Maryland planters—and carried their tobacco back to England.

St. Mary's, the capital of Maryland, lay about three miles

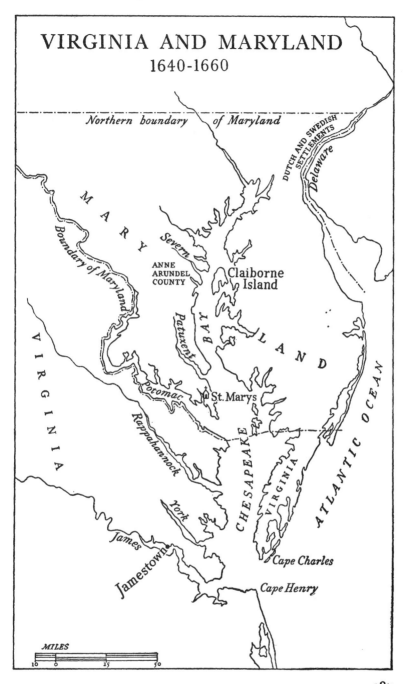

VIRGINIA AND MARYLAND
1640-1660

Northern boundary of Maryland

DUTCH AND SWEDISH SETTLEMENTS

Delaware

M A R Y

Boundary of Maryland

Severn

ANNE
ARUNDEL
COUNTY

Claiborne
Island

Patuxent

B A Y

L A N D

VIRGINIA

Potomac

St. Marys

Rappahannock

CHESAPEAKE

VIRGINIA

ATLANTIC OCEAN

York

James

Jamestown

Cape Charles

Cape Henry

MILES

10   0   25   50

up an inlet on the northerly side of the Potomac River. By water the town was not over twelve miles from the entrance of the Potomac into Chesapeake Bay. Directly overland it was only about four miles from the Chesapeake. Northward, by an Indian path, it was only nine miles from the Patuxent, a deep-water river reaching into the mainland from the Chesapeake. The location gave ready access to all parts of the province; and it was a much more healthful place than Jamestown.[34]

It was at St. Mary's that Governor Calvert made his first settlement in 1634. Six years later the town consisted of about a dozen houses. On the waterfront stood the fort. Adjoining was the home of Governor Calvert. Half a mile to the eastward was the brick house of Thomas Cornwallis, now reconciled to raising the "stincking weed of America." Scattered over an area of roughly a mile square were the homes of the other leaders of the colony—Catholics all. Between them and the Protestant servants and small landholders the social line was sharply drawn. St. Mary's might be a long way from England, but the Calverts, the Cornwallises, and the rest of them lived up to the position they had held in the Mother Country. Their dining tables were covered with fine linens. Silver spoons, cruets and bowls sparkled among the dishes. If the ladies did not have the very latest gowns from London, they made up for it by a display of gold chains, diamonds and other jewels. Virginia could not look down its nose at Maryland.[35]

Near the Governor's house stood the Catholic Chapel. There during certain hours on Sundays Father Fisher celebrated Mass for the Catholic leaders of the colony, and at other hours the Protestant farmers and servants read the Book of Common Prayer. Only once in the six or seven years during which the chapel was used jointly did an untoward incident occur. In 1641 Thomas Gerrard, a prominent Catholic, took away the prayer books and locked the Protestants out of the building. For this act he was fined five hundred pounds of tobacco by a court composed mostly of his fellow Catholics; and it was further stipulated that the fine was to go toward the support of a minister for the Protestants, when they got one.[36]

The Governor's "Castle" at St. Mary's, 1639. Reconstructed by Doctor
Henry C. Forman, Wesleyan College, Macon, Ga.

Right. Anne Arundel,
wife of Cecil Calvert,
Lord Baltimore. The
county of Anne Arun-
del, Maryland, was
named in her honor.
Doubtless the young
ladies at St. Mary's did
their hair in the same
fashion.

289

From St. Mary's the settlements had spread westward up the Potomac, southeastward down the peninsula, and northward to the Patuxent. Across Chesapeake Bay Claiborne's former trading post and plantation on Kent Island (as it was now more commonly called) had been brought to terms and forced to acknowledge the authority of Lord Baltimore.

For administrative purposes Maryland, like Virginia, was divided into counties, though they did not have the same importance as in the older colony. There being no established church in Maryland, there was, of course, no parish government as in Virginia. The local units were called "hundreds," and from them burgesses were elected to a provincial assembly. There the burgesses, together with the Governor's Council, sat in a single body presided over by the Governor. Since the Governor and the members of the Council were appointees of the Proprietor, the proceedings generally went the way he directed that they should go.[37]

To attract planters of limited means Lord Baltimore had made many small grants in fee simple; that is, the owner could mortgage his land, sell it or bequeath it, with no other liens than he himself had placed upon it. Most of the larger plantations, however, were held subject to quitrents—payable annually forever to the Proprietor by whoever held title to the land.[38]

In addition to granting land in fee simple or subject to quitrents Lord Baltimore introduced a feudal system of landholding which was common in England at the time but not hitherto attempted in America. It was a natural thing for him to do. His patent from the King followed the English feudal pattern; that is, he did not own Maryland; he *held* it from the King. The considerations which he gave were his fealty and two Indian arrows to be delivered annually at Windsor Castle. The arrows were of course merely tokens of his dependence upon the King, but by the fact that they were only tokens it was understood that great service was due to his overlord.[39]

The service which Baltimore undertook in behalf of the King was that of peopling and governing the province of Maryland. By his patent he was authorized to depute parts

of his privileges and responsibilities to others who were willing to *hold* small divisions of the province under him—by
oaths of fealty and the payment of rents to himself. These
sub-grants were known as manors; in size they varied from
one thousand to six thousand acres; and the man who held
one became the lord of the manor. Usually the lord reserved
a part of his manor to be farmed by his own servants for the
support of himself and his manor house; the rest he granted
in small parcels to tenants who, in their turn, *held* from him
by oaths of fealty and paid rents to him. Nor were these
rents—paid by the tenants—mere tokens such as Indian arrows; they were substantially equivalent to what the use of
the land was worth.

But there was much more to manorial tenure than the
payment of rents. By the oath of fealty, running in a sequence
from tenant to King, the manor acquired a political status.
Manorial courts, made up of the tenants and presided over
by the lord or his steward, dispensed justice for offenses committed within the manor, settled controversies, and otherwise administered the affairs of the manor, which was, in
short, a small self-contained principality.

During the early years of the colony some sixty such
manors were created around about St. Mary's. Leonard Calvert was lord of Trinity, St. Gabriel's and St. Michael's
manors. Thomas Cornwallis was lord of Cross and Resurrec-
tion manors. Thomas Gerrard was lord of the manor of St.
Clement's. And there with them, as lord of the manor of
Westbury, was Thomas Weston, who more than any other
one man had made possible the sailing of the *Mayflower*.[40]

Weston was now approaching the ripe age of seventy. We
last met him in 1624, in company with the irascible Captain
John Martin, on his way from New England to Virginia.
There he remained a number of years, becoming a member
of the House of Burgesses in 1628. Just when he moved to
Maryland is uncertain, but he was adjudged a freeman in
the provincial assembly of 1642.[41] One may wonder whether,
as he presided over a court-baron on his manor of Westbury,
he ever harked back in memory to his long-lost colony at
Wessagusset—or recalled the day when, on the coast of New

England, he was stripped to his shirt by the Indians. Probably not. More likely he was thinking up some new scheme that was sure to make him rich the next year. However, Westbury seems to have been his last great venture. He died in 1644, and in parting we are moved to say: Well done, old Tom Weston. You dug up the money when it was needed, and you had the courage to risk it. Without you and men of your sort there might have been no English colonies in America.

That Weston held a manor in Maryland does not at all mean that he had accepted Catholicism. True, the colony had been founded by a Catholic as a refuge for Catholics. True too, Maryland was the only place under English rule where the Catholic form of worship could be openly practiced. But Catholicism was not the established church in Maryland. Not only did Baltimore's patent require him to allow the Church of England service but he had gone out of his way to see that the Protestants in his colony were neither persecuted nor offended.

Curiously enough very few of Baltimore's fellow Catholics availed themselves of the haven which he had provided for them. From the first there had been more Church of England people than Catholics among the settlers. As the colony grew, the percentage of non-Catholics also grew. And as the Puritans gained control of the revolutionary movement then in the ascendancy in England, Baltimore made overtures to those of that profession. In 1643 he wrote to Edward Gibbons, at Boston, outlining the attractions of Maryland for any Massachusetts people who might wish to settle there, at the same time giving assurances of freedom in matters of worship. Gibbons will be recalled as a sinner snatched from Morton's Merry Mount by the forceful preaching of Mr. Skelton. Later he became a member of Winthrop's church, and when Baltimore's letter arrived he was one of the outstanding merchants at the Bay. Neither Gibbons nor any of his friends appears to have accepted the invitation, but the fact of its having been proffered probably did no harm to Baltimore's cause when the story got back to England—where the puritanically inclined Earl of Warwick had just been appointed by Parliament to head a commission for the control of colonial affairs.[42]

But with all Baltimore's profession of, and insistence upon, freedom of religion, the fact remained that the actual government of Maryland was firmly in the hands of a small group of Catholics. Provincial assemblies, with Protestant burgesses, might meet and go through the motion of making laws only to be overruled by the Catholic members of the Council or by the Catholic Governor or by the Catholic Proprietor, each and every one of whom owed his estate and his position to the King by an oath of fealty.[43]

This was well known to the Puritan leaders of Parliament, as was also the fact that a good deal of the trade with Maryland was going to Dutch ships operated by English royalists who used the profits to support the King's army.

Caught thus between the forces contending for mastery in England, and with his province at stake, Baltimore summoned his brother, the Governor of Maryland, to England for counsel and advice. Calvert sailed from St. Mary's in April, 1643. During his absence the acting Governor either stirred up or was unable to stop friction between the Catholics and the Protestants of the province. Whether or not Thomas Bushnell actually said, "I hope that there will be ne'er a Papist left in Maryland by May day," the words expressed what was in many minds.[44]

While in England, Governor Calvert probably joined the King in his winter camp at Oxford. Then, if ever, the King needed fealty. Full half of his subjects were arrayed in arms against him. London with all its wealth and trade was in their hands. To Calvert the King gave a commission directing him to go to Virginia and there, with the aid of Governor Berkeley, seize all ships belonging to merchants of London—this because those merchants were carrying on "a great trade in the dominion and colony of Virginia, receiving daily great advantages from thence, which they impiously spend in vast contributions toward the maintenance of an unnatural war. . . ."[45]

But Virginia was having its own troubles that spring of 1644. Old Opechancanough, who had instigated the massacre of 1622, again broke loose. The frontiers suffered severely before the Indians were finally subdued. When word of the disaster reached London, Parliament authorized a number of ships to carry food, clothing, arms and ammunition "for the supply and defense and relief of the planters of Virginia." Among these ships was the *Reformation* commanded by Captain Ingle, who had previously traded at St. Mary's and who was at odds with the officials there.[46]

In the early autumn of 1644 Governor Calvert was back at St. Mary's. Hurriedly putting the affairs of his colony into the hands of a subordinate, he departed for Virginia, presumably to arrange with Berkeley for the seizure of the London ships as ordered by the King. Naturally Claiborne, as Secretary of Virginia colony, learned the content of Calvert's commission. As always, his thoughts turned to the possible recovery of Kent Island. Probably he knew that the majority of the settlers there sympathized with Parliament rather than the King—and here was a chance to oust Calvert. Force was not necessary; the Kent Island people were ready to be persuaded that Calvert was disloyal to Parliament and that not only his authority should end but that his fellow Catholics should be thrown out. One enthusiastic adherent of the new regime went up into the loft of the house of a Catholic planter and, pitching down a number of books, exclaimed, "Burn them Papist Divells."[47]

News of what was happening at Kent Island brought Governor Calvert back to Maryland, but before he had time to restore order on his rebellious frontier, he was confronted by a more serious danger. St. Mary's itself was under the guns of the *Reformation* of London, Captain Ingle master.[48]

Ingle had arrived at Virginia late in 1644 or early 1645. There Claiborne had told him of Calvert's commission to seize all ships out of London and may have suggested turning the tables. It is, of course, just possible that Ingle had been sent over by the Parliamentary party to spike Calvert's proposed activities. In any case, under the pretense of suppressing opposition to the Parliamentary cause, Ingle sailed for St. Mary's. There he captured a ship flying the Dutch flag, but operating for English merchants—doubtless royalists. He next proceeded to stir up the discontented Protestants to join with him in looting the homes and property of the Catholics. For four or five months he and his followers burned and plundered at will; and when, in the summer of 1645 he sailed for England, he carried along as prisoners two or three of the Jesuit priests for trial on charges of treason.[49]

Governor Calvert had fled to Virginia to escape capture. So disturbed were conditions in Maryland that more than a year passed before he could recover control, and then only through the assistance of Governor Berkeley. Nor did the Governor long enjoy his return to authority. On June 9, 1647, he died.[50]

In selecting a successor to his brother, Lord Baltimore acted with considerable political deftness. The charge of Catholic domination was being increasingly leveled against the government of Maryland—and had to be met. Baltimore met it by appointing William Stone, a Protestant, to the governorship. At the same time he protected the Catholic minority in the province. In the oath which the new Governor was required to take upon assuming office was the commitment, ". . . I will not by myself, or any person directly or indirectly, trouble, molest, or discountenance any person whatsoever in the said province professing to believe in Jesus Christ, and particularly no Roman Catholick. . . ."[51]

Baltimore's next move was even more astute. With the Puritan faction unmistakably in control of the government of England, he opened Maryland to the unhappy Puritans of Virginia. The invitation was gratefully accepted and during 1649 a hundred or more Puritan planters with their families, under the leadership of Richard Bennet, emigrated from Virginia to the fertile land on the western shore of Chesapeake Bay, opposite Kent Island. The region was soon organized as a county under the name of Anne Arundel. Today the city of Annapolis lies within the general area.[52]

The admission of these Puritans undoubtedly helped Baltimore's case with Parliament, but it was a foregone conclusion that after the next election in Maryland the Protestants would be in control of the provincial government. Accordingly, while he still had the power, Baltimore prepared and caused the assembly to pass an Act Concerning Religion, which officially extended full toleration to all who professed the Christian religion. The act really did little more than restate the instructions which the Proprietor had given his brother in 1633 and which Governor Stone's oath had confirmed. But the action of the assembly turned an instruction into a law; also it emphasized the fact that Maryland was not a Catholic colony. And by the token that the act extended liberty of worship to all Christians it extended the same liberty to Catholics.[53]

While Lord Baltimore was temporizing with the revolutionary leaders in England, Governor Berkeley of Virginia was standing steadfast in his loyalty to the King—now a captive in the hands of the faction with which Baltimore was dealing. On January 20, 1649, the King was brought to trial before a so-called High Court of Justice. The charge was that he had "traitorously levied war against the Parliament and people of England." His conviction was a foregone conclusion. On January 30 he was beheaded. As the axe fell, a groan of horror burst from the spectators and echoed throughout England.[54]

To the fierce Puritan minority, hoisted to power by its victorious armies and bent on reshaping England according to its particular pattern, the death of the King was a "cruel necessity." The next step was to abolish the office of king as being "unnecessary, burdensome, and dangerous to the liberty, safety and public interests of the people." The government of England became a Commonwealth. Any one who recognized the late King's son, then a refugee, was to be "deemed and adjudged a Traitor to the Commonwealth."[55]

But to Governor Berkeley, of Virginia, and to the Governors of the island colonies of Bermuda, of Barbados and of Antigua, treason lay in recognizing the Commonwealth. To them the son of the dead Charles I was now King; they recognized him as Charles II; and from him Berkeley received, as evidence of royal approval, a commission to continue as Governor of Virginia.[56]

For the Proprietor of Maryland the fugitive King had no kind words. Lord Baltimore "doth visibly adher to the rebels in England and admit all kinde of schismatics and sectaries, and other ill-effected persons into . . . Maryland," said Charles—and, ignoring the Proprietor's rights, he appointed his own Governor for the province. At the same time he encouraged Governor Berkeley to launch an attack on Maryland from Virginia. However, the King's appointee was promptly picked up by a Commonwealth warship, and before Berkeley could move against Maryland he found himself face to face with the punitive power of the Commonwealth.[57]

The leaders of the new government in England had not been unaware of the attitude of Berkeley and the other recalcitrant governors. Also they knew that in Virginia and the island colonies were many former officers of the defeated royalist armies—being hospitably entertained by the planters while they fanned hatred of the Commonwealth government. The fact that the royalists had got across on Dutch ships and that those ships had carried most of the tobacco and other products of the colonies back to Holland made the situation even less tolerable.[58]

Accordingly, on October 3, 1650, Parliament passed an act which, after calling attention to the fact that Virginia, Bermuda, Barbados and Antigua had been founded "at the Cost" of England and "ought to be subordinate to, and dependent upon England," prohibited all trade with them until they recognized the Commonwealth. The act further authorized the Council of State to bring them to terms.[59]

To this Governor Berkeley replied in a hot speech before the Virginia House of Burgesses. "They talk of money laid out in this country in its infancy: I will not say how little, nor how Centuply repaid, but will onely aske, was it theirs? They who in the beginning of this warr were so porre & indigent that the wealth and rapines of three kingdomes & their churches too, cannot yet make rich, but are faine to seek out new Territories and impositions to sustain their Luxury amongst themselves. Surely Gentlemen we are more slaves by nature, then their power can make of us, if we suffer ourselves to be shaken with these paper bulletts & those on my life are the heaviest they Either can or will send us. 'Tis true, with us, they have long threatened the Barbados, yet not a ship goes thither but to beg trade nor will they do to us, if we dare Honourably resist their Imperious Ordinances. . . ."[60]

But Berkeley had underrated the men who were running the government of England. In the autumn of 1651 a war fleet appeared before Barbados, and the island colonies were forced to submit. Early the following March the same fleet was before Jamestown. Berkeley made a show of resistance but prudence prevailed. Virginia surrendered on terms agreed upon between her officials and three commissioners who had been designated by the Commonwealth. Interestingly enough two of the commissioners were far from strangers to Virginia, and those two dominated the proceedings. One was Captain William Claiborne, the long-time enemy of Lord Baltimore; the other was Richard Bennet, who had led the Puritan migration from Virginia to Maryland in 1649.

By the terms of capitulation Virginia agreed to be subject to the Commonwealth; the commissioners granted indemnity to Virginia for past acts of disloyalty to Parliament; the General Assembly of the colony was permitted to function as in the past; no taxes were to be levied without the consent of the General Assembly; the Book of Common Prayer might continue to be read, with the omission of prayers for\ the King; the established ministers were not to be disturbed. Most important, perhaps, among the terms was a clause stating that Virginia should "have and enjoy the ancient bounds and limits granted by the charters of the former Kings, and that we shall seek a new charter from Parliament to that purpose against any that have intrenched upon the rights thereof. . . ." This doubtless was primarily the contribution of Claiborne, and was aimed straight at Maryland. The intent was to reunite Maryland with Virginia—from which it had been carved by Baltimore's patent, or charter, of 1632. Mathews, acting for Virginia, would readily have connived at such a clause. In any case, there it was, and it was a very real threat to Baltimore's proprietary rights.[61]

And there was an even more immediate threat to the rights of Baltimore. Maryland had not been included among

CAPTAIN WILLIAM CLAIBORNE.
Courtesy, Mrs. Alfred Grima (*née* Clarisse Claiborne), New Orleans.

the colonies to be reduced by the fleet, but the instructions had named Virginia loosely as Chesapeake Bay. That was enough for Claiborne and Bennet. Maryland lay in the Chesapeake Bay region, and across the Bay they went to St. Mary's. Governor Stone was compelled to submit and the government of Maryland was placed under a local commission, responsible to the Commonwealth commissioners rather than to Lord Baltimore.[62]

With this taken care of, Claiborne and Bennet returned to Virginia. There, together with the House of Burgesses, they organized a provisional government. Berkeley retired to private life on his plantation. Bennet became Governor of the colony and Claiborne Secretary of State. Captain Samuel Mathews, George Ludlow and other prominent men accepted places on the Governor's Council; and the affairs of Virginia went along much as in the past.[63]

Not even a trade war between England and the Dutch immediately affected the Virginia planters. They had been in the habit of selling their tobacco to the Dutch ship captains, who paid better prices than the English. When, in 1651, Parliament passed a Navigation Act excluding all except English ships from the colonial trade, the planters either ignored the law or sent their tobacco to New Amsterdam from whence it went to Europe in Dutch ships as usual.[64]

All in all the colony was prospering and growing. Wheat was being successfully grown on abandoned tobacco land. Cattle and hogs, running loose and shifting for themselves, brought good prices in the export trade. Population had increased by more than half since 1640.[65]

Meanwhile in England the days of the Commonwealth were numbered. Parliament, a pitiful "rump" of the body that had assembled so bravely in 1640, was trembling before the armed might which it had created. On April 20, 1653, Oliver Cromwell, Commander-in-Chief of the armies of England, strode into the House of Commons. "Come, come," he said, "I will put an end to your prating"—and he did. Eight months later Cromwell became the Protector of England. Government under the pronouncements of the old Parliament had presumably ceased to exist.[66]

To Richard Bennet, as Governor of Virginia, and William Claiborne, as Secretary of the Colony, the change of government in England was not immediately applicable since their offices were by confirmation of the General Assembly of Virginia. But to Richard Bennet and William Claiborne, as Commissioners of the Commonwealth of England, the change spelled the legal end of their authority.

Lord Baltimore was quick to act. He wrote to Stone directing him to resume the governorship of Maryland. St. Mary's and the older counties readily submitted. Not so the Puritan county of Anne Arundel. The planters there stood out for a continuance of the government under the commissioners. Stiffened into action by a sharp letter from Baltimore, Governor Stone got together a force of some two hundred men and in March, 1655, moved northward to compel obedience. On the banks of the Severn River, near the present city of Annapolis, he found the Puritans waiting for him. "In the name of God fall on, God is our strength," ordered the Puritan commander—and God was with them. Stone was completely defeated. Twenty of his men were killed; and, according to one witness, the field of battle was "strewn with Papist beads where they fled."

Following the battle, many prisoners remained in the hands of the victorious Puritans. Several of them were condemned to death by a drumhead court-martial, and four were actually executed. The Puritans were in full control of the province; nor were they nearly so tolerant of the Catholics as the Catholic Proprietor had been of them.[67]

Thus in both Maryland and Virginia the provisional governments organized by Claiborne and Bennet continued to function. Meanwhile, Captain Mathews was in England making every effort to have Maryland rejoined to Virginia as suggested in the terms under which Virginia had submitted to the Commonwealth government in 1652. Mathews attacked Baltimore's patent on the grounds that it applied to lands that were uncultivated and uninhabited whereas Kent Island, lying within the area claimed by Baltimore, had been cultivated and inhabited "long before the name of Maryland was even heard of." Also he made the most of "that old,

great, sad complaint of . . . poor ignorant Protestants" being seduced and ruled over by Papists.[68]

But with everything seemingly in his favor Mathews found
himself outplayed by the shrewder Proprietor. The long fight
to recover Maryland was lost and Mathews finally realized
that fact. On November 30, 1657, he and Baltimore signed
an agreement ending all the differences between the two
colonies. Baltimore had won on every point, even to the re-
tention of the Act Concerning Religion. In the Province of
Maryland, Puritans or any other Christians might practice
their religion, but Catholics could do the same.[69]

Mathews returned to Virginia where, on March 13, 1658,
he was elected Governor. Six months later Oliver Cromwell,
Protector of England, died and was succeeded by his son
Richard. In May, 1659, Richard Cromwell resigned. The
following January Governor Mathews died. England had
no Protector and Virginia had no Governor. In March, 1660,
the General Assembly of the Colony of Virginia met and
declared that, since in England there was no certain, absolute
and acknowledged power, Virginia would act for itself. Sir
William Berkeley was recalled from his plantation and restored to the office of Governor, which he accepted with the
understanding that "if any supreme settled power appears,
I will immediately lay down my commission. . . ."[70]

The revolutionary movement was slowing to a halt in
England. Virginia and Maryland had weathered the storm.
Each had preserved its territory, its identity and its funda-
mental institutions.

North of the Merrimac

I T WOULD HAVE SEEMED only natural for the people of New Hampshire and Maine to have sympathized with the royal cause in the conflict going on in England. And so they probably would have done, had they been left to their own courses. Both colonies had been founded by men who gave unquestioning allegiance to the King and to the institutions for which he stood. The inhabitants were largely of the Church of England persuasion. Their economic welfare depended upon a continuation of the established trade with the Mother Country.

But New Hampshire was, as we have already seen, in a confused condition. Captain Mason, the Proprietor, had died before he received a royal confirmation of his grant from the Council for New England. His heir was a minor. His wife had little interest in the plantation on the Piscataqua River, and soon advised the employees to shift for themselves—which they did. One of them drove a hundred head of Captain Mason's blooded Danish cattle down to Boston and sold them, pocketing the proceeds. Another pulled the cannon off the fort and sold them, for his own benefit. The rest followed suit, and in a short time nothing remained for Mason's heir except the title to the land.[1]

Nor was the title itself safe from grasping hands. Massa-

chusetts looked northward across the Merrimac with covet-
ous eyes. The first move appears to have been the acquisition
by the Bay colony of a questionable right to govern the
plantations which, as will be recalled, Lords Say and Brook
had bought at Piscataqua some years earlier. At the same
time the leaders at the Bay began suggesting to the inhabitants of the New Hampshire towns that it would be to their
advantage to place themselves under the kindly wing of
Massachusetts.[2]

Even Captain Underhill, while acting as Governor of
Dover, joined in urging the people of that little New Hampshire town to accept the offer of the Bay colony. That some,
at least, did not like the idea is evident from an incident
that occurred in the spring of 1641. In his campaign in behalf of Massachusetts, Underhill had enlisted the aid of the
Reverend Hanserd Knollys, leader of the more godly sort
among the inhabitants and later a much-respected minister
in England. Another minister, heading the opposition, gathered up a few of his followers and started to arrest Underhill. The Governor and his cohorts issued forth to meet the
challenge—one man holding aloft a Bible on the point of
a long-handled sword, and Knollys waving a pistol. Faced
with this determined show of strength, the attacking party
gave ground until reinforcements could come up from Strawberry Bank. When things quieted down, a court was organized and Underhill was banished from New Hampshire.[3]

Thus the first gentle approach of Massachusetts failed.
However, when the men of the Bay put their minds to a
problem they usually found a solution, and this was no exception. They examined their patent and surveyed the Merrimac River. The patent placed their northern boundary at
a point three miles north of the Merrimac "or to the norward
of any and every parte thereof," with an implication that
the line ran east and west from sea to sea through this most
northern point. At the time the patent was granted no one
had any idea of the position of the upper course of this river;
in fact, early exploration had shown it turning southward
and the boundary had been looked upon as following the
curves of the river at a distance of three miles. Now, how-

HANSERD KNOLLYS.

He soon lost favor with the Massachusetts leaders. Governor Winthrop tells us that he was "discovered to be an unclean person, and to have solicited the chastity of two maids, his servants, and to have used filthy dalliance with them, which he acknowledged before the church there, and so was dismissed, and removed from Pascataquack."

From this statement we need only gather that Knollys refused to accept the interpretation of the Word then being rigidly enforced at the Bay. The charge of uncleanness was one consistently leveled at those who disagreed.

The portrait is from James Culross, *Hanserd Knollys*.

ever, it was suddenly discovered that the Merrimac again turned northward—how far was still uncertain, but far enough for the present purpose.[4]

On October 7, 1641, the General Court of Massachusetts Bay recorded "Whereas it appeareth that by the extent of the line, (according to our patent) . . . the ryver of Pascataquack is within the jurisdiction of the Massachusets . . . it is now ordered . . . That from hencefourth the said people inhabiting there are, & shalbee, accepted & reputed under the government of the Massachusets." New Hampshire became a colony of Massachusetts colony. The ways of life and of thinking of Massachusetts became the ways of life and thinking of New Hampshire. The Reverend John Wheelwright, who only three years before had established the town of Exeter in New Hampshire as a refuge from the ways of thinking of Massachusetts, found himself again within the power of Massachusetts. He moved northward across the Piscataqua to Gorges' Province of Maine.[5]

The extent to which life and thought in Maine differed from that in Massachusetts is well shown by the experience of a Bay minister on a visit to the northern province. The minister urged his listeners to be more religious; otherwise, he told them, they would "contradict the main end of planting this wilderness," to which a voice from the pews replied, "Sir, you are mistaken, you think you are preaching to the people at the Bay; *our main end was to catch fish.*"[6]

For more than thirty years—ever since the first attempted settlement at Sagadahoc in 1607—Sir Ferdinando Gorges had been godfather of the Maine coast. He had organized the Council for New England, from which every one of the colonies between the Hudson and the Penobscot had sprung. He had expected to be governor-general of all New England. He had seen part after part of his domain snatched from him. However, he was now, by a patent from the royal hand, Proprietor of the territory between the Piscataqua and Kennebec rivers and reaching a hundred and twenty miles inland —"forever hereafter [to] be called & named the Province or County of Maine."[7]

Within the bounds of Gorges' province lay several well-

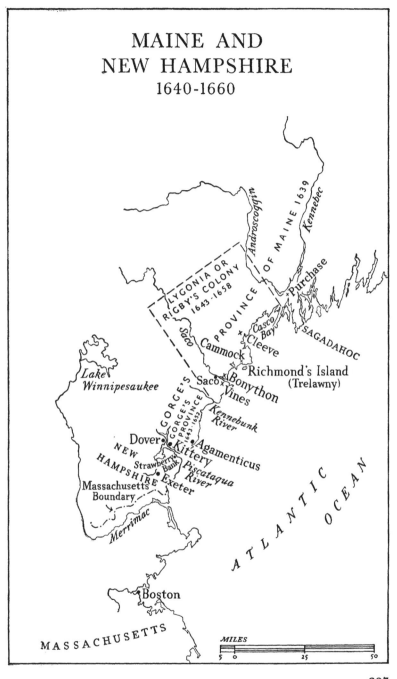

MAINE AND
NEW HAMPSHIRE
1640-1660

Androscoggin

Kennebec

PROVINCE OF MAINE 1639

LYGONIA OR
RIGBY'S COLONY
1643-1658

×Purchase

Saco

PROVINCE OF MAINE

SAGADAHOC

Casco
Bay

Cammock

×Cleeve

Lake
Winnipesaukee

Saco×

Bonython

Richmond's Island
(Trelawny)

Vines

GORGE'S

GORGE'S PROVINCE
1643-1652

Kennebunk
River

Dover•

Agamenticus

•Kittery

NEW

Strawberry
Bank•

Piscataqua
River

HAMPSHIRE

•Exeter

Massachusetts
Boundary

Merrimac

ATLANTIC

OCEAN

•Boston

MASSACHUSETTS

MILES

5 0   25   50

established plantations. At Agamenticus, a few miles northward of the Piscataqua, Edward Godfrey presided over a small settlement that had grown up around a trading post operated for Gorges himself. Twenty-five miles to the northeast—on the southerly side of the Saco River—was Richard Vines. Across the river from Vines was Richard Bonython, whose partner, Thomas Lewis, had just died. A half-dozen miles farther on was the fifteen-hundred-acre plantation of Thomas Cammock. Adjoining Cammock on the mainland and occupying all of Richmond's Island, lying opposite, was the Trelawny plantation. It was managed by John Winter for the owner, a wealthy and influential merchant of Plymouth, England. In Casco Bay, where the city of Portland now stands, was George Cleeve, poor but pugnacious. Still easterly, on the Androscoggin River, was Thomas Purchase.[8]

Gorges, like Lord Baltimore, *held* his province from the King by an oath of fealty and a token payment—eight bushels of wheat, to be exact, though the place of delivery was not specified. What with Indian arrows from Baltimore, the King may have figured that he could get along without having a wagon pull up to Windsor Castle once a year with a load of wheat from Gorges.

Also, like Baltimore, Gorges had full authority to establish a government, administer justice and grant land. And if Baltimore's manors were out of place in Maryland, some of the feudal institutions which Gorges tried to establish in Maine were little less than fantastic. It would have been helpful if Gorges and Baltimore each could have spent a season in their respective colonies. They would have discovered that what worked in England was not suited to a raw country such as America.

As the capital of his province Gorges selected the little settlement of Agamenticus, which he rechristened Gorgeana in honor of himself. On paper he raised the tiny town to the status of a city with more high-sounding offices than there were people in the place. Provision was even made for the appointment of a bishop.[9]

However, the immediate need was not for a bishop but rather for a governor and a government. In the absence of any other authority the people of Maine had, in a number of cases, appealed to the Governor and General Court of Massachusetts for aid in settling their problems—"as if they alone were the supreame lordes of that parte of the world," observed Gorges.[10]

Sir Ferdinando was too old to undertake personally the rigors of life in the New World. Accordingly, he appointed his nephew, Thomas Gorges, as deputy to act in his stead. Governor Gorges arrived in Maine in the late summer of 1640. There he found a large accumulation of sin, controversy and plain human nature awaiting the processes of justice. The new Governor summoned a court to meet at Saco, and plunged in.[11]

On the docket was a complaint against the Reverend George Burdett, of Agamenticus, formerly Governor of Dover, New Hampshire. He was "indicted by the whole bench for a man of ill name and fame, infamous for incontinency, a publisher and broacher of divers dangerous speeches the better to seduce that weake sex of women to his incontinent practises, contrary to the peace of our Soveraigne lord the King." The evidence amply supported the charge. The minister was given a thumping fine and one of his victims was sentenced to "stand in a white sheete publiquely in the congregation at Agamenticus two severall Sabath dayes, and likewise one day at the Generall Courte"—all this six weeks after she was delivered of the child.[12]

Also before the court at Saco appeared the Reverend Richard Gibson and his wife, the former Mary Lewis, daughter of the late Thomas Lewis. They testified that John Bonython, gentleman, the son of Lewis' partner, had called Gibson "a base preist, a base knave, a base fellow" and his wife "a base whore, an impudent whore, a base strumpet, with such other names often repeated with much contempt." Worse yet, young Bonython said he could prove his statements. However, he apparently failed to satisfy the jury—which assessed a good fine.[13]

Most important of the many complaints before the court were those of George Cleeve. From John Winter he demanded damages for the loss of his house and improvements opposite Richmond's Island—out of which Winter had driven him several years earlier; also he asked for a confirmation of his title to land in Casco Bay, out of which Winter was also trying to drive him. The jury awarded damages and confirmed the title.[14]

But being awarded damages and collecting them were two different things—particularly where John Winter was concerned. Cleeve called on the Governor to enforce the award of his court, and the Governor sent the marshal up to Richmond's Island to collect. The marshal reported that Winter beat him off the island. "But no such matter," said Winter, "our men never stroke him, but Carried him out of our house betwixt 3 or 4 of them, he refusing to go out when they bid him to departe out of the house. He told them he would not, so that was the cause they bore him out. So he departed & went away. . . ."

But the marshal did not stay away. He soon came back with thirty armed men while Winter was absent from the island. Winter's men were equal to the occasion; they declined to let the marshal and his men ashore. So the marshal and his band turned back to the mainland and marched to the house formerly owned by Cleeve, and now a part of the Trelawny plantation. No luck there either. One of Winter's men locked himself inside and told them that "if they did breake open the dore they should take what Comes." The marshal decided to let the matter rest—and Winter, egged on by Trelawny, went stubbornly ahead with his efforts to dispossess Cleeve from Casco Bay.[15]

It is evident that Trelawny had an efficient and determined organization at Richmond's Island. There were about thirty men regularly employed. Most of them were under contract, or indenture, to work for a specified length of time —three years on the average. They received agreed upon wages of from two to fourteen pounds per year which was the equivalent of from $45 to $315 as money was valued three hundred years later. They got food, shelter and clothing as a matter of course and received some share in the fishing. They differed from the indentured servants of Virginia in that they were not working out the cost of their transportation to America. They were working for wages, wherever their master directed and sent them. They were not particularly interested in coming to America, and many returned to England when their terms of service expired.[16]

In addition to these regular workmen there were at one time as many as four carpenters engaged in building a ship —which in due time was finished, loaded with fish and sailed to Europe. These carpenters were an independent lot; they would not hurry; and if Winter ventured to urge them to do so, their answer was, "If you do not like us we will be gon."[17]

On the mainland, across from the island, Winter raised corn, wheat, barley, peas and other grain. There, too, he had droves of hogs and some cattle. At first the Indians raided his stock; always the wolves were troublesome; but the increase more than offset the losses.[18]

The trade in furs, which had been profitable in the early 1630's, had now fallen off to a point where it was negligible. Beaver still passed as money but at only eight shillings a pound, and Winter did not think it was worth that. In 1640, when he had a supply of brandy and other desirable trade goods he refused to take beaver at more than six shillings— and was accused of debasing the currency. But the following year, when he had to pay five jars of whale oil and four shillings in money for an otter coat ordered by Trelawny, he observed, "to my thinkinge I pay deare for this."[19]

Whale oil and fish were probably the two most profitable products of the plantation. During the fishing seasons Winter had from three to six boats constantly at sea—each boat manned by three men. Occasionally there was a tragedy— men drowned or frozen to death—but others took their places. Year after year Winter complained that the fishing was poor; but generally, when Trelawny's ships anchored at Richmond Island, there were more fish and oil than cargo space —even after the ships had unloaded everything from boxes of shoes, stockings and soap to gridirons, thread, lamps, guns, kettles and canvas drawers, by which latter name men's pants were called in the seventeenth century.[20]

The great market for the fish was Catholic Spain, but

some were sold at Massachusetts Bay and Virginia. In 1640 Thomas Weston, then living in the southern colony, bought two hundred and thirty-three and a third pounds of fish from Winter at eighteen shillings per hundred. The clothing, tools, utensils and other manufactured goods which Trelawny sent over were in part for trade up and down the coast and in part for use on the plantation. Winter fed and housed his men and supplied some clothing, but whatever extras they wanted were charged against their wages.[21]

A few of the men lived in the old Cleeve house on the mainland, but most of them were taken care of in the big house on the island. This house was forty feet long by eighteen wide, and partitioned into two parts. In one side the men had their bunks; in the other, along with boxes of clothing, of sailcloth, and such, Winter and his wife, his daughter Sarah and a maid had their quarters. Underneath the house was a kitchen where the men ate their meals off wooden platters and drank their beer, the standard beverage of the time, from pewter "cans." The fireplace had a bake oven at either side and over the fire swung a great kettle in which much of the food was cooked.[22]

Mrs. Winter not only managed the house but attended to having the cows milked and the pigs fed. Nor was her job without its troubles. She could not get the maid up in the morning. Often she had to light the fires herself. The maid could not milk the cows; she was "so sluttish" that the men objected to having her do the cooking; nor could she be trusted "to serve a few piggs, but my wyfe most Commonly must be with her," complained Winter. In addition to all her other failings the maid had a habit of going to bed with her clothes on. All in all, Winter could not blame his wife for beating the girl once in a while; "if a faire way will not do it, beatinge must, sometimes, uppon such Idlle girrells as she is." Besides a little beating did her no harm —she was so fat and soggy.[23]

John Winter was having his trouble, too. As Parliament and the King squared off for a finish fight in England, the flow of immigration to America slackened. Ready money became scarce. Prices dropped. There was no market for cattle or other produce, and if Winter did find a buyer, he also found it hard to collect. People would "promyse well, but pay ill." Men who had considered themselves wealthy, found themselves poor. "Theris a great many weary of this Country . . . & now ar goinge for the West Indias to live their," wrote Winter to Trelawny in the spring of 1642.[24]

Nor was Trelawny without troubles of his own. The revolutionary faction had expelled him from his seat in Parliament and clapped him into prison because he questioned their violent procedure. The King could not help him; he had been driven from his capital; all who remained loyal to him were being harried by the radicals. Sir Ferdinando Gorges was unmolested only because he was too old to be worth bothering with.

In all this George Cleeve, of Casco Bay, found a chance to turn the tables on the implacable John Winter. Whether Cleeve himself figured out the details of the scheme upon which he now embarked may be doubted. The Reverend Robert Jordan, who had taken Gibson's place as minister at Richmond's Island, credited Cleeve with being able "to deceave the wisest braine," but there were wiser brains than his at Massachusetts Bay, and in Cleeve they found a useful tool for the accomplishment of their aims.[25]

In June, 1643, Cleeve sailed from Boston for England. There he became the central figure in an exceedingly questionable transaction. From some almost forgotten source there was dug up what purported to be the record of a grant of land for a province called Lygonia. Supposedly the grant was made by the Council for New England in 1630, when the Earl of Warwick was in sole charge and no records were kept, or at least none produced when demanded (see pages 206 and 207).[26]

That some sort of grant was made in about 1630 for a settlement somewhere on the coast of Maine was true enough; a shipload of people had come over, attempted a colony, and melted away. But just where their grant was located or what area it covered is not so certain. Now, however, in 1643, it was claimed that the patent covered an area forty miles square extending from Sagadahoc down the coast.

This neatly covered the whole northern part of the Province of Maine as granted to Sir Ferdinando Gorges in 1639.[27]

The conclusion is inescapable. This Lygonia affair followed the old, familiar pattern by which the Massachusetts Bay Company got its patent of 1628 and by which Lords Say and Brook claimed the Connecticut country. First an elusive grant from the Earl of Warwick; then an extensive claim based upon a non-appearing document; always the Puritan colonizers the beneficiaries; always Gorges the victim.

But in the summer of 1643 Lygonia was very real. And strangely enough at that very time the title fell into the hands of a prominent member of Parliament, one Alexander Rigby, not hitherto known to be interested in colonial ventures. By something more than sheer coincidence Rigby appointed Cleeve as his deputy, and the former poverty-stricken nuisance of Casco Bay returned to Maine as Governor of Lygonia (see map on page 307).[28]

Within this new Province of Lygonia lay the plantations of Trelawny, Cammock, Vines, Bonython and others. Naturally they challenged the validity of the patent on which Cleeve's power was based, but in vain. The final decision lay in the hands of a committee of Parliament presided over by none other than the Earl of Warwick, and he decided in favor of Lygonia. And to the end that Cleeve should know his place, Parliament appointed Winthrop and other worthies of Massachusetts as a committee to direct and advise him. Lygonia became an appanage of the Bay.[29]

This was a bitter pill for John Winter. Worse yet, in 1644 Trelawny died, leaving no one to carry on the business of sending trade goods and supplies to Richmond's Island and to take back the fish, oil and other commodities which Winter's men had collected. The following year Winter, broken and dismayed, passed to his fathers. At about the same time Richard Vines, the pioneer of pioneer settlers on the New England coast, picked up and moved to Barbados. He was "weary" of Maine.[30]

The position of George Cleeve seemed secure. So certain was he of himself that he graciously aided Robert Jordan in establishing his own fortune. Jordan, the minister, had won Sarah Winter for his wife—and she may well have thanked her lucky star that the Reverend Gibson had preferred the Lewis girl. On Winter's death Jordan cast off his ministerial robe and picked up the mantle dropped by Trelawny's manager. Within a short time he had firmly in his hands not only all the property formerly belonging to Winter but all that had belonged to the Trelawny plantation. Along with Trelawny's title Jordan inherited the old claim against Cleeve's land on Casco Bay; and, with ability far beyond that of John Winter, he patiently awaited a favorable moment to strike.[31]

Meanwhile, with the separation of Lygonia from his province of Maine, there remained to Gorges only the narrow wedge between the Kennebunk and Piscataqua rivers. Governor Thomas Gorges had returned to England leaving Edward Godfrey as acting Governor. Gorgeana, the former Agamenticus, still gave little evidence of its status as an episcopal city. At Wells the Reverend John Wheelwright had gathered a small group of followers about him. Along the Piscataqua River there were a few straggling settlements incorporated under the name of Kittery. And that was all that was left of his province when, in 1647, Sir Ferdinando Gorges, more than eighty years of age, poor and puzzled, died.[32]

Three years later Alexander Rigby, the proprietor of Lygonia, died. The time seemed propitious for Massachusetts to again examine her patent and survey the Merrimac River —which she did. The surveyors found that the most northward point of that river was in Lake Winnipesaukee and that an east-west line through that point not only took in all that remained of Gorges' province of Maine but also a good part of Lygonia.[33]

What Massachusetts had in mind was obvious. Godfrey, for Maine, and Cleeve, for Lygonia, both protested—but without avail. There was no one to help them. The King was dead; England was a Commonwealth; Massachusetts was her darling child; and Massachusetts insisted upon her patent rights as she was pleased to interpret them. In one town after another north of the Piscataqua the people grudgingly took the oath of allegiance to the government centering at Boston. Only in the part beyond the Saco, where dislike of Puritanism was intense, did Jordan and his neighbors hold out, preferring even Cleeve to Massachusetts; and Cleeve, the ungrateful rascal, held out with them.[34]

The name of Maine disappeared. In its place there came into being the County of Yorkshire. Not even the name Gorgeana was allowed to remain as a memorial to the god-father of New England; it became York. And there, on June 30, 1653, the commissioners appointed by the Bay held their first court for the administration of justice in the new county.[35]

That a bit of discipline was needed north of the Piscataqua is more or less evident from the case of Joan Andrews, wife of John Andrews of Kittery. At this first court she was presented for having abused a grand-juryman with "threateing & revileing speeches." Four months later she was charged with having beaten up Rice Tommasse; also she was sentenced to stand for two hours in the town meeting at York and the same at Kittery with a paper attached to her forehead acknowledging that she had sold a tub of butter well weighted with stones. The following spring she was sentenced for stealing. Somewhat later she was charged with having been seen unseasonably and too much in company with Gowan Willson "up & downe Pischataqua River about frivelous Occasions . . . to the great discontent of the wife of the said Willson"; also with having threatened Goody White in a "profayne manner." Finally, to make herself thoroughly popular with the justices, she announced that "shee Cared not a Toard for any Magestrate in the world."[36]

And Joan was but one of many who appeared and re-appeared in the court records. Probably some things that would have passed for normal under the former government of Maine were magnified into offenses by the more godly magistrates from the Bay. The number of presentments for failure to attend church indicates an effort to reshape the lives of the people.

But with it all, Yorkshire County enjoyed a more orderly government than it had known before. Justice was impartially administered. Roads were laid out from town to town; bridges were built; ferry service was improved; taverns were strictly supervised. Even the settlers on the other side of the Saco began to recognize some advantages in being subject to Massachusetts.[37]

Steadily but without threats of force the Bay pressed its claim. Then on April 19, 1658, the Earl of Warwick died. Five weeks later the General Court of Massachusetts ordered its commissioners to go into the region beyond the Saco and take "the inhabitants thereof into our jurisdiction." On July 13 the commissioners met with the planters at Robert Jordan's house, on the mainland opposite Richmond's Island. There, after much discussion, an agreement was arrived at. Cleeve, Jordan, and twenty-six others acknowledged themselves "subject to the government of Massachusetts Bay."[38]

Both Cleeve and Jordan accepted official positions under the Bay; in fact, Jordan was given authority outranking that of Cleeve. And then Jordan struck. Inch by inch he challenged Cleeve's title to the land in Casco Bay. In every case the decision went in favor of Jordan. Ruthlessly he seized Cleeve's homestead, his milk cows, his personal property. He even required the constable, according to Cleeve's account, "to goe into my wifes chamber where she was laid on her bedd & very sick who in a Barberous manner pulls her from off her bedd and takes her bedd from under her and the bed clothing and carries all away. My wife being no lesse than fouer score & seven yeares of age."[39]

Nor could Massachusetts help her old ally. In fact, Massachusetts had enough to worry about south of the Merrimac. The revolutionary movement had come to an end in England. The friends of Massachusetts no longer sat in the seats of power. Those likely to have the power had no love for Massachusetts. The heirs of Mason and Gorges were clamoring for a restoration of their rights in New Hampshire and Maine, and Robert Jordan was listening to them rather than to the scared Puritans at the Bay.[40]

The Puritan Colonies

PURITANS WE CALL THEM—the people who settled at Massachusetts and spread through southern New England. But the Pilgrim Fathers did not call themselves Puritans. The people who came to Massachusetts Bay in 1630 did not call themselves Puritans. The people who settled on the Connecticut River in 1635 and at New Haven some three years later did not call themselves Puritans; nor did those who fled from Massachusetts to the Rhode Island country call themselves Puritans. The term was not used in the seventeenth century as it is in the twentieth. Roger Ludlow would have been somewhat puzzled to find an answer had one asked him if he were a Puritan, but he had no uncertainty as to why he and his spiritual brethren had come to New England. It was "to establish the Lord Jesus in his Kingly Throne." The manner in which they strove to do this and the way of life which that endeavor created has, by later Americans, come to be summed up in the convenient word Puritan.

The Pilgrims at Plymouth prepared the way, but the pattern of the Puritan church in America was established at Salem in 1629 (see page 186). This pattern was followed at Charlestown, Boston and other towns as the main body of the Bay settlers arrived in 1630. Each congregation became a separate and independent church gathered about a small group of "visible saints" who had made a covenant whereby they gave themselves "unto the Lord, to the observing of the ordinances of Christ together in the same society."[1]

As new towns came into being, new churches were founded. When some of the towns moved to the Connecticut River, they carried their church organizations with them. When the founders of New Haven Colony settled on Long Island Sound, they followed the practice established at the Bay. First they held "private meetings wherein they thatt dwelt nearest together gave their accounts one to another of Gods gracious worke upon them and prayed together and conferred to their mutual edification." Thus they discovered which were the most godly among them. From those they chose seven "pillars" who became the foundation of the church and who admitted others as by their confessions of faith they proved themselves to be of the "elect."[2]

As the number of congregations increased, there naturally grew up a loosely knit but none the less effective association between them. The ministers would get together and discuss points of doctrine and discipline. Questions of belief or of action would be referred to them by the magistrates for consideration and determination. Those who refused to conform to these decisions were often excommunicated from their churches and sometimes punished or banished by the magistrates.

As a haven for these dissenters from the discipline of the "consociated" churches, Roger Williams had pointed the way to Rhode Island. Many had followed, and by 1640 there were three well-established towns in that region—Providence, Portsmouth, and Newport. In those towns the people had organized churches of their own, "in a very disordered way" as it appeared to the orthodox Congregationalists at the Bay; and, as might have been expected, they "broached new heresies every year."[3]

Most serious of these heresies that swept Rhode Island was one that had to do with the baptism of infants. The older Puritan churches had followed the long-accepted doctrine that if a person had been baptized as an infant, no further baptism was necessary. The Anabaptists, as the followers of the new heresy were called, held that infant baptism was useless and probably a sin; to them baptism must follow a recognition and renunciation of sin. Roger Williams, Mrs. Hutchinson and many others straightway had themselves rebaptized.[4]

Nor was this heresy confined to Rhode Island; it began to show itself here and there throughout the churches of Massachusetts and New Haven. The matter was eternally serious. It was a challenge to the "elect." If the Anabaptists were right, then John Winthrop, John Endecott and even John Davenport, none of whom had presumably been baptized since they were infants, might, in that day for which life is but a preparation, find Roger Williams and Mrs. Hutchinson sitting close up to the Kingly Throne while they themselves were left to cry in the outer darkness—or worse. That the heresy had to be stamped out was obvious to Winthrop, Endecott, Davenport and the other orthodox Puritans.

But local squabbles over matters of doctrine were for the moment overshadowed by news that came out of England late in 1640. The King had been forced to call a Parliament. To the Puritans of New England, whether of Massachusetts, Plymouth, Connecticut, New Haven or Rhode Island, this brought the hope of a thorough reformation in the church government of the Mother Country. The men who would wield power in that new Parliament would be sympathetic to the cause for which the Puritan colonies stood. In fact, Massachusetts had been the laboratory in which many of their ideas had been worked out, and already there was a party in England advocating the adoption there of the New England way of church and civil government.[5]

Soon there came from some of these well-wishers in England a suggestion that Massachusetts send over a few of her leading men to solicit favors from Parliament. The idea seemed a good one and three men were commissioned to go. One of them was Hugh Peter, who will be recalled as a member of one of the early companies from which the Bay Company was formed; later he had taken Roger Williams' place as minister at Salem.[6]

From his old friend, Emanuel Downing, also of Salem, Peter received a parting injunction. "The Bishop," said Downing, "caused a Quo Warranto to be sued forth in the King's Bench against our Patentees, thinking to damme our patent, and put a generall Governour over us, but most of them that appeared I did advise to disclaime, which they might safely doe, being not sworne Magistrats to governe according to the patent; and these Magistrats which doe governe among us being the only parties to the patent were never summoned to appear. Therefore if there be a Judgement given against the patent, its false and erroneous and ought to be reversed, [which] a motion in the Kings benche without any long suite by writt of Error may set right againe." In that statement we get a fleeting glimpse of the legal ability, and ethics, that had guided the patentees of the Bay Company through one of their difficulties. Downing was a brother-in-law of Governor Winthrop; like Winthrop he was a lawyer; he was still in England at the time the Bay Company patent was on trial (see pages 235 and 242); and it is evident that he was one at least who advised the patentees.[7]

Whether due to the insistence of Peter and his associates or to general goodwill for their cause, the Puritan colonies received at the hands of Parliament all the consideration they could wish for, and sometimes more. The Massachusetts patent was "revived and confirmed"—in recognition of which the churches throughout the Bay observed a day of thanksgiving "for the good success of Parliament." Customs duties were removed from all exports and imports between England and New England. The leading ministers of New England were invited to come over and assist in working out a new church government for old England.[8]

This latter request was not an unmixed favor. Already too many New England ministers and other able men had returned to England or were planning to do so. Hugh Peter talked about coming home but never did so. Young George Downing and Nathaniel Brewster, graduates of the first class at Harvard, soon went off to England instead of taking churches at the Bay. John Humphry, who had been associated with the colony since the days of the old Dorchester

THE PURITAN COLONIES
1640-1660

Merrimac

Rowley.

Andover.

Lynn. Salem

Charlestown

Cambridge. Boston

MASSACHUSETTS

.Springfield

Roxbury.

Dorchester.

Braintree. PLYMOUTH Plymouth

Connecticut

Hudson

Windsor.

Hartford.

Wethersfield.

Saybrook

Guilford

New Haven

Stratford

Fairfield

Norwalk

Stamford

Greenwich.

Branford

Southold

Pequot

Providence.

Pawtuxet

Shawomet.

Portsmouth.

Newport

LONG ISLAND

Southampton

New Amsterdam

ATLANTIC   OCEAN

MILES

10 0   25   50

Company, sold his land and returned to England. Many others were doing the same.[9]

More serious at the moment, however, was the economic impact of the impending struggle between King and Parliament. As in Maine so in Massachusetts, Plymouth, Connecticut, New Haven, and Rhode Island. Money almost disappeared. The price of corn, cattle and land fell to a fourth of what it had been. People could not pay their debts. With shipping from England practically at a standstill, there arose the grave question of how the people were to get clothing and other supplies for which they had been dependent upon the English merchants.[10]

There was just one way to meet the situation. The merchants of New England must build their own ships, carry their produce to the best markets and bring back the things that were needed in the colonies. In making that decision and putting it into action New England laid the foundations of her future prosperity. Before the ice broke up in the spring of 1641 there was a ship of three hundred tons on the ways at Salem; a somewhat smaller one was being built at Boston. The following year five ships were built, and from that time onward—from Rhode Island to the Piscataqua—shipbuilding became an established industry of New England.[11]

The voyage of the *Trial,* launched at Boston in the summer of 1642, was typical of the trade developed by these ships built along the shores of New England. With a cargo of fish and pipestaves (barrel staves we call them today) she sailed for the Azores. In those Catholic, wine-making islands the master of the *Trial* sold his fish and pipestaves at a very good price; and taking on a cargo of wine and sugar, which were cheap, he sailed for the West Indies. There he found a ready market at a good price for all the wine he cared to sell. And there cotton and tobacco were cheap. So taking on those products, he headed for Boston—with a handsome profit in goods and some ready money.[12]

This and similar voyages soon provided the colonies with all the necessities and many of the luxuries of life. Fishing ships swept the northern seas and brought their catches to Salem, Boston and other ports. Lumbermen cut trees on the

Piscataqua and floated them down the river to sawmills operated by water power and driving as many as twenty saws at once—the saws made at an ironwork set up at Lynn, Massachusetts, through the efforts of young John Winthrop. Corn and wheat from the farms of Connecticut were heaped on the wharves at Windsor, Hartford and Wethersfield. All these products—fish, lumber and grain—were gathered up by the ships as they coasted from harbor to harbor, and all of them found a sure market in the Azores, Canaries, and even in the ports of Spain. Occasionally an enterprising ship captain would pick up a cargo of negroes at the Canaries or on the coast of Africa, which merchandise brought a better profit than wine when he arrived in the West Indies.[13]

In addition to this triangular trade through the Wine Islands to the West Indies there developed a considerable direct trade with the prosperous English colony at Barbados, where horses and cattle were in constant demand. William Coddington on his farm at Newport in Rhode Island made a fortune breeding horses especially for the Barbados trade. So ample was the cotton brought back by the trading ships that not only were the spinning wheels of the housewives supplied but several mills came into operation. At Rowley, Massachusetts, where experienced spinners from Yorkshire had settled, cloth was soon being turned out in considerable quantity.[14]

Nor did the merchants overlook the possibility of increasing their trade with the Dutch at New Amsterdam, with the Indians in Delaware Bay, and with the English colonists of Maryland and Virginia. But war between England and Holland interrupted the trade with the Dutch; both the Dutch and the Swedes discouraged English efforts to trade in the Delaware; the act of Parliament prohibiting trade with royalist Virginia temporarily put a stop to coastwise voyages to the south. Even less happy was the outcome of an attempt to establish trade relations in the fur-rich region about Nova Scotia, where two Frenchmen were fighting each other for control. The Massachusetts merchants sided with La Tour, who claimed to be a Protestant. He was hospitably entertained at Boston and fitted out with men and ships against his opponent, D'Aulnay. But in the end D'Aulnay won and Captain Gibbons among others lost £2500 (say $50,000) in trade goods. We will hope that he did not regret his failure to seriously consider Lord Baltimore's invitation to settle in Catholic Maryland.[15]

Voyages across the Atlantic sometimes turned out badly, too. New Haven, not to be outdone by the Bay towns, contracted for a ship to be built in Rhode Island. Late in 1645 it was worked down the Sound and tied up in the Quinnipiac River where it was loaded with all the exportable merchandise of the colony, including the manuscript of a book by the Reverend John Davenport. On a cold day in January, 1646, the last barrel of beaver was lowered into the hold. The passengers, some seventy in all, including Mr. Francis Brewster and other leading merchants, were on hand—but the ship could not stir; she was frozen tight in the ice. Men with axes cut a channel three miles to open water; the ship was eased out into the Sound and started on her voyage. More than two years later the startled townspeople of New Haven saw in the sky over their harbor the form of a ship on the poop of which appeared a man with a sword pointing out to sea. And that was the only message that ever came back from the Phantom Ship.[16]

The loss of this ship was a severe blow to the commercial hopes of New Haven, and unquestionably halted its growth. In its first flush years the settlement had attracted both wealth and ability. Several new towns—Milford, Guilford, Branford and Stamford—sprang up along the coast and placed themselves under the government created by Eaton and his associates. Even Southold across the Sound on Long Island had asked to be taken in.[17]

Similar expansions had taken place in the other Puritan colonies. Connecticut, as the associated towns of Windsor, Hartford and Wethersfield were now coming to be called, established new towns at Fairfield and Stratford—on the coast between Stamford and Milford—thus thrusting a wedge between the towns of New Haven Colony. Southampton, a neighbor of Southold on Long Island, threw in its lot with Connecticut, still further confusing the situation. In Massachusetts, settlement had pushed northward toward the Merrimac River, where Wenham, Rowley and other towns came into being.[18]

The process of town settlement was much the same in all the Puritan colonies. A few leaders would pick out a new location that suited them; in Massachusetts, they would ask for and, if approved, receive a grant of the land from the General Court; in Rhode Island or the Connecticut country, where only squatter title existed, they would buy from the Indians or simply take the land and then ask to be received under the wing of one of the stronger combinations of towns.[19]

Those who took original title for a town were in no sense owners of the land but rather trustees for all the inhabitants. They usually assumed the authority to admit or exclude other inhabitants according to their judgment. But once admitted, each inhabitant was entitled to his proportionate part in the division of the town land. To each was allotted, in fee simple, a home lot—for a house, barn and garden— and a field or fields sufficient for his needs. Social position, number of persons in the family, and amount of money or effort expended in getting the town started all had a bearing on the size of the assignments, but there was always an honest effort to be fair to every one.[20]

The home lots were grouped together in a compact body, often around a central "green." The farm land lay at a distance, and the owner of two fields might find one considerably removed from the other; nor was there any regularity as to their shape—the boundary lines might be described as running from a black birch to a boulder to the land of some one else whose bounds were as irregularly marked. Pasture land, also at a distance from the home lots, was held in common for the use of all. Later, as the town grew, there might be a second and sometimes a third division in which both old and new inhabitants shared.[21]

On their home lots in these tight little villages, which sometimes had gates at the ends of the streets, the inhabitants built their houses, barns and outhouses. Each morning their milk cows were driven out of town to the public pasture,

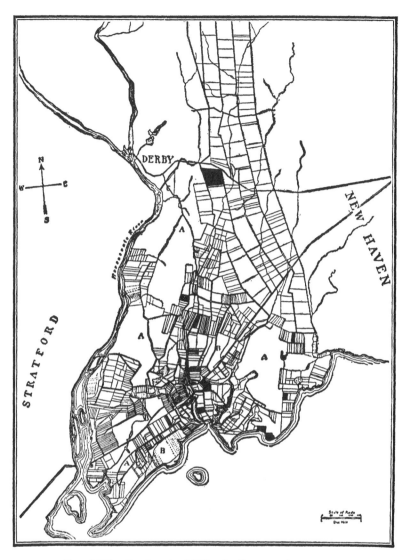

Land Distribution in Milford, Conn., 1639–1700.

    A. Common and Undivided Land.

    B. Sequestered for Special Purposes: church, ferry, common pasture, etc.

From Leonard W. Labaree, *Milford, Connecticut.*

and each evening they were brought home to be milked. Their hogs roamed everywhere, to the constant irritation of those whose gardens were rooted up by their neighbors' swine. To till their land and to harvest their grain the inhabitants trudged out to their fields in the morning and back at night, sometimes relieving the trip by riding a work horse or sitting in the back of a cart. Viewed against the plantation system of Virginia a New England Puritan town was as different physically as the people were different spiritually.[22]

To the Puritan mind, life in such villages seemed the natural way. In part it was what they had been accustomed to at home; in part it provided protection against Indian attack; most important of all, it enabled them to live together as brethren and worship together, which was what they had come to America to do. Those who lived apart were looked upon with suspicion. In the closely associated village life each of the brethren, or sisters, could watch over the thoughts and behavior of his or her neighbors. Whoso strayed from the strait and narrow path was sure to be detected. And it was the duty of any one detecting such an error to report it to the minister or the magistrates, whereupon the delinquent would first be "dealt with" privately "in a church way." If that failed to bring reformation, the erring one would be publicly "admonished"; excommunication from the church and correction by the magistrates were final resorts.[23]

The organization of a church naturally followed the founding of the town. People who did not look forward to living in a church estate were not permitted to found towns in Puritan New England. We have seen how New Haven proceeded with its church organization. In Massachusetts those intending the founding of a new church asked the approbation of the other churches and the magistrates, who required them to publicly confess the faith that was in them. Nor did they always convince their examiners. At Wenham in 1644 "there was a public assembly for gathering a church, but the magistrates and elders present, finding upon trial, that the persons appointed were not fit for foundation stones,

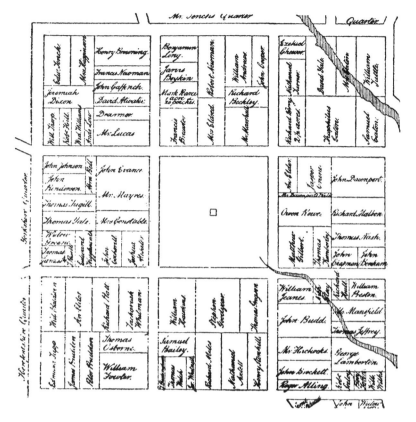

New Haven home lots, laid out around a central "green."

Governor Eaton's lot is in the upper right square. Just south of Eaton is the Davenport lot. Facing the northwest corner of the "green" is the Francis Brewster lot. The church stands in the center of the "green."

Courtesy, The New York Public Library.

they advised them not to proceed. . . ." That same year
when the prospective founders of churches at Andover and
Haverhill "refused to declare how God had carried on the
work of his grace in them" the magistrates and elders declined to permit the churches to be organized.[24]

Usually, however, suitable foundation stones were at hand;
a church would be organized; and additional members would
be admitted, though the doors of the church did not "stand
so wide open, that all sorts of people good or bad, [might]
enter therein at their pleasure. . . ." New members, like
the founders, had to be *"examined & tryed* first; whether
they be fit & meet to be received into church-society, or not."
With enough members to provide for his support a minister
would be called, and a meetinghouse built.[25]

At New Haven the meetinghouse stood on the village
green in the center of the town. The seats were assigned
according to a well-recognized rule of precedence. There on
a Sabbath morning, in the spring of 1646, Mr. John Davenport, the minister, saw immediately before him the Right
Worshipful Governor Theophilus Eaton, flanked by other
visible saints. At one side sat Isaac Allerton, who had come
over on the *Mayflower* twenty-six years before; he had long
since given up trying to make a living in Plymouth and was
now a wealthy merchant with interests in New Haven and
New Amsterdam. Farther back, on one side, were rows of
men, and, on the other, rows of women. Among the latter
was Lucy Brewster, whose husband had sailed the preceding
January on a ship from which no word had come. But for
Mrs. Eaton, the wife of the Governor, no seat had been assigned; she was no longer a member of the church; she sat
with the non-members; she had, in fact, been excommunicated because of her anabaptistical beliefs. Gossip said that
she was asking the Governor for a separate room.[26]

Mr. Davenport spoke from Ephesians 4:12, and from this
text drew a lesson that to most of his listeners brought consolation and assurance of salvation. But to some, including
Mrs. Eaton, the sermon was not so convincing. Neither had
it impressed Mrs. Brewster, as she informed Mrs. Eaton when
later in the week they were calling, together with Mrs.

Above. John Davenport, minister of the church at New Haven.

Courtesy, Yale University Art Gallery.

First Meetinghouse in New Haven. *Courtesy,* Connecticut Magazine.

Moore, at the home of young Mrs. Leach. Mrs. Brewster was quite definite about it; the sermon had made her stomach "womble"; she was "sermon sick." Mrs. Leach could take a disinterested view; she was not a member of the church; she had thought of joining but had found "soe manny untruthes among them" that she decided to stay out. Then Mrs. Brewster had a bright idea: Mrs. Eaton could convert her to anabaptism; she could convert some other woman to that heresy; the other woman could complain against her to the magistrates; she could complain against Mrs. Eaton; and they would both be banished to Rhode Island. The ladies had a good laugh over that, and by the time they parted they had pretty completely settled the affairs of New Haven.[27]

What they did not know was that Elizabeth Smith, Mrs. Leach's maid, had been in the next room listening with both ears; in fact, she had found the conversation so interesting that she had called in Job Hall, her fellow servant, "to heare also, who could better remember the perticulars of such a conference than herselfe." Naturally the story got around and soon reached the ears of the magistrates. They hauled the ladies into court to answer for their remarks, which was a mistake as even the fathers of New Haven should have known. The magistrates' discomfiture is particularly evident in the case of Mrs. Leach, who stood by her reasons for not joining the church and, as the record solemnly informs us, "spake uncomly for her sex & age . . . soe that her carryadge offended the whole court."[28]

Had Mrs. Brewster and Mrs. Leach been less socially prominent they would probably have been browbeaten by the magistrates and publicly whipped for their disrespectful attitude toward the court. But except for Governor Eaton, no man in New Haven had a larger estate than Mr. Francis Brewster; he was one of the few men in the town who rated the title of "Mr."; his house faced on the village green; in his family were nine persons, some of them probably servants and relatives; one of his sons had graduated from the new college at Cambridge in Massachusetts. In his house, in addition to providing for his family, he stored part of his trade

Above. Clark House, Stratford, Conn.

From Edwin Whitefield, *The Homes of Our Forefathers.*

Below. Bedroom. The Thomas Hart House, Ipswich, Mass. About 1640.

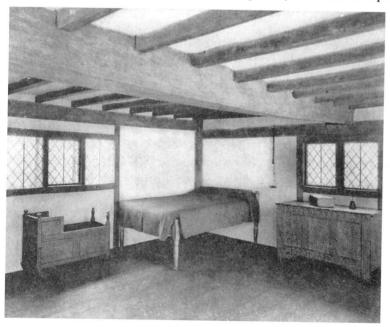

Courtesy, The American Wing, The Metropolitan Museum of Art, New York.

goods. Even the magistrates were in the habit of sending over for a jug of wine now and then when they ran low.[29]

In New England, as in Virginia, the houses varied in size, form, and construction according to the means and tastes of the owners. Governor Eaton, a comparatively wealthy man, lived down the street from the Brewsters in a ten-room house, built in the shape of the letter E, with five chimneys; there was ample space for Mrs. Eaton to have a separate room. Other families in New Haven, Boston and probably elsewhere still lived in cellars. Between these extremes there developed the form of house that has come to be looked upon as typically New England. In general it was built around a huge central chimney, of stone laid in clay mortar and with logs running through it as supports over the fireplaces. The frame of the house was of roughly hewn beams, ten to fifteen inches square, mortised at the joints and held together with wooden pegs. The rafters, too, were joined with pegs at the peak of the roof; nails were scarce and expensive. The outside covering of the house generally consisted of long, heavy, hand-split shingles. Within the house some of the walls were plastered, though partitions and particularly the framing around the chimney were generally of panelling. Above the fireplaces, which opened into each room from the chimney, there were often simple mantels.

The front entrance to the house was through a narrow hallway facing the panel-covered chimney. From this hallway a steep, ladder-like stairway ascended to the rooms or the garret above. At either side, the hall led into the main rooms of the house, one being generally used as a bedroom and the other as a parlor or living room. Back of these rooms lay the kitchen, which was really the living part of the home. Often the back roof of the house was carried downward at a reduced angle to within five or six feet of the ground, making provision for a milk room or storage space. The effect of this roof line when viewed from outside gave the name of "saltbox" to such houses—the shape being similar to the boxes in which the housewives kept their salt.[30]

As in the houses of Virginia, beds were apt to be found in almost any of the rooms. Solid boards, or cords laced from

Above. Kitchen, Abraham Browne, Jr., House, Watertown, Mass.

Courtesy, Society for the Preservation of New England Antiquities, Boston.

Right. Betty Lamp.

Courtesy, Mrs. Insley Blair Collection, Cooper Union Museum for the Arts of Decoration, New York.

335

side to side of the bedstead, provided support for ticks filled with feathers, cotton wadding or straw. The bedstead usually had high corner posts and was shielded with curtains; sometimes there was a canopy in addition. Sheets and pillowcases were used even in the more modest homes. Blankets were plentiful. Against the walls of the rooms stood chests in which table linen, extra bedding and clothing were stored. There were cupboards for dishes and pewter ware. Chairs were somewhat of a luxury; benches and stools served for most homes and for most purposes. Still Governor Haynes at Hartford had nine chairs in his dining room—five of leather and four with rush seats—but he was a wealthy man. Tables were usually of the trestle type—wide boards laid over an upright frame—removable or extendable as occasion required. Brightly colored curtains hung at the windows; equally bright rugs covered the floors; many-hued runners covered the tops of the chests; cushions in a great variety of colors were to be found on the benches, stools, or wherever one might sit. Captain Gibbons had thirty-one cushions in his house at Boston—perhaps a lingering expression of the joyousness which in his youth had caused him to join Thomas Morton's crew at Merry Mount.[31]

Pine knots and candles were used to some extent for lighting; but betty-lamps, in which whale oil or tallow was burned, seem to have been more common (see picture on page 335). Wood was the universal fuel both for heating and cooking. Bread was baked in the ovens at either side of the fireplace. Meat, with a great variety of accompaniments— from dumplings to vegetables—was boiled in kettles hung from cranes in the great kitchen fireplaces. A fat hen was always available from the chicken yard in the back lot; hogs were butchered from time to time; milk came from the barns morning and evening. Vegetables and apples were grown on most of the home lots; John Endecott had early established an orchard and supplied young trees at a price. Other fruits, spices and sugar were freely imported.[32]

Water, if not available from natural springs or a well on the home lot, was carried from the town well, but the drinking of too much water was looked upon as being injurious

WILLIAM PYNCHON.

Puritan merchant, trader and magistrate. Founder of Springfield, Mass.
Note the simplicity of the falling band and coat.

Courtesy, Essex Institute, Salem.

to health. Wine, beer, and "strong water" were commonly drunk by all adults, although excesses were frowned upon. The "drinking" of tobacco, as smoking was called, was also considered healthful, but in Connecticut those who were under twenty years of age or who had not already acquired the habit were required to secure a permit from the court and a certificate of need from a doctor before lighting up. And with a view to promoting home industries, a tax was assessed against any one who "drank" tobacco grown outside the colony.[33]

The clothing of the Puritans differed little from that of the Virginians. They wore the same garments and the same falling bands; they had the same slashed sleeves and the same embroidery. The general effect was doubtless less colorful than in Virginia, in part because the Puritan magistrates forbade undue display and in part because those who could have afforded it were naturally of a sober temperament. None the less excess in dress constantly cropped out, particularly among the women. They would appear in silks and silver laces, and unless they could prove that their husbands' estates amounted to two hundred pounds or more, they were sometimes fined for their vanity.[34]

A fair idea of what the average woman wore may be gained from an inventory of the wardrobe of Blanche Hunt of Connecticut, apparently a spinster and of an estate which would have indicated that she was neither a servant nor an heiress. She had two suits, one of ordinary cloth and the other of worsted; seven petticoats, five of which were old; four pairs of stays; four waistcoats; nine aprons; four hats; three shifts (which we may identify as underwear); a cloak; a pair of shoes; stockings, mittens, and gloves. Certainly Blanche's clothing would have caused no stir among the young men as she walked to church of a Sabbath morning. And we may be sure that she did attend the Sabbath-day services; she, like every other inhabitant of a Puritan town, was "required by wholsome lawes to attend."[35]

However, only a small percentage of the inhabitants were actually members of the church. Many found the door of the church too narrow for them to pass; others, like Mrs.

JOHN UNDERHILL.

Captain of the Massachusetts militia.

Note the embroidered falling band and the slashed sleeve.

From an original portrait in the possession of Mr. Myron C. Taylor, New York.

Leach, did not wish to belong. Why, then, we may ask, were they in New England? The answer is that they were there to make a living. Side by side with the wealthy, church-founding leaders of the colonies were the equally wealthy merchants and traders—too useful to be discouraged so long as they did not openly oppose the ways of the "elect." There were blacksmiths, coopers, carpenters and other artisans who held to their title of "Goodman" as tenaciously as their betters did to the title of "Mr." There were free laborers who worked for whoever would pay them best; there were indentured servants who had sold their time; and there were a few slaves.[36]

The first slaves appear to have been Indians captured at the time of the attack on the Pequots. The Reverend Hugh Peter, of Salem, hastened to write to Governor Winthrop, "Wee have heard of a dividence of women and children in the bay and would bee glad of a share viz: a young woman or girle and a boy if you thinke good." Some years later, when the Bay was considering an attack on the Narragansett Indians, Emanuel Downing offered some advice to the Governor. "If upon a Just warre," he said, "the Lord should deliver them into our hands, wee might easily have men woemen and children enough to exchange for Moores [negroes], which wilbe more gaynefull pilladge for us than wee conceive, for I doe not see how wee can thrive untill wee gett into a stock of slaves sufficient to doe all our buisines, for our children's children will hardly see this great Continent filled with people, soe that our servants will still desire freedome to plant for them selves, and not stay but for verie great wages."[37]

Negro slaves probably were brought into the colonies through the West Indian trade that developed after 1640. Governor Eaton, of New Haven, had a "neager" man as early as 1644, and soon after a "neager" woman. In 1650 an inventory of the property of an inhabitant of Hartford, on the Connecticut River, included "a neager Maide £25." In 1657 Robert Keayne, a Boston merchant, left "2 negros and a negro child."[38]

But the great body of inhabitants of the Puritan colonies

were of the middle class, neither bound to service nor of great estate. Many of them were in full sympathy with the congregational form of church organization, even though they were not church members. Others were scornful. Bamfeild Bell, of New Haven, for example, being reproved by William Paine "for singinge profane songs, answered & said, you are one of the holy bretheren that will lye for advantadge." Peter Bussaker, of Connecticut, went even farther; he set forth that "hee hoped to meete some of the members of the Church in hell ere long, and hee did not question but hee should." He met some of them at the pillory the following Sabbath day, where he was soundly whipped.³⁹

Despite godly example and stern laws young men would get drunk. Theophilus Higginson, son of the Reverend Francis Higginson, had a little too much one night, while in company with Goodman Fancy and some others. One may wonder whether he remembered the day in 1629 when, as a small boy, he stood on the deck of the *Talbot* among the assembled saints and heard his father say, "Farewell, the Church of God in England, and all the Christian friends there! We do not go to New-England as Separatists from the Church of England; though we cannot but separate from the corruptions in it." Other young men and girls, even the daughters of the saints, would slip out at night to venison or watermelon feasts in the country, where "base carryage" and "filthy dalliance" often took place.⁴⁰

Worse yet were the goings-on at New Haven revealed by Goodwife Fancy. She was working for Goodwife Robinson and "being alone in the cellar with Thomas Robinson . . . he tooke hold of her, put downe his owne breeches, put his hand under her coates, & with strength & force labored to satisfie his lust, & to defile her. . . ." Some time later, when she was out in the lot getting a wheelbarrow of firewood, and the corn was high, Thomas made similar advances. Another time, being out in the lot gathering pumpkins, he "attempted the like." Even when she went with him "into the cow howse in the evening to hold the lanthorne while he cought a hen for his wife" he suddenly "darkned the lanthorne, fownd & tooke hold of her in the darke, she crying out, (fearing he would kill her,) what shall I doe; but he put downe his breeches, put his hands under her coats, & gott them upp, thrust her to the wall . . . & endeavored with his boddy to comitt adulterie with her." And so it went on for two years, but always she "resisted & hindered him," so she said. Then the story leaked out, and the magistrates took action. Nor did Goody Fancy get the sympathy that she may have expected. She was sentenced to be severely whipped for concealing Thomas' unseemly behavior. As for Thomas, when the magistrates wished to question him, his wife informed them that he had, the day before, gone forth "in a sadd discontented frame, and as she since heareth, passed over the ferry, but since she hath not heard of him." [41]

If the young carpenters and stone masons sometimes shocked the communities, the servants offended even more deeply. Constantly the charge of bestiality was brought against farm laborers and herdsmen. There may have been some basis of fact in the stories told, but too often they seem to indicate a state of mind in the teller. Governor Winthrop, after recording a most unpleasant episode in Massachusetts, alluded to a similar happening in New Haven: ". . . there was a sow," he says, "which among other pigs had one without hair, and some other human resemblances, it had also one eye blemished, just like one eye of a loose fellow in the town, which occasioned him to be suspected, and being examined before the magistrates, he confessed the fact, for which, after they had written to us, and some other places for advice, they put him to death." [42]

The case seems to be clear enough; the man confessed his sin and on the advice of the elders of the churches of the other towns he was executed. But when we turn to the court record we find that the culprit, a poor dumb clod, denied the charge; that he was bullied by the magistrates; that words were put in his mouth; that he was accused of lying when he denied that he had said things that had been said for him; and that, at the foot of the gallows, with the halter around his neck, he still denied the charge. None the less he was hanged—for a biological impossibility.

Of such a character were the charges against and the

"confessions" blandly credited to scores of persons who proved objectionable to the magistrates or the ministers but who were not otherwise assailable. In the present case it develops that the farm laborer was "prophane"; that he had "scoffed att the Lords day, calling itt the Ladyes day;" therefore, reasoned the magistrates, he would have committed bestiality; the case was clear.[43]

Similarly when the Reverend Stephen Batchellor, over eighty years of age, fell into disfavor with the Bay leaders he was accused of having solicited the chastity of a neighbor's wife, and was said to have confessed. Mrs. Eaton was excommunicated from the church on a charge of lying, while it is amply evident that her conversion to Anabaptism was the real issue. When John Gatchell, of Marblehead, wore his hair in a more stylish manner than his sober neighbors considered proper, he was fined for building on town land, with the proviso that if he would cut his hair "into a sevil frame," the penalty would be abated.[44]

The Puritan fathers did not question the infallibility of their ways of thinking and acting. They were the elect of God; God was on their side and He proved it by making things unpleasant for those who troubled His saints. John Endecott noted that a ship blew up because the sailors jeered at "one of the holie brethren, mockinglie & disdainefullie." John Hull, who made the Pine Tree Shillings, was sure that the reason why another ship company came to grief was because they "did deride the churches of Christ, in our harbor." Governor Winthrop noted that after John Humphry deserted his brethren in New England his corn and hay burned and his daughter, aged seven, took up a life of immorality, the latter related at great length and with all the details. The last entry in Winthrop's journal tells of a child falling into a well and drowning—all because the father worked on the Lord's day.[45]

Women who ventured to disagree with the church, as established in its primitive purity by the elect, were often suspected of having given birth to monsters. Women, too, were susceptible to the insidious wiles of Satan—even to the point of familiarity. The secret practice of witchcraft naturally followed. However, from their friends in England the Puritans had learned how to catch witches; and when, in 1648, Margaret Jones of Charlestown showed signs of possessing the black art she was promptly clapped into prison. There a forcible search revealed "an apparent teat in her secret parts as fresh as if it had been newly sucked." Later, "in the clear daylight, there was seen in her arms, she sitting on the floor, and her clothes up, etc., a little child, which ran from her into another room, and the officer following it, it was vanished." Her behavior at the trial, says Governor Winthrop, "was very intemperate, lying notoriously, and railing upon the jury and witnesses, etc., and in the like distemper she died."[46]

These Puritan leaders—who advocated slavery, who were convinced of their own infallibility, who were sure that Divine Providence stood ready to back them, who believed in witchcraft—were not ignorant men. Many of them were university graduates; most of them were well educated; all of them were able men. Nor were they out of touch with the world. They corresponded constantly with other well-educated, able men in England; they received and read the latest books published in England and on the continent. Hezekiah Usher was running a bookstore in Boston in the 1640's; young John Winthrop and others received hundreds of books direct from their friends in the old country.[47]

Even more to the point, the·New Englanders were writing and publishing books of their own which were widely read both in the colonies and in England. Roger Williams' *The Bloudy Tenent of Persecution,* a plea for religious liberty, was published in London in 1644, and answered by John Cotton, the Boston minister, in *The Bloudy Tenent Washed and Made White* (London, 1647). *The Sound Beleever,* a 317-page, closely reasoned statement of Congregational faith, by Thomas Shepard, minister of the church of Cambridge, appeared in London in 1652. *The Wonder-working Providence of Sions Saviour in New England,* an unique history of early Massachusetts by Captain Edward Johnson of Woburn, was published in London in 1654. And there were many others.[48]

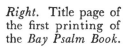

Right. Title page of
the first printing of
the *Bay Psalm Book.*

Courtesy, New York
Public Library.

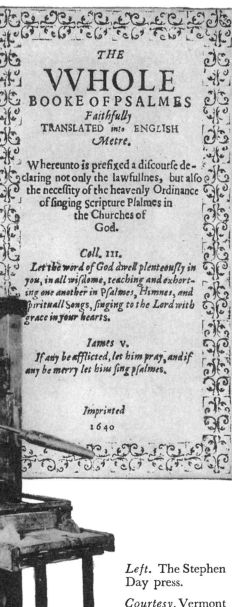

THE
VVHOLE
BOOKE OF PSALMES
Faithfully
TRANSLATED *into* ENGLISH
Metre.

Whereunto is prefixed a difcourfe de-
claring not only the lawfullnes, but alfo
the neceffity of the heavenly Ordinance
of finging Scripture Pfalmes in
the Churches of
God.

Coll. III.

*Let the word of God dwell plenteoufly in
you, in all wifdome, teaching and exhort-
ing one another in Pfalmes, Himnes, and
fpirituall Songs, finging to the Lord with
grace in your hearts.*

Iames v.

*If any be afflicted, let him pray, and if
any be merry let him fing pfalmes.*

Imprinted
1640

Left. The Stephen
Day press.

Courtesy, Vermont
Historical Society,
Montpelier.

In 1638 a printing press, the first in the future United States, arrived at Cambridge, Mass., from England. The following year it was put into operation by Stephen Day and his sons. The first job to be set up and run off was a single sheet containing the freeman's oath. This was followed by an almanac for 1639, and in 1640 appeared *The Whole Booke of Psalmes,* which for more than a century was printed and reprinted in America, England and Scotland.[49]

Nor did the Puritans neglect the education of their children. Teachers, supported in part by tuition and in part by public subscriptions, conducted elementary schools in the Bay towns. Heretical Rhode Island went a step farther; in 1640 the town of Newport called Robert Lenthal "to keep a public school for the learning of youth." The following year New Haven "ordered thatt a free schoole be set up" under the superintendence of Mr. Davenport and the magistrates.[50]

In 1642 Massachusetts made parents and masters responsible for the education of their children and young servants, especially "of their ability to read & understand the principles of religion and the capital lawes of the country." Three years later free schools were established at Boston, Roxbury and other Massachusetts towns, the inhabitants binding their land and houses for the perpetual support of the teachers and the schoolhouse. In 1647 the General Court of Massachusetts directed that every town of fifty or more families should "appoint one within their towne to teach all such children as shall resort to him to write & reade, whose wages shall be paid either by the parents or masters of such children, or by the inhabitants in general." Connecticut, in 1650, adopted an identical provision. The purpose of such public education was clearly stated by both Massachusetts and Connecticut; it was to outwit "that ould deluder, Satan" whose chief project was "to keepe men from the knowledge of the Scriptures."[51]

The instruction was fitted to the purpose. As soon as the pupil learned to read he was introduced to the catechism and the Bible. One of the most popular elementary textbooks of the period was prepared by John Cotton, minister of the

In the portrait *above*, made in 1661, we see a little miss, doubtless in her best attire, and holding a hornbook—from which to learn her ABC's.

From A. W. Tuer, *History of the Hornbook.*

Church of Boston, and printed in London as early as 1646. It bore the intriguing title of *Milk for Babes, Drawn out of the Breasts of both Testaments, Chiefly for the spirituall nourishment of Boston Babes in either England: But may be of like use for any Children.* In it the little ones were introduced to the spiritual facts of life. "Are you then born a sinner?" asked the book, which also furnished the answer for lisping lips, "I was conceived in sinne, & born in iniquity." [52]

A Latin school, supported by tuition after the manner of similar institutions in England, was established in Boston in 1635. It was intended to prepare boys for college. The following year, along with prohibitions against the use of lace on clothing and directions for the regulations of wages, the General Court of Massachusetts "agreed to give 400£ towards a schoale or colledge." Newtown, now renamed Cambridge, became the seat of the new college; John Winthrop, Thomas Dudley, John Davenport, Thomas Shepard, Hugh Peter and seven other leading magistrates and ministers were appointed as a governing board; and by 1638 the new institution of higher learning got under way. That same year John Harvard, a teaching elder in the church at Charlestown, died. By his will Harvard left his library, of some four hundred volumes, and a considerable sum of money to the infant college. On March 13, 1639, the General Court ordered "that the colledge . . . shalbee called Harvard Colledge." [53]

Nathaniel Eaton, a brother of Theophilus, was chosen as first head of the college, but he did not turn out well. He beat up one of his assistants with a club "big enough to have killed a horse"; his wife confessed that the students had received bad food and had been forced to make their own beds—the maid's fault, of course. So Mr. Eaton departed, and Henry Dunster, M.A., Cambridge University, England, was made president in 1640. Under his guidance nine promising young men, suited for the ministry, graduated from Harvard in 1642. [54]

Young women were not admitted to Harvard College; in fact, higher education was a hazard to which the Puritan fathers did not ordinarily subject their daughters. Take the case of Mrs. Hopkins, wife of Governor Hopkins of Connecticut, and a daughter of Mrs. Theophilus Eaton of New Haven. She was, according to Governor Winthrop, "a godly young woman . . . who was fallen into a sad infirmity, the loss of her understanding and reason, which had been growing upon her divers years, by occasion of her giving herself wholly to reading and writing, and had written many books. Her husband, being very loving and tender of her, was loath to grieve her; but he saw his error, when it was too late. For if she had attended her household affairs, and such things as belong to women, and not gone out of her way and calling to meddle in such things as are proper for men, whose minds are stronger, etc., she had kept her wits, and might have improved them usefully and honorably in the place God had set her." [55]

Still, Governor Winthrop may have been wrong in his diagnosis. The wife of another Governor of Connecticut developed similar symptoms—"violent fitts & groaning." In her case, John Winthrop, the Younger, who had considerable reputation as a doctor, was called in to prescribe. His powders were faithfully taken but the malady persisted. Unfortunately, or perhaps fortunately, we do not know what was in the powders. Winthrop's pharmacopœia specified some strange ingredients, including crabs' eyes and vinegar —"two spoonefulls . . . three times a day." Most potent among his remedies was "rubila," provided the patient had "strength to bare it."

The practice of medicine was generally combined with other activities. John Clarke, of Rhode Island, was both a doctor and a preacher. At Hartford, Thomas Lord was engaged by the General Court, at a retainer of fifteen pounds a year, "for the setting of bones and otherwise." For house calls within the town he was authorized to charge twelve pence; if he had to go to Wethersfield, he might charge three shillings; and if to Windsor, five shillings. [56]

Thus life went on in the Puritan colonies. People journeyed from town to town and from colony to colony. Some of the travel was by boat but mostly it was by foot or horseback; John Endecott could not come up to Boston from Salem because he was "unfitt for travaile, having an infirmitie upon mee that I cannot well sitt on horseback nor travaile on foote such a journey." Highways were being built and ferries established; at Windsor the ferry over the Connecticut River charged three pence for a person and eight for a horse; from Portsmouth, R. I., to the mainland the ferry charged six pence per person and four pence for each head of swine or goats. None of the roads was fit for carriage travel; in fact, there were no carriages or coaches in the colonies. In 1646 one of the Earl of Warwick's privateers called at Boston after a successful cruise in the West Indies; the captain spent money lavishly and presented Governor Winthrop with a very handsome sedan which the Viceroy of Mexico had intended as a gift to his sister. Winthrop, in turn, presented the sedan to D'Aulnay, who was demanding redress for the damage done by the Boston merchants to his trade east of Pemaquid. A sedan might appease the irate Frenchman and it was of no earthly use on the muddy streets of Boston.[57]

Even though its streets might be muddy Boston was becoming a large town, the largest by far of any in the English colonies. No longer were hogs allowed to roam the streets without being rung and yoked; goats were banished from the town completely. Boys and young men were no longer permitted to play football in the streets. The inhabitants had to keep their houses within the building line; privies had to be twenty feet back from the highway. When a man cleaned his stable he was no longer allowed to pitch the manure into the street. Butchers were required to find some better place than the dock to throw their "Stinking garbage . . . that such loathsome smells might be avoyded."[58]

And by 1655 Boston had a speed law—probably the first in America. "Whereas," says the town record, "greatt inconveniences may accrew to the towne and inhabitants thereof, especially children, by persons irregular riding through the streetes of the towne, and galloping. Itt is therefore ordered that if any person shall bee seene to gallop through any streete of the town after this day, except upon dayes of military exercise, or any extraordinary case require, every such person shall pay two shillings, sixe pence . . . and itt shall bee lawfull for any person to make stop of such horse or rider till the sayd fine be paid. . . ."[59]

By the 1650's there were many houses of brick or stone construction in Boston, but the majority were still of wood —and pretty flimsy at that. Fire was a continual hazard despite public water buckets and ladders at convenient places. The old town well was no longer adequate. In 1657 Robert Keayne, a wealthy merchant, left a considerable sum to the town for building a conduit to bring water in from outside. Within a short time Boston had a public water supply.[60]

The streets of Boston were lined with busy shops. The waterfront was lined with busy wharves. There were brickworks turning out building material. Ropewalks were turning out cordage—made from hemp raised on the farms of Connecticut. At Lynn and Braintree iron ore was being turned into tools, kettles, pans and other things needed in the colonies. At Stratford on Long Island Sound, Henry Gregory was making shoes by the dozens of pairs. At Salem Emanuel Downing was distilling strongwater which was "desired more & rather then the best spirits they bring from London," as he himself said.[61]

To transact all the business that went on in Massachusetts a dependable currency was needed. English coins were scarce; foreign coins were of uncertain value; beaver and wampum no longer met the situation. On May 26, 1652, the General Court directed that, after the 1st of September following, no other money than that coined by Massachusetts or England should be current in that colony. A mint was established. John Hull was appointed mintmaster and instructed to make shilling, sixpence and three-penny pieces of a specified value. The inhabitants were invited to bring their silver bullion, plate or Spanish coins and have them transformed into the new money. For his labor and expense Hull was to have one shilling out of every twenty that he coined. On October 19 following, the Court further directed that "all peices of mony coined as aforesaid shall have a double ring on either side, with this inscription, Massachu-

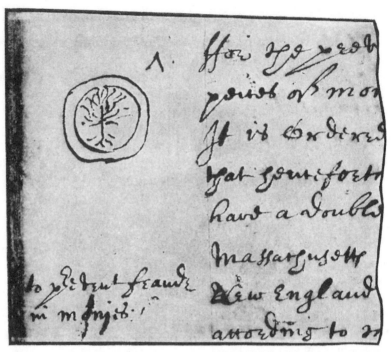

Original design for the Pine Tree Shilling—from the *Massachusetts Colonial Records*.

Pine Tree Shilling as coined in 1652.

Courtesy, The Chase National Bank Collection of Moneys of the World, New York.

setts, and a tree in the center on the one side, and New England and the yeere of our Lord on the other side, according to this draught heere in the margent"—and there in the margin was the sketch shown on page 352. Such was the origin of the famous Pine Tree Shillings which for many years bought mittens, went into the church contribution plates or paid fines in all the towns of Puritan New England.[62]

The town was the important local administrative unit. At town meetings, with all the qualified voters present, the problems of the towns were threshed out and decided. But in New England not every adult male was a voter by any means; in all the towns the franchise was limited to those who paid taxes; in some, church membership was also a requisite; Bamfeild Bell would not have been allowed to vote in New Haven. Selectmen, duly elected at the town meetings, carried out the mandates of the voters and saw to it that the affairs of their town were properly taken care of. One of the important duties of the selectmen was that of admitting or excluding new inhabitants. People did not just move into a New England town; if a newcomer's financial standing was uncertain, he had to find a property owner who would put up a bond securing the town against the possibility of having to support him. The Boston Town Records of the 1650's bristle with such entries as the following: "Jno. Lewes is fyned 5s for Intertaining Francis Burges without libertie from the seleckt men."[63]

The other duties of the selectmen were many and varied; they hired the herdsmen for the town cows; they saw to it that people kept their fences in repair and their chimneys clean; they licensed taverns; they kept the pillory and stocks in repair; they sold land for the benefit of the school; they laid taxes for the support of all these town services; also they laid taxes for the town's proportion in the support of the general government of their colony.[64]

The general government, or general court as it was usually called, was the supreme political power in each of the colonies. It was made up of deputies, or representatives, elected from the various towns at annual town meetings, and of magistrates, including a governor, elected by the deputies.

The Stocks.

The Pillory.

The pictures *above* and *right* are from Justin Winsor, *Memorial History of Boston.*

The Bilboes.

From S. A. Drake, *The Making of New England.*

354

Thus at first sight, it would seem that the general court was based on the will of the people of the colony, but such was far from the case. Even less than in town affairs did the people as a whole enjoy the right to vote for their deputies.

In Massachusetts and New Haven those and only those who were members of one of the Congregational churches, in other words the "elect," had the privilege of voting for deputies; and they were but a fraction of the inhabitants in any of the towns. Nor did the deputies have an open field of candidates from which to select a governor and other magistrates; those higher offices were almost invariably filled from a very small group made up of such men as Winthrop, Endecott or Eaton, who, because of their standing in their respective colonies or their contributions toward public welfare, were the natural and accepted leaders. Thus it came about that in Massachusetts and New Haven the supreme government actually lay in the hands of a very small number of men, all closely concerned in the maintenance of a particular form of church worship, while the great majority of the people were without any say as to the manner in which they were governed.[65]

Connecticut, though in accord with Massachusetts and New Haven in the matter of church organization, did not formally make church membership a qualification for voting. Those who were "admitted Inhabitants in the several towns and have taken the oath of fidelity" were entitled to vote for deputies to their general court; "peaceable and honest conversation" was the test for admission as an inhabitant. In Plymouth colony church membership was assumed rather than demanded in those who voted or held office. And in Rhode Island, where the only combination of towns prior to 1647 was that between Portsmouth and Newport, it was accepted as a principle that religion and government were separate matters.[66]

Between sessions of the general courts the magistrates administered justice. There were, in the early years, no written codes of law to guide and direct them. The Word of God was their code. New Haven, when organizing its government in 1639, stated this plainly: ". . . the worde of God shall be the onely rule to be attended unto in ordering the affayres of government in this plantation." In this, New Haven was but following the procedure already established at the Bay. Naturally the sources to which the magistrates turned for the Word of God were the elders of the churches, meaning, in most cases, the ministers. Accordingly there grew up a system by which, when they needed backing, the magistrates called on the elders for advice; equally, at times, the elders called on the magistrates for action when they felt that the Word was not being enforced as it should be.[67]

Thus developed what came to be known as "The New England Way" in church and state. The elders, *i.e.*, the ministers, became unofficial advisers of the magistrates, always available on call; the magistrates became "nursing fathers" of the churches. When the Humphry girl got into trouble, the magistrates sought "to know the mind of God by the help of all the elders of the country, both our own, and Plimouth, and Connecticut, New Haven, etc.," said Winthrop. When New Haven was faced with the problem of what to do with the man accused of bestiality, the magistrates of that jurisdiction wrote around to the magistrates and elders of the other colonies for advice; when the magistrates and deputies of Massachusetts could not agree, they called in the elders, who, after listening to both sides, retired for consultation. The next day they gave their answer—unanimously in favor of the magistrates.[68]

That the Word was often weighted in favor of the magistrates is an inescapable conclusion. That the elders should have been in accord with the magistrates in most matters was but natural; their authority depended upon the power of the magistrates. The Reverend Thomas Hooker, of Connecticut, expressed himself thus to Governor Winthrop in 1642, "I know my place & I would not abuse your pacience, or hynder greater imployments: my ayme is nakedly this; to be in the number, & to have my voice with those, that whyle your self & your faythfull Assistants . . . be laying the first stone of the foundation of this combynation of peace, I may crye grace, grace; to your indeavors."[69]

This combination of peace to which Hooker cried "grace,

grace" was a proposed confederation between the colonies. The idea had first been broached in 1638 when the Eaton group was preparing to settle at New Haven. Evidently what Massachusetts had in mind at that time was, in effect, simply absorbing Connecticut and New Haven. To this proposal Connecticut refused to listen; Ludlow's reply was "very harsh," Governor Winthrop tells us. In turn Massachusetts got huffy and proceeded to survey the western extension of her southern boundary. The survey showed that Springfield lay within the limits of Massachusetts. This town had been settled as part of the movement that brought Windsor, Hartford and Wethersfield into being, and had associated itself under the government formed by those towns. It now was brought under the government of Massachusetts. The same survey showed that a large slice of Plymouth colony lay within the bounds claimed by Massachusetts, and the Bay people did not hesitate to demand their rights as they interpreted them.[70]

Thus unhappily ended the first approach to a combination among the colonies. However, the project was kept alive and in 1643 articles of confederation were agreed upon between Massachusetts, Plymouth, Connecticut and New Haven. The combination, known as The United Colonies of New England, was intended to be "a firme and perpetuall league of ffrendship and amytie for offence and defence, mutuall advice and succour upon all just occasions both for preserveing & propagateing the truth and liberties of the Gospell and for their owne mutuall safety and wellfare." Each of the four colonies appointed two commissioners, and of those eight the votes of six were to be considered a majority, binding upon the confederated colonies. In all other ways the existing governments of the separate colonies functioned as in the past. With some not unnatural misunderstandings the confederation continued for many years as a useful clearing house for the mutual problems of its members.[71]

The Rhode Island plantations were not asked to join the United Colonies. This was in part because Massachusetts would have nothing to do with the leaders at Providence,

Portsmouth and Newport, most of whom had been banished from her limits for their heretical views, and in part because Massachusetts had plans of her own for bringing Rhode Island into the fold. The first moves were similar to those which at the same time were proving successful in New Hampshire.

Mr. Samuel Gorton, who within a period of three years had managed to get himself thrown out of Massachusetts, Plymouth and Portsmouth, gave the Bay its opportunity. In 1641, while sojourning at Providence, Gorton as usual had gotten into a row with some of his neighbors. Roger Williams had done his best to smooth things over, but a few of the planters appealed to Massachusetts for help. The magistrates at the Bay replied that unless the complainants would put themselves under the government of some orderly colony, such for instance as Massachusetts, nothing could be done for them. A few months later, when the trouble-making Gorton moved to Pawtuxet, three or four miles south of Providence, four of the leading men of that town hastened to offer their land and allegiance to Massachusetts. The offer was promptly accepted and the four men were appointed by the General Court of Massachusetts as justices of the peace —in a town belonging to Providence. One of them, named Benedict Arnold, received an unexplained fee from the Massachusetts Court. Winthrop throws some additional light on the attempted annexation. "This we did," he says, "partly to rescue these men from unjust violence, and partly to draw in the rest in those parts, either under ourselves or Plimouth, who now lived under no government, but grew very offensive, and the place was likely to be of use to us, especially if we should have occasion of sending out against any Indians of Narragansett and likewise for an outlet into the Narragansett Bay, and seeing it came without our seeking, and would be no charge to us, we thought it not wisdom to let it slip." [72]

Gorton paid his respects to Massachusetts in a letter containing too much truth and virulence to be appreciated, and moved on southward to a place called Shawomet, beyond the bounds claimed by Providence or any other town. There he and a group of associates bought from the head chief of the Narragansett Indians a tract of land extending westward from Narragansett Bay. But even in the wilderness they were not safe from pursuit. Massachusetts sent a few men down to Shawomet who rounded up some local Indians and caused them to place themselves, and the land just sold to Gorton, under the government of Massachusetts. Then the General Court of Massachusetts ordered Gorton and his associates to appear before it and answer complaints against themselves.[73]

The Gortonites not only refused to go to Boston but turned loose on the Bay magistrates a barrage of picturesquely unpalatable information about themselves such as they had never before faced. For once the Bay was speechless; anyway the time had come for action. Forty armed men marched southward, through Providence, to Shawomet; Gorton and his followers were seized and dragged back to Boston to answer for their lives. The elders were called in to labor with them, but the Gortonites apparently quoted more Scripture to the elders than the elders could quote to them. Altogether they were the hottest heretics the Bay had met with up to that time. The majority of the magistrates voted for their death, but the deputies of the General Court would not go that far. The final sentence was that they should be heavily shackled, distributed among the towns and put to work. But even that failed to silence Gorton and his associates. Sadly Governor Winthrop notes that they had to be "all sent away, because we found that they did corrupt some of our people, especially the women, by their heresies." However, as a practical matter, the magistrates sent some men down to Shawomet for Gorton's cattle—and Massachusetts retained its claim to jurisdiction over the land sold to Gorton by the chief of the Narragansetts who, incidentally, was knocked in the head on orders from the Commissioners of the newly formed United Colonies—with the advice of the elders, of course.[74]

As Gorton and his friends made their way back to Portsmouth, not even being permitted to stay in their own houses at Shawomet, the finger of time pointed to March 14, 1644.

And on that day, in London, the Warwick Committee on Plantations was passing a patent incorporating the "Providence Plantations, in Narraganset-Bay, in New England."

A few weeks after the formation of the United Colonies, and Rhode Island's omission from that coalition, Roger Williams had quietly sailed from New Amsterdam for England. There he made the most of the coolness that the headstrong behavior of Massachusetts had created among her former friends, and asked for a patent that would protect the Rhode Island settlements from further aggression. The patent was secured, uniting Providence, Portsmouth and Newport "with Full power and Authority to rule themselves, and such others as shall hereafter inhabit within any Part" of the area roughly within the limits of present-day Rhode Island.[75]

With this document, and a letter assuring him of a safe passage through Massachusetts, Williams landed at Boston in the early autumn of 1644. By the same route that he had traveled eight years before, when in the dead of winter he fled from Salem an exile without a home, Williams turned southward to the newly created Providence Plantations. Word of his coming had preceded him. At the Seekonk River he was met by fourteen canoes filled with his cheering townsmen who escorted him in triumph to Providence.[76]

It would have seemed that the patent which Williams received from a committee of Parliament would have settled the status of Rhode Island, but it took more than that to discourage Massachusetts. She still maintained her claim to Shawomet. Equally dogged in opposition to this claim was Samuel Gorton. Late in 1644 he, too, sailed from New Amsterdam for England. The Warwick Committee was going to be called upon to back up its patent.[77]

Meantime, a "democratical spirit" was rearing its ugly head in Massachusetts, to the dismay of the magistrates and the elders. The arbitrary power of the magistrates was being challenged by the deputies to the General Court. And these deputies were the direct representatives of the people of the towns. True, they were elected only by the church members —no one else being allowed to vote—but they were hearing more and more from the many capable men of their towns

who, although not church members and not voters, were not
without influence.[78]

To the end that the decisions of the magistrates might
stand on some more solid authority than their own and the
elders' interpretations of the Word of God, the deputies had
forced the formulation of a code of civil laws. This so-called
Body of Liberties, adopted in 1641 and revised from time
to time, afforded some protection from arbitrary action; but
in 1644 the magistrates were still insisting that "where there
is no particular express law provided" they should "be guided
by the word of God"—with which point of view the elders
agreed without one dissenting voice.[79]

Mrs. Sherman's sow touched off another constitutional
struggle. The sow went for a walk through the streets of
Boston; Mrs. Sherman accused Robert Keayne of butcher-
ing it. The case got into the General Court where, with the
deputies overwhelmingly in favor of Mrs. Sherman, the
decision certainly would have gone in her favor. At that
point, however, the magistrates, sitting with the deputies in
a single body, claimed and exercised a veto power. This
right the deputies denied and the battle was on.[80]

As usual the magistrates called for help from the elders,
who "agreed to deal with the deputies of their several towns."
Apparently they also attempted to deal with some of the
doubtful magistrates; old Thomas Dudley turned on one of
them and said, "Do you think to come with your eldership
here to carry matters." To Governor Winthrop the right of
veto by the magistrates was fundamental; without that right,
he pointed out, the government would be a mere democracy,
and a democracy was "among most Civill nations, accounted
the meanest & worst of all formes of Government." The controversy was patched up in 1644 through a compromise by
which thereafter the magistrates and deputies sat as separate
houses—but the charge of arbitrary government continued.[81]

So far the difficulty had been among the brethren themselves. Then, in 1646, came a movement that threatened to
shake "the New England Way" to its very foundations. William Vassall, a former magistrate, circulated and sent to
Parliament a petition complaining that freeborn subjects of

England were being deprived of the privilege of taking a part in their government solely because they refused to become members of a church whose covenant was contrary to their consciences. At the same time Samuel Maverick, Doctor Robert Child (an "honest man who will bee of exceeding great use if the Country know how to improve him," Hugh Peter had written only a year earlier) and others submitted a similar petition to the General Court. Getting only abuse from the magistrates, they too appealed to Parliament for relief from ministers who "meddled in civil affairs beyond their calling." Nor did this seem a vain appeal. At the moment Parliament contained a majority that might be expected to listen sympathetically.[82]

Right in the midst of this uproar who should step off a ship in Boston harbor but one of Gorton's men with a letter from the Warwick Committee telling Massachusetts to kindly keep out of Rhode Island. Governor Winthrop realized that it was time to have a capable agent in England. The man selected for the job was Edward Winslow, of Plymouth, and an excellent choice it proved to be. Also, the hand of the Lord favored his mission. Shortly after Winslow's arrival in England the party friendly to Massachusetts regained power in Parliament. The Warwick Committee not only refused to act on the petitions of Vassall and Maverick, but also upheld Winthrop's contention that the General Court of Massachusetts was the final court of appeal for inhabitants of the colony. Vassall moved to the West Indies; Child returned to England, as did also Maverick, who had been in Massachusetts long before the Puritans arrived.[83]

While the Bay had effectively disposed of the question of appeal to England from the decisions of her General Court, the protests of Vassall, Child and Maverick, together with the "democratical spirit" of the deputies, served both to liberalize the civil government and to systematize the church government. The unsatisfactory Body of Liberties adopted in 1641 was extensively revised and, as finally approved in 1648, gave the nonfreemen, which is to say nonmembers of the church, privileges of participation in governmental affairs far greater than they had previously enjoyed. And in a synod held at Cambridge that same year of 1648 the elders of the churches of Massachusetts, Connecticut, New Haven and Plymouth agreed upon and published a Platform which, while establishing Congregationalism as the state-church of Puritan New England, reconciled it with the Puritan churches of old England.[84]

Interestingly enough the call for this synod was issued not by the churches, which had no central organization that could have done so, but by the General Court of Massachusetts. There were in the four colonies something over fifty churches. How many sent delegates is uncertain, but the synod was regarded as being representative. It met on August 15. Mr. Allen of Dedham delivered the opening sermon. As the people crowded on the stairs and at the door to listen, a snake crawled in among the elders and curled up on Mr. Allen's vacant chair. "Nothing falling out but by divine providence," observed Governor Winthrop, "it is out of doubt, the Lord discovered somewhat of his mind in it." Mr. Thomson of Braintree, "a man of much faith," was more practical; he "trode upon the head" of the snake, and the synod proceeded. Chapter by chapter the elders agreed upon their Platform: only by a covenant entered into by visible saints could a church come into being; ministers were to be chosen by the congregations and ordained by the imposition of hands; public confession of "Gods manner of working upon the soul" was necessary by those who would pass the narrow door of the church; it was "the duty of the Magistrate to take care of matters of religion"; and so on—a definitive statement of Congregational faith and practice.[85]

With the adoption of the Cambridge Platform, the spiritual quest which had beckoned the Puritans from their homes in old England to the wild shores of New England seemed at last to have been achieved. The following winter John Winthrop died. For almost twenty years he had been the leader of the Puritan experiment. His place as the more or less permanent governor of Massachusetts was taken by John Endecott, but no one could take his place in the hearts and confidence of the people of New England. Slowly a sense of uncertainty and gloom settled over the Puritan colonies. Days

of fasting and humiliation in which to seek the face of the
Lord became frequent.[86]

The old serpent of heresy, ever "trode upon" but never
dead, still turned up in unexpected places. The followers of
Anabaptism, now coming to be called Baptists, increased.
Lady Deborah Moody, "a wise and anciently religious
woman" who had become infected, was now living in the
Dutch colony, but she had left many converts behind, including Mrs. Eaton. The crowning blow came when, in 1654,
Henry Dunster, President of Harvard College, acknowledged
his acceptance of the new faith. He was promptly dismissed.[87]

Witches, too, gave more and more trouble. In 1651 there
was a witchcraft scare in the town of Springfield in western Massachusetts. Somewhat later the little town of Fairfield, in Connecticut, found a suspect in its midst. She was
proven guilty and condemned to death. The whole town
turned out to see the sentence executed. After she was cut
down from the gallows and was "being caried to the grave
side, goodwife Staplyes with some other women went to
search [her] concerning findeing out teats, and goodwife
Staplyes handled her verey much, and called to goodwife
Lockwood, and said, these were no witches teates . . .,"
but all the other women rebuked her and said, "they were
witches teates." Thus justice was vindicated. In 1656 Mistress Ann Hibbins, a member of the church of Boston and
widow of a former magistrate of the General Court of Massachusetts, was found guilty of witchcraft. Governor Endecott
personally pronounced the sentence: she was to go "to the
place of execution, & there to hang till she was dead."[88]

Evangelizing Quakers, "a cursed sect of hereticks lately
risen up in the world," also began an assault upon the Puritan stronghold. The first arrivals were simply shipped away,
but when they came back or more arrived, suitable laws
were enacted. The Quakers were imprisoned; they were
whipped; their ears were cut off. But still they came back,
"reproaching and reviling magistrates and ministers." Massachusetts and New Haven thought they knew a way to stop
that: "they shall have theire toungues bored through with a
hot iron." Connecticut was somewhat milder, but she wanted

none of these strange enthusiasts. Rhode Island, true to form, not only harbored the Quakers, but its people proved fertile soil for the new faith. Mary Dyer, for example, became a convert. She had been an early member of the Congregational Church at Boston; she had been a follower of Mrs. Hutchinson; and like many others she had gone to Rhode Island to live. In 1658 she appeared in New Haven preaching Quakerism and was, of course, expelled. The following year she went to Boston to "bear witness to her faith." She was banished. Within a short time she was back to comfort other Quakers who were imprisoned at Boston. She was arrested and sentenced to be hanged, but was let off and sent to Rhode Island. Back she went to Boston. Again she was sentenced to be hanged, but was offered a reprieve if she would get out and stay out. "Nay, I cannot," she answered, "for in obedience to the will of the Lord God I came, and in His will I abide faithful to the death." And, faithful to the death, she died on the gallows.[89]

Many who had no sympathy with the Baptists or Quakers were disturbed by the fury by which Congregational uniformity was maintained. In fact, the Puritan experiment seemed less attractive than when it was founded as an escape from the persecutions of the Church of England. Now the churches in England opened their doors wider than did the churches of New England—and for men of ability the political and financial opportunities were greater. Edward Winslow, who had gone over in 1646 as agent for Massachusetts, had not returned to New England. Hugh Peter, an earlier agent, still stayed in England—so busy preaching to Cromwell and his Council that he had little time to think of faraway Massachusetts. When he did write to his old friends there, his messages hardly made for contentment. One can imagine the feelings of John Winthrop, the younger, when he opened a letter from Peter and read, ". . . my counsell is that you should come hither with your family for certainly you will be capable of a comfortable living in this free Commonwealth. I doe seriously advise it: & you shall have more by the next if you bee not come away. G. Downing is worth 500£ per annum. . . ." To Winthrop, who had failed in everything he had undertaken in New England, who had been thinking of moving to the Dutch colony of New Netherland, and who was eking out a living at Pequot (present-day New London, Conn.), the possibility of a comfortable life in England must have been a temptation. Particularly he must have compared his situation with that of his youthful cousin, George Downing, who had slipped off to England shortly after he graduated from Harvard, and was now doing so "wonderfull well." [90]

Still Winthrop stuck it out at Pequot. However, his uncle, Emanuel Downing, George's father, packed up and returned to England in 1654. Edward Hopkins, although elected as governor of Connecticut that same year, was already in England, never to return. Even Roger Ludlow, the Father of Connecticut, was lured from his home at Fairfield by offers of position and honor under the Cromwellian government. Nor did new settlers come from England to take the places of those who went back. The stream of Puritan emigration was flowing elsewhere—to the West Indies or to newly subjugated Ireland, which places the Lord Protector of England was interested in settling with English colonists. So far as New England was concerned Cromwell looked upon it "only with an eye of pitie, as poore, cold & useles." [91]

Conditions in New England did not wholly belie Cromwell's estimate. New Haven, which had started off with great promise, was getting poorer year by year. Her inhabitants were seriously thinking of giving up altogether and moving to some other place. Plymouth was practically deserted—left, said Governor Bradford, "like an anciente mother, growne olde, and forsaken of her children." [92]

In Connecticut the situation was little better. Land was worth less than half its former value. The old leaders were gone—Hooker in his grave, Ludlow and Hopkins in England. Still the colony had an abiding vitality; like Massachusetts, Connecticut had in herself the germ of growth. From a beginning in the three River Towns of Windsor, Hartford and Wethersfield, she had reached out to the sea with Fairfield, Stratford and other new towns on Long Island Sound; in 1644 she had bought Saybrook from its proprietors and thus acquired control of the Connecticut River; eastward she had made good her claim to the Pequot country, where young John Winthrop was now making his home.[93]

And in 1657, when things looked darkest for the struggling colonies, Connecticut assured her political future by making young John Winthrop her Governor. He was no longer young except to those who thought of him as his father's son. He was, in fact, fifty-one years of age, discouraged and about ready to give up at Pequot. But he was likable, and he knew most of the people who had influence in both New England and old England. When the time came he well justified his choice. Meanwhile he looked westward toward the Dutch settlements at New Netherland and kept in mind the advice given to Connecticut some years earlier by an English diplomat: ". . . crowd on, crowding the Dutch out . . . but without hostility or any act of violence."[94]

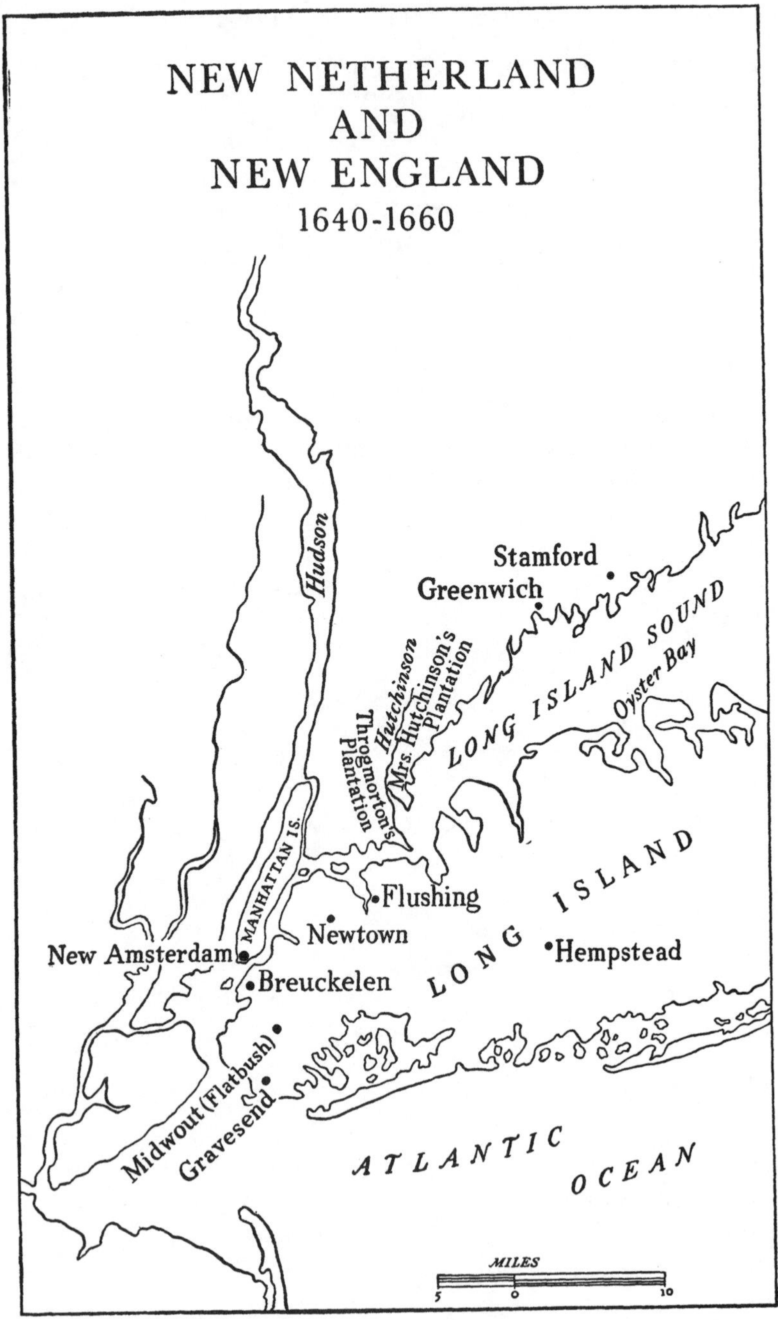

NEW NETHERLAND
AND
NEW ENGLAND
1640-1660

Hudson

Stamford

Greenwich

LONG ISLAND SOUND

Oyster Bay

Hutchinson
Mrs. Hutchinson's Plantation

Throgmorton's Plantation

MANHATTAN IS.

•Flushing

Newtown

LONG ISLAND

New Amsterdam•

•Hempstead

•Breuckelen

Midwout (Flatbush)•
Gravesend•

ATLANTIC OCEAN

MILES

5 · 0 · 10

The Fall of New Sweden

THE DUTCH, after having been pushed steadily westward along the shores of Long Island Sound, finally made a stand at a little place named Greenwich. An English settlement had been made there in 1640 under the leadership of Captain Daniel Patrick and Robert Feake, both formerly inhabitants of the Bay, and the latter related by marriage to Governor Winthrop. In 1642 the Governor of New Netherland forced them to accept the protection of the Dutch colony. If the English would "crowd on," the Dutch were prepared to absorb them rather than be pushed out by them.[1]

Other New Englanders moved inside the borders of New Netherland deliberately, because of a well-founded fear that Massachusetts was laying plans for the annexation of Rhode Island. People who had gone to Providence or Portsmouth to escape from the church government of the Bay had no wish to be brought again under its control. Anne Hutchinson, in 1642 a widow but with a large family, asked and was granted permission to settle within a few miles of New Amsterdam. The location, near the present-day city of New Rochelle, is commemorated in the name of the Hutchinson River Parkway running from New York City toward the New England from which Mrs. Hutchinson fled. John Throgmorton, who had arrived at the Bay with Roger Williams in 1631 and who had followed him to Providence in 1636, was authorized by Governor Kieft to settle thirty-five families on the land just west of Mrs. Hutchinson—which he did in 1643.²

Across the Sound on Long Island two other groups of New Englanders received grants of land from the Dutch in 1642. Francis Doughty, a minister who had been pitched out of his church in Massachusetts because he refused to follow Congregational doctrine, founded Newtown on the northerly side of the island, where he was joined by a group of his followers. Lady Deborah Moody, who had lived at Salem and was credited with having converted Mrs. Eaton to anabaptism, located her people, some forty in all, at Gravesend on the southern side of the island. Two years later a number of Stamford families, unhappy under the godly government of New Haven, received permission to settle at Hempstead, also on Long Island. Thus, within two years, five towns inhabited by English people from New England were established within the Dutch colony of New Netherland.³

Even as Mrs. Hutchinson and the others were getting settled near New Amsterdam, another group of New Englanders, without asking permission, was trying to establish itself in another part of New Netherland. The Delaware River region had long been claimed by the Dutch. True, the Swedes had pushed in and built Fort Christina on the western bank, but Maryland claimed that too. However, when in 1641 George Lamberton, a New Haven merchant, started a settlement at Varkens Kill on the eastern bank of the river, Governor Kieft protested; and when, a few weeks later, Lamberton's people began building a trading post at the mouth of the Schuylkill River, almost directly opposite the Dutch Fort Nassau, Kieft acted. The New Haveners were given a scant two hours in which to pack up their trading goods; their buildings were burned; and they were shipped off to New Amsterdam.⁴

No sooner had the Dutch got rid of the English than the Swedes burst into activity. For four years they had been

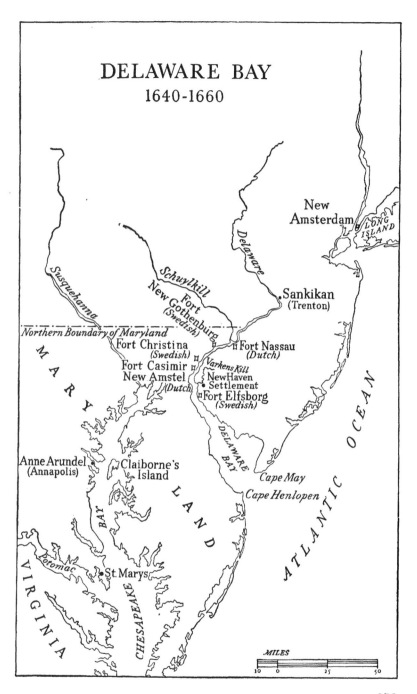

DELAWARE BAY
1640-1660

New
Amsterdam

LONG
ISLAND

Delaware

Susquehanna

Schuylkill

Fort
New Gothenburg
(Swedish)

•Sankikan
(Trenton)

Northern Boundary of Maryland

Fort Christina
(Swedish)

Fort Nassau
(Dutch)

M A R Y

Fort Casimir
New Amstel
(Dutch)

Varkens Kill

NewHaven
•Settlement

Fort Elfsborg
(Swedish)

O C E A N

*DELAWARE
BAY*

Anne Arundel
(Annapolis)

Claiborne's
Island

L A N D

Cape May

Cape Henlopen

A T L A N T I C

Potomac

B A Y

•St.Marys

V I R G I N I A

C H E S A P E A K E

MILES

10 0   25   50

content to do their trading with the Indians that came to Fort Christina; they had brought in a few Finns to supplement the mixed crowd of soldiers, laborers and traders who made up the population of New Sweden—perhaps fifty people in all. Most of their provisions had been bought from the Dutch, a not altogether unprofitable arrangement.[5]

But now, in 1642, the Swedes—disregarding both the Maryland and the Dutch claims—claimed the Indian title to the whole western bank of the river, from Cape Henlopen to present-day Trenton. And early in 1643 a new Governor, Johan Printz, arrived to take charge of affairs in the colony. In addition to his commission from the directors of New Sweden the Governor carried with him physical authority sufficient to impress even an unconquered continent. All contemporaries agree that he tipped the scales at four hundred pounds; and every pound was full of energy. With him the Governor had brought ninety or one hundred laborers and soldiers whom he put to work. Just below the English settlement at Varkens Kill he built Fort Elfsborg and forced the men from New Haven to swear allegiance to Sweden. Up the river, only a little below the Schuylkill, he built another stronghold which he named Fort New Gothenburg. Beside it he caused a two-story mansion of hewn logs to be built for himself, said to be the finest house between New Amsterdam and Virginia—with brick chimneys, glass windows, and furnishings suitable for a colonial governor.[6]

In the midst of all this progress George Lamberton of New Haven came sailing up the river in his little ship *The Cock,* and anchored only three miles above Fort Christina. There he began a brisk trade with the Indians, gathering up the beaver skins that the Swedes themselves expected to buy from their savage neighbors. In the very briskness of the trade Governor Printz found the suspicious circumstance which he needed in order to put a stop to the incursion; he would charge the Englishman with inciting the savages against the Swedes. Lamberton and some of his men were brought ashore to be questioned.[7]

For the evidence which Governor Printz needed, John Woollen, Lamberton's interpreter, seemed a likely source. So he was separated from the others, and the watchman "brought wine and beere and gave him, with a purpose, as he conceived to have made him drunck, and after he had largely drunk there, the Governor sent for him into his owne chamber and gave him more strong beer and wine, and drunk freely with him, entertayning of him with much respect seemingly, and with profession of a great del of love to him, making many large promises to doe very much good for him if he would butt say thatt Georg Lamberton had hired the Indians to cutt off the Sweeds. . . ." This was only the beginning of the beer, wine and strong water proffered to and guzzled by the thirsty prisoner, who, however, to Printz's growing irritation, steadfastly refused to say what the Governor wanted him to say. In the end Printz "was much enraged, and stamped with his feete" which, considering the Governor's four hundred pounds, made quite a noise.[8]

Witness or no witness, the Englishmen had to be found guilty; and with the Governor acting as judge, prosecutor and jury, the necessary legal formalities were easily taken care of. Lamberton was fined enough beaver skins to make the trial profitable, and sent sadly home to New Haven, where he complained to the newly formed United Colonies of New England. Governor Winthrop, as President of that confederation, wrote to the Swede, demanding redress. Printz obligingly reopened the case, carefully examined his handling of the evidence, and not only fully confirmed his verdict but seemingly satisfied Winthrop.[9]

Perhaps Governor Winthrop's conciliatory attitude toward the Swede was prompted by the hope of favors to come. At just this time Massachusetts had been surveying its northern boundary—three miles northward of the most northerly part of the Merrimac River—and the Bay leaders suspected that in their hinterland they might find that elusive Laconia which had so interested Captain Mason and Sir Ferdinando Gorges fourteen years earlier. It might be that the easiest way to get there would be by paddling up the Delaware River. So they fitted out an expedition and in due time this party appeared in the Delaware River armed with a letter of introduction from Governor Winthrop to Governor Printz.

As the boat came opposite Fort Elfsborg, it was hailed by a warning cannon shot. However, when the captain showed his credentials, Printz was most courteous and told him to go right along up the river, at the same time sending word ahead to the Dutch at Fort Nassau asking them to turn him back, which they did. Governor Printz expressed his deep regrets—and presented a bill of forty shillings for the cost of firing his cannon, which bill he made the Englishmen pay before he would let them go back home.[10]

All in all the "Big Swede" seems to have been a jovial character. A story told by the Dutch commander of Fort Nassau confirms this impression. It appears that the Dutchman was dining with Governor Printz and his lady. As usual the conversation got around to the relative claims of the rivals. The Dutchman contended that his people had been on the Delaware long before the Swedes appeared. Printz replied that the Devil was the first owner of Hell, but that he might have to give way to a younger one, "with other vulgar expressions to the same effect."[11]

While these pleasantries were taking place on the Delaware, savage warfare was raging at New Amsterdam. A senseless massacre of unoffending Indians, carried out by Governor Kieft in retaliation for an individual offense, had set the whole native population against the whites. Outlying plantations were devastated; farmers who ventured into their fields were slain; cattle were driven off and buildings burned. Mrs. Hutchinson and her entire family, with the exception of one small grandchild, were murdered—"God's hand is the more apparently seen herein," commented a godly minister of Massachusetts. Many people were killed at the adjoining Throgmorton plantation. Across the Sound on Long Island the settlement at Newtown was attacked; some were killed; Doughty and the rest fled to New Amsterdam. Of the English planters only Lady Moody and her people at Gravesend wholly escaped. They put up so sturdy a defense that the savages were glad to leave them in peace.[12]

So serious was the situation that many of the colonists saw safety only in flight, either to Holland or up the Hudson to Fort Orange and Rensselaerswyck. Roger Williams was in

New Amsterdam at the time, waiting for a ship to take him to England where he hoped to get a patent for Rhode Island. He reported, "mine eyes saw the flames at their towns, and the flights and hurries of men, women, and children, the present removal of all that could for Holland." [13]

Something had to be done. Governor Kieft called a meeting of the burghers of New Amsterdam and asked their advice and help. The decision was for a vigorous offense. Soldiers were raised, and Captain John Underhill, then living in the English town of Stamford, was asked to take command in the Greenwich and Long Island area. In addition, Underhill and Isaac Allerton appealed to the General Court of New Haven for soldiers and money. Although fearful that the outbreak would extend to her own towns, New Haven declined the men but offered a loan provided Stamford would repay it out of any salary which she might have promised to Underhill. Despite this rebuff, the Dutch captains were able to deal with the situation. Underhill and his men hunted the Indians from their lairs, incidentally perpetrating cruelties scarcely less drastic than those which the savages had inflicted upon the whites. The Indians soon had enough and made peace. [14]

Up the Hudson River, where the patroonage of Rensselaerswyck surrounded the West India Company's trading post of Fort Orange, there had been no trouble with the Indians. In fact, the Iroquois Confederacy, which dominated the region, was busy exterminating the Huron allies of the French to the northward—with guns supplied to them by the Dutch. In one of their raids the Iroquois captured Father Jogues, a Jesuit missionary to the Hurons. He was, of course, put to the usual tortures, and news of his situation soon seeped into Fort Orange. The commandant made every effort to secure the Father's release, but in vain. Finally, however, Jogues made his way to the Fort. There he was concealed and cared for by Domine Megapolensis, the Calvinist minister to the upper Hudson. When opportunity offered, the Jesuit was sent down the river to New Amsterdam and on to Europe. However, even as Mary Dyer, the Quakeress, returned to Boston in justification of her faith, so Father Jogues returned to his savage torturers with his message of salvation. And like the Quakeress he paid with his life for his faith. In October, 1646, an Indian tomahawk brought him the crown of martyrdom at a Mohawk "castle" near the present city of Amsterdam, N. Y.[15]

Kieft's mismanagement of the Indian outbreak, on top of other growing dissatisfaction, finally resulted in his recall. In the spring of 1647 a new Governor, Peter Stuyvesant, arrived at New Amsterdam. He found the town in a "low condition." Of the four or five hundred men who, with their families, made up the inhabitants, a large proportion were of other than Dutch nationality; eighteen different languages were spoken; and almost as many different religions and sects were represented. The houses clustered around the fort at the lower end of Manhattan Island—south of a palisade built from river to river along a line later known as Wall Street. Hog pens, often jutting into the streets, dominated the landscape. There was a commodious tavern to take care of the many transients who stopped over on their trading trips between New England and Virginia. The church, begun in 1642, was still unfinished.[16]

Stuyvesant set to work to put the town and colony into some sort of order. The church, Calvinist of course, was completed. A public school was organized. A degree of representative self-rule was granted to the inhabitants, who previously had been subject to the arbitrary rule of the Governor. New towns—Midwout (Flatbush) and others—were established on Long Island. Up the Hudson the village of Beverwyck, which had grown up around the walls of Fort Orange, was separated from the patroonage of Rensselaerswyck and became the nucleus of the later city of Albany.[17]

With the crowding New Englanders to the eastward, Governor Stuyvesant tried to reach an amicable understanding. In the autumn of 1650 the Commissioners of the United Colonies were holding their annual meeting at Hartford, where the Dutch trading post—known as the House of Hope or Fort Good Hope—still stood on the Connecticut River, surrounded by the English town. (See pages 211 and 212.) Stuyvesant took this opportunity to visit Good Hope; and from this bit of Dutch territory he carried on a series of negotiations with the commissioners. He was particularly concerned over the trade practices of William Pynchon and other New Englanders. Pynchon had founded Springfield on the Connecticut River in 1635, and year after year had been pushing his fur-trading operations westward—toward the Hudson River and the Dutch post at Fort Orange. Stuyvesant now charged that Pynchon was paying altogether too much for beaver skins, to the detriment of the Indian trade in general. The commissioners refused to take action on this complaint, but we may be relieved from worry about Pynchon when we find, included in one of his charges against an Indian, the following item: "For your being drunk, 10 shillings."[18]

On two other points the Dutch Governor made more progress. It was agreed that the boundary between the Dutch and the English should be a line across Long Island at Oyster Bay to Greenwich on the mainland and thence northerly at a distance of at least ten miles from the Hudson River. At the same time the Dutch title to Fort Good Hope and the land immediately surrounding it was recognized by the United Colonies.[19]

Fort Good Hope had been a thorn in the side of the Hartford people from the time of their arrival on the Connecticut River. The post was already there and the newcomers could find no equitable excuse for ousting the Dutchmen; however, they did all they could to make life unpleasant for them. When the Dutch tried to plant their fields, the English came with clubs and so frightened the horses that they ran away; they threw the Dutchmen's plow into the river; and they took possession of every cow or hog that wandered away from the immediate vicinity of the post. Through it all the Dutch had held on, and the agreement worked out in 1650 seemed to assure them peaceful possession.[20]

But the following year England passed a navigation act directed against Dutch shipping, and soon the two countries drifted into war. The Dutch West India Company urged Governor Stuyvesant to keep on friendly terms with his English neighbors if possible but, if he could not, then to engage the Indians against them. News of this design of making use of the Indians soon leaked out; some Indians claimed to have been solicited by the Dutch to attack the English settlements; and when the Commissioners of the United Colonies met at Boston in the spring of 1653, the question before them was peace or war with New Netherland. Connecticut and New Haven, the two colonies most exposed to an attack from the Indian allies of the Dutch, were all for war; Massachusetts, which would have had to furnish most of the money and men, held back; Plymouth was neutral. In the end it appeared that seven of the eight commissioners, enough to make the decision binding, were prepared to vote for war. At that point the Massachusetts General Court challenged the power of the commissioners to bind the colonies to an offensive war without the approval of the general court of each colony. From that point on the deliberations of the commissioners degenerated into a row between themselves and Massachusetts. As Jeremiah Jagger of Stamford remarked, the commissioners "satt long, but what did they, he could have three or foure plow-men should doe as much in three or foure dayes." [21]

While the United Colonies wrangled, Captain John Underhill acted. Following his campaigns against the Indians, he had moved from Stamford to the new Dutch town of Flushing on Long Island. There he found a number of other English settlers, while nearby Hempstead, Newtown and Gravesend were almost entirely made up of English. When the war broke out between England and Holland, Underhill denounced "the iniquitious government of Peter Stuyvesant" and urged the Long Island towns to "Accept and submit, ye, then, to the Parliament of England." There being no Parliament at hand, the towns did nothing; Governor Stuyvesant, very much at hand, became unpleasant; and Underhill betook himself hurriedly to Rhode Island, where, from the newly formed Providence Plantations, he received a commission to make war on the Dutch. He had already assured the Commissioners of the United Colonies that he would "be tender in sheeding blood"—and he was. With a few men he proceeded to Hartford and on the door of the temporarily unoccupied Fort Good Hope nailed a notice of the fact that he thereby seized the Dutch post and land with the permission of the General Court of Connecticut, "to remain seized till further determined by the said State." [22]

Connecticut determined the affair by retaining possession of the post. In fact, many of the people of Connecticut were in a humor to attack New Netherland without the help of Massachusetts. The inhabitants of Fairfield held a meeting and voted to "goe against the Duch." Roger Ludlow, leading man of the town, magistrate of the General Court of Connecticut and one of her Commissioners for the United Colonies, accepted command of the proposed expedition. The conclusion of peace between England and Holland was probably all that saved New Amsterdam from capture by the New Englanders in 1654. [23]

From Governor Stuyvesant's point of view the English were probably less troublesome than the Swedes. There were not many Swedes—two or three hundred at the most—but they were laying a solid foundation for a permanent colony on the Delaware River. They had developed a considerable trade with Virginia and were exporting tobacco as well as beaver skins. They were experimenting with tobacco on their own land, and were raising barley, rye and other grains sufficient for their support. They were planting orchards and were well equipped with oxen and cattle. From Fort Christina (present-day Wilmington, Del.) to the mouth of the Schuylkill River (present-day Philadelphia) the western bank of the Delaware was dotted with their settlements. When the Dutch attempted to establish a trading post on the Schuylkill, the Swedes built a larger post directly in front of it, and otherwise made themselves disagreeable. [24]

Finally Stuyvesant decided that the time had come for a showdown. In the summer of 1651 he sent a number of armed ships up the Delaware while he himself marched overland from New Amsterdam with a hundred and twenty soldiers. Then he requested Governor Printz to show title to the lands which the Swedes were occupying. Printz's airy reply that the Swedish limits were "wide and broad enough" did not satisfy the Dutchman; he secured from the always

willing Indians a deed to the western bank of the Delaware southward from Fort Christina, and proceeded to build a new Dutch fort to which he gave the name of Casimir—only five miles below the Swedish fort. Fort Nassau was dismantled; its guns were mounted at Fort Casimir; a couple of armed ships were stationed offshore; and the Dutch were in control of the Delaware River. Whoever or whatever went in or out had to pay respect, and customs, to the government of New Netherland.[25]

For two years New Sweden dwindled. No ships or men or guns came from home with which to humble the now dominant Dutch. In the early winter of 1653 Governor Printz, leaving his office to a deputy, departed for Sweden —carrying with him a tidy fortune made in ways known to all colonial governors of the times. Even as he sailed, a relief expedition was on the way. On a May evening in 1654 the Dutch commandant at Fort Casimir saw a strange sail coming up the river. It was the Swedish ship. Aboard was a new Governor, Johan Rising, who promptly demanded the surrender of the Dutch fort. There was no alternative. "What can I do?—there is no powder," the Dutch commandant replied to those who counseled defense. So for the moment the Swedes controlled both Fort Casimir and Fort Christina—and with these the whole of the Delaware River.[26]

The position of the Swedes seemed secure—so much so that the Parliamentary commissioners for Maryland and Virginia felt that it was high time to present the English claim on the Delaware as granted to Lord Baltimore. Rising countered with the formula which Elizabeth's great minister had used on the Spaniards. "King Jame's donation," he said, "was like the donation given by the Pope in Rome to the Kings of Castilien and of Portugal, the Pope giving what he did not own, nor was able to give." To this, Rising tells us, the English envoy "answered not a word." As a matter of fact the authority of the Parliamentary commissioners was at that very time being challenged by Lord Baltimore, who had more at stake than any other English claimant (see pages 301 and 302).[27]

But it was not with the power of Sweden that the English

were destined to contend. Upon receipt of news of the "infamous surrender" of their fort, the Dutch West India Company directed Stuyvesant to "exert every nerve to avenge that injury." Reinforcements were sent to New Amsterdam, and in September, 1655, seven armed vessels with six or seven hundred men sailed into the Delaware with Governor Stuyvesant in command. Within two weeks, and without a single casualty, the Swedes surrendered Forts Casimir and Christina; Governor Rising and his officers were shipped off to Europe; such of the colonists as wished to accept the sovereignty of the Dutch were allowed to remain. And that was the end of New Sweden.[28]

From the Delaware to Greenwich, from Oyster Bay to Fort Orange, the Dutch ruled supreme. New Amsterdam was the capital of a great trading venture. To it came slavers from the West Indies with negroes for sale; to it came Virginians with tobacco for sale; to it came New Englanders with fish for sale; at it, on their way back and forth along the coast, stopped most of the itinerant traders. The town was full of small merchants and peddlers. A fourth of the one hundred and twenty houses in the town offered brandy, tobacco or beer for sale. Monday was a regular market day during which all the traders exhibited their wares and drove their bargains. There among others Isaac Allerton, formerly of Plymouth, carried on a trade in goods from Virginia and Barbados. Once each year there was a *kermis,* or special fair, lasting several days, with dancing, processions, heavy drinking and a general hilarity sometimes bordering on what the Puritans of New England would have considered impropriety.[29]

New Netherland was not without spiritual nourishment. The established Reformed Church (Calvinistic) of Holland supplied ministers who did the best they could for the scattered population. In the towns on Long Island or along the Sound, where the settlers were mostly English expatriates from Massachusetts or New Haven, various species of Puritan worship were tolerated. We have an account of one of these Sabbath-day meetings in 1656—at the old Throgmorton plantation near the northern boundary of the present-day city of Greater New York. They had no minister. There was a "gathering of about 15 men and 10 or 12 women. Mr. Baly made a prayer, which being concluded, one Robbert Basset read a Sermon from a printed Book composed & published by an English Minister in England. After the reading Mr. Baly made another prayer and they sung a Psalm and seperated." [30]

No one could take exception to such a service. But when, that same year, William Wickendam, "a cobbler from Rhode Island," not only started preaching a new doctrine at Flushing but led his converts to the river and "dipped them," Governor Stuyvesant recognized that he had Baptists in his midst. Wickendam was told to get out, and his followers were fined. [31]

Quakers were even less welcome. In 1657 Dorothy Waugh and Mary Witherhead, who had been kicked out of Boston, arrived at New Amsterdam and began preaching on the streets. They were shipped off to Rhode Island, which, according to Domine Megapolensis, was "the receptable of all sorts of riff-raff people, and is nothing else than the *latrina* of New England." Other Quakers got off less easily, being imprisoned and brutally flogged. [32]

The expedition against New Sweden had involved the Dutch West India Company in a heavy debt. To shift a part of this burden the Company assigned Fort Casimir and the surrounding land to the City of Amsterdam, Holland, which rechristened the area with the name of New Amstel and proceeded with a program of colonization. The first settlers sent over were largely Waldensian refugees—a remnant of the "slaughtered saints, whose bones lie scattered on the Alpine mountains cold," as John Milton, Secretary to the Council of State of the Commonwealth of England, somewhat inaccurately described them. [33]

In the spring of 1657 the exiles from the Alpine Mountains arrived on the Delaware River. There, together with the few Swedes and Finns who had stayed on, they began establishing their new homes. As time went on, a number of shipwrecked Englishmen from Virginia were added to the population and by 1658 New Amstel was "a goodly town of about one hundred houses." But, as so often happened in colonizing ventures controlled from Europe, more people were added to the growing town than it could support. Sickness and want went hand in hand. "Our granary and larder and trust has been only at the Manhattans [New Amsterdam]," wrote the distraught director of New Amstel to Governor Stuyvesant.[34]

At this very moment word spread through the settlement that Lord Baltimore, who was again in control of his province of Maryland, was preparing to exercise his patent rights along the western shore of the Delaware River. Many families moved down into the Chesapeake region; servants began running away to the lower Maryland settlements; and a general state of alarm prevailed. Early in September, 1659, Colonel Utie, a member of the Council of Maryland, came up the Chesapeake and crossed overland to New Amstel with a message from his Governor: the Dutch must either clear out of their town on the Delaware or come under the government of Lord Baltimore. The director of New Amstel temporized until he could get advice, and possibly help, from Governor Stuyvesant.[35]

Stuyvesant was in no position to do more than put up a strong bluff, which, of course, was exactly what Maryland was doing. Some sixty Dutch soldiers were hurried off to New Amstel and an embassy was dispatched to Maryland with a protest against Utie's behavior and a demand for the return of runaway servants; also to find out what the Marylanders really had in mind. This embassy, headed by Augustine Herrman and accompanied by a few soldiers and Indian guides, left New Amstel on September 30. A day's tramp across country brought them to the headwaters of Elk River, a northern affluent of Chesapeake Bay. There they found a boat of doubtful ownership, and, dismissing their escort with the exception of two guides, embarked on their voyage. The boat leaked and had to be constantly bailed out. All one night they paddled down the river, and where it emptied into the Chesapeake they found a plantation belonging to Jan Turner. There, at the Turner place, was "Abraham the Finn" and a Dutch woman—both of them runaways from New Amstel. Worse yet, the Finn claimed their boat, and they had a deal of trouble bribing him to let them use it. Across the narrow neck of the Bay, lying against the western shore, was Colonel Utie's island plantation from whence came the sound of continuous gun fire; the Dutch embassy did not call.

On they went in their crazy little boat. At the northern end of Claiborne's Island, long since transferred from the fiery captain to Lord Baltimore, they spent the night at the home of an English planter. In his employ they found another runaway Dutch woman—not worth her salt, so nothing was done about her return to New Amstel. From their host the ambassadors hired a skiff in which they sailed across the Chesapeake to the Puritan settlement at Anne Arundel (present-day Annapolis) and thence down to the Patuxent. From there they walked overland the nine miles to St. Mary's and presented their credentials to Philip Calvert, Secretary of the Province of Maryland and half-brother of Lord Baltimore.

For two solid weeks, between dinners and other courtesies, the conferences went on. Most of the talk was about the respective titles of New Netherland and Maryland. Herrman contended that the Dutch had been on the Delaware long before Baltimore received his patent; Calvert insisted that the limits named in Baltimore's patent settled the boundaries. The English intent back of all the citation of titles and boundaries came out in one of the conversations. Calvert, quoting the text of the Baltimore patent, stated that Maryland reached to New England, but did not divulge that the patent, intentionally ignoring the existence of New Netherland, had exactly identified the point "where New England ends" as being the fortieth parallel (present-day Philadelphia). Herrman, accepting Calvert's statement as referring to New England as it actually existed in 1659, inquired, "Where would New Netherland be in that case?" to which Calvert answered bluntly: I know not.[36]

God Save the King

IT WAS MAY 23, 1660. An English warship was standing out from the coast of Holland into the North Sea. On the quarter-deck a tall young man walked back and forth followed by a group of admiring men and a dog. Of the lot the dog was probably the only one that the young man really trusted. As he walked he told stories of his experiences after the defeat of the royalists at Worcester: how he had hidden in an oak tree while his pursuers searched below; how he had been roundly scolded by a kitchen wench while disguised as a farm boy.

The ship was named *The Charles;* twenty-four hours earlier it had been *The Naseby,* so christened in memory of the battle in which the royal army had been shattered in 1645. Trailing behind were other warships, their guns roaring in honor of the present occasion. On ahead were still other ships, leading the way down the North Sea to Dover, England. On one of them was George Downing, the former Harvard boy, now England's ambassador to Holland and, by a matter of hours, Sir George, if you please—doing "wonderfull well" as usual. Dukes, duchesses, lords and ladies were scattered everywhere throughout the fleet.[1]

After years of exile Charles Stuart was going home—joyously welcomed by the nation which eleven years earlier had cut off his father's head and which had chased him out of the land. At Dover vast crowds waited to bend their knees to their returning King—Charles II. London had already proclaimed him.

Not everybody was happy, however. Hugh Peter, sometime preacher at Salem in Massachusetts, shivered with apprehension. His sermons had egged on the judges during the trial of Charles I; many royalists believed that he was actually the masked man who swung the axe that cut off the martyred King's head. The Council of State had already ordered his arrest. Edward Whalley and William Goffe, who had sat as judges on the tribunal that condemned Charles I, were aboard a little merchant ship named the *Prudent Mary,* pounding her way westward across the Atlantic. They had heard the cheering throngs; they had seen the bonfires; they knew that it was only a matter of days before Charles II would be in England—and they had no desire to meet him.[2]

News of the King's restoration was received with varying emotions in the different American colonies. The people of Virginia, who had accepted the rule of Parliament only through coercion, gladly returned to their loyalty. Governor Berkeley apologized abjectly for having accepted even temporary authority at the hands of the Assembly, and was as a matter of course confirmed by a new commission from the King. The Assembly, in behalf of the people, asked the King's pardon for having yielded to force which they had not the power to resist. In acknowledgment of their weakness it was decreed that the anniversary of the death of Charles I should "be annually solemnized with fasting and prayers, that our sorrows may expiate our crime, and our teares wash away our guilt." The King, not to be outdone, elevated Virginia to the status of a dominion. But the former parliamentary commissioner, Captain William Claiborne, lost his job as Secretary of the dominion, along with all chance of ever regaining his island up the Chesapeake.[3]

For Lord Baltimore and the people of Maryland the restoration of the King marked an end to a long period of confusion. No longer was it necessary for Baltimore to placate the Puritan faction. In the place of a not-too-loyal Governor he appointed his half-brother, Philip Calvert, a rigid Catholic; and called upon the King for assistance in restoring order, which assistance the King directed Governor Berkeley of Virginia to extend. Nor was Baltimore less prompt in challenging the activities of the Dutch on the Delaware River. In July, 1660, he ordered his agent at Amsterdam to inform the Dutch West India Company that any settlements within the limits of his patent must submit to his government. The Dutch replied that they had been on the Delaware a long time and intended to stay there. Unfortunately for his future rights Baltimore did not press the matter. Instead, in July, 1661, we find Governor Calvert and the Dutch director of New Amstel "making merry" together on the headwaters of the Chesapeake and negotiating a deal whereby the Marylanders offered to deliver two or three thousand hogsheads of tobacco annually to the Dutch in return for negroes and other commodities.⁴

All through 1659 and early 1660 the leaders of the Puritan colonies had watched the course of events in England with growing concern. In January, 1660, John Hull, the mintmaster at Boston, wrote in his diary, ". . . there came in a ship from London, and brought us intelligence of the state of our native land, which was very sad . . . as if the reformation, purchased by so much war and blood, should be given up again to heretics and Papists. . . ." Definite word of the King's impending restoration was slow in reaching New England. Late in April John Davenport at New Haven heard a rumor, by way of Virginia, that Charles was in London, but he put no stock in it. A week after Charles had sailed from Holland, the people of Massachusetts were observing a solemn day of humiliation on account of the "sad & deplorable condition of our deere native countrie. . . ." Some time in July Governor Winthrop, of Connecticut, had a report on the situation in England for the week of May 3 to May 10, which indicated that the restoration would occur soon. He sent a transcript to Davenport, but the preacher was still not wholly convinced; he was much more interested in getting some of Winthrop's rubila pills for his wife, who was ailing.⁵

On July 27 the *Prudent Mary,* after a long voyage, docked

at Boston. From its passengers the people of Massachusetts learned what was going on in England at the time of their departure on May 14, and the rest could be inferred. Doubtless, too, there were confidential reports from John Leverett, who had taken the place of the late Edward Winslow as agent for the colony.[6]

Among the passengers who arrived on the *Prudent Mary* were Goffe and Whalley, under assumed names of course, but known to so many people as to leave little mystery as to their identity. They were hospitably received by the leaders of the Bay government; they lived at the home of one of the magistrates; they were honored guests at the dinner tables of prominent ministers and of the president of Harvard College. Davenport extended an invitation for them to visit New Haven. It did not seem to occur to any one that the King's arm might reach to New England. In fact, the general feeling was that the Restoration was but another disorder which the Mother Country must temporarily bear. When an English ship captain suggested that the two regicides, as the King's judges were coming to be called, be arrested as traitors, he was rebuffed—"grinned" at and told not to "meddle."[7]

But as autumn turned into winter, disturbing reports began coming out of England. Leverett wrote to Governor Endecott that complaints were being made against the colony— for its annexation of Maine, for its treatment of the Quakers —and that a defense was advisable. Accordingly, on December 19, an address to the King was drafted and forwarded to Leverett for delivery. Endecott and the magistrates asked for a continuation of their patent rights; they excused their treatment of the Quakers; about the regicides in their midst they said not a word.[8]

However, they were hearing enough about the regicides who had been caught in England. Twenty-nine had been tried and condemned to death; several had already paid the full penalty prescribed for treason: they had been hanged, drawn, and quartered. To Hugh Peter the same punishment had been meted out. On October 16 he was taken to Charing Cross, London, and hanged until he choked. Then, while

Octob.
1660

Etatis
Suæ 61.

J.F Sculp

HUGH PETER.

From *A Dying Fathers Last Legacy to An Only Child: or, Mr. Hugh
Peter's Advice to His Daughter. Written by his own Hand, during his
late Imprisonment in the Tower of London; And given her a little
before his Death.*

Courtesy, The American Antiquarian Society, Worcester.

still alive, he was cut down; his private members were cut off; he was sliced through his middle; his entrails and heart were "drawn" out, held before his eyes and thrown in the fire; his head was cut off and set on a pole on London bridge; the rest of his body was hacked into "quarters" and hung at the gates of the city—all this as a moral lesson to those who might contemplate treason.[9]

When the news of this sad end of their former minister reached the Bay, it caused Governor Endecott and his fellow magistrates to do some hard thinking. At about the same time there arrived a royal proclamation offering a reward for the capture of Goffe and Whalley, which must have suggested some unpleasant possibilities to the two regicides. They decided to accept Davenport's invitation to visit New Haven, where they were lodged in the guest room of the minister's house. After they were well out of Massachusetts, Governor Endecott issued a warrant for their arrest.[10]

On April 28, 1661, Endecott received a royal warrant addressed to all the magistrates of New England, commanding that Goffe and Whalley be "apprehended, and with the first opportunity sent over hither under a strict care, to receive according to their demerits." Outwardly Endecott acted with all sincerity. He deputized two avowed royalists, Thomas Kellond, a merchant, and Thomas Kirke, a ship captain, to search for and apprehend the fugitives. In addition he insisted upon providing the deputies with letters of introduction to the governors of Plymouth, Connecticut, New Haven and New Netherland, and with printed copies of the King's warrant. The printing took several days—during which word of what was going on certainly reached New Haven.[11]

On May 7 Kellond and Kirke galloped westward from Boston along the well-beaten Bay path toward Springfield on the Connecticut River. From that place they followed the road along the river to Hartford, where they arrived on May 10. The total distance was perhaps one hundred and twenty-five miles. To a merchant and a ship captain this probably seemed fast riding, but it would not have prevented a good rider from covering the same distance well ahead of them.[12]

At Hartford, Kellond and Kirke were told that the regicides were in New Haven. Accordingly they proceeded to
Guilford, where Deputy-governor Leete of New Haven Colony lived—Governor Eaton had died three years before.
News of their errand soon spread. Worse yet, it was the
Sabbath eve; and no good Puritan, much less the Deputy-
governor, could think of taking action on mundane affairs,
though some riders did mysteriously disappear from Guilford that evening. The following Monday morning Kellond
and Kirke went on to New Haven—fifteen miles to the westward. There later in the day they were joined by Leete.
Much futile conversation ensued as to whether and how
the magistrates of New Haven Colony could assist in the
search. Nor could the two regicides be found. No one had
seen them—recently; no one knew where they were. They
were, as a matter of fact, only a couple of miles from the
village—in a cave on a high hill known as West Rock. However, after diligent inquiry from the townspeople Kellond
and Kirke came to the conclusion that their quarry had fled
to the Dutch colony. So they rode hopefully westward to
New Amsterdam and presented their credentials to Governor
Stuyvesant. Goffe and Whalley climbed down from their
perch and during the next three years lived more or less
openly at the town of Milford a few miles west of New
Haven.[13]

While New Haven was thus resisting the King's authority,
the other Puritan colonies were officially recognizing him
and professing their loyalty. The Providence Plantations
(Rhode Island) had acted with little delay; they had publicly proclaimed the King in October, 1660. By March 5,
1661, Plymouth Colony was conducting her courts in the
name of her "sovereign lord the Kinge." On March 14 the
General Court of Connecticut acknowledged its "loyalty &
allegiance" to Charles and assured him that the inhabitants
of the colony were "his Highnes loyall and faythfull subjects"; also the Court authorized Governor Winthrop to proceed to England to "petition his Majesty for grace and
favour." Although Massachusetts had addressed the King
the preceding December, she now, on August 8, formally

proclaimed him. Finally New Haven, uncertain and fearful, fell in line; at nine o'clock in the morning on August 22, with the military company drawn up to solemnize the occasion, she acknowledged Charles to be her "Soveraigne Lord and King." Too poor to send an agent of their own to England, the New Haven magistrates decided to ask Governor Winthrop of Connecticut to petition the King in their behalf. But Winthrop had already sailed—very quietly from New Amsterdam.[14]

Had the New Haven magistrates known the nature of the instructions which Winthrop carried with him from his General Court they would have been less trustful of his assistance. He was directed to ask for a patent with bounds extending from Massachusetts on the north and Plymouth on the east to the Delaware River on the south. This would have taken in all of Rhode Island, all of New Haven and all of New Netherland.[15]

Upon his arrival in England Winthrop made the most of his father's old friends and particularly those associated under the elusive patent said to have been granted to Lords Say and Brook in 1632 (see page 229), the rights of which had been purchased by Connecticut. In his address to the King the Governor departed slightly from his instructions. He did not ask for all of Rhode Island, but only for that part lying west of Narragansett Bay. On the south he was more specific than his instructions; Connecticut's southern boundary was the fortieth parallel—"where New England ends" as it had been phrased in Lord Baltimore's patent. Westward the colony swept across the continent to the Pacific. These bounds Winthrop coolly based on the Say and Brook patent—"lost in a Fatall Fire at Saybrook fort," according to his statement.[16]

It was a lucky rather than a "Fatall" fire that kept the old Say and Brook patent from being put in evidence. If it ever existed, of which there is considerable doubt, it certainly gave no such limits as those cited; and no one knew this better than Winthrop, who, back in 1635 and 1636, had been the first and only Governor under that patent. None the less his petition was successful, and on April 23, 1662, Connecticut received her new patent or charter. The description of the southern boundary was somewhat less definite than Winthrop requested, being merely identified as "the sea." That might, with good luck, be interpreted as meaning Delaware Bay; an excellent case could be made for the inclusion of Long Island; there could be no question that the bounds extended to Long Island Sound. And Connecticut thus swallowed up New Haven, which latter colony was most unhappy about the whole business and acquiesced only after a long and acrimonious wrangle.[17]

While in London Governor Winthrop met John Clarke, the doctor-preacher who in 1638 had delivered Mrs. Hutchinson of the "monster." Clarke had been in England for several years, acting as agent for the Providence Plantations (Rhode Island), and was in 1662 engaged in securing a royal patent for that colony, in confirmation of the one granted by the Warwick Commission in 1644. The Connecticut patent had already been approved before Clarke discovered that its eastern boundary had been placed at Narragansett Bay. Naturally he protested, and delivery of the Connecticut patent was withheld until the controversy could be threshed out. Both Winthrop and Clarke agreed to abide by the decision of a board of arbitrators. The decision went against Connecticut; and on July 8, 1663, Rhode Island got her patent, her boundaries, and her permanent name of Rhode Island. Also she received the guarantee "that noe person within the said colonie, at any time hereafter, shall bee any wise molested, punished, disquieted, or called in question, for any differences in opinione in matters of religion."[18]

Winthrop and Clarke were not the only American colonials in London during the early years of the Restoration. Governor Berkeley of Virginia was there to solicit favors for his colony and for himself; he became one of the proprietors of a new colony to be known as Carolina. Others were there just to solicit favors for themselves. Among the latter was "Captain" John Scott of Long Island. A former indentured servant, Scott had resided for a number of years at Southampton, on the eastern end of Long Island. From making his living as a blacksmith he had branched out into the

JOHN WINTHROP, the Younger.
Governor of Connecticut.

Courtesy, Connecticut State Library, Hartford.

business of buying land titles from the Indians and selling them to the unwary. With the return of Charles II to royal power Scott sensed the opportunities that might present themselves to one near the throne, and sailed for England. What he had in mind appears to have been nothing less than being made lord proprietor of the whole of Long Island.[19]

And except for the presence of Governor Winthrop in London at the same time, Scott might conceivably have had his wish. He had wormed his way into places of influence, and a good-natured King would have been an easy prospect for his plausible tongue. However, Winthrop wanted Long Island for Connecticut, and the former blacksmith from a town under Connecticut jurisdiction knew when to bide his time. So Scott waited until Winthrop left for home in the spring of 1663, and then presented to the newly formed Council for Foreign Plantations a complaint against New Netherland in general. Apparently Samuel Maverick, late of Massachusetts, and Captain George Baxter, sometime English secretary to Governor Stuyvesant but now in England helping John Clarke get the Rhode Island patent, had expressed similar opinions. Anyway the three of them were directed to prepare a detailed statement of the English right to the territory occupied by the Dutch, and "of the means to make them acknowledge and submit to His Majesty's government."[20]

All in all Scott's trip to England had not been unprofitable. True, he had failed to get Long Island, but he had hobnobbed with the great; his advice had been asked by the King's council; no one knew just how much authority he might have; and he would make the most of it. On the financial side he had done very nicely, too. From a trusting Quaker tradesman of London, with a yearning for Long Island acreage, he had extracted a considerable sum of ready cash. So when he arrived at Long Island in the autumn of 1663, Scott was a personage of consequence and in funds.[21]

Governor Winthrop, too, was home. But the General Court of Connecticut had not awaited his return to begin the expansion permitted by the new patent. Nor did the court feel bound by Winthrop's agreement with Clarke concerning the

Rhode Island boundary; the towns west of Narragansett Bay were warned against admitting authority from any other source than Connecticut. So far as New Haven was concerned, her protests could be ignored; one by one her towns —Guilford, Stamford, Southold and others—were breaking away from the old confederation and asking to be taken in under the more liberal government of Connecticut.[22]

Against the Dutch colony Connecticut "crowded" down the mainland past Greenwich to within a dozen miles of New Amsterdam. In 1654 a few English families, without asking permission from Governor Stuyvesant, had settled at Westchester, where Mrs. Hutchinson and Throgmorton had had their plantations eleven years earlier. The leader of the movement was Doctor Thomas Pell, who had come to America as surgeon at Saybrook fort. Later he had lived at New Haven, where he married the widow of Francis Brewster, she who had found Davenport's sermons a little trying to her stomach. We have already witnessed one of the Sabbath-day services at Westchester (page 383), which we may hope was more to Mrs. Pell's taste. Whatever the advantages spiritually, the settlers were, in 1656, compelled to place themselves under the rule of the Dutch government. But when news of the new Connecticut patent spread through the settlements, Westchester appealed to Hartford and on October 9, 1662, was formally added to the growing colony.[23]

Across the Sound, on Long Island, Connecticut moved more slowly but left no question as to her claim or intention. Then into the scene popped "Captain" John Scott. Under just what authority, if any, he acted is difficult to judge. He set forth that the King had granted all of Long Island to the Duke of York; he formed a "combination" of Hempstead, Gravesend, Flushing and other towns inhabited by English but hitherto unquestionably under Dutch authority; and he undertook to act as their "President" until the Duke might further manifest his wishes. Early in January, 1664, with "60 or 70 horsemen and as many foot, with colors flying, drums beating and trumpet sounding" he marched on the towns wholly inhabited by Dutchmen, even to the ferry where Brooklyn stands today. There was much talk but no bloodshed, though Scott threatened to pursue the townspeople with "fire and sword" if they did not acknowledge the authority of the Duke.[24]

This was all very disturbing to Governor Stuyvesant. It was even more disturbing to Governor Winthrop and the General Court of Connecticut, who figured that Long Island belonged to their colony. This talk about the Duke they looked upon as simply a device by Scott for stealing Connecticut's newly won domain across the Sound. An indictment against the interloper was promptly found: Scott stood charged by the General Court of Connecticut with "Speaking words tending to the defamation of the Kings Majesty"; with "Seditious practices and tumultuous carriages"; with "Acting treachourously to the Colony of Connecticut"; with "Usurpeing authority, upon pretense of a commission"; and with divers other crimes including "Grosse and notorious prophanation of God's holy day." Every peace officer in the colony was instructed to bring in the malefactor wherever found. Connecticut wanted John Scott in the jail at Hartford; not at large on Long Island.[25]

Nor could all Scott's horsemen and footmen, flying colors, drummers and trumpeters save him. From the Connecticut marshal we have an account of the capture. As the marshal and his deputies approached the house where Scott was staying, they saw his supporters gather to his defense. Scott ordered the marshal to stand at his peril; he said that he would "sacrifice his heart's blood upon the ground" before he would yield; he dared them with "a flourish" to lay hands on him; he said, "lett them take me if they dare"; he questioned whether "the proudest of them all dearst for to lay hands on him." And then the marshal arrested him and took him to Hartford.[26]

Two days after Connecticut ordered the arrest of Scott there passed the Great Seal of England a patent from the King to his "Dearest Brother James Duke of York" which justified all that Scott had been saying and that ended forever Connecticut's dream of greatness. To his brother the King granted not only all of Long Island but the rest of

New Netherland, a large slice of Connecticut and the northern part of Maine.[27]

Nor, except for some geographical details, was this grant to the Duke a capricious action; it was the logical result of several well-considered economic formulas which added up to a new colonial policy. To begin with, the government of Charles II needed money. The King's advisers saw plainly enough that customs duties derived from trade were the only practical source from which the money could be had. Accordingly the existing trade and navigation laws were reenacted and strengthened. A Council for Foreign Plantations was created to enforce and systematize the new regulations. All cargoes between England and her colonies were to be carried in English ships and required to pay duties according to schedules devised to bring in what the traffic would bear. Obviously this was a blow at the Dutch, whose ships had long dominated the seas. There was in fact a group, led by Sir George Downing, openly committed to breaking the Dutch trade even if it led to war; and they hoped it would. With this group the Duke of York joined—because in its activities he saw an opportunity to make the money which he, himself, wanted desperately.[28]

Against these diverse English interests the Dutch colony of New Netherland stood as an obstacle and a temptation. So long as it remained in the midst of the English colonies the enforcement of the navigation acts would be almost impossible; opportunities for evasion, by buying or selling in the nearby Dutch towns, would be easy. Therefore, New Netherland must be brought under English control.[29]

Grounds for seizure of New Netherland were easily found. It was not in reality a Dutch colony; it was a trading post, without boundaries or title to land, belonging to the Dutch West India Company. The area which it occupied had long been claimed by England; it had in fact been included in the grant made by King James in 1620 to the Council for New England; and so far as Long Island was concerned that area had been granted in 1635 by the Council to the Earl of Stirling, who, through land sales, had amply established a claim to proprietorship.

So it came about that the Duke started his operations with the heir of the Earl of Stirling. From him he bought—with promissory notes which were never paid—the title to Long Island and upper Maine. To this the King added the rest —from Connecticut River to the Delaware River and well up into present-day New York State and Vermont. That the Duke's bounds west of the Connecticut River clearly over-lapped those granted to Connecticut only two years before apparently bothered the King not at all. Only through a sense of justice on the part of the King's commissioners, sharpened by a bribe of five hundred bushels of corn, did Connecticut finally retain her permanent bounds.[30]

The existence of the Duke's patent and his intent to reduce New Netherland were known only to a limited circle. When, in the spring of 1664, four warships sailed from England, it was given out that their sole purpose was to escort commis-sioners appointed by the King to investigate conditions in New England. It was quite true that aboard the fleet were four commissioners with orders to investigate boundary dis-putes, observe the administration of justice, arrange for the collection of customs, make inquiries about the regicides, and generally correct any existing abuses. Heading this commis-sion was Richard Nicolls, who also had a commission for the capture of New Netherland. Another of the commissioners was Samuel Maverick, who had been fur trading at Massa-chusetts Bay long before the Puritans arrived and who in 1646 had been forced out of the colony because of his de-mand for the right to vote without having to be a member of the Congregational church.[31]

In July two of the ships arrived at Boston and the other two at Piscataqua. From the latter place Maverick sum-moned Robert Jordan, successor to John Winter at Rich-mond's Island, to meet him—doubtless for advice regarding conditions in Maine. At the same time Maverick sent a mes-sage to the Governor and General Court of Massachusetts telling them to "take care how they dispose of such things as may bee out of their bounds and not fit for them to take cognisance of," by which he meant that they were to cease exercising authority in Maine; title to that province was being handed back to the heir of Sir Ferdinando Gorges.[32]

At both Boston and Hartford the real purpose of the military expedition was revealed to the magistrates, and troops were requested. While Massachusetts procrastinated, Governor Winthrop, with volunteers from Connecticut and eastern Long Island, hastened to join the invading force before New Amsterdam. And as the Connecticut volunteers marched southward, the two regicides, Goffe and Whalley, marched in the opposite direction. From Milford they went to the frontier town of Hadley, on the Connecticut River twenty miles north of Springfield, where they lived for many years in the home of the Reverend John Russell. At about the same time John Scott broke jail at Hartford, leaving behind for his keeper only an unpaid board bill.[33]

Governor Stuyvesant had been warned of the real purpose of the English fleet but apparently allowed himself to be lulled into inaction by assurances that Nicolls and his fellow commissioners were concerned only with bringing Massachusetts and Connecticut to terms. He was soon disillusioned. Late in August Nicolls anchored his ships at the entrance to the harbor of New Amsterdam—just north of Coney Island. On the Long Island shore, near Brooklyn, English volunteer companies gathered to help in the capture of the Dutch colony. Some were from Connecticut under the command of Governor Winthrop; others were from the Long Island towns—those towns such as Flushing and Hempstead at which the Dutch had allowed the Englishmen to settle when they had been unable to live with their fellow Englishmen in Massachusetts and New Haven. And there among them, with his company of armed men, was Captain John Scott, late of the jail at Hartford.[34]

To Nicolls' demand that New Amsterdam be surrendered Governor Stuyvesant could do little but stall for time. His fort was short of powder. His soldiers were ready to mutiny. The townspeople were in deadly fear of the New Englanders —waiting at the Brooklyn ferry for a chance to loot the rich stores and homes on Manhattan Island. On September 6th terms of capitulation were agreed upon. Two days later Stuyvesant and his officers marched out of the fort; a small

English guard marched in; and the colors of England fluttered over the old Dutch trading post. New Amsterdam became New York. Fort Orange, up the Hudson, became Fort Albany. New Amstel, on the Delaware, became New Castle. From Maine to Virginia England ruled the coast of America.[35]

Unto All Ages

MUCH HAD HAPPENED since those days when Coronado and De Soto led their expeditions through the future United States, and Francis Drake touched upon her coasts. Yet there were doubtless many men still alive whose grandfathers had marched with the Spanish captains; there were men living in Virginia and Massachusetts who well might themselves, as young boys, have seen Drake.

But the lands explored or viewed by those great pioneers still lay practically unconquered by white men. At Santa Fe in New Mexico, there were a Spanish governor and two or three hundred soldiers who with their wives and servants, many of which latter were natives, made a town of perhaps a thousand souls. Most of their supplies came up from Mexico in annual caravans; some cattle went back for sale. However, the settlement was not self-supporting; it existed primarily as a guard for a dozen or so Catholic missionaries who labored with the Indians at the pueblos along the Rio Grande where, according to Father Benavides, the whole land was "dotted with churches, convents, and crosses."[1]

On the coast of Florida, at St. Augustine, there was a ragged Spanish garrison; elsewhere about the peninsula a few Franciscan friars strove, not too successfully, to christianize the unstable natives. Roanoke Island lay as bare as when Raleigh's men arrived there in 1585, though the Virginians were pushing along the coast in that direction. In California nothing remained to commemorate Drake's brief visit except perhaps a piece of engraved brass, passing from one Indian tribe to another. Down the great central valley of the continent, over the moldering bones of De Soto, the Mississippi rolled to the Gulf unvexed by the petty doings of white men.[2]

Only along the middle Atlantic seaboard had the Europeans taken root. And this had come about not from colonizing programs carried out by the rulers of the countries from which the colonists came, but rather from the efforts of privately financed companies actuated by the hope of profit—either to the purses or the souls of the backers. Thousands of people had died to make Virginia habitable; countless thousands of pounds sterling had been lost to make it profitable. New England had had its starving and its dying times, but the survivors had hung on; more people had taken the places of those who perished; salvation was the reward.

But, with the colonies once established, the trading companies had served their purpose. Virginia had been taken over by the King. Massachusetts had avoided the same fate only by the accident of a civil war in England. Never again would a colonizing venture be entrusted to a company dependent upon subscribers for its funds, and directed by elected officers. The proprietary grant made to Lord Baltimore in 1632 had established a new pattern for the founding of colonies; the grant to the Duke of York had followed that pattern; those yet to come would be of the same sort—direct from the King to a proprietor or group of proprietors who would be directly responsible to the King.

This was in line with a colonial policy glimpsed by Charles I, and consistently followed by Charles II. The colonies were to be knit into an imperial scheme, held together by a uniform system of trade, molded into a uniform system of government. The Mother Country would profit; the colonies might at times suffer; but for the empire as a whole the program would be advantageous.[3]

Already Virginia and Maryland were feeling the teeth of

the new system of customs and shipping. Tobacco was bearing so heavy a burden in duties and freight that little was left for the planters; the profits that formerly went to them were now going to enrich the merchants of England or the favorites of the King. The small planter was having a hard time making a go of tobacco; servants freed from service were not taking up land as in the past; rather the land was falling into the possession of large planters who had the capital with which to buy cheaper labor. In ever-increasing numbers the places of the indentured servants and the free white laborer were to be taken by negro slaves—slaves supplied by the Royal Adventurers to Africa, of which company the principal stockholder was the King's "dearest brother," the Duke of York.[4]

Spiritually too there was a new imperial policy, gently but steadily enforced, very different from that attempted by Charles I and Archbishop Laud. So far as the colonies were concerned, dissenters from the Church of England would be tolerated provided they did not interfere with those who wished to conform to the established church of the Mother Country. The Congregational church organization of New England was allowed to continue, but Massachusetts was required to repeal the law which restricted citizenship to the members of that church; also she was called upon to permit the use of the *Book of Common Prayer* by those of her inhabitants who preferred the episcopal service.[5]

To Governor Endecott this was a bitter pill, but his sands were run; he died in 1665. Some of his fellow leaders had already sensed the flaw in Puritanism; human nature could be repressed only so far and so long. Governor Bradford, meditating on the reasons for the increase of sin in so pious a community as Plymouth, had commented, ". . . as it is with waters when their streames are stopped or dammed up, when they gett passage they flow with more violence, and make more nois and disturbance, then when they are suffered to rune quietly in their owne chanels."[6]

And now Governor Bradford was gone. Gone, too, was the elder Winthrop; gone was Thomas Dudley; gone was Roger Ludlow; gone were Edward Winslow, Theophilus Eaton,

John Cotton, Thomas Hooker—all the old leaders. It was a new age. On the throne of England sat a King who had come into the world at the very time that the great Puritan fleet was crossing the western sea to escape from "the bishops" of old England.

Charles II could no more understand the fear which the Puritans had of "the bishops" than he could understand his father's unyielding support of episcopacy. He would not jeopardize his throne, much less his head, for a mere principle. If the Puritans wanted a congregational form of church, let them have it. If the Quakers wanted to rant, let them rant. If the restored Church of England yearned for altars and surplices and bishops, let it have them. Even for the Catholic form of worship Charles had great sympathy, if not more; but since the great majority of his subjects disliked Romanism, he would not push the matter.

The new King knew a better way of gripping the people to his throne than by meddling with religious doctrines—with which most of them were thoroughly weary anyway. He would amuse them, give them some risque stories to laugh over while he and his ministers would patiently, during long hours of which his subjects knew nothing, build a British imperial system—based on trade, seemingly easy-going, tolerant, but with a jealous eye to profits for those whose support was needed to uphold the throne.

No more than their King could the younger people of America understand their fathers. The sons of the foundation stones of the Puritan churches found themselves unable to make that profession of spiritual regeneration expected from a "visible saint." Try as they might to believe all that they had learned in *Milk for Babes* they could not be sure that they were of the "elect." Within nine years of the adoption of the Cambridge Platform the churches were forced to liberalize their requirements for admission; it was that or the churches would have been empty.[7]

Other young men worried not at all about spiritual regeneration. They took the King for their model. What he did, or what they thought he did, they too would do. Thus four young blades of Westmoreland County, Virginia, joined in

building a temple dedicated to pleasure. There each in his
turn acted as master at a feast to which the wives, sweet-
hearts and friends of each were invited. Music, pleasant re-
freshments and dancing doubtless made the occasions not
unworthy of comparison with those enjoyed by the young
King in London.[8]

One of the members of this gay quartet was named Isaac
Allerton. His father had come to America on the *Mayflower*.
His mother was Fear Brewster, shadowy daughter of Elder
Brewster, the spiritual leader of the Pilgrims. Young Allerton
had been born at Plymouth; his early life had been spent
at Plymouth.[9] One may speculate whether, as he sat at the
banquet table in the temple dedicated to pleasure, there on
the balmy shores of the Potomac, he thought for a fleeting
second of his mother and his grandfather lying in the weed-
grown plot by the chilly harbor far to the north. As he joined
in the round of festivities, surrounded by the wit and beauty
of Virginia, perhaps singing the latest London catch song—

> Hang sorrow, cast away care,
> Come let us drink up our sack;
> They say it is good
> To cherish the blood,
> And eke to strengthen the back;

> 'Tis wine that makes the thoughts aspire,
> And fills the body with heat,
> Besides 'tis good
> If well understood
> To fit a man for the feat . . ."[10]

did there perchance, at such a time, come to his ears in
memory the voice of his grandfather, leading his little flock
in the long, stern roll of Old Hundred—

> Confess to him, bless ye his name.
> Because Jehovah he good is:
> his mercy ever is the same:
> and his faith, unto all ages.

Bibliography

IN general the reference numbers are placed at the end of the paragraphs concerned. In some cases, where several paragraphs are plainly derived from or supported by the same source or sources, the reference number is placed at the end of the last paragraph bearing on the subject. Where a short title seems sufficient, the full title and description are given the first time the citation appears, and the statement is made that thereafter it will appear by the short title as given; also the full title and description are usually repeated the first time the citation appears in each subsequent chapter.

CHAPTER 1. THE KIVA

1. *U. S. Senate Executive Document No. 64, 31st Congress, 1st Session.*
2. Fewkes, J. W., *Antiquities of the Mesa Verde National Park,* Bureau of American Ethnology, Bulletin 51 (Washington, 1911) ; Chapin, F. H., *The Land of the Cliff-Dwellers* (Boston, 1892).
3. *U. S. Geological and Geographical Survey of the Territories,* Tenth Annual Report (Washington, 1878), 383–478.
4. Fewkes, J. W., *Antiquities of the Mesa Verde National Park,* Bureau of American Ethnology, Bulletins 41 and 51 (Washington, 1909 and 1911) ; Roberts, Jr., Frank H. H., *Early Pueblo Ruins in the Piedra District, Southwestern Colorado; The Ruins at Kiatuthlanna, Eastern Arizona; The Village of the Great Kivas on the Zuni Reservation, New Mexico;* being Bureau of American Ethnology Bulletins 96, 100 and 111 (Washington, 1930, 1931 and 1932) ; Pepper, G. H., *Pueblo Bonito,* Anthropological Papers of the American Museum of Natural History, Vol. XXVII (New York, 1920) ; Watson, Don, *Cliff Palace, The Story of an Ancient City* (Ann Arbor, 1940).
5. Hewett, Edgar L., *The Chaco Canyon and Its Monuments* (Albuquerque, 1936), 127–131.

CHAPTER 2. THE CROSS

1. The *Relacion* of Cabeza de Vaca was first printed in Spain in 1542. The present chapter follows the English translation as printed in *Spanish Explorers in the Southern United States, 1528–1543* (New York, 1907, in the Original Narratives of Early American History series, Barnes & Noble, publishers).
2. This account is based upon "The Narrative of the Expedition of Hernando de Soto, by the Gentleman of Elvas" as printed in *Spanish Explorers in the Southern United States, 1528–1543,* from an English translation made in 1866. The Gentleman of Elvas was a member of

the De Soto expedition. His Narrative was first published in Portugal in 1557.

3. There are a number of first-hand accounts of the Coronado Expedition. The one followed in the present chapter is that of Pedro de Castaneda, as translated into English by George Parker Winship and printed with an introduction in the *Fourteenth Annual Report of the American Bureau of Ethnology* (Washington, 1896).

CHAPTER 3. THE HERETIC

1. Burrage, Henry S., ed., *Early English and French Voyages, 1534–1608* (New York, 1906, in the Original Narratives of Early American History series), 4–102.
2. *Dictionary of American History,* Vol. II (New York, 1940), 133; Andrews, C. M., *The Colonial Period of American History,* Vol. I (New Haven, 1934), 13–15.
3. Williamson, James A., *Sir John Hawkins* (Oxford, 1927), 111.
4. *Dictionary of American History,* Vol. I (New York, 1940), 144.
5. Winsor, Justin, ed., *Narrative and Critical History of America,* Vol. II (Boston and New York, 1886), 260.
6. Parkman, Francis, *Pioneers of France in the New World,* Vol. I (Frontenac Edition, New York, 1915), 35–42.
7. Hakluyt, Richard, *The Voyages, Navigations, Traffiques & Discoveries of the English Nation,* the Third and Last volume (1600), 314–315.
8. Parkman, Francis, *Pioneers of France in the New World,* Vol. I, 43–47.
9. Williamson, James A., *Sir John Hawkins,* 96.
10. Parkman, Francis, *Pioneers of France in the New World,* Vol. I, 48–89.
11. Williamson, James A., *Sir John Hawkins,* 97, 100–110.
12. Parkman, Francis, *Pioneers of France in the New World,* Vol. I, 89–93; Williamson, James A., *Sir John Hawkins,* 110–113.
13. Parkman, Francis, *Pioneers of France in the New World,* Vol. I, 93–95.
14. *Pedro Menendez de Aviles,* A Memorial by Gonzalo Solis de Meras. Translated by Jeannette Thurber Connor (Deland, Fla., 1922), 80–179; Parkman, Francis, *Pioneers of France in the New World,* Vol. I, 109–151.
15. Lanning, John Tate, *The Spanish Missions of Georgia* (Chapel Hill, 1935), 41–54.

CHAPTER 4. THE ENGLISH

1. Williamson, James A., *Sir John Hawkins* (Oxford, 1927), 142–202; Burrage, Henry S., ed., *Early English and French Voyages, 1534–1608* (New York, 1906, in the Original Narratives of Early American History series, Barnes & Noble, publishers), 137–148.
2. Wagner, Henry R., *Sir Francis Drake's Voyage Around the World* (San Francisco, 1926), 42–169; Burrage, Henry S., ed., *Early English and French Voyages,* 153–173.
3. *Dictionary of American History,* Vol. II (New York, 1940), 165.
4. *Dictionary of National Biography* (Oxford since 1917), Vol. VII, 1206–1209; Winsor, Justin, ed., *Narrative and Critical History of America,* Vol. III (Boston and New York, 1884), 86.

5. Burrage, Henry S., ed., *Early English and French Voyages*, 177–222; Gilbert's patent is printed in *Sir Humfrey Gylberte and His Enterprise of Colonization in America* (Boston, 1903, Prince Society), 96–102.

6. *Dictionary of American History*, Vol. I (New York, 1940), 266.

7. Brown, Alexander, *The Genesis of the United States*, Vol. I (Boston and New York, 1890), 9–10.

8. Thorpe, F. N., ed., *Constitutions, Colonial Charters, and Other Organic Laws*, Vol. I (Washington, 1909), 53–57; Burrage, Henry S., ed., *Early English and French Voyages*, 227–241.

9. Burrage, Henry S., ed., *Early English and French Voyages*, 245–268; Winsor, Justin, ed., *Narrative and Critical History of America*, Vol. III, 108–112.

10. Hakluyt, Richard, *The Voyages, Navigations, Traffiques and Discoveries of the English Nation*, The Third and Last Volume (London, 1660), 546–547; Barrow, John, *The Life, Voyages and Exploits of Francis Drake* (London, 1844), 91–93.

11. Burrage, Henry S., ed., *Early English and French Voyages*, 268–271, 277.

12. *Ibid.*, 277–278.

13. *Ibid.*, 281–300.

14. *Ibid.*, 303–323.

15. *Dictionary of American History*, Vol. II, 109; Sparkes, Boyden, "Writ on Rocke," *The Saturday Evening Post*, April 26, 1941.

CHAPTER 5. THE KING IS DEAD

1. Lanning, John T., *The Spanish Missions of Georgia* (Chapel Hill, 1935), 82–110.

2. Bolton, Herbert E., *Spanish Exploration in the Southwest, 1542–1706* (New York, 1916, in the Original Narratives of Early American History series, Barnes & Noble, publishers), 199–280, also 176–179, where, from the Narrative of Espejo, we find a description of the pueblos along the Rio Grande as they doubtless appeared to Onate; Chapman, C. E., *History of California, The Spanish Period* (New York, 1921), 124–136.

3. Chapman, C. E., *History of California, The Spanish Period*, 189–191.

CHAPTER 6. "THE MEANS, UNDER GOD"

1. Burrage, Henry S., ed., *Early English and French Voyages, 1534–1608* (New York, 1906, in the Original Narratives of Early American History series), 355–394.

2. Parkman, Francis, *Pioneers of France in the New World*, Vol. II (New York, 1915, Frontenac Edition), 68–80; Grant, W. L., ed., *Voyages of Samuel de Champlain, 1604–1618* (New York, 1907, in the Original Narratives of Early American History series), 56–79.

3. Brown, Alexander, ed., *The Genesis of the United States*, Vol. I (Boston and New York, 1890), 126.

4. *Massachusetts Historical Society Collections*, Third Series, Vol. VI (Boston, 1837), 50–51.

CHAPTER 7. JAMESTOWN AND SAGADAHOC

1. *Massachusetts Historical Society Collections,* Third Series, Vol. VI (Boston, 1837), 51.
2. Brown, Alexander, ed., *Genesis of the United States,* Vol. I (Boston and New York, 1890), 46.
3. *Ibid.,* 52–63.
4. *Ibid.,* 61.
5. Baxter, James P., ed., *Sir Ferdinando Gorges and His Province of Maine,* Vol. III (Boston, 1890), 122–126; Brown, Alexander, ed., *Genesis of the U. S.,* Vol. I, 65–75.
6. Baxter, James P., ed., *Sir Ferdinando Gorges and His Province of Maine,* Vol. II, 9–11; Burrage, Henry S., ed., *Early English and French Voyages* (New York, 1906, in the Original Narratives of Early American History series, Barnes & Noble, publishers), 394.
7. Grant, W. L., ed., *Voyages of Samuel de Champlain* (New York, 1907, in the Original Narratives of Early American History series), 77.
8. Brown, Alexander, ed., *Genesis of the U. S.,* Vol. I, 76.
9. *Ibid.,* 79–85.
10. Tyler, Lyon Gardiner, ed., *Narratives of Early Virginia* (New York, 1907, in the Original Narratives of Early American History series), 5–15, 121–126.
11. *Ibid.,* 15–19.
12. *Ibid.,* 125–132; Brown, Alexander, ed., *Genesis of the U. S.,* Vol. I, 105.
13. Gardiner, S. R., *History of England, 1603–1642,* Vol. II (London, 1883), 11; Brown, Alexander, ed., *Genesis of the U. S.,* Vol. I, 106–108.
14. Burrage, Henry S., ed., *Early English and French Voyages,* 399–419; Banks, Charles E., "New Documents relating to the Popham Expedition, 1607," in the *Proceedings of the American Antiquarian Society* for October, 1929.
15. Banks, Charles E., "New Documents relating to the Popham Expedition, 1607"; Burrage, Henry S., ed., *Early English and French Voyages,* 417–418; Brown, Alexander, ed., *Genesis of the U. S.,* Vol. I, 145–146.
16. Baxter, J. P., ed., *Sir Ferdinando Gorges and His Province of Maine,* Vol. III, 154–160.
17. Arber, Edward, ed., *Travels and Works of Captain John Smith* (Edinburgh, 1910), Vol. I, lxx–lxxiii, 13, Vol. II, 391–402.
18. Brown, Alexander, ed., *Genesis of the U. S.,* Vol. I, 116–124.
19. Arber, Edward, ed., *Captain John Smith,* Vol. I, 9–19.
20. *Ibid.,* Vol. II, 531, see also 400.
21. *Ibid.,* Vol. I, 20–23, 98–103; Brown, Alexander, ed., *Genesis of the U. S.,* Vol. I, 176.
22. Arber, Edward, ed., *Captain John Smith,* Vol. I, 103–120, Vol. II, 412–433.
23. Burrage, Henry S., ed., *Early English and French Voyages,* 418–419; *Massachusetts Historical Society Collections,* Third Series, Vol. VI, 56.
24. Arber, Edward, ed., *Captain John Smith,* Vol. I, 121–131, Vol. II, 433–447.
25. Brown, Alexander, ed., *Genesis of the U. S.,* Vol. I, 206–237.
26. *Ibid.,* 248–249, 252–253, 273.

27. Andrews, C. M., *The Colonial Period in American History*, Vol. I (New Haven, 1934), 108–109; Brown, Alexander, ed., *Genesis of the U. S.*, Vol. I, 345, 376–384.

28. Arber, Edward, ed., *Captain John Smith*, Vol. I, 131–160, Vol. II, 446–478.

29. Arber, Edward, ed., *Captain John Smith*, Vol. II, 476; Brown, Alexander, ed., *Genesis of the U. S.*, Vol. I, 343–344.

30. Brown, Alexander, ed., *Genesis of the U. S.*, Vol. I, 345–347; Arber, Edward, ed., *Captain John Smith*, Vol. I, 161–162, Vol. II, 478–480.

31. Grant, W. L., ed., *Voyages of Samuel de Champlain*, 157–169.

32. *Dictionary of American Biography*, Vol. IX (New York, 1932), 339; Jameson, J. Franklin, ed., *Narratives of New Netherland* (New York, 1909, in the Original Narratives of Early American History series), 16–28.

33. Arber, Edward, ed., *Captain John Smith*, Vol. I, 167–170; Brown, Alexander, ed., *Genesis of the U. S.*, Vol. I, 334.

34. Arber, Edward, ed., *Captain John Smith*, Vol. I, 170, Vol. II, 497.

35. *Ibid.*, Vol. I, 161–170, Vol. II, 478–498.

36. Brown, Alexander, ed., *Genesis of the U. S.*, Vol. I, 350, 376–384.

37. *Ibid.*, Vol. I, 401; Arber, Edward, ed., *Captain John Smith*, Vol. II, 498–499.

38. Brown, Alexander, ed., *Genesis of the U. S.*, Vol. I, 400–401.

39. *Ibid.*, 402–408.

40. *Ibid.*, 354–356.

CHAPTER 8. VIRGINIA AND NEW ENGLAND

1. Brown, Alexander, ed., *The Genesis of the United States*, Vol. I (Boston and New York, 1890), 392.

2. *Ibid.*, 343.

3. *Ibid.*, 340.

4. *Ibid.*, Vol. II, 552, 570–571; Bruce, P. A., *Economic History of Virginia in the Seventeenth Century*, Vol. II (New York, 1895), 275–278.

5. Brown, Alexander, ed., *The Genesis of the U. S.*, Vol. I, 506–507.

6. Arber, Edward, ed., *Travels and Works of Captain John Smith*, Vol. II (Edinburgh, 1910), 511; Force, Peter, *Tracts*, Vol. III (Washington, 1844), 9–19.

7. Arber, Edward, ed., *Captain John Smith*, Vol. II, 507–509.

8. Brown, Alexander, ed., *The Genesis of the U. S.*, Vol. I, 507–524; Davis, William T., ed., *Bradford's History of Plymouth Plantation* (New York, 1908, in the Original Narratives of Early American History series), 75; Andrews, C. M., *The Colonial Period of American History*, Vol. I (New Haven, 1934), 146.

9. Arber, Edward, ed., *Captain John Smith*, Vol. II, 516.

10. *Dictionary of American Biography*, Vol. XVI (New York, 1935), 117–118.

11. Brown, Alexander, ed., *The Genesis of the U. S.*, Vol. II, 643; Arber, Edward, ed., *Captain John Smith*, Vol. II, 511–513.

12. Tyler, L. G., ed., *Narratives of Early Virginia* (New York, 1907, in

the Original Narratives of Early American History series, Barnes & Noble, publishers), 239–244.

13. Arber, Edward, ed., *Captain John Smith*, Vol. II, 514; Tyler, L. G., ed., *Narratives of Early Virginia*, 251 n.

14. Arber, Edward, ed., *Captain John Smith*, Vol. II, 517–519, 525; *Dictionary of American Biography*, Vol. XV (New York, 1935), 18–19.

15. Brown, Alexander, ed., *Genesis of the U. S.*, Vol. II, 700–734; Parkman, Francis, *Pioneers of France in the New World*, Vol. II (New York, 1915, Frontenac Edition), 124–142.

16. Arber, Edward, ed., *Captain John Smith*, Vol. I, 187–192, Vol. II, 697–702.

17. *Ibid.*, Vol. II, 698.

18. Baxter, J. P., ed., *Sir Ferdinando Gorges and His Province of Maine*, Vol. I (Boston, 1890), 207; *Massachusetts Historical Society Collections*, Third Series, Vol. VI (Boston, 1837), 70.

19. Arber, Edward, ed., *Captain John Smith*, Vol. II, 698–699; Baxter, J. P., ed., *Sir Ferdinando Gorges*, Vol. I, 209–210; Davis, W. T., ed., *Bradford's History*, 111–112.

20. Grant, W. L., *Voyages of Samuel de Champlain* (New York, 1907, in the Original Narratives of Early American History series, Barnes & Noble, publishers), 285–297.

21. O'Callaghan, E. B., *History of New Netherland*, Vol. I (New York, 1845), 67–80.

22. *Mass. Hist. Soc. Col.*, Third Series, Vol. VI, 57.

23. Brown, Alexander, ed., *The Genesis of the U. S.*, Vol. II, 775–779; Arber, Edward, ed., *Captain John Smith*, Vol. II, 536; Kingsbury, Susan M., ed., *The Records of the Virginia Company of London* (Washington, 1906), Vol. I, 350–351, Vol. II, 401–405.

24. Winsor, Justin, ed., *Narrative and Critical History of America*, Vol. III (Boston and New York, 1884), 141–142; Campbell, Charles, *History of the Colony and Ancient Dominion of Virginia* (Philadelphia, 1860), 124–128; Arber, Edward, ed., *Captain John Smith*, Vol. II, 540; Tyler, L. G., *Narratives of Early Virginia*, 282–283; Andrews, C. M., *The Colonial Period of American History*, Vol. I (New Haven, 1934), 120–123; Kingsbury, Susan M., ed., *Records of the Virginia Company of London*, Vol. II, 400–405.

25. McIlwaine, H. R., ed., *Journal of the House of Burgesses of Virginia, 1619–1658/9* (Richmond, 1915), 36.

26. Arber, Edward, ed., *Captain John Smith*, Vol. II, 542.

27. Tyler, L. G., ed., *Narratives of Early Virginia*, 249–278.

28. Arber, Edward, ed., *Captain John Smith*, Vol. II, 541–542; Kingsbury, Susan M., ed., *Records of the Virginia Company of London*, Vol. II, 402.

29. Arber, Edward, ed., *Captain John Smith*, Vol. II, 543.

30. *Ibid.*, Vol. II, 543; Kingsbury, Susan M., ed., *Records of the Virginia Company of London*, Vol. I, 255–256, 269, 270–271, 566; Andrews, C. M., *Colonial Period of American History*, Vol. I, 134.

31. Kingsbury, Susan M., ed., *Records of the Virginia Company of London*, Vol. I, 94–95, 303, 350, 562.

32. *Ibid.*, 221, 228.

CHAPTER 9. THE PILGRIMS

1. Davis, William T., ed., *Bradford's History of Plymouth Plantation* (New York, 1908, in the Original Narratives of Early American History series, Barnes & Noble, publishers), 79, hereafter cited as *Bradford's History.*
2. *Ibid.*, 23–31.
3. Howell, T. B., *State Trials and Proceedings for High Treason and Other Crimes and Misdemeanors*, Vol. II (London, 1816), 85–86.
4. Davis, W. T., ed., *Bradford's History*, 31–49, 79; Hebrews, 11, from the text of the Geneva Bible of 1560.
5. Davis, W. T., ed., *Bradford's History*, 49–65.
6. *Ibid.*, 65, 69–70; Kingsbury, Susan M., ed., *The Records of the Virginia Company of London*, Vol. I (Washington, 1906), 321; Farnham, Mary F., ed., *Documentary History of the State of Maine*, Vol. VII (Portland, 1901), 15–18.
7. Davis, W. T., ed., *Bradford's History*, 66–67.
8. *Ibid.*, 67–78.
9. *Ibid.*, 79–80; Baxter, James P., ed., *Sir Ferdinando Gorges and His Province of Maine*, Vol. II (Boston, 1890), 30–31.
10. Davis, W. T., ed., *Bradford's History*, 80–92. The day of sailing was September 6 Old Style, or September 16, New Style dating.
11. *Ibid.*, 92–94; *Dictionary of American History*, Vol. III (New York, 1940), 361; Andrews, C. M., *The Colonial Period of American History*, Vol. I (New Haven, 1934), 268–272.
12. Farnham, Mary F., ed., *Documentary History of the State of Maine*, Vol. VII, 20–45; Kingsbury, Susan M., ed., *The Records of the Virginia Company of London*, Vol. I (Washington, 1906), 411.
13. Davis, W. T., ed., *Bradford's History*, 94–95, 106–107.
14. *Ibid.*, 95–97; Young, Alexander, ed., *Chronicles of the Pilgrim Fathers* (Boston, 1841), 120.
15. Young, Alexander, ed., *Chronicles of the Pilgrim Fathers*, 125–162; Davis, W. T., ed., *Bradford's History*, 97–105.
16. Young, Alexander, ed., *Chronicles of the Pilgrim Fathers*, 163–173.
17. *Ibid.*, 173–182; Davis, W. T., ed., *Bradford's History*, 115.
18. Young, Alexander, ed., *Chronicles of the Pilgrim Fathers*, 182–196; *Dictionary of American Biography*, Vol. XVII (New York, 1935), 487; Davis, W. T., ed., *Bradford's History*, 110–114.
19. Young, Alexander, ed., *Chronicles of the Pilgrim Fathers*, 197–200; Davis, W. T., ed., *Bradford's History*, 108–109, 115–116.
20. Young, Alexander, ed., *Chronicles of the Pilgrim Fathers*, 199; Davis, W. T., ed., *Bradford's History*, 115, 122.
21. Davis, W. T., ed., *Bradford's History*, 122–123.
22. Davis, W. T., *Ancient Landmarks of Plymouth* (Boston, 1883), 40–44.
23. O'Callaghan, E. B., *History of New Netherland*, Vol. I (New York, 1845), 399–407.
24. Davis, W. T., ed., *Bradford's History*, 116, 270–271, 407–414; Young, Alexander, ed., *Chronicles of the Pilgrim Fathers*, 197–199; *Dictionary of American Biography*, Vol. XX (New York, 1936), 393–394.

25. The text of "Old Hundred" is from the Ainsworth *Psalms in Metre,* published at Amsterdam in 1618.
26. Davis, W. T., ed., *Bradford's History,* 115–116.
27. *Ibid.,* 121; Young, Alexander, ed., *Chronicles of the Pilgrim Fathers,* 224–229.
28. Davis, W. T., ed., *Bradford's History,* 121; Young, Alexander, ed., *Chronicles of the Pilgrim Fathers,* 234–235.
29. Davis, W. T., ed., *Bradford's History,* 122–125.
30. *Ibid.,* 125–130; the "Narrative of Phinehas Pratt" in Levermore, C. H., ed., *Forerunners and Competitors of the Pilgrims and Puritans,* Vol. II (Brooklyn, 1912), 809–810.
31. Davis, W. T., ed., *Bradford's History,* 137–138; Kingsbury, Susan M., ed., *The Records of the Virginia Company of London,* Vol. I, 534, 554, 562.
32. Winsor, Justin, ed., *Narrative and Critical History of America,* Vol. III (Boston and New York, 1884), 142–145.
33. Arber, Edward, ed., *Travels and Works of Captain John Smith,* Vol. II (Edinburgh, 1910), 572–578.
34. Davis, W. T., ed., *Bradford's History,* 138; Young, Alexander, ed., *Chronicles of the Pilgrim Fathers,* 292–294; Levermore, C. H., ed., *Forerunners and Competitors of the Pilgrims and Puritans,* Vol. II, 810. Bradford, who consistently belittles Weston's aid, states that the Plymouth men went to Damariscove in their own boat, piloted by the *Sparrow's* shallop. Pratt, who presumably had no prejudices in the matter, states definitely that the Plymouth men went in the *Sparrow's* shallop. Winslow, who went, does not say whose boat was used.
35. Davis, W. T., ed., *Bradford's History,* 138–139.
36. *Ibid.,* 132–137; Young, Alexander, ed., *Chronicles of the Pilgrim Fathers,* 296–297.
37. Davis, W. T., ed., *Bradford's History,* 139; Young, Alexander, ed., *Chronicles of the Pilgrim Fathers,* 298; Kingsbury, Susan M., ed., *The Records of the Virginia Company,* Vol. I, 534, 554, 562.
38. Davis, W. T., ed., *Bradford's History,* 140.
39. Young, Alexander, ed., *Chronicles of the Pilgrim Fathers,* 299.
40. Davis, W. T., ed., *Bradford's History,* 410–414; Deuteronomy 4:31.

CHAPTER 10. FISH AND FURS

1. *Records of the Council for New England* (Reprinted from the Proceedings of the American Antiquarian Society for April, 1867), 16–18, 35, 39–40.
2. *Ibid.,* 11–48[4]; Baxter, J. P., ed., *Sir Ferdinando Gorges and His Province of Maine,* Vol. II (Boston, 1890), 55–56; Insh, G. P., *Scottish Colonial Schemes, 1620–1686* (Glasgow, 1922), 41–50; Arber, Edward, ed., *Captain John Smith,* Vol. II (Edinburgh, 1910), 706.
3. Dean, J. W., ed., *Capt. John Mason* (Boston, 1887), 11–17, 170–183.
4. *Ibid.,* 17–18; Baxter, J. P., *Christopher Levett, of York* (Portland, 1893), 90.
5. *Records of the Council for New England,* 27–28; Burrage, H. S., *The Beginnings of Colonial Maine, 1602–1658* (1914), 166.

6. Baxter, J. P., ed., *Sir Ferdinando Gorges*, Vol. II, 49–54.

7. *Records of the Council for New England*, 38–40; Rose-Troup, Frances, *John White* (New York, 1930), 58–60.

8. *The Planters Plea* (London, 1630), as reprinted in Mass. Hist. Soc. publication entitled *The Founding of Massachusetts* (Boston, 1930), 189–191.

9. Kingsbury, Susan M., ed., *The Records of the Virginia Company of London*, Vol. I (Washington, 1906), 416, 428; Winsor, Justin, ed., *Narrative and Critical History of America*, Vol. III (Boston and New York, 1884), 307; Baxter, J. P., ed., *Sir Ferdinando Gorges*, Vol. II, 32–46.

10. Davis, W. T., ed., *Bradford's History of Plymouth Plantation, 1606–1646* (New York, 1908, in the Original Narratives of Early American History series, Barnes & Noble, publishers), 140–144; The Narrative of Phinehas Pratt as printed in Levermore, C. H., ed., *Forerunners and Competitors of the Pilgrims and Puritans*, Vol. II (Brooklyn, 1912), 807–822; *Good Newes from New England* (London, 1624), as reprinted in Young, Alexander, ed., *Chronicles of the Pilgrim Fathers* (Boston, 1841), 327–334.

11. Davis, W. T., ed., *Bradford's History*, 143–144; Young, Alexander, ed., *Chronicles of the Pilgrim Fathers*, 331–343.

12. Davis, W. T., ed., *Bradford's History*, 144–145.

13. *Ibid.*, 146–147.

14. *Ibid.*, 151–152.

15. *Ibid.*, 152–157; Young, Alexander, ed., *Chronicles of the Pilgrim Fathers*, 351–353. C. E. Banks (*Planters of the Commonwealth*, Boston, 1930, page 55) believes that Roger Conant reached New England in one of Weston's ships.

16. Davis, W. T., ed., *Bradford's History*, 158–159; Bolton, C. K., *The Real Founders of New England* (Boston, 1929), 48; Andrews, C. M., *The Colonial Period of American History*, Vol. I (New Haven, 1934), 340–341.

17. Davis, W. T., ed., *Bradford's History*, 159.

18. *Ibid.*, 159–163.

19. Levett, Christopher, *A Voyage into New England* (London, 1628), as reprinted in Baxter, J. P., *Christopher Levett, of York*, 90–91.

20. Baxter, J. P., ed., *Sir Ferdinando Gorges*, Vol. I, 131, 234–237; *Records of the Council for New England*, 36–37.

21. Baxter, J. P., ed., *Sir Ferdinando Gorges*, Vol. I, 132; Davis, W. T., ed., *Bradford's History*, 163; Andrews, C. M., *Colonial Period of American History*, Vol. I, 339–341.

22. Baxter, J. P., *Christopher Levett, of York*, 91–109.

23. *Ibid.*, 24–26; Baxter, J. P., ed., *Sir Ferdinando Gorges*, Vol. I, 133–152; Dean, J. W., ed., *Capt. John Mason*, 20–21.

24. O'Callaghan, E. B., *History of New Netherland*, Vol. I (New York, 1845), 95–104; *Dictionary of American History*, Vol. IV (New York, 1940), 107–108.

25. Mass. Hist. Soc., *The Founding of Massachusetts*, 191–192; Rose-Troup, Frances, *John White*, 62–67.

26. McIlwaine, H. R., ed., *Minutes of the Council and General Court of Colonial Virginia, 1622–1623, 1670–1676* (Richmond, 1924), 25–26;

Mass. Hist. Soc. Proceedings, Vol. XLIII (Boston, 1910), 493–496; *Mass. Hist. Soc. Proceedings,* Vol. LVIII (Boston, 1925), 147–193; Davis, W. T., ed., *Bradford's History,* 236–237.

27. Arber, Edward, ed., *Travels and Works of Captain John Smith,* Vol. I (Edinburgh, 1910), 92, 104, 107, 161; Tyler, L. G., ed., *Narratives of Early Virginia* (New York, 1907, in the Original Narratives of Early American History series), 253–255, 260–262; Kingsbury, Susan M., ed., *The Records of the Virginia Company of London,* Vol. I, 594–596, 609–615, Vol. II, 509–510; McIlwaine, H. R., ed., *Minutes of the Council and General Court of Colonial Virginia, 1622–1623, 1670–1676,* 25–26; *Mass. Hist. Soc. Proceedings,* Vol. XLIII, 493–496.

28. McIlwaine, H. R., ed., *Minutes of the Council and General Court of Colonial Virginia, 1622–1623, 1670–1676,* 25–26; Young, Alexander, ed., *Chronicles of the Pilgrim Fathers,* 296, for the identification of the *Swan* as Weston's ship; Davis, W. T., ed., *Bradford's History,* 159, 161, 236–243.

29. McIlwaine, H. R., ed., *Minutes of the Council and General Court of Colonial Virginia, 1622–1623, 1670–1676,* 28–29, 61; Campbell, Charles, *History of the Colony and Ancient Dominion of Virginia* (Philadelphia, 1860), 170–174; Andrews, C. M., *Colonial Period in American History,* Vol. I, 173–179.

30. Davis, W. T., ed., *Bradford's History,* 166–188.

31. *Ibid.,* 200; *Dictionary of American Biography,* Vol. IV (New York, 1930), 336–337; Rose-Troup, Frances, *Roger Conant and the Early Settlements on the North Shore of Massachusetts* (Printed by the Conant Family Association, Inc., 1926), 6.

32. Davis, W. T., ed., *Bradford's History,* 197–199.

33. *Ibid.,* 201–205.

34. *The Planters Plea* as reprinted in Mass. Hist. Soc., *The Founding of Massachusetts,* 192–193; Rose-Troup, Frances, *Roger Conant,* 6–9; Rose-Troup, Frances, *John White,* 81–93; Davis, W. T., ed., *Bradford's History,* 201.

35. Davis, W. T., ed., *Bradford's History,* 208.

36. Rose-Troup, Frances, *John White,* 91–92; Mass. Hist. Soc., *The Founding of New England,* 192–194.

37. Rose-Troup, Frances, *John White,* 91–106.

38. Burrage, H. S., *The Beginnings of Colonial Maine, 1602–1658,* 179–183; Davis, W. T., ed., *Bradford's History,* 211–212.

39. Davis, W. T., ed., *Bradford's History,* 212–216.

40. *Ibid.,* 222–227, 234; Jameson, J. Franklin, ed., *Narratives of New Netherland* (New York, 1909, in the Original Narratives of Early American History series, Barnes & Noble, publishers), 109–112.

41. Davis, W. T., ed., *Bradford's History,* 233–236.

42. Morton, Thomas, *New English Canaan* (Amsterdam, 1637), 137, 149, 183.

43. Davis, W. T., ed., *Bradford's History,* 236–238.

44. Morton, Thomas, *New English Canaan,* 132–134.

45. *Ibid.,* 139–143; Davis, W. T., ed., *Bradford's History,* 239–243.

46. Morton, Thomas, *New English Canaan,* 139–140; Young, Alexander, ed., *Chronicles of the First Planters of Massachusetts Bay* (Boston,

1846), 48, 375; *Dictionary of American Biography,* Vol. II (New York, 1929), 319, Vol. XII (New York, 1933), 432.

47. Rose-Troup, Frances, *John White,* 104–105, 109, 114–116.
48. *Ibid.,* 107–114; Andrews, C. M., *Colonial Period of American History,* Vol. I, 352–361.
49. Shurtleff, N. B., ed., *Records of the Governor and Company of the Massachusetts Bay in New England* (Boston, 1853–1854), Vol. I, 53, hereafter cited as *Mass. Col. Rec.*
50. Rose-Troup, Frances, *John White,* 111–113; *Mass. Col. Rec.,* Vol. I, 40.
51. Young, Alexander, ed., *Chronicles of the First Planters of the Colony of Massachusetts Bay* (Boston, 1846), 13, 30–31; *Mass. Col. Rec.,* Vol. I, 25; Rose-Troup, Frances, *John White,* 116–117; Andrews, C. M., *Colonial Period of American History,* Vol. I, 361–362; Jameson, J. Franklin, ed., *Johnson's Wonder-Working Providence* (New York, 1910, in the Original Narratives of Early American History series), 44.

CHAPTER 11. THE GREAT MIGRATION

1. Davis, W. T., ed., *Bradford's History of Plymouth Plantation* (New York, 1908, in the Original Narratives of Early American History series), 238; Rose-Troup, Frances, *John White* (New York, 1930), 118–122.
2. Young, Alexander, ed., *Chronicles of the First Planters of the Colony of Massachusetts Bay* (Boston, 1846), 374.
3. Davis, W. T., ed., *Bradford's History,* 260–261; Morton, Thomas, *New English Canaan,* edited by Charles Francis Adams, Jr. (Boston, 1883), 298.
4. Davis, W. T., ed., *Bradford's History,* 242, 250–251; Andrews, C. M., *Colonial Period of American History* (New Haven, 1934), 363 n.
5. *Mass. Col. Rec.,* Vol. I, 3–20, 387.
6. Rose-Troup, Frances, *John White,* 86, 108, 111, 117; Young, Alexander, ed., *Chronicles of Massachusetts,* 106, 303–304, 317–318; *Dictionary of American Biography,* Vol. V (New York, 1930), 484–485; Brydges, Sir Samuel E., ed., *Collins' Peerage of England,* Vol. II (London, 1812), 208–209; Cokayne, G. E., *The Complete Peerage,* revised and enlarged by the Hon. Vicary Gibbs, Vol. VII (London, 1929), 693–696. To be wholly exact, Humphry (his name is spelled variously: Humfry, Humfrey, Humphreys) was courting the Lady Susan in 1629. The marriage took place the following year.
7. *Dictionary of American Biography,* Vol. XI (New York, 1933), 493–494, Vol. XX (New York, 1936), 408–411; Winthrop, R. C., *Life and Letters of John Winthrop,* Vol. I (Boston, 1864), 305–332.
8. *Mass. Col. Rec.,* Vol. I, 3–20.
9. *Ibid.,* 29, 388–390, 398.
10. *Ibid.,* 23–38; *Higginson's Journal* as printed in *The Founding of Massachusetts* (Mass. Hist. Soc., Boston, 1930), 61.
11. Mass. Hist. Soc., *The Founding of Massachusetts,* 61–62; *Mass. Col. Rec.,* Vol. I, 386, 389–390, 396–397.
12. Mass. Hist. Soc., *The Founding of Massachusetts,* 61–75; Davis, W. T., ed., *Bradford's History,* 245; Young, Alexander, ed., *Chronicles of Massachusetts,* 209–212, 216 note 5, 262, 317.

13. Young, Alexander, ed., *Chronicles of Massachusetts,* 221 note 1.
14. Mass. Hist. Soc., *The Founding of Massachusetts,* 73 note 34; Morton, Thomas, *New English Canaan* (Amsterdam, 1637), 157; Davis, W. T., ed., *Bradford's History,* 251.
15. Mass. Hist. Soc., *The Founding of Massachusetts,* 73, 84, 93; *Mass. Col. Rec.,* Vol. I, 23.
16. Young, Alexander, ed., *Chronicles of Massachusetts,* 243–246, 261; Mass. Hist. Soc., *Founding of Massachusetts,* 84–85.
17. Mass. Hist. Soc., *Founding of Massachusetts,* 93; *Mass. Col. Rec.,* Vol. I, 387, 399.
18. *Mass. Col. Rec.,* Vol. I, 403–404; Davis, W. T., ed., *Bradford's History,* 261–262; Young, Alexander, ed., *Chronicles of Massachusetts,* 209–212, 316 note 3.
19. Mass. Hist. Soc., *Founding of Massachusetts,* 93; Young, Alexander, ed., *Chronicles of Massachusetts,* 383–384 note 12.
20. *Mass. Col. Rec.,* Vol. I, 51, 54, 60–61, 407–409; Mayo, L. S., *John Endecott* (Cambridge, 1936), 42–44.
21. *Collections of the Mass. Hist. Soc.,* Fourth Series, Vol. VI, 30; Winthrop, R. C., *Life and Letters of John Winthrop,* Vol. I, 303–332.
22. Winthrop, R. C., *Life and Letters of John Winthrop,* Vol. I, 284–287, 296; *Dictionary of American Biography,* Vol. XX (New York, 1936), 408–411.
23. Winthrop, R. C., *Life and Letters of John Winthrop,* Vol. I, 304, 344–345.
24. *Mass. Col. Rec.,* Vol. I, 49–51.
25. *Ibid.,* 58–69.
26. Baxter, J. P., ed., *Sir Ferdinando Gorges and His Province of Maine,* Vol. II (Boston, 1890), 59–60.
27. Parkman, Francis, *Pioneers of France in the New World,* Vol. II (New York, 1915, Frontenac Edition), 261–273; Dean, J. W., ed., *Capt. John Mason* (Boston, 1887), 54–55; *Dictionary of American History,* Vol. III (New York, 1940), 226.
28. Dean, J. W., ed., *Capt. John Mason,* 183–189; Baxter, J. P., ed., *Sir Ferdinando Gorges,* Vol. I, 152.
29. Dean, J. W., ed., *Capt. John Mason,* 189–197; Baxter, J. P., ed., *Sir Ferdinando Gorges,* Vol. I, 152–153; Andrews, C. M., *Colonial Period of American History,* Vol. I (New Haven, 1934), 49–50, 308–311, 318–319.
30. *Dictionary of American Biography,* Vol. III (New York, 1929), 428–429; Wilhelm, Lewis W., *Sir George Calvert* (Baltimore, 1884); 121–142; *Maryland Archives,* Vol. III (Baltimore, 1885), 15–16.
31. McIlwaine, H. R., ed., *Minutes of the Council and General Court of Colonial Virginia* (Richmond, 1924), 480, 484.
32. *Mass. Col. Rec.,* Vol. I, 69–70; Young, Alexander, ed., *Chronicles of Massachusetts,* 347; Winthrop, John, *The History of New England,* edited by James Savage (Boston, 1853), Vol. I, 33, hereafter cited as Winthrop, *History;* Mass. Hist. Soc., *Founding of Massachusetts,* 186.
33. Winthrop, *History,* Vol. I, 1–7; Young, Alexander, ed., *Chronicles of Massachusetts,* 311.
34. Young, Alexander, ed., *Chronicles of Massachusetts,* 295–298.
35. *Ibid.,* 347; Winthrop, *History,* Vol. I, 29–32; *Mass. Col. Rec.,* Vol. I, 75.

36. Hutchinson, Thomas, *The History of the Colony of Massachusetts-Bay*, Vol. I (Boston, 1764), 19; Young, Alexander, ed., *Chronicles of Massachusetts*, 312–314, 350–351, 378–381.

37. *Mass. Col. Rec.*, Vol. I, 42–43, 399; Wertenbaker, T. J., *The First Americans* (New York, 1927), 56–57.

38. *Mass. Col. Rec.*, Vol. I, 73.

39. Winthrop, *History*, Vol. I, 36–39.

40. Young, Alexander, ed., *Chronicles of Massachusetts*, 331–332.

41. *Ibid.*, 316–319, 325; Winthrop, *History*, Vol. I, 40, 44.

42. Young, Alexander, ed., *Chronicles of Massachusetts*, 351–352.

43. *Ibid.*, 315, 330, 352–353; Winthrop, *History*, Vol. I, 52–54.

44. Winthrop, *History*, Vol. I, 43, 49, 57, 58, 65, 67; Young, Alexander, ed., *Chronicles of Massachusetts*, 338–339.

45. Young, Alexander, ed., *Chronicles of Massachusetts*, 170 n., 313, 320, 339, 381; Winthrop, *History*, Vol. I, 46; *Mass. Col. Rec.*, Vol. I, 75.

46. *Mass. Col. Rec.*, Vol. I, 73–79.

47. Winthrop, *History*, Vol. I, 65–66, 68; Davis, W. T., ed., *Bradford's History*, 286–288; Young, Alexander, ed., *Chronicles of Massachusetts*, 333–335; *Mass. Col. Rec.*, Vol. I, 83; *Dictionary of American Biography*, Vol. VII (New York, 1931), 135–136; Libby, C. T., ed., *Province and Court Records of Maine*, Vol. I (Portland, 1928), 64–65.

48. *Mass. Col. Rec.*, Vol. I, 11–12, 79–80.

49. *Ibid.*, 87, 366.

50. *Ibid.*, 86.

51. *Ibid.*, 88; Young, Alexander, ed., *Chronicles of Massachusetts*, 361–362.

52. Dean, J. W., ed., *Capt. John Mason*, 57–67, 72–73; *Dictionary of American History*, Vol. V (New York, 1940), 187–188.

53. Burrage, H. S., *Beginnings of Colonial Maine* (1914), 201–202, 207, 211–214, 216–222, 242; Farnham, Mary F., *Documentary History of the State of Maine*, Vol. VII (Portland, 1901), 112, 117–125, 137–142, 152–161, 165–172, 177–179.

54. *Records of the Council for New England* (Reprinted from the Proceedings of the American Antiquarian Society for April, 1867), 49–58; Baxter, J. P., ed., *Sir Ferdinando Gorges*, Vol. II, 62–64.

55. *Records of the Council for New England*, 59.

56. *Ibid.*

57. *Ibid.*, 60–62.

58. W. L. Grant and James Munro, eds., *Acts of the Privy Council of England, Colonial Series*, Vol. I (1908), 183, 184–185; Andrews, C. M., *Colonial Period of American History*, Vol. I, 408–411; Winthrop, *History*, Vol. I, 122–123.

59. Winthrop, *History*, Vol. I, 119, 122–124.

60. Winthrop, *History*, Vol. I, 104, 107–108; *Mass. Col. Rec.*, Vol. I, 63–66.

61. *Ibid.*; Young, Alexander, ed., *Chronicles of Massachusetts*, 322–323; Winthrop, *History*, Vol. I, 127; Davis, W. T., ed., *Bradford's History*, 330.

62. *Mass. Col. Rec.*, Vol. I, 404; Young, Alexander, ed., *Chronicles of Massachusetts*, 137, 313 note 4, 374, 404; Winthrop, *History*, Vol. I, 69.

63. Winthrop, *History*, Vol. I, 133–134; O'Callaghan, E. B., *History of New Netherland*, Vol. I (New York, 1848), 99–130, 139; Dean, J. W., ed., *Capt. John Mason*, 298.

64. O'Callaghan, E. B., *History of New Netherland*, Vol. I, 112–139; *Dictionary of American History*, Vol. IV (New York, 1940), 225–226, Vol. V (New York, 1940), 515.
65. O'Callaghan, E. B., *History of New Netherland*, Vol. I, 129–136.
66. *Ibid.*, 141–146.
67. Winthrop, *History*, Vol. I, 134–135.
68. Farnham, Mary F., ed., *Documentary History of the State of Maine*, Vol. VII, 108–116.
69. Baxter, J. P., ed., *Documentary History of the State of Maine*, Vol. III, the Trelawny Papers (Portland, 1884), 19, 53, 219.
70. Davis, W. T., ed., *Bradford's History*, 252–257, 262, 269, 272–273, 285–286, 299–301, 318; Burrage, H. S., *The Beginnings of Colonial Maine*, 189; Winthrop, *History*, Vol. I, 125, 132, 134–135.
71. Davis, W. T., ed., *Bradford's History*, 301–302.
72. *Ibid.;* O'Callaghan, E. B., *History of New Netherland*, Vol. I, 153–155.

CHAPTER 12. MARYLAND

1. Tyler, Lyon G., ed., *Narratives of Early Virginia* (New York, 1907, in the Original Narratives of Early American History series, Barnes & Noble, publishers), 431–460.
2. Brigham, Clarence S., ed., *British Royal Proclamations Relating to America* (Worcester, 1911), 52–55.
3. Saunders, W. L., ed., *Colonial Records of North Carolina*, Vol. I (Raleigh, 1886), 5–11.
4. McCrady, Edward, *The History of South Carolina under the Proprietary Government* (New York, 1897), 49; *South Carolina Historical Society Collections*, Vol. I (Charleston, 1857), 199–200.
5. Andrews, C. M., *Colonial Period of American History*, Vol. III (New Haven, 1937), 189–190.
6. *Ibid.*, Vol. II (New Haven, 1936), 278–279.
7. *Ibid.*, 279–285.
8. Hall, C. C., ed., *Narratives of Early Maryland* (New York, 1910, in the Original Narratives of Early American History series, Barnes & Noble, publishers), 101–112.
9. *Ibid.*, 29, 70–71; Sainsbury, W. N., ed., *Calendar of State Papers, Colonial Series*, Vol. I (London, 1860), 171; *Maryland Historical Magazine*, Vol. I, 352–353; *Dictionary of American Biography*, Vol. XX (New York, 1936), 87.
10. Hall, C. C., ed., *Narratives of Early Maryland*, 101.
11. *The Calvert Papers*, Number One (Baltimore, 1889), 131–132.
12. *Ibid.*, 133; Hall, C. C., ed., *Narratives of Early Maryland*, 31–39.
13. Hall, C. C., ed., *Narratives of Early Maryland*, 18, 39–40.
14. *Ibid.*, 39; *Dictionary of American Biography*, Vol. IV (New York, 1930), 114–115.
15. Hall, C. C., ed., *Narratives of Early Maryland*, 40–42, 71–77, 91.
16. *The Calvert Papers*, Number One, 141–149; *Maryland Archives*, Vol. IV, 22, Vol. V, 157–239; Scharf, J. T., *History of Maryland*, Vol. I (Baltimore, 1879), 109–110; Campbell, Charles, *History of the Colony and Ancient Dominion of Virginia* (Philadelphia, 1860), 192.

17. Andrews, C. M., *Colonial Period of American History*, Vol. I (New Haven, 1934), 194–205.
18. Bruce, P. A., *Institutional History of Virginia*, Vol. II (New York, 1910), 355–357; Campbell, Charles, *Colony and Ancient Dominion of Virginia*, 195; Scharf, J. T., *History of Maryland*, Vol. I, 111–113.
19. Hall, C. C., ed., *Narratives of Early Maryland*, 75–77; *The Calvert Papers*, Number One, 176.

CHAPTER 13. "AGAINST ALL OPPOSERS"

1. Winthrop, John, *The History of New England from 1630 to 1649*, edited by James Savage, Vol. I (Boston, 1853), 159–160, 172, hereafter cited as Winthrop, *History*.
2. *Mass. Col. Rec.*, Vol. I, 79, 116–121; Winthrop, *History*, Vol. I, 85–88, 152–153, 157–158.
3. Hutchinson, Thomas, *History of the Colony of Massachusetts-Bay*, Vol. I (Boston, 1764), 502–506.
4. Winthrop, *History*, Vol. I, 164, Vol. II, 233–235.
5. *Ibid.*, Vol. I, 160–161, 163.
6. *Ibid.*, 163–164, 170–171; *Mass. Col. Rec.*, Vol. I, 123–130, 137.
7. *Mass. Col. Rec.*, Vol. I, 129; Winthrop, *History*, Vol. I, 160, 162, 167–169; Andrews, C. M., *Colonial Period of American History*, Vol. I (New Haven, 1934), 496.
8. Winthrop, *History*, Vol. I, 176–177.
9. *Ibid.*, 137, 185.
10. *Ibid.*, 160–161; Trumbull, Benjamin, *History of Connecticut*, Vol. I (New Haven, 1818), 495–496.
11. Coleman, R. V., *The Old Patent of Connecticut* (Westport, 1936), 9–50.
12. Farnham, Mary F., ed., *Documentary History of Maine*, Vol. VII (Portland, 1901), 111; Winthrop, *History*, Vol. I, 163.
13. *Records of the Council for New England* (Reprinted from the Proceedings of the American Antiquarian Society for April, 1867), 66–70; Coleman, R. V., *The Old Patent of Connecticut*, 20–22.
14. *Records of the Council for New England*, 71–81; Andrews, C. M., *Colonial Period of American History*, Vol. I, 420–421.
15. *Mass. Col. Rec.*, 145–148; Mass. Hist. Soc., *Proceedings*, Vol. LVIII, 450–458; Winthrop, *History*, Vol. I, 188.
16. *Mass. Col. Rec.*, Vol. I, 145; Davis, W. T., ed., *Bradford's History* (New York, 1908, in the Original Narratives of Early American History series), 323.
17. *Mass. Hist. Soc. Col.*, Fifth Series, Vol. I (Boston, 1871), 216–217; *Mass. Hist. Soc. Col.*, Fourth Series, Vol. VI (Boston, 1863), 579–581.
18. Trumbull, Benjamin, *History of Connecticut*, Vol. I, 58–68.
19. Davis, W. T., ed., *Bradford's History*, 326–327.
20. Brodhead, J. R., *History of the State of New York*, First Period (New York, 1853), 254–255.
21. Trumbull, Benjamin, *History of Connecticut*, Vol. I, 497–498.
22. Andrews, C. M., *Colonial Period of American History*, Vol. I, 420–421.
23. Winthrop, *History*, Vol. I, 202–203, 207–208; Trumbull, Benjamin, *History of Connecticut*, Vol. I, 61.

24. Winthrop, *History*, Vol. I, 207–209.
25. Parkman, Francis, *Pioneers of France in the New World*, Vol. II (New York, 1915, Frontenac Edition), 280–281; Kellogg, Louise P., *The French Regime in Wisconsin and the Northwest* (Madison, 1925), 65–83.
26. Winthrop, *History*, Vol. I, 163, 223; Dean, J. W., ed., *Capt. John Mason* (Boston, 1887), 55–80.
27. Bartlett, John R., ed., *Narragansett Club Publications*, First Series, Vol. VI (Providence, 1874), 335–336; Winthrop, *History*, Vol. I, 49–50, 63, 145–147, 188, 193–194, 198, 204, 209–210; *Dictionary of American Biography*, Vol. XX (New York, 1936), 287–289; Davis, W. T., ed., *Bradford's History*, 299; *Mass. Col. Rec.*, Vol. I, 160–161; Andrews, C. M., *Colonial Period of American History*, Vol. II (New Haven, 1936), 4–5; Arnold, S. G., *History of the State of Rhode Island and Providence Plantations*, Vol. I (Providence, 1899), 38–40.
28. Winthrop, *History*, Vol. I, 203, 477–478.
29. *Mass. Col. Rec.*, Vol. I, 170–171; Trumbull, J. Hammond, ed., *The Public Records of the Colony of Connecticut, 1636–1665* (Hartford, 1850), 1, hereafter cited as *Conn. Col. Rec.;* Winthrop, *History*, Vol. I, 219.
30. Winthrop, *History*, Vol. I, 204, 223; Trumbull, Benjamin, *History of Connecticut*, Vol. I, 62–63; *Mass. Hist. Soc. Col.*, Fourth Series, Vol. VII, 52–55.
31. Winthrop, *History*, Vol. I, 225–228.
32. Underhill, John, *Newes from America* (London, 1638), as reprinted in *Mass. Hist. Soc. Col.*, Third Series, Vol. VI (Boston, 1837), 1–11.
33. *Ibid.*, 11–12.
34. *Conn. Col. Rec.*, Vol. I, 9; *Mass. Hist. Soc. Col.*, Third Series, Vol. VI, 16, 23–25.
35. Trumbull, Benjamin, *History of Connecticut*, Vol. I, 89–93; De Forest, J. W., *History of the Indians of Connecticut* (Hartford, 1851), 140–152; Coleman, R. V., *The Old Patent of Connecticut*, 44–45.
36. Andrews, C. M., *Colonial Period of American History*, Vol. I, 420–421; W. L. Grant and James Munro, eds., *Acts of the Privy Council of England*, Colonial Series, Vol. I (London, 1908), 217; Sainsbury, W. Noel, ed., *Calendar of State Papers*, Colonial Series, 1574–1660, Vol. I (London, 1860), 256–257.
37. Baxter, J. P., ed., *Sir Ferdinando Gorges and His Province of Maine*, Vol. I (Boston, 1890), 178–180.
38. Calder, Isabel MacB., *The New Haven Colony* (New Haven, 1934), 28–54.
39. Winthrop, *History*, Vol. I, 284–286, 292–301, 304, 306–307, 309–311; *Mass. Col. Rec.*, Vol. I, 207, 211–212, 225–226; *Dictionary of American Biography*, Vol. IX (New York, 1932), 436–437, Vol. XX, 62–63.
40. *Dictionary of American Biography*, Vol. XX, 62.
41. *Mass. Col. Rec.*, Vol. I, 69, 211, 223, 225; *Dictionary of American Biography*, Vol. IV (New York, 1930), 258–259.
42. Andrews, C. M., *Colonial Period of American History*, Vol. II, 8; Winthrop, *History*, Vol. I, 313–317, 326–328.
43. Winthrop, *History*, Vol. I, 324–326.

44. Winsor, Justin, ed., *Memorial History of Boston*, Vol. I (Boston, 1880), 418.

45. Winthrop, *History*, Vol. I, 338.

46. W. L. Grant and James Munro, eds., *Acts of the Privy Council of England*, Colonial Series, Vol. I, 229.

47. Burrage, H. S., *The Beginnings of Colonial Maine* (1914), 233–234.

48. Libby, C. T., ed., *Province and Court Records of Maine*, Vol. I (Portland, 1928), 1–2; Baxter, J. P., *George Cleeve of Casco Bay* (Portland, 1885), 26–53; Burrage, H. S., *Beginnings of Colonial Maine*, 210–211, 221–227; Baxter, J. P., ed., *Documentary History of the State of Maine*, Vol. III, being the Trelawny Papers (Portland, 1884), 101–105.

49. Libby, C. T., ed., *Province and Court Records of Maine*, Vol. I, lxii; Baxter, J. P., *Documentary History of the State of Maine*, Vol. III, 86–87.

50. Bouton, Nathaniel, ed., *Documents and Records relating to the Province of New-Hampshire*, Vol. I (Concord, 1867), 108–131.

51. *Mass. Col. Rec.*, Vol. I, 117, 225, 232, 242, 279.

52. *Mass. Hist. Soc. Col.*, Fourth Series, Vol. VI, 186–187; Andrews, C. M., *Colonial Period in American History*, Vol. II, 7; Arnold, S. G., *History of the State of Rhode Island and Providence Plantations*, Vol. I, 104–105; Winthrop, *History*, Vol. I, 340–341.

53. Arnold, S. G., *History of the State of Rhode Island and Providence Plantations*, Vol. I, 124–143.

54. Coleman, R. V., *A Note Concerning the Formulation of the Fundamental Orders Uniting the Three River Towns of Connecticut, 1639* (Westport, 1934), 3–10; *Conn. Col. Rec.*, Vol. I, 20–25.

55. *Mass Hist. Soc. Col.*, Fifth Series, Vol. I, 260–261.

CHAPTER 14. THE DUTCH AND SWEDES

1. Campbell, Charles, *History of the Colony and Ancient Dominion of Virginia* (Philadelphia, 1860), 195; O'Callaghan, E. B., *History of New Netherland*, Vol. I (New York, 1848), 189; Brodhead, J. R., *History of the State of New York*, First Period (New York, 1853), 280–282; *Dictionary of American History*, Vol. IV (New York, 1940), 113.

2. Brodhead, J. R., *History of the State of New York*, First Period, 282–284; Ward, Christopher, *The Dutch & Swedes on the Delaware* (Philadelphia, 1930), 87–89.

3. *Dictionary of American History*, Vol. IV, 113.

4. O'Callaghan, E. B., *History of New Netherland*, Vol. I, 190–192.

5. Brodhead, J. R., *History of the State of New York*, First Period, 222–225, 275–276, 283.

6. *Ibid.*, 276–279.

7. Andrews, C. M., *Colonial Period of American History*, Vol. III (New Haven, 1937), 83–85. For the detailed records of Rensselaerswyck see *Van Rensselaer Bowier Manuscripts*, edited by A. J. F. van Laer, Albany, 1908.

8. Jameson, J. Franklin, ed., *Narratives of New Netherland* (New York,

1909, in the Original Narratives of Early American History series, Barnes & Noble, publishers), 139–157.

9. Ward, Christopher, *The Dutch & Swedes on the Delaware*, 91–96.
10. Brodhead, J. R., *History of the State of New York*, First Period, 287–292; Shelley, H. C., *John Underhill* (New York, 1932), 290; Fernow, B., ed., *Documents relative to the Colonial History of the State of New York*, Vol. XIV (Albany, 1883), 26.
11. Brodhead, J. R., *History of the State of New York*, First Period, 293–296; Trumbull, Benjamin, *History of Connecticut*, Vol. I (New Haven, 1818), 118–119.
12. Brodhead, J. R., *History of the State of New York*, First Period, 297–301; Calder, Isabel MacB., "The Earl of Stirling and the Colonization of Long Island" in *Essays in Colonial History, Presented to Charles McLean Andrews by his Students* (New Haven, 1931), 74–95; Adams, James Truslow, *History of the Town of Southampton* (Bridgehampton, 1918), 45–53; Craven, C. E., ed., *Whitaker's Southold* (Princeton, 1931), 53–55.

CHAPTER 15. THE TOBACCO COLONIES

1. Statements as to the population of the colonies during the middle seventeenth century are at best only estimates. For varying estimates see Bureau of the Census, *A Century of Population Growth* (Washington, 1909), 9; Adams, J. T., *The Founding of New England* (Boston, 1921), 120; Wertenbaker, T. J., *The First Americans* (New York, 1927), 313. Hugh Peter, in 1641, stated that there were fifty thousand English in America (O'Callaghan, E. B., ed., *Documents Relative to the Colonial History of the State of New York*, Vol. I, 367) and, considering the size of the families and the number of children, this estimate may be more nearly correct than has generally been believed.
2. Bruce, P. A., *Economic History of Virginia in the Seventeenth Century*, Vol. I (New York, 1895, as reprinted in 1935), 512–527, 556–558 —hereafter cited as Bruce, *Economic History of Virginia*.
3. *Ibid.*, Vol. I, 217–218, 300–308, 324, Vol. II, 495–496; Campbell, Charles, *Colony and Ancient Dominion of Virginia* (Philadelphia, 1860), 207.
4. Bruce, *Economic History of Virginia*, Vol. I, 321–323.
5. *Ibid.*, Vol. I, 296, 492–495; Andrews, C. M., *Colonial Period in American History*, Vol. I (New Haven, 1934), 206; Neill, Edward D., *Virginia Carolorum* (Albany, 1886), 133; Campbell, Charles, *Colony and Ancient Dominion of Virginia*, 224.
6. Coleman, R. V., *Roger Ludlow in Chancery* (Westport, 1934), 18–19; *Mass. Hist. Soc. Col.*, Fourth Series, Vol. VI (Boston, 1863), 212, 256.
7. Bruce, *Economic History of Virginia*, Vol. II, 139, 145–147, 151–159.
8. *Ibid.*, 135–139, 157.
9. *Ibid.*, 160–184.
10. *Ibid.*, 184–196.
11. *Ibid.*, 534, 545; Bruce, P. A., *Social Life of Virginia in the Seventeenth Century* (Lynchburg, 1927), 174–177.
12. Bruce, *Economic History of Virginia*, Vol. II, 197, 211–231; Hall, C. C., ed., *Narratives of Early Maryland* (New York, 1910, in the Original

Narratives of Early American History series, Barnes & Noble, publishers), 298.

13. Bruce, P. A., *Institutional History of Virginia in the Seventeenth Century*, Vol. I (New York, 1910), 45–50, 55–56, 62, 73, 83–85, 98–99, 131–176—hereafter cited as Bruce, *Institutional History of Virginia*.

14. Bruce, *Economic History of Virginia*, Vol. II, 1–3.

15. Hall, C. C., ed., *Narratives of Early Maryland*, 289.

16. Bruce, *Economic History of Virginia*, Vol. II, 1–2 note.

17. *Ibid.*, 41–42, 45–46; Hall, C. C., ed., *Narratives of Early Maryland*, 292.

18. Bruce, *Economic History of Virginia*, Vol. I, 574; Neill, Edward D., *Virginia Carolorum*, 133.

19. Wertenbaker, T. J., *The First Americans*, 25, 47–48; Bruce, *Economic History of Virginia*, Vol. II, 89, 96.

20. Campbell, Charles, *Colony and Ancient Dominion of Virginia*, 209.

21. Bruce, *Institutional History of Virginia*, Vol. I, 323–325.

22. *Ibid.*, 331–342.

23. *Ibid.*, 350–356, 360.

24. *Dictionary of American Biography*, Vol. II (New York, 1929), 217–218, Vol. XII (New York, 1933), 405–406; Scharf, J. T., *History of Maryland*, Vol. I (Baltimore, 1879), 111–113.

25. Bruce, *Institutional History of Virginia*, Vol. II, 301, 342, 344; Hening, W. W., ed., *The Statutes at Large, Being a Collection of All the Laws of Virginia*, Vol. I (New York, 1823), 280–282.

26. Bruce, *Institutional History of Virginia*, Vol. II, 368–370, 403–406, 417–422; Andrews, C. M., *Colonial Period of American History*, Vol. I, 194–203.

27. Andrews, C. M., *Colonial Period of American History*, Vol. I, 204–205.

28. Bruce, *Institutional History of Virginia*, Vol. II, 294–295, 405–406, 409–410, 426–428.

29 *Ibid.*, Vol. I, 82, 484–486, 540–549, 660, 681, 690; Bruce, *Economic History of Virginia*, Vol. II, 12; Hall, C. C., ed., *Narratives of Early Maryland*, 294.

30. Bruce, *Institutional History of Virginia*, Vol. II, 522–569.

31. *Ibid.*, Vol. II, 345, 566–569; Hening, W. W., ed., *The Statutes at Large; Being a Collection of All the Laws of Virginia*, Vol. I, 281.

32. Bruce, *Institutional History of Virginia*, Vol. I, 690; *Dictionary of American Biography*, Vol. II, 217.

33. Winthrop, *History*, Vol. II, 93–94; Bruce, *Institutional History of Virginia*, Vol. I, 217, 254–255.

34. Hall, C. C., ed., *Narratives of Early Maryland*, 300–301, 363–364; *The Calvert Papers*, Number One (Baltimore, 1889), 176; Steiner, B. C., *Maryland during the English Civil Wars*, Part II (Johns Hopkins University Studies, Series XXV, Nos. 4–5, Baltimore, 1907), 15; Forman, H. C., *Jamestown and St. Mary's* (Baltimore, 1938), 177.

35. Forman, H. C., *Jamestown and St. Mary's*, 207; Steiner, B. C., *Maryland during the English Civil Wars*, Part II, 54.

36. Hall, C. C., ed., *Narratives of Early Maryland*, 134–135; Steiner, B. C., *Maryland during the English Civil Wars*, Part I (Johns Hopkins University Studies, Series XXIV, Nos. 11–12, Baltimore, 1906), 31.

37. Hall, C. C., ed., *Narratives of Early Maryland*, 304; Andrews, C. M.,

Colonial Period of American History, Vol. II (New Haven, 1936), 300–301.

38. Wertenbaker, T. J., *The First Americans,* 27–28; Hall, C. C., ed., *Narratives of Early Maryland,* 91.

39. Hall, C. C., ed., *Narratives of Early Maryland,* 101–112.

40. Andrews, C. M., *Colonial Period of American History,* Vol. II, 292–298; Forman, H. C., *Jamestown and St. Mary's,* 177, 254–255, 309–318; *Maryland Historical Magazine,* Vol. V (Baltimore, 1910), 172.

41. *Dictionary of American Biography,* Vol. XX (New York, 1936), 20–21; Steiner, B. C., *Maryland during the English Civil Wars,* Part I, 45.

42. Winthrop, *History,* Vol. II, 179–180; Savage, James, ed., *A Genealogical Dictionary of the First Settlers of New England,* Vol. II (Boston, 1860), 245.

43. Birch, Thomas, ed., *Collection of the State Papers of John Thurloe, etc.,* Vol. V (London, 1742), 486.

44. Steiner, B. C., *Maryland during the English Civil Wars,* Part II, 7, 32–39.

45. Birch, Thomas, ed., *Collection of the State Papers of John Thurloe, etc.,* Vol. V, 484; Steiner, B. C., *Maryland during the English Civil Wars,* Part II, 43.

46. Campbell, Charles, *Colony and Ancient Dominion of Virginia,* 203–204; Steiner, B. C., *Maryland during the English Civil Wars,* Part II, 48.

47. Steiner, B. C., *Maryland during the English Civil Wars,* Part II, 42–46, 60–62.

48. *Ibid.,* 47–50.

49. *Ibid.,* 50–56; Scharf, J. T., *History of Maryland,* Vol. I, 145–149.

50. Steiner, B. C., *Maryland during the English Civil Wars,* Part II, 51, 63–70.

51. *Ibid.,* 102, 105–106; Scharf, J. T., *History of Maryland,* Vol. I, 173.

52. Steiner, B. C., *Maryland under the Commonwealth* (Johns Hopkins University Studies, Series XXIX, No. 1, Baltimore, 1911), 10–11; Hall, C. C., ed., *Narratives of Early Maryland,* 301–302; Andrews, C. M., *Colonial Period in American History,* Vol. II, 312.

53. Steiner, B. C., *Maryland during the English Civil Wars,* Part II, 114–118; Scharf, J. T., *History of Maryland,* Vol. I, 174–176.

54. Cross, A. L., *History of England and Greater Britain* (New York, 1914), 507; Gardiner, S. R., *History of the Great Civil War,* Vol. IV (London, 1893), 293–323.

55. Gardiner, S. R., *History of the Great Civil War,* Vol. IV, 329; Gardiner, S. R., *History of the Commonwealth and Protectorate,* Vol. I (London, 1903), 1–9; Firth, C. H., and Rait, R. S., eds., *Acts and Ordinances of the Interregnum,* Vol. I (London, 1911), 1263–1264, Vol. II (London, 1911), 122.

56. Gardiner, S. R., *History of the Commonwealth and Protectorate,* Vol. I, 316; Campbell, Charles, *Colony and Ancient Dominion of Virginia,* 212–213.

57. Neill, Edward D., *Virginia Carolorum,* 211; Hall, C. C., ed., *Narratives of Early Maryland,* 179–180; Steiner, B. C., *Maryland under the Commonwealth,* 12.

58. Campbell, Charles, *Colony and Ancient Dominion of Virginia,* 213–

215; Harlow, V. T., *A History of Barbados, 1625–1685* (Oxford, 1926), 48–70.

59. Firth, C. H., and Rait, R. S., eds., *Acts and Ordinances of the Interregnum*, Vol. II, 425–429.

60. Neill, Edward D., *Virginia Carolorum*, 212–216.

61. Harlow, V. T., *A History of Barbados*, 69–82; Campbell, Charles, *Colony and Ancient Dominion of Virginia*, 216–221; Andrews, M. P., *History of Maryland: Province and State* (New York, 1929), 116.

62. Steiner, B. C., *Maryland under the Commonwealth*, 53–58.

63. Campbell, Charles, *Colony and Ancient Dominion of Virginia*, 222–223.

64. Bruce, *Economic History of Virginia*, Vol. I, 349–356; Fernow, B., ed., *Documents relating to the Colonial History of the State of New York*, Vol. XIV, 500.

65. Bruce, *Economic History of Virginia*, Vol. I, 315, 329, 333, 336.

66. Abbott, W. C., *The Writings and Speeches of Oliver Cromwell*, Vol. II (Cambridge, 1939), 641–645; Gardiner, S. R., *History of the Commonwealth and Protectorate*, Vol. II (London, 1903), 262–265, Vol. III, 1.

67. Campbell, Charles, *Colony and Ancient Dominion of Virginia*, 228–229; Andrews, C. M., *Colonial Period of American History*, Vol. II, 316–320; Hall, C. C., ed., *Narratives of Early Maryland*, 204, 237–244, 303–305; Steiner, B. C., *Maryland under the Commonwealth*, 84–101.

68. Steiner, B. C., *Maryland under the Commonwealth*, 101–112; Birch, Thomas, ed., *Collection of the State Papers of John Thurloe*, etc., Vol. V, 482–487.

69. Browne, W. H., ed., *Maryland Archives*, Vol. III (Baltimore, 1885), 332–335.

70. *Dictionary of American Biography*, Vol. XII, 406; Campbell, Charles, *Colony and Ancient Dominion of Virginia*, 242–244.

CHAPTER 16. NORTH OF THE MERRIMAC

1. Hammond, Otis G., *The Mason Title and Its Relations to New Hampshire and Massachusetts* (Reprinted from the Proceedings of the American Antiquarian Society for October, 1916), 5–6.

2. Winthrop, *History*, Vol. II (Savage edition of 1853), 45, 50–51; *Mass. Hist. Soc. Col.*, Fourth Series, Vol. VI (Boston, 1863), 106–107.

3. *Mass. Hist. Soc. Col.*, Fourth Series, Vol. VII (Boston, 1865), 178–179; Winthrop, *History*, Vol. II, 32–33; Bouton, N., ed., *Documents and Records relating to the Province of New Hampshire*, Vol. I (Concord, 1867), 122–124.

4. *Mass. Col. Rec.*, Vol. I, 7.

5. *Ibid.*, 342; *Dictionary of American Biography*, Vol. XX (New York, 1936), 62.

6. Mather, Cotton, *Magnalia Christi Americana*, Vol. I (Hartford, 1820), 62.

7. Farnham, Mary F., ed., *Documentary History of the State of Maine*, Vol. VII (Portland, 1901), 223–243.

8. Burrage, H. S., *Beginnings of Colonial Maine* (State of Maine, 1914),

197–225, 243; Libby, C. T., ed., *Province and Court Records of Maine,* Vol. I (Portland, 1928), 54.

9. Farnham, Mary F., ed., *Documentary History of the State of Maine,* Vol. I, 226; Baxter, J. P., ed., *Sir Ferdinando Gorges and His Province of Maine,* Vol. I (Boston, 1890), 185–187.

10. Baxter, J. P., ed., *Sir Ferdinando Gorges and His Province of Maine,* Vol. III (Boston, 1890), 294.

11. Winthrop, *History,* Vol. II, 11–12; Libby, C. T., ed., *Province and Court Records of Maine,* Vol. I, 36–56.

12. Libby, C. T., ed., *Province and Court Records of Maine,* Vol. I, 74–75.

13. *Ibid.,* 68–69.

14. *Ibid.,* 62–64.

15. Baxter, J. P., *Documentary History of the State of Maine,* Vol. III, being the Trelawny Papers (Portland, 1884), 252–254, 273.

16. *Ibid.,* 259, 288–295.

17. *Ibid.,* 216, 243, 258, 288.

18. *Ibid.,* 30, 57–58, 102, 203–204, 216, 281.

19. *Ibid.,* 27–29, 53, 202–203, 209–213, 254–255.

20. *Ibid.,* 57, 107, 157, 200–204, 215, 242, 259, 281, 296–307.

21. *Ibid.,* 290–295, 302, 321.

22. *Ibid.,* 31–32, 307.

23. *Ibid.,* 166–168.

24. *Ibid.,* 218, 224, 249, 259, 281, 309.

25. *Ibid.,* 319.

26. Baxter, J. P., *George Cleeve of Casco Bay* (Portland, 1885), 116–123.

27. Winthrop, *History,* Vol. I, 69, Vol. II, 390–391; Farnham, Mary F., ed., *Documentary History of the State of Maine,* Vol. VII, 134–136.

28. Baxter, J. P., *George Cleeve of Casco Bay,* 118, 124.

29. *Ibid.,* 130–151, 278–280.

30. Baxter, J. P., ed., *Documentary History of the State of Maine,* Vol. III, xxv, 365 note 2; Baxter, J. P., ed., *Sir Ferdinando Gorges and His Province of Maine,* Vol. I, 194.

31. Baxter, J. P., *George Cleeve of Casco Bay,* 152–154.

32. Burrage, H. S., *The Beginnings of Colonial Maine,* 309–310, 341; Williamson, W. D., *History of the State of Maine,* Vol. I (Hallowell, 1832), 303–304; Baxter, J. P., ed., *Sir Ferdinando Gorges and His Province of Maine,* Vol. I, 196.

33. Baxter, J. P., *George Cleeve of Casco Bay,* 155; *Mass. Col. Rec.,* Vol. III, 278, 288.

34. Baxter, J. P., *George Cleeve of Casco Bay,* 156–167; *Mass. Col. Rec.,* Vol. III, 288; Burrage, H. S., *Beginnings of Colonial Maine,* 367–377; Libby, C. T., ed., *Province and Court Records of Maine,* Vol. II (Portland, 1931), 5–10.

35. Libby, C. T., ed., *Province and Court Records of Maine,* Vol. II, 11.

36. *Ibid.,* 12, 20, 22, 31, 55–56.

37. *Ibid.,* 6, 13–15, 29, 63, 65, 68–69.

38. *Mass. Col. Rec.,* Vol. IV, Pt. I, 338, 357–358.

39. Baxter, J. P., *George Cleeve of Casco Bay,* 169–186, 306–307, 313–318; *Mass. Col. Rec.,* Vol. IV, Pt. I, 359–361.

40. Baxter, J. P., *George Cleeve of Casco Bay,* 187–205.

CHAPTER 17. THE PURITAN COLONIES

1. Young, Alexander, ed., *Chronicles of the Pilgrim Fathers* (Boston, 1841), 426; Walker, Williston, *Creeds and Platforms of Congregationalism* (New York, 1893), 205, 207–208.
2. Hoadly, C. J., *Records of the Colony or Jurisdiction of New Haven, 1638–1649* (Hartford, 1857), 15, 20–hereafter cited as *New Haven Col. Rec.*, Vol. I.
3. Winthrop, *History*, Vol. I, 356–358, Vol. II, 46. Note that the edition referred to throughout is that edited by James Savage (Boston, 1853).
4. *Ibid.*, Vol. I, 352–353, Vol. II, 46.
5. *Ibid.*, Vol. II, 25.
6. *Ibid.*, 29–30, 37.
7. *Mass. Hist. Soc. Col.*, Fourth Series, Vol. VI (Boston, 1863), 58.
8. Winthrop, *History*, Vol. II, 50, 91–92, 118–119; Firth, C. H., and Rait, R. S., eds., *Acts and Ordinances of the Interregnum*, Vol. I (London, 1911), 571.
9. *Mass. Hist. Soc. Col.*, Fourth Series, Vol. VI, 108–112; Sibley, J. L., *Biographical Sketches of Graduates of Harvard University*, Vol. I (Cambridge, 1873), 15, 68–72; Beresford, John, *The Godfather of Downing Street* (Boston and New York, 1925), 43–51; Young, Alexander, ed., *Chronicles of the First Planters of the Colony of Massachusetts Bay* (Boston, 1846), 106 note; Winthrop, *History*, Vol. II, 346.
10. Winthrop, *History*, Vol. II, 21, 25, 103; Trumbull, J. H., ed., *The Public Records of the Colony of Connecticut, 1636–1665* (Hartford, 1850), 69–hereafter cited as *Conn. Col. Rec.*, Vol. I.
11. Winthrop, *History*, Vol. II, 29, 37, 79.
12. *Ibid.*, 91, 114.
13. *Ibid.*, 186, 269, 291–292, 298–299; *Conn. Col. Rec.*, Vol. I, 59–60, 116; Weeden, W. B., *Economic and Social History of New England*, Vol. I (Boston and New York, 1891), 162, 174, 177–178; *Mass. Hist. Soc. Col.*, Fourth Series, Vol. VI, 61, 76, 80.
14. Winthrop, *History*, Vol. II, 144, 380; *New Haven Col. Rec.*, Vol. I, 337; Weeden, W. B., *Economic and Social History of New England*, Vol. I, 158, 176–177.
15. Winthrop, *History*, Vol. II, 106–107, 109, 128–139, 150–154, 162–163, 219–221, 232, 241, 290–291, 334–336.
16. Trumbull, Benjamin, *History of Connecticut*, Vol. I (New Haven, 1818), 161; Winthrop, *History*, Vol. II, 325–326, 336–337, 399–400; Jacobus, Donald L., *History and Genealogy of the Families of Old Fairfield* (New Haven, 1930), 101.
17. Trumbull, Benjamin, *History of Connecticut*, Vol. I, 155, 161–162; *New Haven Col. Rec.*, Vol. I, 110–111, 463.
18. *Conn. Col. Rec.*, Vol. I, 35–36, 53, 86, 566–568; *Mass. Col. Rec.*, Vol. I, 271, 279.
19. *Mass. Col. Rec.*, Vol. I, 271; *Conn. Col. Rec.*, Vol. I, 42, 52–53; Arnold, S. G., *History of the State of Rhode Island and Providence Plantations*, Vol. I (Providence, 1899), 108–109.
20. *New Haven Col. Rec.*, Vol. I, 25, 41–43, 47–48; *Mass. Col. Rec.*, Vol. I, 271.

21. Labaree, L. W., *Milford, Connecticut*, a publication of the Tercentenary Commission of the State of Connecticut (New Haven, 1933), 1–29.
22. *New Haven Col. Rec.*, Vol. I, 24, 81, 154; *Boston, Second Report of the Record Commissioners of* (Boston, 1881), 84, 88, 92, 104, 109, 123; Arnold, S. G., *History of the State of Rhode Island and Providence Plantations*, Vol. I, 132; *Conn. Col. Rec.*, Vol. I, 41.
23. Winthrop, *History*, Vol. I, 217, 325, 380, Vol. II, 215, 278; Walker, Williston, *Creeds and Platforms of Congregationalism*, 227–228; *Mass. Col. Rec.*, Vol. I, 274.
24. Walker, Williston, *Creeds and Platforms of Congregationalism*, 232, 234–235; Winthrop, *History*, Vol. II, 217, 238.
25. Walker, Williston, *Creeds and Platforms of Congregationalism*, 221–222.
26. *New Haven Col. Rec.*, Vol. I, 242–243, 269–270, 302–304; *Papers of the New Haven Colony Historical Society*, Vol. V (New Haven, 1894), 133–148.
27. *New Haven Col. Rec.*, Vol. I, 242–257.
28. *Ibid.*
29. *Ibid.*, 93, 173, 250; Sibley, J. L., *Biographical Sketches of Graduates of Harvard University*, Vol. I, 15; Jacobus, Donald L., *History and Genealogy of the Families of Old Fairfield*, 101.
30. *New Haven Col. Rec.*, Vol. I, 31, 32, 46, 47; Halsey, R. T. H., and Cornelius, C. O., *A Handbook of the American Wing* (Metropolitan Museum of Art, New York, 1932), 8. The description of a typical New England house is based on the author's personal acquaintance with many of them. For details of construction see Kelly, J. F., *Early Domestic Architecture of Connecticut* (New Haven, 1924).
31. *Conn. Col. Rec.*, Vol. I, 496–497, 501, 504; Halsey, R. T. H., and Cornelius, C. O., *Handbook of the American Wing*, 12–30, 77; Weeden, W. B., *Economic and Social History of New England*, Vol. I, 215, 229; Lockwood, L. V., *Colonial Furniture in America*, Vol. II (New York, 1926), 244–248.
32. *Mass. Hist. Soc. Col.*, Fourth Series, Vol. VI, 146–147; Weeden, W. B., *Economic and Social History of New England*, Vol. I, 188; *Mass. Col. Rec.*, Vol. I, 186.
33. *Boston, Second Report of the Record Commissioners of*, 141; *Conn. Col. Rec.*, Vol. I, 53, 153–154.
34. *Mass. Col. Rec.*, Vol. I, 126, 183, 274; Winthrop, *History*, Vol. I, 331; *Conn. Col. Rec.*, Vol. I, 64; Weeden, W. B., *Economic and Social History of New England*, Vol. I, 227.
35. *Conn. Col. Rec.*, Vol. I, 457; Walker, Williston, *Creeds and Platforms of Congregationalism*, 200.
36. *Mass. Col. Rec.*, Vol. I, 109, 186, 223; *Conn. Col. Rec.*, Vol. I, 65, 105; *New Haven Col. Rec.*, Vol. I, 44, 77.
37. *Mass. Hist. Soc. Col.*, Fourth Series, Vol. VI, 65, 95.
38. *Papers of the New Haven Colony Historical Society*, Vol. V, 142; *New Haven Col. Rec.*, Vol. I, 296, 335; Weeden, W. B., *Economic and Social History of New England*, Vol. I, 149 note 3.
39. *New Haven Col. Rec.*, Vol. I, 173; *Conn. Col. Rec.*, Vol. I, 168.
40. *New Haven Col. Rec.*, Vol. I, 81, 84, 229, 327.

41. *Ibid.*, 233–236, 239.
42. Winthrop, *History*, Vol. II, 58–60, 73.
43. *New Haven Col. Rec.*, Vol. I, 62–73.
44. Winthrop, *History*, Vol. I, 210–211, Vol. II, 53–54; *Papers of the New Haven Colony Historical Society*, Vol. V, 133–148; Weeden, W. B., *Economic and Social History of New England*, Vol. I, 225.
45. *Mass. Hist. Soc. Col.*, Fourth Series, Vol. VI, 142; *Transactions and Collections of the American Antiquarian Society*, Vol. III (1857), 169; Winthrop, *History*, Vol. II, 15, 54–57, 411–412.
46. "Diary of John Hull," in *Transactions and Collections of the American Antiquarian Society*, Vol. III, 188–189; Winthrop, *History*, Vol. I, 313–316, Vol. II, 397–398; *Mass. Col. Rec.*, Vol. III, 126.
47. Wright, T. G., *Literary Culture in Early New England* (New Haven, 1920), 15–18, 25–81; Andrews, C. M., *Colonial Period of American History*, Vol. I (New Haven, 1934), 505.
48. Wright, T. G., *Literary Culture in Early New England*, 82–95.
49. *Dictionary of American History*, Vol. IV (New York, 1940), 344–345; Winship, G. P., *The Cambridge Press* (Philadelphia, 1945), 1–34; Wright, T. G., *Literary Culture in Early New England*, 92.
50. Winsor, Justin, ed., *Memorial History of Boston*, Vol. I (Boston, 1880), 123; Arnold, S. G., *History of the State of Rhode Island and Providence Plantations*, Vol. I, 145; *New Haven Col. Rec.*, Vol. I, 62.
51. *Mass. Col. Rec.*, Vol. II, 8–9, 203; Winthrop, *History*, Vol. II, 264; *Conn. Col. Rec.*, Vol. I, 554–555.
52. Wright, T. G., *Literary Culture in Early New England*, 23–24, 108–109.
53. *Dictionary of American History*, Vol. III, 250; *Mass. Col. Rec.*, Vol. I, 183, 208, 217, 253; *Dictionary of American Biography*, Vol. VIII (New York, 1932), 371–372.
54. Winthrop, *History*, Vol. I, 370–376, Vol. II, 105; *Dictionary of American Biography*, Vol. V (New York, 1930), 524, 611.
55. Winthrop, *History*, Vol. II, 265–266; *Papers of the New Haven Colony Historical Society*, Vol. V, 133.
56. *Mass. Hist. Soc. Col.*, Fourth Series, Vol. VII (Boston, 1865), 452–467; *Connecticut Magazine*, Vol. V (Hartford, 1899), 36–37; *Conn. Col. Rec.*, Vol. I, 234.
57. *Mass. Hist. Soc. Col.*, Fourth Series, Vol. VI, 150b–151; *Conn. Col. Rec.*, Vol. I, 51, 174–175; Arnold, S. G., *History of the State of Rhode Island and Providence Plantations*, Vol. I, 146; Winthrop, *History*, Vol. II, 322, 335.
58. *Boston, Second Report of the Record Commissioners of*, 68, 70, 91, 92, 97, 109, 112, 131, 139, 141.
59. *Ibid.*, 129.
60. *Ibid.*, 114, 116, 122, 138; Winsor, Justin, ed., *Memorial History of Boston*, Vol. I, 482; *Transactions and Collections of the American Antiquarian Society*, Vol. III, 174, 179; *Mass. Col. Rec.*, Vol. IV, Pt. I, 99–100.
61. Winsor, Justin, ed., *Memorial History of Boston*, Vol. I, 499; *Boston, Second Report of the Record Commissioners of*, 87, 91, 93; Winthrop, *History*, Vol. II, 261; *Mass. Hist. Soc. Col.*, Fourth Series, Vol. VI, 71,

80; *Conn. Col. Rec.,* Vol. I, 61, 64, 79; *New Haven Col. Rec.,* Vol. I, 345–346.

62. *Mass. Col. Rec.,* Vol. IV, Pt. I, 84–85, 104.

63. *Mass. Col. Rec.,* Vol. I, 161; *New Haven Col. Rec.,* Vol. I, 110–111; Boston, *Second Report of the Record Commissioners of, passim.*

64. Boston, *Second Report of the Record Commissioners of, passim.*

65. *Mass. Col. Rec.,* Vol. I, 87; *New Haven Col. Rec.,* Vol. I, 15, 17, 112.

66. *Conn. Col. Rec.,* Vol. I, 21, 23, 96, 290, 331; Arnold, S. G., *History of the State of Rhode Island and Providence Plantations,* Vol. I, 149.

67. *New Haven Col. Rec.,* Vol. I, 21; Walker, Williston, *Creeds and Platforms of Congregationalism,* 211–212, 234–236; Winthrop, *History,* Vol. II, 140.

68. *Mass. Hist. Soc. Col.,* Fifth Series, Vol. I (Boston, 1871), 383; Winthrop, *History,* Vol. II, 55–57, 73, 250–251.

69. Winthrop, *History,* Vol. II, 278; *Mass. Hist. Soc. Col.,* Fourth Series, Vol. VI, 390.

70. Pulsifer, David, *Records of the Colony of New Plymouth,* Vol. IX (Boston, 1859, being Vol. I of the *Acts of the Commissioners of the United Colonies of New England),* ix; Winthrop, *History,* Vol. I, 341–344, 365; Davis, W. T., ed., *Bradford's History of Plymouth Plantation* (New York, 1908, in the Original Narratives of Early American History series), 349–352.

71. *Acts of the United Colonies,* Vol. I, 3–8; Winthrop, *History,* Vol. II, 102–103.

72. *Dictionary of American Biography,* Vol. VII (New York, 1931), 438–439; Arnold, S. G., *History of the State of Rhode Island and Providence Plantations,* Vol. I, 110–111; Winthrop, *History,* Vol. II, 69–71, 102; *Mass. Col. Rec.,* Vol. II, 26–27.

73. Arnold, S. G., *History of the State of Rhode Island and Providence Plantations,* Vol. I, 175–179; *Mass. Col. Rec.,* Vol. II, 35; Winthrop, *History,* Vol. II, 144–148.

74. Arnold, S. G., *History of the State of Rhode Island and Providence Plantations,* Vol. I, 179–189; Winthrop, *History,* Vol. II, 157–158, 165–169, 171–179; *Acts of the United Colonies,* Vol. I, 14–15.

75. Thorpe, F. N., ed., *The Federal and State Constitutions, Colonial Charters, etc.,* Vol. VI (Washington, 1909), 3209–3211; Arnold S. G., *History of the State of Rhode Island and Providence Plantations,* Vol. I, 113.

76. Arnold, S. G., *History of the State of Rhode Island and Providence Plantations,* Vol. I, 114–115; Winthrop, *History,* Vol. II, 236–238.

77. Arnold, S. G., *History of the State of Rhode Island and Providence Plantations,* Vol. I, 190–191.

78. Winthrop, *History,* Vol. II, 140–141.

79. *Ibid.,* 66, 251.

80. *Ibid.,* 83–86, 139.

81. *Ibid.,* 140–144, 193; Winthrop, R. C., *Life and Letters of John Winthrop,* Vol. II (Boston, 1867), 430.

82. Winthrop, *History,* Vol. II, 319–321, 346–359; *Mass. Hist. Soc. Col.,* Fourth Series, Vol. VI, 108.

83. Winthrop, *History,* Vol. II, 332–334, 340–344, 346, 359–367, 389–391.

84. *Mass. Col. Rec.,* Vol. II, 61, 239, 246, 263; *The Laws and Liberties*

of *Massachusetts,* Reprinted from the copy of the 1648 edition in the Henry E. Huntington Library, with an Introduction by Max Farrand (Cambridge, 1929), 51; Walker, Williston, *Creeds and Platforms of Congregationalism,* 159–188.

85. *Mass. Col. Rec.,* Vol. II, 154–156; Walker, Williston, *Creeds and Platforms of Congregationalism,* 174, 203–237; Winthrop, *History,* Vol. II, 402–403.

86. *Mass. Col. Rec.,* Vol. IV, Pt. I, 52–53, 108–109, 195, 276, 347–348; *Conn. Col. Rec.,* Vol. I, 170, 206, 228, 251, 293, 323; *New Haven Col. Rec.,* Vol. II (Hartford, 1858), 132, 154, 194.

87. Winthrop, *History,* Vol. II, 148–149; *Mass. Hist. Soc. Col.,* Fourth Series, Vol. VI, 148; *Dictionary of American Biography,* Vol. V, 524.

88. *New Haven Col. Rec.,* Vol. II, 80–83; *Dictionary of American Biography,* Vol. IX (New York, 1932), 2; *Mass. Col. Rec.,* Vol. IV, Pt. I, 73, 269.

89. *Mass. Col. Rec.,* Vol. IV, Pt. I, 277–278, 308–309; *New Haven Col. Rec.,* Vol. II, 238; *Conn. Col. Rec.,* Vol. I, 324; *Dictionary of American Biography,* Vol. V, 584.

90. *Dictionary of American Biography,* Vol. XX (New York, 1936), 393–394; *Mass. Hist. Soc. Col.,* Fourth Series, Vol. VI, 81, 114; *Mass. Hist. Soc. Col.,* Fifth Series, Vol. I, 368–370.

91. *Mass. Hist. Soc. Col.,* Fourth Series, Vol. VI, 84, 291; *Dictionary of American Biography,* Vol. IX, 207–208; Coleman, R. V., *Mr. Ludlow Goes for Old England* (Westport, 1935), 21–30.

92. Trumbull, Benjamin, *History of Connecticut,* Vol. I, 161–162; Davis, W. T., ed., *Bradford's History,* 391.

93. *Conn. Col. Rec.,* Vol. I, 119–122, 185.

94. *Ibid.,* 297, 565–566.

CHAPTER 18. THE FALL OF NEW SWEDEN

1. O'Callaghan, E. B., *History of New Netherland,* Vol. I (New York, 1845), 252; O'Callaghan, E. B., ed., *Documents Relative to the Colonial History of the State of New York,* Vol. II (Albany, 1858), 144.

2. Brodhead, J. R., *History of the State of New York,* First Period (New York, 1853), 333–334; Winthrop, *History,* Vol. I (Savage edition, 1853), 50; Arnold, S. G., *History of the State of Rhode Island and Providence Plantations,* Vol. I (Providence, 1899), 100.

3. O'Callaghan, E. B., *History of New Netherland,* Vol. I, 257–258, 317–318, 427.

4. *New Haven Col. Rec.,* Vol. I, 56–57; Fernow, B., ed., *Documents Relative to the Colonial History of the State of New York,* Vol. XII (Albany, 1877), 23–24; O'Callaghan, E. B., *History of New Netherland,* Vol. I, 231–232, 253–254.

5. O'Callaghan, E. B., *History of New Netherland,* Vol. I, 365–366.

6. *Ibid.,* 366–367; Ward, Christopher, *The Dutch & Swedes on the Delaware* (Philadelphia, 1930), 107–111, 113.

7. *New Haven Col. Rec.,* Vol. I, 106–108; Brodhead, J. R., *History of the State of New York,* First Period, 382–383.

8. *New Haven Col. Rec.,* Vol. I, 106–108.

9. Ward, Christopher, *The Dutch & Swedes on the Delaware*, 118–122; Pulsifer, David, ed., *Records of the Colony of New Plymouth*, Vol. IX, being Vol. I of *Acts of the Commissioners of the United Colonies* (Boston, 1859), 13; Brodhead, J. R., *History of the State of New York*, First Period, 382–383.

10. Winsor, Justin, ed., *Narrative and Critical History of America*, Vol. IV (Boston and New York, 1884), 456–457; Brodhead, J. R., *History of the State of New York*, First Period, 383; Winthrop, *History*, Vol. II, 218–219.

11. Ward, Christopher, *Dutch & Swedes on the Delaware*, 131.

12. Brodhead, J. R., *History of the State of New York*, First Period, 347–360, 366–368; Winthrop, *History*, Vol. II, 163–164.

13. Brodhead, J. R., *History of the State of New York*, First Period, 354–355.

14. *Ibid.*, 386–392; *New Haven Col. Rec.*, Vol. I, 116–117.

15. Brodhead, J. R., *History of the State of New York*, First Period, 345–346, 373, 422–423.

16. *Ibid.*, 335, 373–374, 392, 432–433, 465; O'Callaghan, E. B., *History of New Netherland*, Vol. II (New York, 1848), 24.

17. Brodhead, J. R., *History of the State of New York*, First Period, 467, 476, 533–537; *Dictionary of American History*, Vol. IV (New York, 1940), 94.

18. *Acts of the Commissioners of the United Colonies*, Vol. I, 171–176; Weeden, W. B., *Economic and Social History of New England*, Vol. I (Boston and New York, 1891), 161.

19. *Acts of the Commissioners of the United Colonies*, Vol. I, 188–190.

20. O'Callaghan, E. B., ed., *Documents Relative to the Colonial History of the State of New York*, Vol. II (Albany, 1858), 141–143.

21. Brodhead, J. R., *History of the State of New York*, First Period, 546–547; *Acts of the Commissioners of the United Colonies*, Vol. II, 3–112; Coleman, R. V., *Mr. Ludlow Goes for Old England* (Westport, 1935), 17.

22. Shelley, H. C., *John Underhill* (New York, 1932), 345–346, 360–367, 372; O'Callaghan, E. B., ed., *Documents Relative to the Colonial History of the State of New York*, Vol. II, 151–152; *Acts of the Commissioners of the United Colonies*, Vol. II, 52.

23. Coleman, R. V., *Mr. Ludlow Goes for Old England*, 12–18; *New Haven Col. Rec.*, Vol. II, 37–38; *Conn. Col. Rec.*, Vol. I, 254, 275.

24. Winsor, Justin, ed., *Narrative and Critical History of America*, Vol. IV, 459–466; Ward, Christopher, *Dutch & Swedes on the Delaware*, 132–135.

25. Brodhead, J. R., *History of the State of New York*, First Period, 528–530; Ward, Christopher, *Dutch & Swedes on the Delaware*, 147–151.

26. O'Callaghan, E. B., *History of New Netherland*, Vol. II (New York, 1848), 272–275; Ward, Christopher, *Dutch & Swedes on the Delaware*, 152–162, 174–176.

27. Johnson, Amandus, *Swedish Settlements on the Delaware* (New York, 1911), 572–573.

28. Brodhead, J. R., *History of the State of New York*, First Period, 601–606; Myers, A. C., ed., *Narratives of Early Pennsylvania, West New*

Jersey and Delaware (New York, 1912, in the Original Narratives of Early American History series), 170–176.

29. Brodhead, J. R., *History of the State of New York*, First Period, 487, 489, 697; Bowman, G. E., ed., *The Mayflower Descendants*, Vol. II (Boston, 1900), 155–156.

30. Brodhead, J. R., *History of the State of New York*, First Period, 614–616; O'Callaghan, E. B., ed., *Documentary History of the State of New York*, Vol. III (Albany, 1850), 923.

31. Brodhead, J. R., *History of the State of New York*, First Period, 626; Fernow, B., ed., *Documents Relative to the Colonial History of the State of New York*, Vol. XIV (Albany, 1883), 369–370.

32. Brodhead, J. R., *History of the State of New York*, First Period, 636–637; Hastings, Hugh, ed., *Ecclesiastical Records of the State of New York*, Vol. I (Albany, 1901), 399–400.

33. Brodhead, J. R., *History of the State of New York*, First Period, 629–632; Fletcher, H. F., ed., *Complete Poetical Works of John Milton* (Boston and New York, 1941), 133.

34. Brodhead, J. R., *History of the State of New York*, First Period, 633, 651, 661; Fernow, B., *Documents Relative to the Colonial History of the State of New York*, Vol. XII, 235–242.

35. Fernow, B., ed., *Documents Relative to the Colonial History of the State of New York*, Vol. XII, 242–243, 245–251; Brodhead, J. R., *History of the State of New York*, First Period, 663–666.

36. O'Callaghan, E. B., ed., *Documents Relative to the Colonial History of the State of New York*, Vol. II, 88–98, Vol. XII (Fernow, B., ed.), 261–262.

CHAPTER 19. GOD SAVE THE KING

1. Wheatley, H. B., ed., *The Diary of Samuel Pepys*, Vol. I (London, 1924), 140–150.

2. *Dictionary of National Biography*, Vol. XV (London, 1921–1922), 955–963; Welles, L. A., *History of the Regicides in New England* (New York, 1927), 23–24.

3. Winsor, Justin, ed., *Narrative and Critical History of America*, Vol. III (Boston and New York, 1884), 149; Hening, W. W., ed., *The Statutes at Large; Being a Collection of all the Laws of Virginia*, Vol. II (New York, 1823), 49; *Dictionary of American History*, Vol. IV (New York, 1940), 170.

4. Andrews, C. M., *Colonial Period of American History*, Vol. II (New Haven, 1936), 323; Brodhead, J. R., *History of the State of New York*, First Period (New York, 1853), 697; Winsor, Justin, ed., *Narrative and Critical History of America*, Vol. III, 524; O'Callaghan, E. B., ed., *Documents Relative to the Colonial History of the State of New York*, Vol. II (Albany, 1853), 116–120, Vol. XII (Fernow, B., ed., Albany, 1877), 356–357.

5. *Mass. Col. Rec.*, Vol. IV, Pt. I, 367, 417–418; *Transactions and Collections of the American Antiquarian Society*, Vol. III (1857), 190–191; *Mass. Hist. Soc. Col.*, Vol. VII (Boston, 1865), 511, 515–516.

6. Welles, L. A., *History of the Regicides in New England*, 25.

7. *Ibid.*, 26–29; *Documents Relative to the Colonial History of the State of New York*, Vol. III (Albany, 1853), 39–41.

8. Hutchinson, Thomas, *History of the Colony of Massachusetts-Bay*, Vol. I (Boston, 1764), 210–211; *Mass. Col. Rec.*, Vol. IV, Pt. I, 449–453.

9. Welles, L. A., *History of the Regicides in New England*, 30; Wheatley, H. B., *The Diary of Samuel Pepys*, Vol. I, 239–242; *Dictionary of American Biography*, Vol. XIV (New York, 1934), 498; *An Exact and Most Impartial Account of the Indictment, Arraignment, Trial, and Judgment (according to Law) of Twenty nine Regicides, etc.* (London, 1660), 282.

10. Welles, L. A., *History of the Regicides in New England*, 30–32.

11. *Ibid.*, 33–34; *Documents Relative to the Colonial History of the State of New York*, Vol. III, 41–42.

12. Welles, L. A., *History of the Regicides in New England*, 34.

13. *Ibid.*, 35–72.

14. Arnold, S. G., *History of the State of Rhode Island and Providence Plantations*, Vol. I (Providence, 1899), 274–275; Shurtleff, N. B., *Records of the Colony of New Plymouth*, Vol. III (Boston, 1855), 210; *Conn. Col. Rec.*, Vol. I, 361–362, 368; *Mass. Col. Rec.*, Vol. IV, Pt. II, 30–31; *New Haven Col. Rec.*, Vol. II, 423; *Mass. Hist. Soc. Col.*, Fourth Series, Vol. VII, 548–550; Brodhead, J. R., *History of the State of New York*, First Period, 695.

15. *Conn. Col. Rec.*, Vol. I, 579–581.

16. Bates, A. C., *The Charter of Connecticut* (Hartford, 1932), 14–15; Coleman, R. V., *The Old Patent of Connecticut* (Westport, 1936), 50–52.

17. Coleman, R. V., *The Old Patent of Connecticut*, 53–54; *New Haven Col. Rec.*, Vol. II, 517–530; Trumbull, Benjamin, *History of Connecticut*, Vol. I (New Haven, 1818), 515–521.

18. Andrews, C. M., *Colonial Period of American History*, Vol. II, 40–46; Sainsbury, W. N., ed., *Calendar of State Papers*, Colonial Series, Vol. V (London, 1880), 127–128; Thorpe, F. N., *Constitutions, Colonial Charters, etc.*, Vol. VI (Washington, 1909), 3211–3222.

19. Campbell, Charles, *History of the Colony and Ancient Dominion of Virginia* (Philadelphia, 1860), 252, 257; McCrady, Edward, *History of South Carolina under the Proprietary Government* (New York, 1897), 61–68; Abbott, W. C., *Colonel John Scott* (New Haven, 1918), 3–15; *Documents Relative to the Colonial History of the State of New York*, Vol. III, 105.

20. Abbott, W. C., *Colonel John Scott*, 15, 21–22; Arnold, S. G., *History of the State of Rhode Island and Providence Plantations*, Vol. I, 383; *Documents Relative to the Colonial History of the State of New York*, Vol. III, 46.

21. Abbott, W. C., *Colonel John Scott*, 16–18, 23–25; *Documents Relative to the Colonial History of the State of New York*, Vol. III, 47–48.

22. *Conn. Col. Rec.*, Vol. I, 386–389, 407.

23. Schenck, Eliz. H., *History of Fairfield*, Vol. I (New York, 1889), 68 note; Fernow, B., ed., *Documents Relative to the Colonial History of the State of New York*, Vol. XIII (Albany, 1881), 64–66; Brodhead, J. R., *History of the State of New York*, First Period, 595, 598, 616, 618–619, 626–627, 703, 709; *Conn. Col. Rec.*, Vol. I, 387–388, 406.

24. *Conn. Col. Rec.*, Vol. I, 410; Brodhead, J. R., *History of the State of*

New York, First Period, 719–727; O'Callaghan, E. B., ed., *Documents Relative to the Colonial History of the State of New York,* Vol. II, 234, 374–375, 393–409, 506–507.

25. *Conn. Col. Rec.,* Vol. I, 420–423.

26. Abbott, W. C., *Conflicts with Oblivion* (New Haven, 1924), 312–313; *Connecticut Archives, Towns and Lands, 1629–1790,* Series I, Vol. I, Doc. 31, page a.

27. O'Callaghan, E. B., ed., *Documents Relative to the Colonial History of the State of New York,* Vol. II, 295–298.

28. Andrews, C. M., *Colonial Period of American History,* Vol. III (New Haven, 1937), 39–42, 49–53, Vol. IV (New Haven, 1938), 53–57; *Dictionary of American History* (New York, 1940), Vol. II, 71, Vol. IV, 73–74.

29. *Documents Relative to the Colonial History of the State of New York,* Vol. III, 45.

30. Andrews, C. M., *Colonial Period of American History,* Vol. III, 58 note 1; Trumbull, Benjamin, *History of Connecticut,* Vol. I, 272–273; *Conn. Col. Rec.,* Vol. I, 433; *Documents Relative to the Colonial History of the State of New York,* Vol. III, 106.

31. Brodhead, J. R., *History of the State of New York,* First Period, 735–736; *Documents Relative to the Colonial History of the State of New York,* Vol. III, 51–65.

32. *Transactions and Collections of the American Antiquarian Society,* Vol. III, 212; *Documents Relative to the Colonial History of the State of New York,* Vol. III, 65.

33. *Documents Relative to the Colonial History of the State of New York,* Vol. III, 63; *Mass. Col. Rec.,* Vol. IV, Pt. II, 120–126; *Transactions and Collections of the American Antiquarian Society,* Vol. III, 212; Welles, L. A., *History of the Regicides in New England,* 73–90; *Conn. Col. Rec.,* Vol. I, 436.

34. Brodhead, J. R., *History of the State of New York,* First Period, 736–743; Andrews, C. M., *Colonial Period of American History,* Vol. III, 60–61; Abbott, W. C., *Conflicts with Oblivion,* 316.

35. Brodhead, J. R., *History of the State of New York,* First Period, 738–745; O'Callaghan, E. B., ed., *Documents Relative to the Colonial History of the State of New York,* Vol. II, 250–253, 429–447.

CHAPTER 20. UNTO ALL AGES

1. Hodge, F. W., Hammond, G. P., and Rey, Agapito, eds., *Fray Alonso de Benavides' Revised Memorial of 1634* (Albuquerque, 1945), 68, 80, 172.

2. Lanning, J. T., *The Spanish Missions of Georgia* (Chapel Hill, 1935), 168–170.

3. Andrews, C. M., *The Colonial Period of American History,* Vol. IV (New Haven, 1938), 50–84.

4. Bruce, P. A., *Economic History of Virginia in the Seventeenth Century* (New York, 1935), Vol. I, 357–362, Vol. II, 76–89; Hening, W. W., ed., *The Statutes at Large; Being a Collection of all the Laws of Virginia,* Vol. II (New York, 1823), 515–516; *Virginia Magazine of*

History and Biography, Vol. I (Richmond, 1893–1894), 142–155; *Dictionary of American History*, Vol. I (New York, 1940), 19.

5. *Mass. Col. Rec.*, Vol. IV, Pt. II, 117–118, 192, 200, 220–221.

6. Davis, W. T., ed., *Bradford's History of Plymouth Plantation* (New York, 1908, in the Original Narratives of Early American History series, Barnes & Noble, publishers), 364.

7. See "Halfway Covenant" in *Dictionary of American History*, Vol. III (New York, 1940), 5–6.

8. *Virginia Magazine of History and Biography*, Vol. VIII (Richmond, 1900–1901), 171–172.

9. Allerton, W. S., *History of the Allerton Family* (1888), 29, 49–51; *Same*, Revised and enlarged (Chicago, 1900), 31–32; Sibley, J. L., *Biographical Sketches of Graduates of Harvard University*, Vol. I (Cambridge, 1873), 253–256.

10. *The New Academy of Complements, Erected For Ladies, Gentlewomen, Courtiers, Gentlemen, Scholars, Souldiers, Citizens, Countreymen, and all persons, of what degree soever, of both Sexes. Stored with variety of Courtly and Civil Complements, Eloquent Letters of Love and Friendship. With An Exact Collection Of the Newest and Choicest Songs à la Mode, Both Amorous and Jovial.* Compiled By L. B. Sir C. S. Sir W. D. and others, the most refined Wits of this Age (London, 1671), 117.

Index

Index